To Rachele,

Stay pretty, and let God guide your footsteps.

I DID NOT KNOW

By Brian Irons

From B von Irons

Copyright © 2007 by Brian Irons

ISBN 0-7414-4207-8

Published by:

INFINITY
PUBLISHING.COM

1094 New DeHaven Street, Suite 100
West Conshohocken, PA 19428-2713
Info@buybooksontheweb.com
www.buybooksontheweb.com
Toll-free (877) BUY BOOK
Local Phone (610) 941-9999
Fax (610) 941-9959

Printed in the United States of America

Printed on Recycled Paper

Published May 2008

Table of Content

"I DID NOT KNOW"- 2nd edition
Author: Brian Irons
Editor: Brian Irons

Introduction

What caused you to pick up this book! Did the book's cover design grasp your attention? You were probably drawn unto this book, as metal does when near a magnet. Did you pick up this book because of its title... "I Did Not Know". If so, then it is certain you are wondering what I Did Not Know actually means. The book cover is very charming to the sight, and as the people say, "never judge a book by its cover". However, just the title alone has your mind in great wonder. Well, in the next two paragraphs, they are going to provide you with true information concerning this book's thesis.

This book speaks about me being the greatest athlete in the world. Well, I may not be the "greatest" athlete in the world, but it is for certain, that I am one of them. In life, my athletic talents and skills were fascinating. Not too many athletes on earth are in comparison. Five different sports, I could have played professionally. Without a doubt, from my displayed talents and skills, I could have earned a position on one out of five different professional league sports. I could have played in the NFL as a quarterback. I could have played MLB as a pitcher. I could have played in the NBA as a shooting guard or point guard. I could have fought in a rink as a pro boxer; and I could have played in the NHL as a goalie. Yeah, when it comes to sports, my talents and skills proved to be worthy of it all. However, from the bad choices I made in life, I messed up the opportunity to play in either one or two Major League Sports. I never signed a financial contract for a team, therefore, I never became known unto the world, as "the greatest athlete who ever lived". Well, have you made your decision to purchase this book? If not, read the next paragraph.

One day, I was in-taking drugs, of course, into my

brain. This day, I had been with several different friends. We all were putting drugs into our brains. Drug intoxicants will always awaken evil experiences. Once a person puts any drug into the brain, an evil spirit then comes alive. Well, me, and only me, experienced a wicked and evil tragedy. My heart had stopped operating for 11 minutes, which means, my brain stop its animated performance. When my brain stopped performing, it was all because drugs had forced it do so. My brain is the controller of my lungs and brain stem, which both enables breathing to be active. For 11 minutes, my breathing came to a moment of halt. When my breathing had ceased, I went into a cardiac arrest. Then, immediately, my brain went into a coma. My conscious center (mental awareness) had been knocked out. I had no active sense or knowledge while in this coma. For ten days, my brain slept in this horrible coma. When this horrible experience had happened, it hit me unexpectedly, and all of a sudden. Nevertheless, I DID NOT KNOW there would be a special day that drugs would cause damage to my brain's function, and destroy my sport dreams both at the same time. As of now, by God's prevailing mercy, my brain functions have been restored, but my sport dreams have not. Sports are over for me, and this evil experience reminds me of that every single day. Well, have you made a decision to purchase this book? If you feel this story is not for you, then I am sure there is a person whom you know who needs to read this book. In fact, purchase this book, and as you walk through your local mall, give it to a teenager and say, "God bless you, please read this book".

Before I go any farther in the story, I do want to say this; I believe I did an incredible job with writing and editing my own book. Writing this book was not hard to do. The editing was ten times harder as it was writing it. It was not easy smoothing the rough spots in this book, until I was somewhat well pleased. I really did want someone to edit this book for me, but I could not afford to pay a story editor, so I did it myself. The editor of this book is Brian Irons. However, soon, and very soon, I will be able to afford a book editor.

If a person has gone through what I went through, and has accomplished a task such as writing a book, that individual should be very happy. Indeed, I am very happy. People just never know what a person has gone through, while on the journey of writing a particular book. If you've ever written a book, after being in a pit, then you should give yourself a pat on the shoulders. Not too many people in the world can write a book, but I happen to be a man that can.

As I was living on earth, many evil and disastrous experiences paraded into my living. No one is to be blamed for these evil experiences, but me. Me, not even knowing, that these experiences where hindering, and forming data of corruption into my living. In the military, all the soldiers march side by side, while listening to their instructor or drill sergeant say, "hut-2-3-4. In my life, so many wicked experiences marched into my living, as if they were soldiers being instructed while in training. Hut-2-3-4, all of my experiences stomped into my living. These experiences became territorial. They marked my life. These experiences kept coming and coming as cars do while in the "Rush hour of the day". They became my schoolmaster, because in the end, a lesson was learned. Some of my experiences were light and soft, while others were rough and harsh. This book will not only explain why wicked experiences had prevailed in my living, but also, it will enlighten others to understand why wicked experiences are touching their lives as well. If wicked experiences are touching your life, this book will explain why it is so.

Many of the experiences I've encountered are equivalent too a great number of people who are living on the earth. However, in this life, most earthly beings have not encountered such experiences I've witness. As a person strolls down the road and unexpectedly stumbles and falls, many hectic experiences fell into my living. All experiences operates by schedule; they begin from appointments; they have a program, and truly, the "Will of God" is before them all. Just as birds are programmed by its maker (God) to chirp in the morning, evil experiences are programmed to soar into person's unrighteous living. By divine appointment, I experienced cognitive shutdown. Yes, truly, these harsh experiences soared into my life, because the "Will" of God" required it to be so.

This book will be mentally persuasive to the simple minds and hearts of all those who read this graphic story. Within the mind, this book will paint a colorful picture about life. The knowledge written in this book will leave nothing to the imagination. You will get the full point, which I am soon to get across unto you. All the members of your inner being will become familiar with this book's power. Emotionally, you'll feel the pain thereof. Psychologically, you'll become sensitive, and spiritually you'll be persuaded to change your life's mental and physical habits. Therefore, to all the readers of this book, grab a seat, and as you read this graphic story, buckle yourself up, and enjoy the journey of traveling through this awesome nonfiction story. Yes, this story is going to drive the mental section of you on the ride of its life. The recorded words in this book are going to run rapidly into your mind, and mobilize your thoughts into another dimension. If your mind is hit by the spoken comments in this story, remember, I have previously given you my foretold warning. Again, buckle yourself up, and enjoy the brainwork of reading this powerful story.

The writing in this book will miraculously draw your attention, and amazingly cause you to gain a sense of understanding to realize that the invincible funeral-planning enemy (Satan) is located within your local neighborhood (city and state). This book will explain unto you how Satan operates, and how his powers are brought into existence. Satan cannot perform nor do anything, until he captures a living man or woman to work his evil powers through. Once Satan captures a person to work his evil powers through, as well as in, an evil work will be performed. Satan (the devil) does not care who he kills; nor does he care how an assassination takes place. Once Satan convinces a person to commit a murder or break the law, his work of evil has just been accomplished. Through human bodies is how Satan lives, and becomes puffed up on the earth.

Here on earth, the physical man (the body) has become people's utmost and greatest concern in life. At times, we've become depressed after viewing ourselves through a full body size mirror. Mentally, our appearance strikes us down. The full size mirror, which shows the evidence of your entire physical being, tells it all. Neither man nor woman has to inform you how you look, because the full size mirror just did. Each and everyday, our hearts and minds have become bothered because we go over board trying to keep the body in tiptop shape. When we look at our image through the mirror, we want it to provide us with a complimentary look. We want to impress the mirror, so it can show us some satisfaction. Throughout the years, we have handled and treated our bodies as if it was U.P.S. mail…first-class. We lotion our skin daily; we constantly spray fragrances on it, because we are highly fascinated with our physical being. Besides, we all love to look great, and nothing else truly matters.

All the times, our bodies must look good! We have heard information through our ears about how to keep the body "tight and right". We have studied information with the mind on how to keep the body in "high standards". Together we have physically gathered in groups, and have inserted dancing steps into exercises. While being at home, people have taken a position, and have played "follow the leader" with a fitness instructor. People watch physical fitness programs on cable TV, VCR tapes, and or DVD's. We have joined local gyms, and signed our full name on financial contracts and agreements to participate in a variety of exercising programs. At some point in our lives, we all have done one of the above. Our minds have been strictly concerned about the outside (body) looks. All of our lives, mentally, we have given the physical look a high praise. High above the stars, high above the heavens, the physical body has been widely cared for.

However, after you have completed reading this book, much knowledge will be given unto you. As you are reading this book, it will teach you that the intelligent human brain is the true strength for the entire body. The intelligent human brain is everything; it is the greatest of all. This book will teach you that if your brain is not healthy, then the body will never experience the true nature of health. True strength and health lies in the power of the brain, which is your internal or inner man. When a brain is healthy, it will miraculously keep the body healthy, too. A healthy brain is automatically linked to a healthy body. Since your brain belongs to you, that means, only you have the power to either keep it healthy or cause it to be unhealthy. If your brain is unhealthy, most of the times, your living has made it that way. This book will lead you to a place, and to a man, who has the power to teach you how to protect your healthy brain.

God's expressive anger from heaven is completely different from human active anger on earth. God's anger, and human's anger, both communicates differently. When humans become angry, their emotions become greatly bothered. It will not take long until a human's fierceness is exposed. Eventually, that individual's aggressive emotions will spring out. When a person's emotions are operating in anger, that individual will stay upset or decomposed until an opportunity for revenge comes about. Once a person's mind creates a way to strike back, through his anger, the destroying of the "World Trade Center" or the "Twin Towers" will be brought down. That is humanity's way, through anger, of getting payback, which is completely different from God's way.

God's anger is always attached to mercy. Even while God is angry with a person, his compassion will still displayed. God, in his anger, never seeks revenge. However, if you keep on bothering and testing the anger of God, he will give you what you deserve. God's anger awakens when people continue to perform certain deeds (breaking his laws and commands). The whole plan of God showing mercy in abundance towards a human being is to send signals, signs, and ongoing warnings. Mercy from God is performed because he desires to have a relationship with you. A relationship with God is deeper than that of a married couple. When God has mercy on an individual's evil situation, his purpose for doing so is to turn that individual's spirit (brain) towards him. Put it like this; mercy is God's invisible power that he uses to give every human being chance after chance, after chance to get his or her thoughts and life connected to his blessed plan for living. Mercy is one of the daily-operated tools from heaven that the entire world has become prisoner too.

Later, in this interesting and remarkable nonfiction story, I will explain unto you how mercy and grace both differs. Through my writing, God is going to explain unto you how grace and mercy operates from two different standpoints. In life, mercy is first presented, and then afterwards, grace is inserted in. Mercy is freely given unto us all, without human works, while grace has to be found or granted. Human works will not earn grace into your life. However, every man must be willing to receive it. Actually, the only works a person has to do to get a hold onto grace is to press his or her way through the evil walls of life. Never is it easy accepting the power of grace into your life. Just as its not easy being freed from mental addictions, well, in the same sense, it is not easy grasping your hands around the power of God's grace.

Evil performances are volunteered willful lawbreaking deeds. Anything done by personal consent is done so voluntarily. All my thoughts in life were criminal minded. When my thoughts became criminal persuasive, voluntarily I broke many laws. Criminal activities became a daily task in my living for a great number of years. If the criminal activities we do today are contrary to the laws written in the world, then most certainly the same committed actions are contrary to the laws written in the bible. Many or most laws, which have been rehearsed into the earth, they come directly from the bible. Unfortunately, humankind tries their best to change the heavenly meaning of the biblical laws just to satisfy their personal mental pleasures. People

7

who are in high position on the earth, that agree or veto certain laws to pass, might cause millions of humans to agree, but if it is against the bible, it will not stand in the eyesight of God Almighty. The laws that are written in the bible cannot be disannulled nor can they be changed. No one can change the meaning thereof, and none can turn it from its force and purpose! There is only one lawgiver, and that is God. When God speaks, who can shut him up? On the other hand, who can change God's sayings after his throat has uttered out words.

For instance, passing a law to accept homosexuality and lesbian relationships are against God's biblical laws and righteous principals. In the bible, homosexuality and lesbian relationships are against God's blessing plan for human living. Yet and still, humankind has voted and has passed an agreeable law in certain cities for such activity to carry on. Since the bible is against such activity, (same sex relationships), if agreed on earth by any party of people, that does not mean God has pleasure in same agenda relationships. Humankind has allowed it, but God has always disproved it. When a law has been passed on earth for the same sex agenda to have relation, someone in high position on earth is trying to satisfy his or her own personal ignorance. People of the world, you need to read God's word (bible) for yourself, and learn its statues (laws) for your own good.

We teach in the church world, that sin is sin no matter what evil act has been committed. Any unrighteous act that has been committed is a sin. During the daytime, the light from the sky shines upon all committed sins performed. During the nighttime, the moon shines upon all wicked acts done. In the sky, God created a variety of lights, and all of them will shine upon all sinful deeds performed. 24 hours a day, one or two lights from the sky will shine on all performances done on the earth.

Judgment time! Many people will think God has been unfair with his righteous judgments. Before being judged, many people will try to fight against their upcoming sentence. Within a person's mind, he or she might think that certain judgments were beyond reason. Therefore, when people disagree with certain judgments, they either try to fight against it, or try to justify themselves. Every human being on earth will be brought under a period of judgment. Whether a person has done righteousness, (uphold the law by doing good deeds in life) or whether a person has done unrighteousness (breaking the law), a time for judgment will always be rendered (given) to the inhabitants of the earth. Righteous people have a calendar day for judgment, and so do the people who are counted as "unrighteous". Whichever type of judgment (verdict) is to be pronounced in your living, whether it's against you or for you, the judgment from God will always be righteous and accurate. Before judgment takes place, God will always investigate or analyze the situation. In judgment, God never make mistakes! Never, never, ever!

The Day of Judgment dashes into our lives at appointed times. People have not the power to choose a day to be judged. The Day of Judgment chooses and selects its own moment and time to come. Earthly time, such as pacific, eastern, standard or mountain means nothing when it comes to the Day of Judgment. We never know when the "Day of Judgment" is set to examine us. The "Day Of Judgment" comes upon us like a thief in the night. Just as someone will break into a person's home unexpectedly, in the same sense, "The Day of Judgment" will break into your life unexpectedly, too. God always provides warnings before judgment takes place. If we do not take heed to life's warnings, then the Day of Judgment will creep into our lives, as a thief does creeps into someone's home. When judgment comes at you, it will hit you unexpectedly. Therefore, neither will a person be prepared physically, nor mentally, because the Day of Judgment comes out of nowhere, and slams a conviction of sentence upon your life.

There are evil works that people (and myself) can perform with the hands. In the bible, it speaks about what will happen to people who do evil with their own hands. *Psalms 28: 4- Give them according to their deeds, and according to the wickedness of their endeavors: give them after the works of their own hands; render to them their desert*. This scripture speaks about a punishment being rendered to people who perform wickedness with their own hands. The word endeavor means- actions, or activities. Mainly, all actions and activities involve hand movement. In other words, endeavor means; physical activities. Yeah, the physical body, preferably the hands, has done an act contrary to God's rules, and the person has been punished because of it. *Psalms 28:4* is a foretold prophecy, which speaks about punishments due unto those who exercise wickedness with their hands as if its a sport. People who have committed their hands to doing wickedness, and are having cheerful delight in doing it, will receive a justified judgment. If you are committing wickedness every single day, God looks at it as if you are having fun doing it. Your hands have become stapled to the activity of wickedness.

After a person eats a meal, usually, dessert is eaten afterwards. In the same sense, after a person's hand has done much wickedness, judgment comes after, and that is his or her desert. The cake for dessert may taste good to the body, but judgment never does. Nevertheless, every time a person has been judged, he has been given his or her desert. A person might not be able to taste judgment from the mouth, but when one has been pronounced upon a person, the heart tastes it, and his or her life feels bitter. Nevertheless, people are always judged because of the wicked activities performed by the physical body. People are never judged because of mental thoughts; they are judged shortly after performing wickedness with their hands (physical body).

From the demonic powers, that my life became subject unto, my brain and bodily limbs became slaves to the forces of evil. This book will enlighten your heart and mind to understand that demonic powers and curses still exist in our present world. If any man is involved in demonic powers, his or her program of life will swiftly. Demonic powers will actually strengthen a person to do unhealthy deeds against his or her own body. Demonic powers are in

10

our land, and can be actively living in your personal home right now today as I speak. This written book will teach your inner being to understand that demons can be walking with you as you go to work or anywhere your brain leads your body. Many people do not have the understanding to realize that demons are in their home sleeping right next to them. Yeah, demons can be in the same building were you relax, and lay your own head. Demons can be that close to you, and you not even knowing it. Demons are smart and clever. When it is time, they will humble themselves just to relationship you. Then, when you marry them, resentment, and all forms of misery breaks loose. Once demons work a work of humbleness to get into your life, when they really get a hold of you, it becomes hard to be liberated (free).

This story vouches and speaks for itself; it needs not human approval, nor an earthly witnesses. It has been designed, and written to prove a declared point. Unfortunately, every human has his or her own personal opinions and facts about the history of substance abuse usage. We all have personal opinions about what is true (real) and what is not true (counterfeit). Whether a drug is prohibited or legal, everyone has a right to post his or her own reply. However, I have a fact or an opinion that will always remain to be true; "There is nothing like a true story (my personal experience) to read, which will overwhelmingly reveal unto the world that such a drug mishap can come into a living man's existence. This written novel will do just that; "it will bring true revelation to the world concerning drugs. There's no need to protest, no need for debates, and no need to do a research online. When it comes to facts about drugs, this book is the absolute truth revealer concerning drugs, and their power. While you are reading this book, it will speak for itself.

This book is the type of nonfiction story that every race, nation, and every creed or church dogma should read. All 50th states, and the hundredths and thousandths of cities/countries should have a copy of this miraculous report. This nonfiction story is not for a certain sect of people, or a certain color of race, it is prescribed to the world as a whole.

The same way that drugs will perform an act on one person of color, or race, is the same evil act that it will forcefully perform on a different nationality. There is not one human being on the planet (earth) that is exempt or that can hide from the forceful power and terror of drugs. If a person is Black, White, Indian, or from over seas, I realize that drugs has the power to do them all the exact same way. No matter where a person is from, or what nationality he or she may be, every brain still operates the same. Every person's brain has the same portion of meat (flesh) within it. The same way a black man's brain functions and operates, is the same way that a Chinese brain functions and operates. Therefore, drugs have the shrewd power to destroy over a billion brains, which God has formed in different colors of people, and different cultures of races.

I was very talented in sports. It was the merciful work of God, which created all my brain's talents. My only work was to guard my talent (brain), which exposed my physical skills. In other words, I should not do anything that will motivate a sudden attack or injury to my mental status. I am supposed to take care of my brain, as a mother does with her newborn child. As I take care of my brain, I am taking care of my talent holder. I have another book in the makings, it'll be published in "2010", and it is called, "Keep Your Vision".

As you read this book, take your time. I hope you read it from the beginning to the end. I am not trying to persuade you in reading the entire book, but if you don't, you just may miss something vital for your soul. If you do not read the entire book, then how can you criticize this story? If it takes 3 to 6 months to read this book, please read this book in its entirety. This book will snatch your soul from being sent to live in the torture of eternal hell. Well, since "hell" itself is trying to receive many people as possible, then you need to read this entire book A.S.A.P. After you are done reading this book, for the rest of your life there will always be a person you will speak to concerning this particular story. As you read this book, put your feet in my shoes. Walk with me down the path of goodness. Then walk with me down the path of danger. Feel my hurt! We all have walked down the road of ignorance before. You truly are no different from me. To all the preachers in the world, in many sentences were I used the word "drugs", I want you to change it to the word, SIN. This book will touch your ministry, and provide you with loads of biblical sermon topics. Actually, you can read one full page, and a sermon topic will be registered within your mind that fast. If you've read this story from the beginning so far, then already you have a few sermon topics.

Wow! Who would have ever thought, that God would use Brian Irons to teach a world of people a thing or two. I never thought that I would ever be the one to write a book. Not only that, but also, I am actually teaching the people who are in the world about life. To all the current readers of this book, every single one of you has become my student, and class is now in session. Sit at your desktop; sit on your living room couch, or wherever is comfortable for you. While you are sitting and reading this novel, it's going to teach you how to turn God's anger off. If you want to know how to please God, the answer to such is written in the book. I am going to educate you, and teach you about the necessities of life. If you can copy my style of writing, consider it a blessing. However, I do want you to know this; there is none like me on the earth.

Chapter 1

Growing Up in a Neighborhood Plagued by Wickedness

The City of St. Louis is considered extremely dangerous. Because of the danger, St. Louis is known as an unsafe and untamed city. St. Louis has gotten out of control. Neither by storm, nor by tornado, St. Louis is filled with the wind of danger. A person blows out candles by the wind of his breath, however, in the same sense; danger has been blown throughout the plains of St. Louis. This city has become so dangerous and treacherous, that those words just might be understatements.

Anytime danger is prevailing in any area, that environment soon becomes a place of hazardous, and a territory engulfed with evil. How remarkable it is that every state on the US map has a city immersed with danger. The more millions of cash a person adds to his or her bank account; the richer the individual becomes. In the same sense; the more dangerous a city becomes; being unsafe will be its fulfillment.

St. Louis City has become a place that can be threatening to a person's life. It's a battlefield, and as they say, "only the strong will survive". Just as it is life threatening to take a bath while lightning and thundering is active in the sky, well, walking through the streets of St. Louis can be life threatening as well. Unexpectedly, trees and houses are sometimes struck down by lightning. However, when a person takes a simple stroll through the streets of St. Louis; his or her life can unexpectedly be struck down as well.

Why is St. Louis filled and labeled to be a dangerous and violent city? Actually, the City of St. Louis has progressive reasons for being labeled dangerous and violent. A City and or state is not dangerous or violent until something or someone causes it to become that way. The people who gather in numbers are the ones who have persuasively caused St. Louis to be looked upon as a dangerous city. Danger or violence does not operate without help. If people would not carry on with certain group activities, then danger would not be the city's shadow. Before danger and violence is brought into any city's existence, a certain physical activity is first performed.

Since people are the ones who brought danger into St. Louis, however, from the bringing of it, violence came, too. Violence is a physical force that awakens danger. Violence is so wrapped up in the people; they are the one's who made St. Louis to be labeled as a place of danger. Through people, violence became an active and ongoing movement in St. Louis. For decades, crime on crime scenes from human bodies has been in session in this city. When the ignorant practices of crime scenes are continually exercised, soon and very soon, danger awakens.

Wherever there are people engaging in violent activities, that area is a place where peace has been destroyed. Wherever violent activities are being glorified, that is a place where peace has been nullified. In your neighborhood, if peace and quietness has been stripped from it, then the nature and movement of violence has performed that work. When violent activities are being uplifted, then the operation of peace has been shut down. Violence empowers people to walk all over peace as if it is a piece of trash. Peace never invites violence; violence powerfully welcomes itself. As a bomb explodes, and destroys the area, however, when violence has been brought into play, peace will be destroyed as well. By Brian K. Irons

Peace and violence are both contrary one to the other. Peace operates in quietness and humbleness, while violence operates to be ignorantly heard and seen. Peace and violence cannot and will not ever abide in the same place, nor will they operate at the same time. When violence creeps into any neighborhood, soon, peace is forced to leave. After peace has been forced to leave the premises, violence will plague that entire region and or environment.

All four sides, or regions of St. Louis are heavily active with violent activity. Everywhere in St. Louis, a violent activity has taken place. Not long ago, on the north side, a murder was committed. Just the other day, on the Southside, a rape was committed. Just last week, on the eastside, a "gang" had beaten a man unconscious. On the Westside, a man was stabbed with a knife. Since all four sides of St. Louis is active with violence, then danger has become its plague. At one point, although, the entire City of St. Louis was filled with violence, however, a certain side of it is considered most dangerous. Yeah, the north side of St. Louis is the side that's considered the most dangerous.

In St. Louis, I grew up on the north side in a neighborhood called, "The Vaughn Projects". Since the Vaughn Projects is a neighborhood located in St. Louis, then violence is active within it. As you are reading this book, it will explain unto you that wherever there are performances of violence, there will also be a displaying of wickedness. Wickedness and violence always dwell in the same area and or location. You are about to mentally learn that wherever there is wickedness, and a performance of violence, that chemical controlled substances are definitely in the area.

Wickedness itself is an activity. The word wickedness means to "perform" an outrageous act that is against the law. Wickedness, in addition, also can mean to cause bodily harm, pain, or introduce someone's life to a state of misery. Meaning, someone has seriously changed a person's life to experiencing an event for the worst.

Let's just say that a man's leg has been cut from his body. 9 times out of 10, this man's life has immediately changed toward the worst. If a human being has performed an act on this man, which caused amputation to be done to his leg, then an outrageous act of wickedness had been performed. Whether a person shot bullets in his leg, or physically damaged it, still an act of wickedness had been performed.

Every time a person transgresses the law, he or she

16

has just performed an act of wickedness. When a person is breaking the law, his or her body is committing a prohibited act. When a person intentionally breaks the law, or does any actions through stupidity and ignorance, usually, "wickedness" is the title of such works.

When a human being breaks the law, the human eye can view such a work in progress. The sight from another human can stare and watch lawbreaking activities in motion. When a person watches another person do illegal activity, he or she is observing a law-breaking maneuver, which is an act of wickedness. Wickedness and lawbreaking deeds go hand and hand. Nevertheless, the keen eyesight of God sees every act of lawbreaking deeds done upon the earth. Just as violence and danger are synonyms, however, wickedness and lawbreaking activities share the same definition. Therefore, when you see a person breaking the law, you are actually watching a person perform an act of wickedness.

Wickedness and violence are like twins born on a certain day. When twin babies are born, one infant comes out before the other. I have two cousins who are twins, Jermeine and Jermaine. Jermaine was born before Jermeine. These twin cousin's of mine were born on the same day, but the timing of birth differs. Jermaine could have been born at 9:30 am, while Jermeine was born at 10:00 am. It is the same given birth with violence and wickedness. Wicked intensions can be in a person's thoughts at 9:30 a.m., and at 10:00 a.m., a violent act can be brought forth. Therefore, wickedness and violence are birthed in people's lives on the same day, just as Jermeine and Jermaine Irons were.

When a person walks into a store, picks up a product from its place, and then walks out of the store without paying for it, an act of wickedness has just been performed. Although, a stolen product may only cost $1, however, if you take a product out of a store without paying for it, you have just caused your hands to perform a wicked deed. Why? Because stealing is against the law, and if performed by anyone, an act of wickedness has been committed. The price of the stolen item means nothing. The only thing that matters is the simple fact that the item was taken out of the store without payment. It is written and record in the bible as one of the 10 commandments saying, **"Thou shall not steal".** In life, if you have ever stolen anything from a fashion store, a friend, or anywhere, you have willingly committed an act against the command of God, which was truly a deed of wickedness.

When any person performs an act of wickedness, a name is immediately registered unto him or her. When a person has been empowered to steal, the name given to such a one is to be called, "thief". Yes, the person who has stolen a product inherits full rights to be called a "thief". For the thief, "wicked" is his first name, and thief is the last name. The person who steals; name shall be called, "Wicked Thief". The bible has a name and a charge of commandment for every wicked and evil act done under the sun by mortals.

Listen here people of the earth; stop the wickedness and the violence, because there is a name for every wicked deed you commit. Wickedness wants to give you a new name. At this stage and age in my life, my name is **Brian K. Irons**. However, later on in my life, wickedness is going to give me a new name.

I also knew if a person has committed a murder, that a judgment and penalty must be rewarded. The murderer must suffer the consequences for committing the act of murder. The court of law is the place where all murderers will hear a judgment, which will be their reward. The murderer performed a work of evil, and a payment must be given. Usually, freedom is taken away when a person commits a murder. He or she becomes a slave to the prison system for a very long time. Therefore, a known killer must be verbally tried in the court of law, judged, convicted, and sentence the capital punishment for this wicked act committed. The person who kills will also receive a name for the evil crime committed. Just as the person that steals is called a "thief", however, the person who kills another human is called, "a killer" or "murderer".

The projects, where I'm living, is filled with so much

wickedness, that if wickedness could be weighed on a global scale, the atomic numerical weight of it would be innumerable. There were numerous acts of wickedness being performed consistently. Somewhere in the "Vaughn Project", either an act of violence was being displayed, or a breaking of the law being performed. In the atmosphere of the projects, is nothing but the breath of evil. Wickedness became a heavy force in the projects, and the strength of man could not lift or cast it out. As a bird flies around in its cage, wickedness has encircled itself in the projects.

Other people from different locations would be in drastic fear when walking through my neighborhood. They would be in fear because of the violent and bad activities that would surprisingly transpire. Unexpectedly, and unrehearsed, an evil episode would bring its attention in the neighborhood. It would be a person's luck just to walk through the projects, and suddenly, become face to face with horrible scenery. If a certain wicked deed was not being performed in the projects, then a different event of evil was being brought into view. However, you can most definitely believe that someone somewhere in the projects was performing an act of evil.

One of the evil activities I remember being performed in the projects were brutal fist fighting. These fistfights were harsh; they were cruel, and some were horrible to see. There were many extreme fistfights active in the "Vaughn Projects". Either my ears heard about these cruel events, or my eyes watched physical battles in session. With my own two eyes, one day, I stood and watched a man bleed badly as he fought another man. With the fighting being displayed in the projects, from those actions of performances, this neighborhood appeared to be possessed with the force and strength of evil. From all of the mental anger, fussing, and verbal cursing being active in the area, wickedness through human violence filled the neighborhood with its presence. The people's mental tempers and evil thoughts were quick in leaning to negativity, rather than activating positive movements.

Often times, people shot guns in the Vaughn Projects. Mainly, at night, the sounds of gunshots were heard. Many times, as I lay in my bed for sleep, I would suddenly hear a deadly pebble size piece of metal being triggered through the barrel of a gun. It seemed like, that a gun would be shot at least once or twice a week. From one side of the town to the next, bullets were shot though the Vaughn Projects, and I heard it many times.

Gunshots have a deep and distinguishing sound. Sometimes it is hard to determine if a gunshot was fired, or if a firecracker had been lit and popped. Then there are those moments and events that you just know that gunshots were fired. It is so scary, that something (a bullet), which is so tiny to the sight, and yet, it can cause a person's body to be seen in graveyard clothes.

Even as a child, I realized why gun-shooting episodes became activate. Gun shooting episodes became active through two people who held mental disputes against one another in their mind and heart. As the people in the world say, "it takes two to tango". The people in the world also say, "It takes two ignorant people to go get guns for one ignorant situation". When I heard the gunshots, of course, I DID NOT KNOW what the disputing was about, however, I did know that a human's hand was in charge of this activity. When bullets are being released in any area, then peace is not in operation. When gun shootings are in action, it is because; a quarrel has been created.

The word quarrel means to have a dispute or disagreement with another. Continually having unsuccessful debates, is quarrelling; Quarrel also means: to find a way to prove that your complaint is right, and nothing else matters. People, who seek to find fault in someone, are actually creating a quarrelling ordeal. Everyone loves to find fault in others just to satisfy his or her own personal emotions. As people have quarrels with one another, arguments will soon come alive. Oscar Wilde, of the 1800's quoted; "arguments are to be avoided; they are always vulgar and often unconvincing". In other words, Oscar Wilde is saying, "refrain yourselves from quarrellings; don't even waste your time, because the battle will never end.

Disagreements are never solved through the acts of arguments. Most arguments can go on and on and never come to a position of halt. You might have an argument in the noonday, or even before bedtime, however, when you awake, the dispute can still be there. Having arguments will only elevate the situation to anger. Then, anger will pass it on to physical brutality. Maybe anger or resentment from a fistfight eagerly persuaded the people to bring violence and gun shooting in the midst of the projects. Whatever happened, which caused that episode to come active, however, guns and a dime size piece of metal (bullet) appeared on the scene. Nevertheless, mental disagreements and disputes brought violence and hostility into my neighborhood's presence.

Anyway, the powerful sounds from continual gun shooting would disturb me. As my ears were experiencing the loud sounds of gunshots, sometimes, I would wrap myself up in my bed's blankets. Hiding under the blankets was supposed to shield my fear. I covered myself in fear, thinking a bullet just might journey through my window. Although, a blanket cannot stop a bullet from penetrating, however, taking cover under a blanket is probably something that all kids do.

Sometimes, when bullets would be shot and heard, I would roll out the bed onto the floor. I learned that hiding technique from my parents, and from watching television. When my parents heard gunshots in the neighborhood, they always said, "Get down on the floor and stay away from the windows".

So another day came, and again gunshots were fired throughout the neighborhood. One by one, a deadly dime size piece of metal was triggered through the barrel of a gun. After I heard the gun shooting this time, I heard a man yelling and screaming. Whole words were not said. Only loud a loud voice, pitched with pain. This man was hollering as if he was being physically beaten right on the spot. When

I had gained enough boldness to get up out of the bed, to look out the window, I saw a man's body lying across the concrete. When a bullet hits a person's body, 9 times out of 10, the individual will scream in drastic fear. As this man was on the ground screaming, one of his hands held onto one of his legs. I suppose he had been shot in the leg by the gun shooter. This gun-shooting incident appeared on the scene, because of the prevailing power of wickedness.

Every time a gun (which is a weapon that performs actions of wickedness) is triggered and fired, most of the times city help (police or ambulance) would eventually be sent to the scene. Once the sirens of police cars or sirens of emergency care (ambulance) are heard, the neighborhood is then filled with the city's "protection and care". Since performances of wickedness will bring the police and the ambulance to your town, then wickedness itself is filled with the power to cause such an activity to take place. For the present moment, let's not lean on the fact that gunshots were fired; let's draw our minds on the fact that wickedness is in the man, which empowered him to shoot a gun.

Since wickedness will cause the police force and emergency medical help to come into the community, then wickedness itself has tremendous physical power. Wickedness had caused three events to take place in a matter of minutes. 1^{st-} the person whose mind was filled with wickedness, actually pulled the lever on a handgun, and shot a bullet into the flesh of a human being. 2nd-the police force arrived on the scene to surround the area with city or state protection. 3^{rd-} registered RN's arrived on the scene to present the wounded man with medical assistance. The ambulance and the police were both sent to check on this brutal scene of crime on crime. From the three activities (gunshot shooting, police arrival, and medical assistance) that had taken place, a number of laws were broken during this horrible event.

The law was broken, because it is against the law for anyone to carry a concealed weapon, which is for the gun carrier's personal use. The second law broken is called, "assault and battery" or "unlawful use of a weapon". It is against the laws of God for any man or woman to seek personal judgment by a bullet. No matter how angry you become, you are never suppose to pull out a gun and shoot a living man. Anytime a person pulls out a gun, and shoots bullets at another human being as pay back, God does not take pleasure in such activity. Besides, guns and violence operates from wickedness, and God never encourages people to do actions of evil. God hates wickedness and evil.

We hear all the time from other people saying, "Only God can judge me". Not only do other people say it, but you say it, too. When most people say that quote, they are trying to over look being wrong. They know something wrong was done, that's why they say that quote. Many people live their entire lives saying, "Only God can judge me". I suppose it brings comfort to the table of their hearts. No one wants to be judged, and no one wants to admit being wrong.

Therefore, put far away from among you the lethal weapons (guns and bullets). Let God be the judge. God is the one who holds all the authority to judge every man according to what he has done. Let each individual stop pursuing after personal gratification. Weapons should not be used as instruments of judgment, or as a tool for payback. Put away the weapons, and put away the bullets, lest you find yourself reaping from that very same act.

(A biblical verse) _Romans 12:17 recompense no man evil for evil._ In other words, the bible is saying, "do not perform evil on a person as a work of compensation" (payback). Do not shoot bullets at a person as reimbursement. Therefore, when people use weapons for payback, they are using evil tactics to repay someone. When done so, you are using evil to solve an evil dispute. God is the one who provides a work of recompense to every person. Also, it says in the book of _Romans 12:19 "vengeance is mine, I will repay, saith the Lord._ Since God is the judge of all the earth, people must sit back ands let him pronounce sentencing and convictions.

Only God knows how to provide a person with

precise judgment. The young man who had been shot by a bullet, his experience probably went beyond means. It probably did not have to go as far as bullets being active in the event. Although, a disagreement and an argument transpired between two people, however, neither of the two have rights to shoot bullets. Only the law enforcers (police officers) have rights to insult the body with bullets. When people recompense someone for evil for evil, they go beyond the point of making it a fair and equal judgment. Since the world is filled with wickedness, from it, people are led to recompense one another from their own personal and evil suitable tactics. *James 1:20 says, For the wrath of man, worketh not the righteousness of God.*

Humankind does not know how to recompense no one. The only thing humankind know to do is to harm or kill one another. Humans' way of recompense is to use weapons of war. In our neighborhoods, bullets are always used as a skill for recompense. Nevertheless, the command of God (the bible) says; *recompense no man evil for evil.* Not by human might, nor by physical strength, *recompense no man, evil for evil*. Evil activities will never solve any problem.

This is my definition of a bullet; a bullet is a tiny piece of iron that has a point at the end. Many bullets are shorter than an inch in size, while some are as long as an inch. Whether a bullet is as small as an inch, or as long as an inch, every bullet serves one purpose. Bullet's purpose is to cast out harm. When bullets get into the hands of wicked people, they are used to harm one another.

When a person puts bullets in a gun's clip, each bullet placed in it counts the number of wickedness. If your you put 9 bullets in the clip, then that is nine times for the trigger of wickedness is planned to be used. Every time a person pulls the trigger of a gun, the activity of wickedness increases. Meaning, if the first bullet does not hit your desired target, you will keep shooting the murder weapon until a bullet enters into the flesh of a living man. People who hold on to such a tradition, their minds are filled with the mental thoughts of wickedness. Wickedness has taken over the mind of such people who has pleasure in the physical involvements of gunplay. As God (the bible) says, _recompense no man evil for evil._ That is a command, not a quote of personal choice. The command is this; stop using guns and bullets to solve problems in life. Stop utilizing weapons!

Wickedness will always bring mathematics and numbers into a person's life. When a person performs an act of wickedness, additions of evil will soon enter into one's life. Like the kindergarten song says, "one little, two little, three little Indians", in the same sense, one bullet, two bullet shots to the body can righteously sentence the gun shooter with a 2 to 3 life sentence in prison, without parole. Actually, if a person triggers one bullet to the body of another human being, that display of action can impressively sentence someone to live in prison for evermore. One bullet shot to the body is all it takes for a person to hear a "judgment" in court, which will sentence the individual to live behind bars for the rest of his or her life. All because of wickedness being active in a person's life, that individual can share a "prison cell" with another man or woman until the day he or she dies. Right now today, there are many people locked up in prison, serving life without parole. All because wickedness had empowered someone to shoot bullets at a living being, freedom has been snatched away.

When I was a child, I thought if a bullet enters into the body of a person or any living species, that he or she would inevitably die soon afterwards. I psychologically thought that once a bullet has penetrated through the flesh of living being, that it would remain inside of the body forever. I use to think the bullet would be lost inside of a person body, and that it could not be found. At this particular time in my life, I was child; therefore, I DID NOT KNOW too much about guns and or bullet wounds.

Movies, TV shows, and live scenes in the projects taught me about guns and violence. From the five senses located within the body, two of them became active learning tools for me. My hearing and sight senses learned about the actions of violence. The same actions of violence I've seen at the movie theatre, and on television, are the same motions of violence that was being performed in my neighborhood. I use to think that the violence, which has been rehearsed by humans to be presented on the television screen, was only performed on TV. However, from the violent scenes I have viewed in the projects, I can now see that gun shooting and violence is active off the screen as well. My young mind had been mentally enlightened that, if I saw anything violently horrible on television, then it is possible to witness the same violent activity in the projects.

I watched a TV show one night, which showed scenes of physical violence and random gun shooting. Then the following day, I witnessed the same act of violent encounter in my neighborhood. Wickedness (violence) had been performed on TV, and wickedness had been performed in the projects. Therefore, the actions of violence done in projects, or in reality, are the same performed wickedness I've viewed on the television screen. Television and the projects have something in common, which is, they both displays actions of violence, which is a performance of wickedness. In other words, you can just about view "Wicked" actions being demonstrated everywhere. On your television screen and in your local neighborhood, wicked and evil actions can be viewed. Wickedness, wickedness, wickedness, is there an answer to cease people from the performance of wickedness.

When I was a child, if I saw someone with a handgun, I would be very fearful to draw near it. In fact, I couldn't even empower myself to even look at the barrel of a real gun. Just the sight of seeing the round barrel of a handgun made me tremble inside. Just the thought of intentionally harming someone with firearm, I could not bare to think considering. The thought of me purposely aiming and pulling the trigger to send bullets at someone to kill, made my inner being shiver. I said to myself frequently, "I would never want to be a victim to ever shoot bullets at a living human being. I could not see myself receiving the mental courage, and the boldness of physical strength to raise my hand with a gun in it to shoot someone. As of now, I have the mind of a child with a simple and merciful heart; therefore, evil thoughts of street wickedness do not have a home within my mind. However, keep reading the story, and you will see how my life shifted from a decent way of living, to the worst way of living possible. You will see how the handling a handgun tested my life.

Once a human being possesses a pistol, for some reason it mentally empowers that individual to want to experience pulling and releasing the trigger. In many neighborhoods, were unpleasant situations and disputes are in progress, eventually, the thoughts of owning a handgun will quickly dash into people's mind. Although, when I was a child, I do not remember hearing the law or the commandment that plainly says, "*Thou shall not kill*"; however, I inwardly felt within my heart that it was wrong to murder a human being.

Many people in the world think that weapons are the best solution to their ongoing problems. People also think that continued physical violence is a natural solution to solving their problems as well. An iron piece of metal (handgun) has never been a solver of any minor or major problem; guns and violence will only enhance or intensify the problem or situation that is in view. Guns and violence only alters problems, and escalate them to a higher degree. When a lethal weapon is utilized as a problem solver, cruel violence and unprepared deaths will be the promotion of such activities. Evil activities will never solve a problem, because, many times it was wickedness that brought the disagreeing situation into existence. People really need to definitely get a tight grip on reality, and comprehend within their minds that weapons and continued violence only leads to more violence. Problems are never solved, and peacemaking is never birthed. Guns and violence will absolutely add to the problem or will unexpectedly create a new one. Since guns and violence begets more violence, that means that they both together will add another problem to the situation.

Once a person fires a bullet at his enemy, the enemy immediately tells his relatives or his homeboys. Then before you know it, two groups of people are having a quarrel. Once the 2 groups have finally come face to face, the situation has just been escalated. An argument jumps off first, after that, physical violence then comes into action. Then, just that fast, and just that quick, gunplay marches in at attention. The more people added to the problem, the bigger a violent mess it becomes. The more people added to the problem, the stronger the power of wickedness gets.

Take heed to this mathematical equation; it will teach you that guns and violence will never solve any problem in life; violence + guns = unresolved problems. Also, violence + guns = continued problems. Whatever relates to a continuation of wickedness will never solve any problem in life. If wickedness has created the problem, never think that wicked tactics is the answer to solving it. Wickedness only begets more wickedness, and from wickedness, out comes the violence and evil. Wickedness will never bring any current problem to a state of halt (end). Its intention is to add more problems into your life, until it either kills you, or lead you to kill someone. How can evil events be purposely prevented from being active? How can wickedness be solved? We need an answer, and we need one right now?

Here is one of the answers to destroying crime on crime scenes, and wickedness. When people activate their gifts and talents, the population will began to change tremendously. Guns and violent activities will soon detour from the land, if we use not our gifts and talents. When you activate your gifts and talents, then guns and violence will become immobile. Then the world will experience the value of goodness. People need to allow their gifts and talents to be seen, so that guns and violence will stray away from the land. When people expose their gifts and talents upon the earth, they will stop recompensing one another *evil for evil*. Just as a man in the military is placed on active duty, in the same sense, people need to put their talents and gifts on active duty as well.

Once we utilize our talents and gifts, which come from within, they will speak for them selves. When people are seeking to live better their lives, they should bring alive their gifts and talents. If people would seek to exercise their gifts and their talents that God has absolutely given unto them, then wickedness, violence, and weapons of war will loose its daily ratings. Then the world would not be polluted with ongoing performances of wickedness. Find out within your heart and mind what it is that you are gifted in. Seek to find precious pleasure from your gifts and talents. Then activate them immediately.

Let us all stop the madness, which tends to lead to violence. God has provided us all with personal gifts and talents. However, people's disturbed minds have become so wickedly stressed out, that they seek weapons of war to soothe their angered minds. Anyone can shoot a gun; anyone can stimulate violence, but let us activate our gifts and talents that God have so generously provided. There are gifts and talents inside your human brain right now. Search within yourself, and find that God given talent. Use your God given talent for your benefit. Not only for your personal benefit, but also, for the prevailing of peace. God did not give anyone a gun to be assessed as a gift nor a talent. Vengeance belongs to God. He is the one who gives pay back to all living beings. Just as you went to the streets and easily found guns to display, however, if you go into your mind, you will easily find your gift and talents, which are waiting to be activated. If people would stop the madness, and become inactive to violence, then their gifts and talents will be exalted.

Take a moment and think about the many events that the performances of wickedness have taken your life through. Whether wickedness took you through something mental or physical, think about it. Then envision within your mind what wickedness is doing to every community in the land. When you do that, then you can see what wickedness will do unto you. Your community is like the shadow of your body. If actions of wickedness are destroying your community, then it can destroy your body as well. If actions of wickedness are killing the nations, then it can kill you also. Whatever performance of wickedness happens in your city or community, the same type of reaction can be displayed upon your body. Just as violence and wickedness will take peace out of your community, it will take peace out of your life. Whatever wickedness and evil does to your community, whether big or small, it holds the same power to perform the very same act within your body. Yes, wickedness wants to get personal with you! Wickedness wants to live inside of you, and later in life, it wants to kill you.

Although, the police force might not see you performing prohibited or wicked actions, however, GOD is most definitely viewing everything done under the moon and under the sun. On earth, people are able to hide their wicked deeds from the police. We as a world need to stop worrying about the police; we need to begin worrying about being seen by God Almighty. People might be able to hide from the police, but never can they hide from God. There is nothing held or done in secret that the Almighty God cannot see. A blizzard, a hurricane, a tornado, not even a big bright star can hinder God's vision from seeing what humanity is doing upon the earth. Therefore, if a concealed weapon is a part of your life, the police might not see it, but God sees the object just as it is. Now use your gifts and talents, which will put a smile on God's face.

God has been watching evil and wickedness live in human bodies since the days of Adam and Eve. From the days of Adam and Eve, up until **Brian K. Irons** has been upon the earth, God has been viewing actions of wickedness. As God Almighty sat and rested in the place of power, which is on his throne in heaven, he has been watching the world of people live evil and wicked lives. For 2000 years, and even longer, God's eyes have been fastened on the performances of wickedness. Yeah, for centuries and centuries God Almighty has been watching wickedness take place. Below, I have a biblical scripture for you to read.

Genesis chapter 6:5 And God saw that the wickedness of man was great in the earth, and that every imagination of the thoughts of his heart was only evil continually. Although, that biblical scripture was originally spoken and recorded in the bible more 2000 years ago, however, the same performances of "wickedness" is still active in our land today. Yep, wickedness is still here, and being operated on the earth. The true reason why wickedness is still mobile in our land is that it lives in the people. Once wickedness lives inside of you, it then has a way to operate. What God has been viewing thousand of years ago; he is still viewing the exact same actions being executed through human beings today. Imagine God watching people do wickedness for hundreds and thousands of years. Do you think that God has had it up to the neck with watching people perform deeds of wickedness? For more than 2000 years, wickedness has been in session, and that's a very long time. To put a scare in you; we are living in these last and evil days, and God is soon to do something drastic, and you had better be ready. When God does something drastic, and if your life is entangled with wickedness, then you will receive drastic effects.

God has been watching people use weapons of war back in the olden days too. God has been observing people do actions of evil since the day Noah's ark was made. I suppose that the people, back in the days of Noah, were fighting, cussing, killing, and allowing wickedness to be performed in their neighborhoods. In the sight of God, wickedness is wickedness, nothing more and nothing less. The day, or the time of the year does not make wickedness any different that what it is. There is only one type of wickedness, and only one type of evil. Therefore, if people today are living wicked lives, and more than 2000 years ago lives were wicked, then law-breaking activity has been in motion for a very long time. People were murdering back then, and in today's society, murdering is still an event. Nevertheless, God's mercy has been operating on the earth for more than 2000 years. Does God have a plan to force evil to stop in its tracks? Is there an answer to cease wickedness, and bring it to a state of death?

I have another scripture, which is the next scripture from the one just written. *Genesis 6:7 And the LORD said, I will destroy man whom I have created from the face of the earth; both man, and beast, and the creeping thing, and the fowls of the air; for it repented me that I have made them.* God spoke this scripture during the days of Noah, which means, it was spoken more than 2000 years ago. Why did God plan to destroy every living mechanism that had life on earth? All because of people living in wickedness, God purposely destroyed the earth, along with the living. Actions of continual wickedness touched God's emotional side, and his anger was displayed from heaven.

Oh my goodness, you mean to tell me that God became that angry, that it repented him that he ever made humankind. God became so sorrowful and grieved that he made a person who is similar to you and I. Wow, back in Noah's day, the people must have really been wicked. Better yet, people did that much performances of wickedness, that it opened God's mouth to say, "*I will destroy man whom I have created.* Need me to remind you, that this comment was spoken from the mouth of God himself. Nevertheless, the thing (wickedness), which caused God to destroy the earth, along with humankind, is the same active thing that is in our land today... WICKEDNESS!

When God said, "*I will destroy man whom I have created*", he did just that, destroyed them. However, Noah and his family were saved because they decided to accept the righteous ways of God. Nevertheless, God destroyed the earth and the people by the water of a flood. God rained water from heaven, until a flood was developed, and all the humans that loved to do wickedness drown in it. The flood of water became a pool filled with wicked people. Just like people get angry and seek to harm the life of a living being, well, God got angry and destroyed every living species too. God's mercy supplied these people with chance after chance to get their lives together, but they wanted to stay connected to the activity of wickedness. It sounds like God hates to see the performances of wickedness. What do you think? Anytime God is moved in heart to destroy something, most of the times, it is always something that pertains to wickedness. I am not going to write unto you all the wicked deeds that were done by the people 2000 years ago. However, I will say this; the same evil acts that you hear and see being performed in today's society, are the same action of wickedness that was performed more than 2000 years ago.

Well, I thank God that he came up with another systematic plan to destroy the works of wickedness. Instead of God destroying wickedness and humankind both together, he supplied the earth with his traveling mercy along with his blessed plan. His divine plan is to destroy the works of wickedness, which is the substance that creates evil. In a later chapter, I will expose and explain unto you the plan that God came up with to destroy wickedness alone, and not humankind with it. Don't worry; I will remind you when I am about to openly reveal unto you the new plan of God, which is to destroy wickedness and evil, and it alone. God's new plan will creatively cause safety and peace to become available unto us all. Well, thank heaven that the bible says, *God is plenteous in mercy, and slow to anger.* HALLELUJAH! Mercy is exactly what God has been displaying in the Vaughn Projects and even throughout the world today.

As I was growing up in this violent neighborhood, outdoors was still my play area. In the neighborhood, I enjoyed playing a variety of activities. Staying in the house was too boring to me. I considered myself a youngster who enjoyed the outdoors because there was so much to do. Therefore, I went outdoors to entertain myself on a regular basis.

While I would be outdoors, I would see tiny objects lying around on the ground. The way the object looked, it could've pass as a stem from a cigarette. However, for some reason, I distinguished within myself that it was not a cigarette. I instantly realized that it was not a cigarette

33

because it was extremely thin and rough looking. Cigarettes are smooth and perfectly round in shape. Besides, I have seen dozens of cigarettes in people's hands as they put them to their mouth's to be smoked. Therefore, I already knew what a cigarette looked like. However, this lumpy shape cigarette looking object, I DID NOT KNOW its official name. Since I was a child, I suppose that is the reason why I DID NOT KNOW what the name of it was called.

For years, as I have occasionally walked pass this thin lumpy shaped object, I became suspicious about its name. I knew that a human being had smoked it because the tip of it had been burnt. I was still puzzled because I DID NOT KNOW the name of this thin object. Well, when I grew older in life and became a teenager, I found out the name of that funny looking object. It is called, "weed or marijuana", which is a chemical controlled substance or mind alternating drug. Therefore, I saw marijuana for the very first time in my life while I was living in the projects.

In my outdoor playing area, there was another object lying on the ground as well. This second object was in the form of a capsule or tablet. This capsule was opened, and completely empty. It looked as if someone had poured the inside (powder) out of it. It made me think someone was in ferocious pain or wanted to be healed right away. I could not understand why the capsules had been opened in the first place. I thought capsules were to be closed, and not to be tampered with. I thought capsules were to be swallowed whole, and not to be pulled apart. Another thing that amazed me was the fact that the capsules were outdoors, opened and empty. Well, nevertheless, I thought that the capsules were for medical healing purposes for the sick body.

The reason why I mentally thought those capsules were for medical purposes is because; those capsules visually looked like the same form of objects that I would see in my parent's medicine cabinet (bathroom). I did not pay to much attention to the capsules lying on the ground; I only saw that they looked like medical capsules. The capsules or medicine that my natural parents kept in their medicine cabinet had names printed on them, and most of times they were kept in boxes or containers. Some of the names were Anacin, Buffering, and a few others. However, the capsules that were outdoors had no names on them. I never touched any of those objects that I saw in the projects, I only looked at them. Well, later on in my ordinary life, as I grew older, I found out that the capsules were from a drug called, "heroin".

Now that I am a lot older, I learned that those two objects (marijuana & heroin) are street drugs. I now understand why so much brutality (violence), gunshots, homicides, and police sirens were definitely in high pursuit in the projects. I now understand why police officers were chasing people by foot through the neighborhood; I now see why murdering and law-breaking actions were at its fullest. It was all because, drugs had performed its power through the brain and bodies of the people who dwelled in the area.

As I was growing up in this neighborhood (Vaughn Projects), which is a place plagued with wickedness, it was still my playing grounds. Actually, my play area is filled with used dope items. Although, the Vaughn Projects was evilly filled with drug users who performed violence and wickedness on a daily basis, outdoors I still had to see. I physically ran around through this neighborhood as if peace and harmony was constantly flowing within it. I was a kid; so therefore, I DID NOT KNOW that drugs were the main reason, why the Vaughn Projects was so triumph with wickedness.

There was one particular game I enjoyed playing. Whenever I had the opportunity to play it, that's what I did. No matter what season of the year it was, or what type of weather was in the air, I still went outdoors to play my personal thought of game. The game that I am about to describe unto you was my favorite activity as I was growing up in the project. Well, to me it was a game and activity, but you might not think so. It was like an active sport to me because it entertained me. Mainly, this game involved rocks and bottles.

I would walk around the neighborhood searching for rocks and bottles. Once I gathered up a number of rocks, I would then set them in a pile beside me. Sometimes I'd collect 20 or more rocks, and put them all in one pile. The bottles, I lined up against one of the buildings in the projects. Once I found a great number of bottles and rocks, it was then time to get my game started.

In this game, I would throw rocks at the bottles to burst them. As I would throw a rock at the bottle, sometimes I would go through the baseball pitcher's wind up as if I was pitching to a baseball batter. I learned the pitcher's wind-up from watching baseball on television every now and then. As I threw the rock, sometimes I made it curve towards the bottles for contact. I also throw "sinker pitches" with the rocks as well. It is a normal throwing action to throw a rock and make it travel straight towards the bottle, but to make it curve and do other air movements, I call that "raw talent". To be able to throw a rock, and cause it to curve in the air like a baseball was a special gift that was placed inside of me. I am sure that many people in the world can do that as well, however, I happen to be the "one" with that talent. The only baseball pitch I could not throw with a rock was a "knuckle pitch". However, any other pitch, I was able to throw with a smooth stone.

My first learning experience of throwing curves and sinker pitches, I learned by throwing stones at bottles and other targets. I thought it was unique and awesome to throw a sinker or curve with a rock, and then watch it make contact with the bottle. Throwing hundreds of rocks at bottles were improving my level of "throwing accuracy". As a kid, I was not thinking about bettering my throwing accuracy, all I wanted to do was have fun as I entertained myself outdoors. Nevertheless, my throwing accuracy was being improved to a higher level of performance just by throwing rocks at bottles and I DID NOT KNOW it. From throwing rocks all year round, that is how and why I learned to throw "curves and "sinkers". Also, that is how and why my throwing accuracy became so precise.

Oftentimes, I would cunningly talk other kids to play a game with me that I called, "rock fight". Just the sound of the game, "rock fight" appears to be a bit dangerous to imagine, I suppose. Nevertheless, the kids would willingly accept the offer and play "rock fight" with me. Here we are, hurling rocks at one another. Of course, I would win because my throwing aim was so straight. I even caused a few heads to be bloody in those days, for real. I would send kids running home to their parents, with slashes in their head from the contact of a rock.

Many times, my parents would hear about drastic things I did when throwing rocks. Because of my rock throwing habits, I would be put on a house punishment all the times. Rock throwing was truly an addiction unto me.

Sometimes, as I would be playing my rock throwing game, I would see people running from a far off. Then all of a sudden, I would hear gunshots being fired. After the gunshots were fired, my mother would also hear the gunshots from her apartment. After she heard the gunshots, she would immediately call my name so I would come unto her for shelter and safety. However, little did my mother know, as soon as I overheard gunshots, I would immediately run to the stairs that led to our apartment. Hearing one gunshot usually does not force people to run and hide. One gunshot usually captures a person's attention. On the other hand, when a person hears back-to-back shots of bullets, that's when it is time to pick up the pace and head for shelter.

When drug chemicals are active in the brain of people, the dope itself will motivate humans to shoot the death contributor (gun). No matter who is in the area, when drugs are controlling a brain, it will cause harsh things to appear in the view of anyone. Here I am in the neighborhood trying to entertain myself, and then human bodies' shows up bringing violence into my view. Drugs powerful force was sending people up and down the neighborhood in strict motions of rage. Of course, it is rage when two people are shooting guns at one another to cause injury or possible bring death on the scene. Drugs will create that sort of out rage when it is in the brain of normal human beings. I was an innocent child out there, and yet, I had to duck, and take cover and run home because of what drugs empowered mental minds to think and contemplate on.

Many neighborhoods are filled with small children all over the globe. Every year a great number of innocent children are killed because of drug led activities. I heard a story about a woman that was sitting in her own living room, watching TV, minding her own business, and suddenly a bullet traveled through the front door and grazed her forehead. That could have been a murder done to an innocent life. An innocent life was almost snatched from the face of the earth all because of certain individuals ignorantly loving to do wicked performances.

Drugs have become "big timers" in this evil world. Drugs have become very popular on the streets throughout the world. It is possible that, in every home in the world, someone in the household knows about the personal affiliations of drugs. Whether drugs has been utilized in a person's brain, or heard about them, however, someone in your home knows about the scheming tactics of drugs. Drugs have increasingly prospered its way through the earth for generations. Generations after generation drug affiliations have been passed on. In every state, wherever a homicide has been charged to a person's criminal record, I believe 9 times out of 10 drugs played a leading role in the act.

Here I am living in St. Louis, Missouri, hearing, and seeing people on the news being brutally murdered, or being physically beaten badly. However, the newscasters fail to mention, or fail to realize that many harsh acts performed are because of a person's mental substance abuse. Well, I do not know too much about the other 49 states, but here, in St. Louis, Missouri, the streets are possessed with drug trafficking, and bodily drug abuse activity.

At this youthful age in my life, since <u>I DID NOT KNOW</u> the name of those two drugs (marijuana & heroin), of course, <u>I DID NOT KNOW</u> the criminal seriousness or the drastic effects these drugs will motivate the brain to think, and lead the body to do. I've heard different people say that drugs kills. People have said that drugs will lead a human being to do bad things. Since I have witnessed so many violent events performed in my neighborhood right before my very eyes, I now believe that chemical usage is the reason for these current wicked events.

Let me give you one or two examples about activation: example 1. When you desire to iron your clothing, normally you plug your iron into an electrical current to generate its power. Once the iron has been plugged into an outlet, the power for it to receive heat is then activated. After the power of heat has surged into the iron, your clothes may then be iron. In other words, if there's no current flow of electric surging into the iron, then there will be no power to cause the iron to perform. The reason why the iron has received heat and ready to operate is because; the iron has received activation through electrical circuits.

Example 2. When driving your automobile, there will always come a time for it to be refilled with gasoline. Gasoline has power because it keeps the car activate and rolling. Although, your vehicle has a motor built within, the car will not stay mobile or stay in operation without gasoline. Having gas in the car will activate the engine and give the vehicle the power to roll.

Gasoline and drugs both have the power to bring about activation. Without a brain and a body, dope cannot generate its motivated power. Drugs are the electrical current that charges up the brain to think negative thoughts. Without a brain, drugs have not the power to contaminate and influence it to lean towards the thoughts of violence. Drug scenes, and violence scenes, which are dope created activities, will not be witnessed, until chemical substances successfully find a brain to instruct continued violence too. When a brain is not filled with drugs, there will be a high dropping rate of crimes committed, and a tremendous drop of homicide cases being tried at court. When drugs aren't in the brain, then wickedness, and lawbreaking activities will cease. Drugs charge the brain up, and then empowers the body to activate evil. **Say No To Drugs!** When you say no to drugs, you are saying no to the performances of wickedness.

While I was living in the projects, a relative of mine had been gunshot and murdered. My immediate family never found out the ultimate reason why he had been murdered. However, since drug usage leads to wickedness and unmerciful actions, substance abuse could have been the explanation for my family member's death. I am not saying that drugs were the true reason, however, from statistics on earth, it could have been. Nevertheless, the man who killed my cousin was filled with the unmerciful ways of wickedness. Yes, wickedness slaughtered my cousin's life many years ago.

I absolutely believe that 90% of killings or homicides, which are committed around the world, are the ending results from drug's intoxicants being active inside of a person's brain. When people's mortal minds are overflowing with drug intoxicants, they make themselves a prime target for violence and unlawful performances to be active their lives. Every time drugs cause an unexpected death, it has hit its unshielded targets (people). It has fulfilled its utmost purpose. Drugs ultimate purpose is to aim and hit the human brain, and lead the human body to suffer the drastic effects. If any drug is inside your anatomy (brain & body), you have already been hit. Once drug intoxicants hit the brain, it has a great chance to crucially damage your body or inwardly persuade you to commit a homicide (young black men really sufferer from this). Although, other races are not exempt from the power of drugs, however, I am commandingly speaking to my young and older black men, because we have allowed drugs and money to become our utmost concern in life. Many people thought that they were only going to get high from drugs, but they had no idea, that being associated with drugs would control their hand to commit a murder.

Have you ever viewed a dart-throwing match in progress? I've watched this indoor game being played were different people toss darts at a game board as a competition.

The game board has many targets on it to be hit. One of the targeted areas on the game board is called, "the bull's eye". Hitting the "bull's eye" will rack up large amounts points for the dart thrower. The dart throwing game that people voluntarily participate in is a competitive game, and it is called, "dart throwing".

The dart thrower's ultimate goal is to hit the bull's eye as many times as possible. Competitors stand behind a line and toss darts at the game board chance after chance, trying their best to hit the bull's eye. The tossed dart can land on a spot that could be worth any number of points ranging from 1 to 40. Yet, the bull's eye (heart of the board) is worth the most at 50 points. The more points accumulated; then the higher the score becomes for the competitor to have the opportune chance to win the dart throwing competition. There is nothing like hitting the heart of the board (bull's eye), and afterwards, listening to the game board play musical sounds of joyful celebrations.

Although, your body is the target drugs are aiming to hit, however, I specifically need to let you know that every target has a bull's eye. Drugs aim to do the exact same thing that the dart thrower desires to do in the dart throwing competition. The dart thrower aims to hit the center of the board, which is the "bull's eye", and drugs aim to hit the center of the body, which is the human heart. Just as the dart thrower will eventually hit the bull's eye, however, drug's crafty power will eventually hit the human heart. Somehow or someway, drugs are going to hit the bull's eye (heart) in the drug seller or dope user's life. Either a drug handler will be robbed, beat up, or assassinated, however, one way or another drugs are going to hit its target (the heart) or (the human brain which is the bull's eye).

My helpful warning and suggestion to the world is this; do not allow drugs to make a direct contact with your anatomy (brain and body). Do not allow the arrow, dart, or missile of drugs to hit your life. Run, run, run for your life because drugs desire to strike you and seriously cause ruin to happen in your life. *STAY AWAY FROM DRUGS, I SAY,*

STAY AWAY!

Speaking about darts, I want to tell you about a dart being sent through my parent's front door, in the form of a bullet. As my parents and I were living in the projects, someone shot a bullet through the front door of our apartment. I pretty much knew that neither of my parents were drug dealers. This gun shooting incident happened by "chance" from wicked ignorant people. However, wickedness and stupidity entered into our apartment in the form of a bullet. My family and I overheard people running through the halls on our floor. Then suddenly a bullet was fired from a gun. One bullet entered into our home. At the time that the bullet was shot through our front door, my little sister (Neco) was happily playing while walking in her baby walker. She was walking around the house in her "baby walker" having kiddy kid fun. Then suddenly, a person who is filled with the pleasure of wickedness sent a violent bullet into her play area. Just that fast, and just that quick, an innocent infant could have been severely injured or even killed. Now that I am thinking about that situation, I thank God for his mercy in our home at that particular time.

Throughout the years, St. Louis has earned wicked rights to be called, "The number 1 city of crime and murder". When it comes to law breaking maneuvers, from statistics, the people have brought nothing but judgments into this city. The Bronx, New York, and Oakland, California, and many other cities were once rated number 1 for crime on crime scenes. However, from the ongoing performances of wickedness, my city (St. Louis) has earned the rating for violent activities. St. Louis is now the most violent city in the world. Since St. Louis is the greatest city of violence, then it is a city grossly filled with law breaking people. Because of the performances of wickedness, St. Louis has been diagnosed as a place full of fierce danger.

Remember this, drugs leads to violence, and violence leads to the grave. Also, remember this, everything that pertains to a breaking of laws is considered a form of wickedness, and is an evil act in the sight of God Almighty.

As I was in the land or neighborhood of drugs, <u>I DID NOT KNOW</u> that drugs could cause so much havoc in one neighborhood. <u>I DID NOT KNOW</u> that wickedness would become so mighty and active when drugs share a space in the brain and body of living human beings. Well, as you have just read, from the venom of drugs, the entire neighborhood had been poisoned. The neighborhood has been poisoned with wickedness. Drugs creepily bossed over the entire projects, and God saw it all. **SAY NOT TO DRUGS!**

Chapter 2
Parents Raising Their Children

In the projects, as my sisters and I were growing up, we were being raised in what I would like to call, "a drug free home". To the naked eye, our home was not seen under the power of chemical control substances. My sisters and I never eye witnessed our parents indulging in drug activity Well, put it like this, I cannot remember any moments of seeing drug usage or drinking alcohol being active by neither my dad nor my mom. My parents did not smoke drugs, sniff dope, nor drank alcohol while relaxing in the house.

Although, my dad did drink intoxicating beverages (alcohol), he never drank his liquor in front of my sisters and me. What my dad did out doors, he kept that activity outdoor. That is what I mean when I say my sisters and I were raised up in a drug free home. Neither chemical control substances, nor alcoholic beverages were found taking up space in our home. Marijuana stems were not found in the ashtrays, nor were there half filled bottles of liquor kept in the refrigerator. I am not saying that my parents were perfect or never used chemicals, however, I am saying this; our home was drug free to the human sight.

A mother or father who raises a child or children in a drug-free home shows a significant amount of love within the household. Raising your kids in a drug-free home will also show a great deal of respect towards the children. When parents consume alcohol or smoke dope in the view of their children, that shows a lack of love and respect on their parental behalf. I am not saying that a mother or father who smokes or drinks in the view of their kids do not love their toddlers, however, what I am saying is this; parents should not walk through the house shoving chemicals in their brains in the presence of their children. For years, and years, parents has been passing drug usage activity to their kids. Using drugs in front of the children has become so common to people, that they actually forget it is affecting their kids.

If parents allow their residence to become a "drug trafficking" home, then that house is not concealed with the maximum insurance of true love. When parents express love towards their children, devotional care must be in action. When true love is concealed in the house, certain activities should not be presented or performed in the home. The kids should not see works of wickedness through drug usage. Drug usage is one of the physical activities that should not be performed in the home. If drugs are in your home, then your house is not filled with the true sincerity of love.

When parents raise their children in a drug free home, usually, they do not allow certain activities to take place. A lane for human drug trafficking will not be engraved at the front, back, or side door. Not only will it stop excessive drug trafficking, but also, it will prevent evil activates from spreading abroad in the home. What I mean by the phrase "drug trafficking"; is when people invite themselves to your home on a regular basis, to put the "violence enhancer" (drug) into their brains. A drug free home will stop drug abusers from approaching the home. When a residence becomes a "drug tracking" home, that house becomes unstable in all its ways.

Not only does the home become unstable, but also, in due time it will loose its peace as well. Your home is just like your community (neighborhood), whatever drugs do to your community, the same event can happen unto your home. Everyone goes to the neighborhood to intake drugs into their brain, and people will congregate at your house to do drugs as well. Therefore, if your home is full of drugs, people will congregate in your home just to get high. Drug usage is displayed in the neighborhood, and if, drug usage is active in your home, then your house has become the neighborhood drug parlor.

Drug users will visit your home, and will begin to bang on one of your door at any given time of the day. From sun up to sun down, people will ball their hand up, make a fist, and bang on your door. No matter how late in the day it is, a drug user will boldly imprint his or her footprints onto your front porch. Drug users will desperately bang on your door at 3 o'clock in the morning just too serve their brain that evil and lawbreaking substance.

A dope-craving individual will be lead to disrespect your home one way or another. No matter how many times you command a drug user not to come to your personal residence after midnight, he or she will still disobey your commands. The dope head will still proceed to your house as if you said nothing about it. Your words mean nothing. More also, you mean nothing. The only thing matters is, the person's brain is yearning or feigning for dope intoxicants to be put into it.

A drug seller or dope user characteristic is a mental trait that the children should not witness from their parents. When kids frequently perceive dope characteristic in the home on a routine basis, they (children) will start to become rebellious to the commands of the parents. That is not always true, but in most cases, it's a rational fact. The children will start to "gradually develop" what is called a "rebellious spirit or a "stubborn attitude". Once the children pick up that rebellious spirit, in so many ways, it came into their lives, because of drug trafficking. I am not saying that because of drug characteristics being displayed in the home, that it will automatically cause the kids to become rebellious, however, when drug habits and manners are being mobile in the home, I am sure it is a part of the child's outward rebellion towards their parents. Therefore, keep the drug characteristic out of the home. It is time for the loving parents to be identified as true leaders.

A parental leader is a responsible person who often leads, guides, and becomes a role model or an inspiration unto his or her children. The formal leader must been seen as an upright individual in the view of his or her pupils. Leaders normally lead his or her followers (children) down the "right pathway". The leader must continuously guide followers to the road of victory. They must set the stage for the children, and present unto them a pathway of righteousness. The leader must do everything from a sincere heart of love, and not through hideous ways of deceit. Alert the kids unto righteousness, and not unto the uprising of stupidity. You are supposed to be responsible, therefore, lift up a standard of righteousness in your home.

Another bad characteristic that should not be displayed in the home is this; parents should not escort or command their company (drug using friends) to go to another room so that they can flush drugs into their brain and body. That procedure usually does not work. Unfortunately, people and parents assume that commanding their company to another area of the house before utilizing drugs is a good tactic. Well, actually, going to a different area in the home does hide the physical activity of drug usage from the children's sight. However, there is another "mental sense" in the child's brain that will be alerted and active. To all parents who believe that "going to a different room to use drugs is a good tactic, that is a scheme learned from the power of wickedness. Being filled with wickedness will cause parents and people to scheme and plan a number of things, and then believe it is a good plan.

Although, the children might not see what their parents are doing, however, the aroma from dope will expose the hideous ways that the parents are doing something in secret. Once the children smell the scent of dope, immediately, they become suspicious. The reason for your children becoming suspicious is, for one, your company has been asked to go to another area of the home. Secondly, the smell of dope will alert your child's intellect to know that mommy or daddy is doing something abnormal. Then the children will begin to wonder why mother or father's company always travels to another room, every time certain people visits.

The bodily eyes and ears on all children are their main tools for learning. Those two bodily functions (eyes and ears) are vital participants while being taught. When your children watch you do unrighteous or righteous actions, it is like viewing an event on your TV screen. Many children continuously learn how to count numbers, and or the official order of the ABC's from watching "Sesame Street", which is a TV program. When a television show has taught your child a thing or two, that child has intelligently learned from what was seen and heard. Parents, remember every action or willful episode being performed, either by mouth or by physical movement, your children are observing, listening, hearing, and more so, learning.

When people have kids, the children become their students. Just as a student sits in a classroom to be taught by the schoolteacher, a child sits at home to be taught by the father and or mother. A teacher educates students from the knowledge learned from reading and the studying books. A mother or father will instruct the child, and give knowledge from experiences that have been encountered in life. Teachers pass out book assignments so that the students may comprehensively learn; on the other hand, a parent will give living examples to teach the child what independent living is all about. A teacher asks for obedience and participation from the students, while a parent asks for strict obedience and high honor from the child. Those facts, which are mentioned in this paragraph, ought to be performed by the father or mother as being a teacher, and or a parental leader.

So loving parents, tell me, where is the influential leadership? Where is your performance of unconditional love and cherishing affection? Do you as a father or mother feel as if you are a leader in your home? Whether you feel as if you are a leader or not, when your adorable baby was born, you automatically became an ultimate leader. You took the time to have sexual relation to produce the infant, now you have to take the time to direct the child's life. Parents must show influential leadership to their kids. Telling your children not to do drugs is showing true leadership. However, if chemical usage is active in the home, then you are not being a great leader. Stop allowing wickedness to come into your home in the form of chemical control substances.

The bible says, *in 1ˢᵗ Corinthians 13:13 and now abideth faith, hope, and charity; but the greatest of the three is charity (love).* This biblical scripture means more of what I am about to express unto you, however, I wanted to use it as a love token for your parental understanding. Parents can have faith for their child's success; parents can have hope for their kids to have a decent living, however, if you are not teaching and expressing love in the home, then nothing else really matters. From the mouth, parents always tell their children, "I love you" nevertheless, actions speak louder than words.

Have you ever heard the phrase; actions speak louder than words". If you have not told your kids that you love them, then your performed actions will speak for you. People say, "I love you" all the time, but if they are not showing love in physical form, then true love is not at work. When a person is trying to prove his or her love, it must be demonstrated, and shown in action form. When you speak from the mouth that you love your kids, then outwardly it must be proven. Speaking love, and showing love, both must be at work. 1 plus 1 is 2, and speaking love plus showing love is the greatest addition of all. Therefore, let the house abide in love by keeping evil substances out of it.

There are two types of love, which needs to be demonstrated in the home among your children. There is a critical time for tough love to be demonstrated, and there is a precious moment for soft love to be assessed. Every mother and every father must have an understanding heart to discern precisely which type of love is to be presented or displayed before the children. When tough love is to be expressed, charge in with tough love. When soft love is to be performed, hold on to that. Tough love and soft love is part of the package when becoming a natural parent or an official leader.

If parents do not express, and exalt true love among their children, many times the children will venture out into the world searching for "love". When your children seek or search for true love, it is greatly possible they will find love the "wrong way" or in the "wrong places". Not only must parents display acts of continual love, but also, a high level of care must be connected as a link. Without true care, there is no true love. Vice versa; without performance of care, there is no true love. The type of love you plant inside your children's mind, is the same physical performance of love that the kids are going to display in public areas.

Respect your home, and respect your children. Although, parents may own the home and pay all the bills, they still need to respect their kids. The reason why children do not respect their parents these days is because; parents do any and everything in the view of their children. A smart and respectful parent will not do any and everything in front of their children's sight. Many actions that the parents do in front of their kids, will cause their children to grow up and copy the same performances seen. Its almost like monkey see, monkey do. If the children occasionally see the father or mother using drugs, then eventually the child is going to grow up in life, and do drugs too. In most cases, that is a known fact. For example, if the parents speak abusive language and disrespect one another, eventually, at a young age the children are going to perform the exact same actions.

Children should always remember the counsels that their natural parents or any guardian has given them. So, when any deeds have been performed, it will be approved by the parent. When a child has done a particular deed that the parents have taught, it will put a beautiful smile on mommy and daddy's face. However, if a father or mother has seen or heard about a bad situation that has been performed by their birth given child, parents think back, did the child view it being done by you? If so, then the parents cannot be upset at the child. If any parent intakes drugs at home, and later on in life, mom or dad has witnessed or found out that their child intake drugs, then the parent should not be disappointed. The child is only repeating the activity seen by mother and or dad. Therefore, not only does counseling with words teaches the children, but also, as I said before, whatever the parents do in the view of children will educate them as well.

I truly wonder how many front and back doors have been kicked in by the police force (the law) because of the evil presence of drugs. I wonder how many times a door has surprisingly been knocked off its hinges while infants were present in the home. When the police force has been commanded to tear into your home for a drug bust, they come without warning. The same entrance that drug associates use to enter into your home is the same pathway the local police force will use to barge into your home.

Drugs have the power to create a pathway of wickedness. The law follows wickedness wherever it is being performed. Whether it is by prophecy or a constitution written in a book, one thing that is for certain, the law will follow you. In a later chapter, I will explain unto you, concerning the phrase, "the law will follow you" everywhere you go".

Since it is against the law to have drugs in your possession (home), whenever the police busts in it, it is not the physical men (police) breaking into your home to find drugs. It is the law that boldly proceeds into your home to righteously convict and judge you if drugs (wickedness) is found within it. Since the law clearly and forcefully speaks against having drugs in your home, then the law must do its job by seeking righteousness, which is to convict you and find you guilty. It is the law that orders men (police force) to unexpectedly barge into your residence to search out your home. Actually, since God is the one who has foreordain the laws, then he is the one who unexpectedly enters into your home. When the law (police) boldly rushes into your home, it comes to imprison you, and make your life miserable. If any wickedness (drugs) is found in your home, immediately the law is empowered to embrace a number of convictions (judgments) upon you for your illegal actions done. Therefore, purposely keep drugs out of your brain, and deliberately keep them out of your home.

The law uses human beings (police) to carry out its work. When the police force barges into your home for a drug search, they do not care what happens to your home.

When the police are in your home searching for drugs, by rights, they can tear into your big radio speakers. The law is on a divine search for narcotics, and nothing else matters. Anything of value in your home, can loose its market price if the police are sent into your residence for a drug search. The police, through the law are on a mission to find you guilty with possession of narcotics. Nothing else matters but to find in your home what the law is looking for (hidden drugs). Therefore, the police are true workers for the laws of God. Some police are cool, and some are crooked, however, to the crooked ones, they have a Day of Judgment coming to them too.

However, if any chemical control substance (drug) is hidden in your home, then your house is plagued and affected with wickedness. Just by bringing drugs into your home, the dope itself brings wickedness along with it. Drugs and wickedness are attached one to another. Just as an unborn infant is attached to the belly of the mom, drugs are attached to the associations of wickedness. You will never find any street drug that does not carry wickedness along with it. They stay connected for life. Therefore, when you are hiding drugs in your home or possession, you are hiding wickedness as well. In fact, drugs give birth to wickedness, remember. Once your life has been filled with drugs, violence next becomes birthed. After birth, every act of wickedness that could be done under God's blue heaven is brought forth. Once you begin to make love to drugs, they will turn around and then make love to you, and less than 3 minutes later, wicked acts will be birthed. Actually, as soon as you put drugs in your hands, wickedness has already been birthed. Therefore, keep drugs out of your home because wickedness will be the birth, and evil experiences will be your children.

Not only will the local police break into a "drug trafficking" home, but also, brain chemical addictive people will break into your residence as well. Drug heads (people who put drugs in their brains) will break into your residence and rob you at gunpoint. Either they are coming to rob you, or steal your possessions. You can be at home, or away from home, however, the law, or drugs filled brains (evil men) will barge in. If the law is not after you, then drug users will be after you. Either the police or drug heads will be plotting to come into your place of dwelling without any given notice. Therefore, neither can you dodge the law, nor can you hide from drug users. Everyone as well as the police knows you have drugs. The law's job is to judge you, and the dope head job is to feed his or her addiction.

Hey, parents do not think that you have the house in control when drugs are in the home. Having drugs in your home will cause you to loose control over it. A package of drugs will only cover about 5 inches of space in your entire home, but from its explosive and evil power, it will take over the entire residence. Every parent who congregates drugs in their home thinks they have the house in order. Thinking you have the house under your authority when drugs are in your home is the wrong mind set to have. Any form of evil can break loose in your home when drugs share couple of inches of space within it.

There are many unpleasant events that all children will experience, which could have truly been avoided. If children (me especially) would have kept their parents counseling and instructions, then probably we could have lived better lives. Counseling from our parents is given unto us so that we will gain an understanding of the things that could happen unto us if we continue to be disobedient.

Parents, give your kids ongoing personal counseling as much as you can. Regardless of how hard the struggle may seem to be, never give up on your child. As long as your child is living under your roof, and eating the food you've purchased, you have complete official rights to call for a moment of counseling. Send your child away with lively counseling. When the child packs up and move out of your home, and begin to live on his or her own, you are "righteously" free from any of the child's worldly experiences.

If we kids do not keep our parents counseling, when

awful experiences approach our lives, we will look back over our lives and say, "mother and father" told "me" not to do that. Many actions and performances that kids have performed, our parents never thought we would have done some of the things we've done. Many parents never thought in a million years that their child would walk down a certain path in life. Although, our parents have explained unto us the first hand consequence we might face if we did certain things, however, we did them anyway. Some of our disobedient actions we are suffering from right now, has force us too say comment such as this; "I wish I could start life all over again." As I grew up in life, and has experienced many things, I said that often to myself. I also said, "I cannot believe that I spent so many years of my life doing a whole lot of nothing".

Every child will receive a reward for his or her own personal actions and mistakes that have been made. No one is committed to suffer someone else's mistakes. If you have willingly committed the act, then you are the one to take the full blame. If a boy or girl suffers from a lawbreaking act, he or she must bare the full guilt. The child's consequence would be his or her judgmental reward.

Every bad and repeated action that youths willfully commit will haunt him or her in the near or future. When a child has submitted to performing actions that break the laws (which are wicked deeds), those wicked deeds will eventually haunt him or her. Its like a spirit ghost has been following you for years and years, and then unexpectedly, it becomes visible, then grabs you, and bruises you. When this invisible character finally grabs you, you have been captured by what I call, "The Wicked Ghost Chaser".

When kids or people do unlawful actions, and it comes back to "haunt" them for punishment, that is called, "reap what you sow". However, I call it "The Wicked Ghost Chaser. That rule (reap what you sow) most definitely implies to the entire world of different people. Every creed and race will reap whatever he or she has sown in life. The "reap what you sow" law does not care how old you are; if you have sown it, then guess what, you must reap it. No age or mind smartness of a human being can cleverly walk around or dodge the prophetic law, which says, "You reap what you sow". God has provided the world with that law; therefore, when it is time to reap, yes, you will reap whatever has been sown.

A child might be able to conceal his wicked deeds (wrong actions) from the parent, but none can hide from the "reap what you sow" law. A child cannot hide from reaping what has been sown, nor can he or she hide from the binocular vision God. Reaping what you sow is a spiritual law from God, therefore, when it is time for you to reap, God is going to allow you to reap what you deserve. Young girl or young boy, whatever evil action you are doing, your future will act horribly sour against you.

Children, in order to be successful in your personal living, a work of obedience must be in session. You need to be obedient to your parents as well as being obedient unto God's laws. It is a good thing to be obedient unto your parents, but it is even greater to be obedient to God, because he is the judge of all the earth. Therefore, not only should kids obey their parents, which are the leaders that control the earthly home, but also children need to obey God, which has the power and control over the entire universe.

Obedience is the master key that will open the doorway to prosperity. In this life, no one will see full future prosperity unless a form of obedience is taken into action. For example, let's say that you applied for a particular job, and the job requires that your body (system) be free from drugs. In order to earn the employment, you have to obey the rules by having a drug free system (body). Therefore, you cannot intake dope into your body. Once you have passed the drug test and have gained the position, you have just walked into the ways of prosperity. Regardless of how much money the occupation pays you, however, prosperity is not measured by financial gross. Prosperity comes when you've been obedient to the rules that have been set before you. By being obedient to the rules set before you, you have earned the position or the job that your heart has desired. Therefore, you have stepped into the world of prosperity because obedience. No matter what you desire to do in this life, in order to be prosperous, obedience must become the "primary" sacrifice. My 3rd book, which is titled, "Keep Your Vision" is a good book concerning being obedient in order to gain what your heart desires (prosperity).

This is to all the caring parents who have amazingly demonstrated true love and have raised their kids in a drug-free home. Although, you have been a great drug free leader in before your children's sight, if or when your kids grow up, and become something that you have not raised them to become, that type of reaction you truly cannot prevent. You know that drug habits were not physically access in your home because you were a drug free leader. Therefore, if your child grows up in life and begin to place drugs in his or her brain, the blame should not be upon your heart. You, the parent, did what you had to do in order to keep drugs out and away from your children's sight. If you as a parent have kept drugs out of the kid's sight, and out of the home, then you have done a great job.

On the other hand, if you are a parent, and drug activity has been mobile in the home, then you share a portion of the child's reason for drug usage. The child watched you intake drugs, and that same activity has been passed on. How are you going get upset at your child, when you do drugs too? Now a day's all parents says, "I do not want my child going through what I went through with drugs". Yet, you still use dope in the presence of the child. These days, most parents are so hypocritical, and they know it not. Most parents are phony, and most are complete fakes.

Chapter 3
My Sports Position

From all the wickedness, and drug trafficking being mobile throughout the Vaughn Projects, and the ongoing physical violence, actions of wickedness was always in session. By the power of wickedness and evil, human bodies were empowered to activate works of unrighteousness continually. While playing my rock and bottle game, often times I became interrupted. The Vaughn Projects was heavily plagued with the works of wickedness, and it was very dangerous for me to play my rock and bottle game.

It is also possible that my parents thought to put me on a sport team because my rock throwing habits were horribly ridiculous. Whatever reason it was, that caused my parents to take me to a youth sports program; here I am about to sign up for a team.

When my mother and I stepped foot into the boys club, I became very nervous. The boys club was packed with little league athletes. I soon realized that all these young boys were here for the same reason I am here for. It was probably more than 25 young athletes in this club, along with their parents. Each athlete looked at one another. After about 10 to 15 minutes had passed, relaxation kicked in, and I became calm.

This club is called, "Mathews Dickey's Boys Club". Mathews Dickey's Boys Club is a well-known and respected sport program in the St. Louis City area. At this boys club, I participated in football and baseball. For many years, I played those two sports for Mathew's Dickey Boys Club. Therefore, the name **Brian Irons** became a regular signature on two different sport's team roster.

I played football first, and when the football season was over, I then participated in baseball. As I played sports year after year, my sport skills became better and better. I felt like I was the man. My sport talents and skills that I utilized in game situations, made me feel as if there was none like me. My athletic statistics proved unto me that I was at least an awesome sport competitor. Even in playing sports, the phrase, "actions speak louder than words" is a great factor. Well, in a minute, I am about to explain my sport skills unto you in wordbook form.

As my parents and I stood in line, we met the boy's club organizer. This first day at the boys club was a visitation to sign my name to a team try-out roster. I signed my name on the Mathews Dickey's Cardinals baseball team. Therefore, after signing my name on the roster, my mom and I were told to return to the boy's club on a certain day, so that we could meet the baseball coach face to face.

A day or two later, my parents and I drove back to the boys club to meet the coach. When my mother and I met the coach face to face, we all shook hands, and verbally introduced our selves. I told the coach my name is **Brian Irons**, and he said; call me "coach" or "Mr. Kenny Younger". Once my mother and I met Mr. Younger, he then gave us a short speech concerning his rules.

These rules were for each athlete to abide by in order to make the team. Every parent was present with their child, so we all heard the coach's speech and rules at the same time. (Good Lord, my parents have rules, my baseball coach has rules, and God has rules (his laws). (It seems like everybody in the world has rules).

The coach also told the players and their parents that he does not want any foolishness on the baseball field. The coach said, "If foolishness is being mobile on the baseball field, that the player will be asked to get off the baseball field, sit on the bench, and wait for the parent to arrive. The coach also said, "The player's name will be deleted from try-out list if disobedience is in action. I guess the coach-wanted tryouts to be over with, so he could begin to work on the chosen players for the season.

Then the coach gave my mom and I a sheet of paper,

which had the team's practice schedule on it. Every day of the week, the players had to practice. Monday through Friday, the athletes are supposed to met up at handy park for practice.

During practice session, we practice 3 to 4 hours. Sometimes practice session was longer. Every now and then, practice was schedule on weekends.

Well, here I am on the baseball field. As I ran out on the baseball field for practice, I immediately ran to an outfielder's position. Any outfielder's position is where I wanted to play. In baseball, my heart was set on playing the outfield, and nothing else. I did not care if it was left, right, or centerfield, I only wanted to play one the outfielder's position.

As I positioned myself in the outfield, there were so many rocks and clods of dirt clustered together. It was almost as if the rocks had a mouth, and were saying, "pick me up, pick me up". Once I looked at a rock, my mind became intrigued. The temptation was so strong, I could not bear it. Therefore, I picked up a few rocks, and began to lay them in a pile next to me.

Then I picked up a rock, and launched it at a player on the baseball field. After I had thrown a rock at a player, I then acted as if I was in my baseball pose waiting for the ball to be hit towards my way. I was leaning forward, with my hands on my knees as an outfielder does when waiting for a ball to be hit towards his way. I DID NOT KNOW any of these players, but here I am launching rocks at them. I threw rocks at a different athlete almost every practice session.

Soon, the players found out that I was the ignorant person who was hurling rocks at them. After the players realized I was the fellow throwing rocks at them, they went and told the coach about it. After the coach had been told the word, I thought I was going to be either sent home or deleted from the squad. I thought my rock throwing habit had messed up my opportunity to play little league baseball.

So the coach yelled out my name saying, "Irons, come here". His voice traveled through the air loudly, and my ears heard the pitch thereof. It seemed like his voice was a physical movement, because when I heard it, my body shook, as it does when a person sneaks up from behind. Suddenly, I became frightened, because it sounded like the coach was a little angry. Besides, I did not want to be cut from the squad (team). With a belt, or whatever was in her presence, my mother would have spanked the living flesh off me. If throwing rocks was the true reason for me being "cut" from the team, I do not know what my mother would have done.

As I was jogging in towards the coach, the closer I got into his presence, the more I trembled inside. I am now face to face with him. He looked straight into my eyes and said, "Irons", since you like to throw rocks so much, "pitch". Then he took off his baseball glove, tossed me the baseball, and I began to pitch to the other players on the baseball team. From that day forward, and throughout my little league baseball career, I became the first string pitcher for the team. I was the starting pitcher for the Mathews Dickey's Cardinals baseball team for the next 7 years. After a while, I emotionally fell in love with the pitcher's position. The pitching position did fit me, since I did like to throw rocks every day. I joined the team to play the outfielders position, however, I DID NOT KNOW that I would be a team's pitcher.

In my first baseball season as a pitcher, my brilliant record was very successful. My first year's pitching record, not counting the playoff games, was 15-1. My second season as a baseball pitcher, my awesome record was 14-2. As you can see, the first 2 years of my pitching career were successful seasons. All my 7 years of pitching, my team's winning record stayed highly above the average of .500. I was a tough baseball pitcher and I have stats to prove it.

My first two seasons, I pitched in 32 games, and only lost 3. Not only that, but I pitched every game in its entirety. My records proved to me that I was a successful little league baseball pitcher. Since my first pitching season had a record of 15-1, I actually almost had a perfect winning season record. If I count the playoff games too, my first year record was 20-1 (20 wins, and one loss). The second season record was 19-2 (19 wins, with 2 losses). Yeah, I am the greatest; I am the best, and there's none like me.

My pitching skills had been voiced all over the youth boy's club. It was said that I was one of the best pitchers in my league and age bracket. I believe, I became a tough and dominant pitcher because of all those rocks I had thrown in the projects, while playing my "rock and bottle" game. I am convinced that I had thrown dozens of rocks on the regular. Although, I was throwing curves and sinkers with rocks, I was still able to move that same throwing talent to a baseball. The same way I threw a sinker or a curve with rocks is the same skill that I utilized to throw with a baseball. Of course, I had to grasp each object (rock or ball) differently, but the flick of the wrist was still the same. To me, it was very easy; I had a special sophistication, and I had no problems at all throwing like that. I know it sounds untrue or unrealistic to throw sinkers and curves with rocks, but I had a skill and a talent, and throwing anything was a "piece of cake". I can also throw curves and sinkers with pennies, nickels, and quarters. Yeah, I even put money in the game, so I know my skills are awesome (talented).

In my first 2 years as a baseball pitcher, my strikeout average was about 9 to 11 players per game. My strike out average is the true reason why my team's winning average stayed highly above .500 every year. In little league baseball, there were only 7 innings per game. Each inning I had to pitch against 3 batters. In a complete 7-inning game, all I had to face were 21 batters from the start. If there are 7 innings in each game, and every inning I pitched to 3 batters, and every GAME I struck out 9 to 11 batters, then that is an average of 3 whole innings without the opposing team hitting the baseball. When the opposing team's player did hit the ball; the ball was hit in the air, and caught by one of my team players'. Or the ball was hit in the infield, and the batter was thrown out at first base. If I am not mistaken, in my 2 years of pitching 32 seasonal games, I believe, I pitched about 15 games were the opposing team did not score a point at all. I've pitched so many "no-hitter" games during my little league baseball career, it's ridiculous.

There was this one team called the "Mathew Dickey's Eagles". The Eagles were the talented squad that caused flaws to be collected upon my record. The Eagles had some very tough hitters on their team. Almost every year, my team (Cardinals) had to play against the Eagles in play-off competition. This team, the Eagles would make it to the playoffs because of their hitting ability. However, my team would make it to the playoffs because of my pitching skills. My team was filled great hitters as well, but when a team has a pitcher (me) on the mound striking out 3 innings worth of batters, it became easy to win. Nevertheless, I became the team's star pitcher, and had to face the fascinating ball hitting Eagles, often.

I had loyal fans who traveled to watch me pitch. Many of my fans would ask my coach, "when is the next scheduled game" so they could come watch me pitch. They wanted to sit on the sidelines, and watch me do what I do best…. pitch. My fans knew they were about to watch an awesome game, so they all came with furniture to keep them comfortable. Some came to the game with lawn chairs, and some even came with blankets to lay on. All through the game, my fans would yell out, "strike him out too, and get this game over with".

My fans, my team players, and my family members gave me a pitcher's nickname. "The junk pitcher" is the name they called me. They called me the "junk pitcher" because the pitches that I threw in game situation had great air movement. I was 7 years of age throwing pitches that lead people to give me a meaningful name, "The junk pitcher".

The talent and gift that God gave me was far advanced for my age limit. Although, I was 7 years old, I pitched as if I was a teenager. I did not have the teenage throwing power (velocity), but making the ball do tricks was a skill and talent that I possessed. I had about 6 different pitches that I learned to throw at the age of 7. Three to four of my pitches were different levels of curves alone. Having many levels of pitches that I could throw, that is what made me an awesome pitcher. My pitching skills were totally unique, and truly "one" of kind.

I remember a championship game my team was scheduled to play. This game was a season's final. After this game is played, the baseball season will be over. The team that wins this game is going to be the team to receive 1st place trophies. Each player on the team has the rights to collect a trophy one by one, after the game has been won. Therefore, the team that wins this game will be traveling home with smiles and grins on their faces.

My team and I went through the playoffs unbeaten and had advanced to the finals. The play-off was tough, but we made it to the finals. I had pitched all season long, and my pitching skills elevated us to this point. Taking my team to the championship finals, to me it was very easy. I performed a work of pitching success because my team is now in the finals. Well, here we are about to play in the championship game, and show off our skills.

As this championship game was in progress, my team's score was trailing our opponent. From the beginning of the game up until now, my team's score stayed under our opponent. Although, my team was trailing in points, the score was still a close. This game was filled with a high level of intensity. My team was nervous, the other team was nervous, but there will be only one winner. Even though this was a close scoring game, my team was putting up a good fight to stop us from loosing. This game was very important to us just as it was for our opposing team.

While this game was in progress, I was sitting on the bench watching. In such a big way, I was actually a spectator. Therefore, another pitcher was on the mound pitching. He was giving his best performance as he pitched. He was doing his very best to prevent us from loosing the chance to win those 1st place trophies. As I was sitting on the bench, the game was not looking to good to my sight. When a team is trailing their opponent's score the entire game, it makes the athletes worry.

Indeed, we wanted to grasp our hands around those 1st place trophies. Besides, we wanted those 1st place trophies to be placed in our homes on shelves. There is nothing like celebrating a win in the last game of the season. No one enjoys loosing; everyone only enjoys winning.

Somehow, my team scrambled back, and the score became tied 8 to 8. A championship game cannot end with a tie; therefore, we had to keep playing until a team's player scored. When my team had finally tied the score 8 to 8, of course we were happy. Not only did my team finally catch up with the opposing team's score, but also, the other team was at bat with the bases loaded. The bases were loaded, and there were no outs. If one of the players of our opposing team hits the ball, it is very possible that they will score, win the championship, and take home those 1st place trophies. Then, they will be crowned the championship champions for this year's championship game. A game, which is as important as this one, my team wanted me to be the pitcher on the mound. In fact, I was scheduled to pitch this game, but another pitcher played, because I injured my pitching hand a few hours before the game.

Whenever my team had an important game, the coach would always tell my parents to "keep an eye on me" so I that would not injure my pitching hand. However, as my mom and I were over my uncle's house, my mother was inside. I was outdoors by myself being a kid, playing by myself.

I had an accident the same day of the championship game. This accident happened about 3 or 4 hours before game time. This accident had unexpectedly happened at my relative's house. My mother and I went to my uncle's house for a short visitation before the game.

Outside in the front yard, there was an old skateboard in the grass. I picked the skateboard up, placed it in the streets, and began to ride it. There was a ridiculous steep hill in the street where my uncle lived. The hill was steep, and it looked like a roller coaster. It had sharp turns, and it kept going downward. The hill was so steep, that after I rode it down the hill, I had to get off the skateboard, and walk back up it.

As I was rolling down this steep hill, I was probably rolling about 5 to 10mph. That's a fast speed to be on a skateboard, and going downhill. As I was riding the skateboard down the hill, I was coasting on the skateboard moving faster and faster. Suddenly, a fast moving vehicle was rolling up the hill and traveling towards my way. It visually seemed like the moving automobile came swiftly from out of nowhere. Unexpectedly, the car appeared. A quick mind alternating decision had to be made. Either I was going to jump off the skateboard, and land on the hood of the rolling car, or leap and land in the dirt and grass. I did not have much time to decide on what should be done. It was like; wham bam and the car came. Less than two seconds, a choice had to be made. Therefore, I made a quick decision, and decided to jump off the skateboard. I landed in the grass and dirt. After I hit the grass, I began to slide. I slid through the glass about 5 yards.

One of the first defensive reactions people do when falling or sliding headfirst is to lay their hands and arms out before them. Well, as I dove into the lawn, I became superman. My body was airborne about a second and a half. In mid air, I stretched my arms and hands out before me. Then I landed on the earth's grass. As I was sliding in the grass, the flesh of my right hand (pitching hand) encountered a piece of glass that had a sharp edge on it.

The sharp piece of glass had thrashed through the palm of my right hand. To my hand, the glass did a work of flesh separation. When the glass split the flesh of my pitching hand, blood began to gush out. I then ran into the house, crying in fear because of all this blood. I ran into my uncle's house crying, and in fear watching blood leak from my hand. When I finally entered into the house, my mother wrapped up my hand with gauge. Then she drove me to the hospital, so I could be provided with professional medical care.

When my mother and I arrive at the hospital, I was handled and treated immediately, because my injury was a right now active one. So a doctor came and got me, took me to a patient room, and sowed my hand with stitches. After the doctor stitched my hand together, I then left the hospital.

When my coach had heard what happened unto my hand, he became very frustrated and worried. He was probably wondering why my mother allowed me to ride a skateboard on championship competition day. As a kid, I just wanted to have some fun; I was not thinking about a baseball game. Besides, <u>I DID NOT KNOW</u> that riding a skateboard was going to cause an injury to my hand.

As this playoff game was in its first extra inning, the other team was at bat, with the bases loaded. It was either we are going to win or lose. Whichever team scores first will fairly win the "championship competition game". So there I was, on the bench about to watch my team probably loose because the bases were loaded and there were no outs.

Well, the coach turned his head and looked at me. As the coach's eyes were fastened upon me, he then said, **"Brian Irons**, how is your hand? Is there any pain in it? Can you pitch? We need you! I replied and said, "No", my hand does not have pain in it, and yes I can pitch". Now that I think about what I just did, I have great courage, and a strong heart. I mean really, this is a championship game, and if the team hits the ball and score, it would be as if I lost the game. Although, I did not pitch in the beginning of this game, however, I came in the game where the heat is on. If the team hit the ball and score, I will probably cry, and my team will too. I could have lied and said, "My hand is too painful to throw". The coach would have had no other choice but to believe my words. But my heart and courage spoke up and said, "Yes, I can pitch".

It is baseball's rule that a pitcher cannot pitch with a wrapped up hand. The reason for this rule is because; the batter might have trouble watching the ball in the air as if leaves the pitcher's hand. Therefore, I un-wrapped the medical gauge from my hand. I took a quick looked at the stitches. I opened and closed my hand, to give it a little stretch. Then I jogged on the baseball field to the pitcher's mound.

I then picked up the baseball. I squeezed it with the inured hand a couple of times. Then I began to play catch with the catcher on my team. As I was loosening up my throwing arm, slight pains of throbbing began to travel through my hand. Nevertheless, I did not mention the pain to my coach because I wanted to rescue my team so that we could earn those first place trophies.

As I was warming up, the entire team gathered around me. The team was whispering in my ears saying, "Irons" strike these dudes out because we want those 1st place trophies. Little did my teammates realize that they were putting more pressure on me by saying such words. They also said, "We know your hand is messed up, but we need you to come through for us. I remember one player whose name is Kenneth Morris (first base player); he would always encourage me in close game situations.

After the opposing team had seen me take the gauge off my hand, they immediately realized that I was a wounded pitcher. Even before the game started, when the other team's coach had found out that I was not going to pitch because of an injured hand, he highly felt that his team had a 90% chance of winning. Actually, the entire opposing team was happy that I did not start as the pitcher in this game. This coach, along with his team players knew that I was the Mathew Dickey Cardinals star pitcher. Nevertheless, they still had to get past the champion of throwing (me) in order to wrap their hands around those 1st place trophies. Therefore, they had to face me anyway. Yeah, they had to face **Brian Irons**, who is the "grand wizard" of throwing.

After I finished loosening up my pitching arm, it was time to get the game started again. During this particular time in the game, the infielders and outfielders all came closer toward the plate. We knew that, if our opponent's bat connects with the ball in any kind of way, that the other team's coach is going to direct the 3rd base runner to head for home plate for the chance to win the championship game. Even if a ball is hit to the outfield, the 3rd base runner can tag up and head for home plate for a score. Therefore, if any player or batter hits the ball on the field, that hit will probably cause us to loose the championship game. Then my team will not be leaving the baseball field with those 1st place trophies, the other team will. Well, here I am, about to pitch with a sore and bruised up hand filled with stitches. This was the biggest test that I had to take throughout my entire season of pitching. Because, not only were the bases loaded, but also, there were no outs, and then I came into the game and had to face the top of the line-up.

The top of the line-up, which is the first 3 batters on any team, is usually the best hitter's of the team. Therefore, I had to face the best hitters on the team, with the bases loaded, and no outs. Here I am about to pitch in the championship game, with stitches in my throwing hand.

The first batter walks up to the plate seeking to hit a base hit to win the championship competition game for his team. I looked him in the eye and he looked me in the eye. Then I went into the pitcher's wind up and pitched him the ball. The first pitch I threw was a curve ball, he swings and miss, so that is strike one. The next two pitches were also curve balls; the batter swings at them both and misses…strike three, one out! The second batter walks up to the plate seeking to be the champion of the game. I hurled 3 different types of curveball pitches at him and struck him out too. The third batter comes to the plate; I threw 3 different type of curveball at him, and struck him out too. I struck the first batter out, the second batter, and the third batter, and the inning was over. I came into the game, and pitched 3 straight outs just that fast. I am the best, I am the greatest, and there's none like me.

My reader, you would have been astonishingly amazed at how precise my throwing accuracy really is. My mental will power is high tech as well, because I was not worried at all pitching against those three batters. Although, I was a little nervous, however, I did not mentally fret. I went into the game, and threw only 9 pitches that turn out to be 3 outs. I am skillful, I am talented, I am the best the best in the business, and I was born with this amazing ability.

If I make it to Major League Baseball, I am confident that I will have the most strikeouts in baseball's history. There is none like me, well, not too many athletes are as gifted as I am. I hope someday soon that I will be able to say what Ali said, "I shook up the world, and I'm a bad man".

After the 3 outs from the strikeouts were executed by my pitching skills, it was then my team's turn to bat. To make a long story short, my team scored, and we won the championship competition game. We won the championship finals, and we all received those 1st place trophies on the baseball field. One by one, we lined up on the baseball field, and received our awards (trophies).

As little league athletes, after winning big games, such as championships, we would gather around one another, sing victory songs, eat chips, eat brownies, and drink sodas. This competitive game goes down on record as one of my best baseball pitching performances ever. My one-inning game performance became a splendid lifetime memorial experience for me. Everything I do goes down as a memorial. Why? Because I am the greatest! However, personally, throughout my career of pitching, I earned three most valuable player trophies. Yeah, three trophies had the name **Brian Irons printed** on them, along with MVP letters.

In life, as I became older, in my neighborhood, I would play cork ball with friends. Cork ball was played with a tennis ball. Yes, I was a pitcher in most of these games. As I pitch in cork ball, sometimes I pitched with my right hand, and sometimes I pitched with my left. Although, my right hand threw more accurate and harder, however, I can pitch with my left too. Not too many baseball pitchers in the world can do that. A person might be able to toss a ball with either hand, but to make the ball curve or sink with either hand, not to many pitchers can do that.

In the neighborhood, as I became older, many people would say unto me, Lytskin (my street name), you need to go to Busch Stadium and sign up for the St. Louis Cardinals baseball team as a pitcher. They also said," you will be the leagues star pitcher, and be the one to win championship games for our city and state team. Yeah, everyone saw the pitching talents and skills that my brain possessed. In my youth days of pitching, I have been named after a few MLB pitchers.

Well, baseball season has ended, and now it is time for me to participate in another sport. After baseball season had ended, my mother took me back to the youth boy's club so I could sign up for football. As I was signing up for the football team, my mother, and I met the football coach. After we all introduced our selves, the coach provided us with his rules, and the boy's club regulations. In other words, just as my baseball coach had rules, my football coach had rules too.

My first year of playing football, I was a starting safety. I was 7 years old at the time. I was a tough safety. I injured many athletes while playing the position of safety. However, let me tell you about my second year of playing football.

I was 8 years old at the time; I signed my name on the football's try-out sheet. I jotted down that I specifically wanted to try-out for the wide receiver's position. I felt within myself that I could catch a football very well. Since I can throw with either hand, then both of my hands were talented for grasping. In addition, I knew that I had great visual judgment of the ball as it traveled while being in the air. For some reason, I like catching balls (football and baseball) as they traveled through the air. That is why I wanted to play outfield in baseball.

The football try-out list is filled with a great number of little league football players. Therefore, the coach was focusing on each athlete to see who had the talents and skills to make the football team. In other words, the team roster sheet needed some names to be put on it. As the coach was watching us, we were physically exposing our very best performance. Each needs to look good before the coach, so that he would be counted as a player for the team. Therefore, every athlete must give his best skillful impression unto the coach.

Another day of football practice had come. The coach was observing and watching the players display their talents and skills on the football field. This particular day the coach had given the try-out athletes a specific task to perform. The athletes were told to line up, and run out for a pass. The coach physically drew a mark on the football field so that the players would see how far to run. The coach was looking to see who was talented enough to play as a wide receiver. I patiently waited for this day to arrive because I wanted to play football as a wide receiver.

So here I am sprinting out on the football field about to show off my catching skills ability. Every time I dashed out on the football field for a pass, I dropped not one. There were no juggling catches; nor were there almost misses. Every pass I caught was solid skillful grabs. I caught every pass with my hands, and no catches were caught with the help of my body. This particular day I was perfect at catching the ball. I even caught a few passes by diving for the ball on purpose. I also caught a couple of passes with one hand, which was also on purpose too. I am talented, and yes, I am the best in business.

The other players were having great difficulties with catching the ball. After I had repeatedly seen the other players having trouble catching the ball, I decided to show off a little. I ran out for a pass farther than what was required for me to do so. Instead of running 10 to 15 yards on the football field, I ran about 30 yards out. Actually, I ran double the amount of yards that the coach had given us. As I ran out for the pass, the coach hurled the ball to me with no hesitation. Yes, I caught that deep pass as well.

After catching that particular pass, it turned out to be a big mistake. The mistake was when I hurled the ball back to the coach from that length of distance. I threw the football to him 10 times better than he had been throwing the football to us. I threw him the ball in a perfect spiral. As I was jogging in to line up for another pass, the coach said, "Young man", I then looked, and he threw me the football. After he tossed me the ball, he replied, "Try this position". That position was quarterback. From that day forward, I became the starting quarterback for the Mathew's Dickey Bulldogs. I was the starting quarterback for the next 5 years. I wanted to be a wide receiver, yet, I DID NOT KNOW that I would be the star quarterback for the team.

In size, I was a little person, so my football's division was called, 8 lights". In my little league years of playing football as quarterback, I earned two trophies labeled MVP (most valuable player). In my days of quarterbacking, I've been called to be the next, "Terry Bradshaw". Also, I was called, "The next Roger Staubach". I have been called dozens of pro league quarterbacks.

Playing sports taught my mind how to be useful in two different ways. When I was a pitcher, my mental status learned how to be tough on the defensive side. When I was quarterbacking, my mind learned how to be tough on the offensive side. Therefore, in my life, just by playing sports, my brain already knows how to be defensive, and it knows how to be offensive. Whether offensive or defensive, I had learned them both from two different points of views. Therefore, in life, as I grow older, I will know how to be offensive and defensive both at the same time.

When I became older in life, high school sports became my next activity. I played football when I was a freshman in high school. I played baseball as a freshman and junior. After football and baseball seasons were over during high school, I quit playing those two sports for teams forever. Although, those two sports were my activities from youth, I fell out of love with playing them both. I fell completely in love with another sport called, "basketball".

All my four years of playing basketball in high school was at Lindbergh Sr. High. Within myself, I held a high level of love for this sport. The love that I held for basketball became greater than the love that I had for any other sport (football or baseball). Football and baseball were okay, but basketball became my new athletic career, and daily participation. The sport of basketball took over my athletic life, and yes, I desire to play in the N.B.A, so that I could play against the professionals.

I was a 1st string shooting guard some of my freshman year. I was a starting shooting guard the entire season as a sophomore and as a senior. I had many great game experiences as I played basketball in high school. Some were victorious, and some were heart hurting.

Let me tell you about one of my basketball experiences I encountered during high school. My team was playing against "Oakville Sr. High School". Oakville and Lindbergh were two schools of rivalry. Just as the Cowboys and Redskins are competitive rivalries, well, Lindbergh and Oakville are rivalries too. In this game, playing against Oakville, I became hyped on the court. I was envisioning myself creating a steal in the game, and then dashing to the goal to get my first high school dunk. I have dreamed of doing this for years. Well, it happened, I stole the ball from Oakville's possession. I begin to dribble the ball towards my goal to get my first dunk in game situation. I felt that I could at least try it once, since we had a ten-point lead going into the fourth quarter. As I went up to perform my first dunk, I missed it; the ball hit the back of the rim and flew into the air. From the missed dunk, the coach became mentally heated, and he snatched me out of the game, and sat me on the bench. I guess it was supposed to teach me a lesson. As I sat on the bench, the other team scrambled back and took the lead. After a while, I guess the coach figured that he should forget about the fact I missed a dunk, and get me back into the game.

Then the coach looked at me, and said, "Irons go back into the game". Well, to make a long story short, I stole the ball twice from Oakville, and led my team to victory. Yeah, my mind is already being defensive because I stole the ball twice from Oakville's possession. I am the best, I am the greatest, I shook up the world, and there is none like me. I am skillful and talented to the fullest. If you come up against me, I guaranteed you, you going down for the count.

There was nothing in the world that had strength to prevent me from playing the game of basketball. I gave basketball my all in all. I was very talented and good at playing basketball. I was the athlete who would take the last second shot some times.

When I played street basketball in many neighborhoods and gyms, different people use to say exalting words about my court performance. Many said I had too many tricks under my sleeves. In other words, there was no way I could be contained on the court. They said, I had too many moves, which is a true statement, because I can do it all with my left arm or my right arm. They said I was too quick. They said, they said, they said it all, and I overheard it all.

As I played the game of basketball, people (my fans) have compared me to many N.B.A. players of today, and from the past. As I was being compared to these N.B.A. stars, it was then given unto me their name. I have been compared to Michael Jordan all my basketball career life. I was compared to Jordan because of the creative moves that I would perform to get a shot off while driving to the hole. I have been compared to Scottie Pippen as well. This is really talent right here; I have been called, a Michael Jordan and a Scottie Pippen put together all in one. When a person compares someone with two professional athletes in one, that individual is very talented. Well, since I was the one said to be two athletes in one, then, I guess I was just that good and talented. I have been compared to Wilt Chamberlain. I have been compared to George (The Iceman) Gervin. I have even been compared to the Kareem Abdul Jabbar because of my either arm skyhooks. Oh yeah, I can shoot accurate hooks with either arm, in the paint and out of the paint. I have been compared to Dr. J (Julius Ervin). I have been compared to Larry Bird because of my long distance shooting. I have even been called, Magic Johnson and Isaiah Thomas. I've been called, Clyde "The Glide" Drexler. If there is a great basketball player that has been seen as a dominant player, then you can bet, I was compared to him too. All of those skills that were attached to the basketball players were seen in one man, and that man is I. Meaning, people have seen **Brian Irons** do it all on the basketball court. Think about it, I am only one man, and I have been compared to dozens of N.B.A stars. That's crazy! No, it's not crazy, it only means, I am just the greatest, and that's it.

My basketball talents and skills were awesome. The way my left hand operated on the basketball court, and I appeared to be a dominant right-hand shooter, confused everyone. Sometimes, I would take a shot with my right hand, and then the next shot would be taken with my left. In basketball, both, my talents and skills were seen and stimulated. With talents and skills such as mine, the people could not help but notice the gifts, which I attained in my body. I can purposely shoot a basketball from the old N.B.A. 3-point range with either arm. That is a skill and a talent that I have not seen in many basketball athletes as of yet.

My arm talent or gift is different from 90% of the basketball athletes who are in the world today. The evenhanded talent that I possessed is actually the true reason why I was so dominant on the b-ball court. There were not too many weaknesses in my skills when it comes to my basketball performance. It was hard for people to stop or contain me on the basketball court. My opponents never knew which hand I was going to use to release the basketball to take the next shot. No matter how far from the goal I planned to take a shot, my opponents never knew which hand was going to release the ball.

It was basic instinct for an athlete to attempt to block my shot on my right side because I was a right-handed shooter. On the other hand, it was basic instinct for me to switch hands and shoot the ball with my left. I thought it was unique to be an evenhanded basketball player. Being able to change hands in mid air to take a shot from any distance on the basketball court was raw talent given unto me. I am not talking about switching hands in the paint near the rim, I am talking about switching hands from anywhere on the basketball court. The basketball gifts and talents my brain possessed, none of the N.B.A. players have it, sorry to say. I am the best, I am the greatest, there is none like me, and they call me "Lytskin".

Not that I am thinking about my basketball skill and talents, I really wonder what it is going to be like after I've trained with professional exercising instructors. If people have already compared me to dozen N.B.A. stars, then surely, I was playing pro level on the streets. Well, just wait till they see me after N.B.A. professional training have gone forth. In fact, I have not seen my talents perform to its maximum ability yet. Wow, when I made it to the N.B.A, I guaranteed you, there will be none like me.

I displayed my basketball skills all over the city of St. Louis. I knew that I was skillfully good in playing basketball, and I have what every athlete in the world desires to have, and that is to be an either-handed sport player. I use to love going to different street courts or basketball gyms to "hoop" were other athletes knew anything about me.

Many times when a person was choosing four players to play on the team with him, I would not be one of the choices. I would not be picked because; the person that picked the team does not know me. The true reason why many people did not choose me to play on their team is that, when they look at me, I look like a long skinny man who probably was not too good in playing basketball. When an athlete goes to any gym to play basketball, and the people in the gym do not know him or her, normally a person is picked to play because of his appearance. However, personally speaking, I love when people did not pick me because of my skinny appearance. It only empowered my mind to embarrass people when I finally step on the basketball court. However, when I really wanted someone to pick me, of course, I would try to talk the person into picking me because sometimes there would be so many people waiting to play.

If I could not talk anyone into picking me to play on the team, I would generously ask a person who has the basketball to toss it to me. Then once I received the basketball ball, I would dash toward the rim and perform a "Jordan Dunk". This dunk is a dunk were both of Jordan legs are moving back and forward as he is in mid air, and the ball is cuffed in his hand and wrist as he slams it through the rim. I called it, "the North Carolina fast break dunk". That "dunk" alone usually wins an opportunity for me to be picked on a team. Only if you could have seen me dash to the basketball rim, leap, and soar through the air to perform that Jordan dunk. Jordan is 6'6 and I am only 6'1. Therefore, it looked like I was soaring, because I was only 6'1. Oh yeah, I am a leaper too, indeed I am.

One day, I remember going to play basketball without my friends traveling along with me. Even then, I would dominate the basketball court skillfully with finesse. No matter where I played basketball at, talking trash to competitors was one of my greatest motives. I was on the basketball court doing what I do best...talking trash, and manipulating athletes with my talents and skills. While I was on the court skillfully punishing my opponents, I overheard a few dudes on the sideline talking about hurting me. I heard them say, "he think he better than everyone, we going to see how good he is after the game, since he talking all that trash". I kept on playing the game as if I didn't hear them. Then I began to miss shots on purpose. I was by myself in their neighborhood, and it was obvious that these guys' minds were operating from the power of jealousy. Since I was in their neighborhood, then I was in the territory. Therefore, I was a little scared. To make a long story short, I took a deep deep shot, and as the ball traveled in the air, I dashed to my car for an escape. Whether those guys were serious or not, they did not know me to be speaking words like that about me. People can't say comment like that to an unknown person, and that individual takes their comments as a joke. These people probably never saw me before in their lives, and I have never seen them neither; therefore, I took their words very seriously. To me, I ran for my life. People have been jealous of me all my basketball career life.

In my heart, I was thinking that if I kept on damaging the athletes on the court with my awesome talents and skills, that those guys on the sideline were going to pick a fight with me. I've walked onto many basketball courts that I talked "trash" on, and afterwards I had to leave early or run to my car because of people being jealous of my basketball talents and skills. I really experience jealous folks like that in my life. I can't help it, if the next man is not talented the way I am.

I traveled to many basketball gyms, and demonstrated my physical talents and skills. My talents, skills, and techniques that my body possessed, can make an entire team look horribly bad. I went to Vashon Center one day, and skillfully demolished teams that I played against. I became so great in this gym; other athletes would sign their name on the player's list after mine. Every athlete had to sign his name on the paper in order to play. The next five players on the list will play the winning team. I suppose the people felt if they had me on their team, it would be a good chance that I would help the team win a number of games, so they can continue to play. Well, it was true, I would keep my team on the court for about 2-3 games before we lost and had to get back in line. After the games were over, many athletes would come up to me, and shake my hand. They would embrace me with exalting words before I left out of the gym. This gym of athletes compared me to many N.B.A stars. One person said I played like Jordan; another said I shot hooks like Kareem, another said, "When I soar through the air, that I look like Scottie Pippen".

I went and played basketball at Gamble Center, and my talents and techniques trampled over everyone and every team that came up against me. I went and played at Cherokee center and demonstrated a tremendous amount skill performance. I played at Cherokee one day, and this guy asked me to play on his team (basketball league). I said, "Yes". In this league, the first game I played was at Tangy Gym. I scored 26 points in the first game. If I can remember correctly, each quarter in the game was 10 or 12 minutes.

Yeah, I hurt the opposing team bad. Nobody could stop me. The people watched me run up and down the basketball court, as if they were watching a man from the N.B.A.. Do you know how it feels, when you are playing a game of basketball, and no one can stop you?

I played at Buder Recreation Center, which is my neighborhood gym, and truly, I was a "pro" in that place. I dunked on **Anthony Davenport** a few times in this gym. In Buder's gym, I experienced signing my first autographs after playing basketball. Well, not so much as much signing autographs, but I was asked by some high school students to sign my name on their possessions. Four students walked up to me and asked, "Can I have your signature? Therefore, I grabbed a pen, and signed my name on their books and papers. When the people in the gym had seen me signing my signature on those student's books, they all looked at me with amazement. People usually never ask an athlete for his signature after playing street basketball, unless that particular individual is already famous, or is a well known. I may not have been famous at the time, but since I actually signed my name on those students' books and papers, I am professional level rated. Have you ever been asked to sign your name on anything after playing street ball, probably not?

I went to every Y.M.C.A. gym in city St. Louis, and wrecked the court. I remember playing at the Y.M.C.A, and I hit the first 8 points. Every score was worth 1 point; therefore, my first eight shots were successful results. Just by me thinking about hitting 8 straight points in a roll, I have to get this off my chest; I am the greatest, I am the best, and there's none like me.

I went and played at Marquette Gym and skillfully smashed the competitors who were in there too. This gym of athletes set a 6'6 player on me, and my talents and skills crushed him. Competing against an athlete taller than me only pumps me up to show off. It only roughly ignites my skills to show the gym that, I do not care if he was 7'6; he is not going to stop me. My talents and skills know how to adjust when playing against someone taller than myself.

With such basketball talents and skills as mine, the N.B.A. needs to experience the chance of catching a glimpse of this good stuff.

I went to 12th and Park gym, and pulverized the court. I played at Terry Park, and bruised my opponents. I played basketball at Whol center a few times, and my talents and skills performed mightily in this place. I remember, when everyone on the entire team had the opportunity to try to contain me (check me). Meaning, neither can one team nor one individual defensive player can contain me. It felt good within myself to know that the entire team tried to check me one by one. Maybe, each individual thought that he could do better than what the last man did. Please, I don't care if you put the whole team on me, I can't be stopped, I cant be contain, I am the best, as Ali would say it, I shook up the world, I'm a bad man. I might not have shaken up the world, but I shook up every basketball gym in St. Louis, Missouri.

My coordination, skills, and talents were tremendously a great gift within my body. My talents and skills that were in my body made me feel like I could challenge or play against any number of basketball athletes at one time. Playing against more than one athlete in a basketball game really advanced my talents and techniques.

I have played against 3 to 4 athletes in a straight game of basketball. As I was playing against these athletes, I would make a risky bet or a financial deal. The deal or bet would be, "if they beat me in a game of 4 on 1, or 3 on 1, I would freely give them $20. Before the 4 on 1 game would be in progress, sometimes I would give the $20 to someone who is watching the game, to give my opponents the insurance that the money is up for grabs. I did not ask my opponents to put any money up. Only I put the money up in the pot. In other words, if I win, the only thing I get is a mental rush of being a great basketball player. If my opponents win, they get a mental rush, and my money. However, guess what, I would actually beat 3 or 4 athletes in a game of basketball. I would win my own money and put it back into my pockets.

Whenever I had the opportune chance to play against these athletes, I would challenge them on the spot. I played against about 20 different teenagers all year round. I am not talking about teenagers who played against me only for the money. These guys love the game of basketball just as much as I did. Not only that, but they were truly good basketball players, too. I am talking about teenagers who were starters when they went to high school and college. These guys were very good, but my talents and skills proved to be the best.

Many times, they approach me, wanting revenge; however, I would beat the again. I beat them so many times, they became frustrated. Then they began to practice as a team. They wanted to earn a win somehow someway. How would you feel if a guy keeps beating you, and your 2 friends? I don't care how many athletes I play against; if my brain wanted to play against a group of basketball players, then it actually believes within itself, that it can win. If I can beat 4 male teenage basketball players, then I am sure I can beat 5 ninth grade girls. I am not putting you down ladies, but it is what it is.

No matter what season of the year it was, we still played basketball. I beat them in a game of basketball in the summer; in the fall, in the winter, and I beat them all year round. From January to December, I beat these guys. I will admit, I do remember loosing one game against them. They finally won the $20 dollar bet. At one point, I remember keeping a record of the games that we played. The record that I remember in my mind was, 5-1. Yes, I won five games and they only won one. I am sure we played more than 6 games in total, but I remember holding a record in my head that was 5 and 1. But you know what, since I played more than 20 games against these teenagers, then I would like to say that my recorded is actually this; 25-1. I know it sounds real, but it is so true, I really won many games them.

Just the other day, I came across one of the teenagers whom I played basketball against. He was telling one of his friends that, "him and all his friends used to play basketball against me, and how they never won a game". Then he said,

"I think we beat him one game out of about 20. Here are some of the names of the athletes I played against, and beat: Gary, Jarnell, Terry, Mike, Andrew, Big Head James, Lex, Moneer, tall skinny James, Sameo, and many others. Yeah, these guys were my students; they learned from me. They learned from the best. They all grew up wanting to be like "Lytskin".

If I can bravely challenge four talented boys in a game of basketball, and literally beat them game after game, then I had to be very talented, skillful, creative, and good. I knew that every time I had the ball in my possession, I needed to score at least 4 to 5 points right away in order for me to have a chance to beat them. When I was on defense, I could not go to far from the goal. I had to stay near it, hoped for a miss, so I could get the rebound. I did everything I could to stop them from scoring. When one of them would take a shot, I would yell out very loud, saying, "Boo, that's off". I screamed at them the entire game just to throw off their shooting concentration. Sometimes it worked, and sometimes it didn't.

Every game we played, we always played until the first team scores 16 points. Each score was worth one point. A few games, we actually, kept playing for the scoring tiebreaker. In other words, there were many close games were the score was tied 15 to 15. I did not set any new rules to my advantage; I did not cheat to win, I literary took my talents and skills at them and played heads up basketball, 4 on 1, or 3 on 1. I played against two athletes before many times, but that was too easy. I always won when playing against 2 players.

Challenging and playing against multiple basketball athletes really made it hard for one individual to check me in a real game. What I am plainly saying unto you is this; if am able to fancy dribble and get pass four basketball athletes to get an easier shot off, then dribbling pass one man is definitely too easy. When I played in that one gym (Whol Center), the entire team took turns trying to contain me. One man trying to contain me is almost impossible. If it is hard for four defenders to contain me, then truly it is horribly hard for one to contain me. Therefore, when I am playing in a real game, and only one defender is checking me, he has no chance; I would potentially crush the poor kid. If I dribble to my left, I can shoot with my left. If I dribble to my right, I can shoot with my right. Answer this: Who can stop an athlete that has the talent of a robot?

I have played in gyms were people have told me face to face that they have never seen a man hoop like me before in their life. I know you thinking to yourself that, I cannot be that good to be better than your star basketball athlete; however, sorry to say, when the people said, "they have never seen a man play ball like me before, that includes your N.B.A star too.

However, this is how you can compare me to a basketball player; you go and find the best right-handed basketball player, and the best left hand player, and then you have me. The best right hand player + the best left hand player = **Brian K. Irons**. You can't really compare me to a one hand basketball shooter, because I am a two handed shooter. Therefore, you have to compare me with another two-handed player. Whatever a right-handed N.B.A star player can do, I can do. However, not all N.B.A right-handed shooters can do what I can do with my left-hand. I am not putting down any athletes, nor their athletic skills, because I have seen a great number of basketball players who are very awesome. However, until you find someone, that can shoot 3-pointers with either arm, or find someone that can throw a football down the field with either arm, or can pitch with either arm, then I have a match. Until then, I am the greatest athlete in the world when it comes down to brain talents. Other athletes might be more skillful that I am in a certain sport; but when it comes down brutal talent, which is provided to the brain, I am the greatest. Later in this book, I am going to explain another sport talent that I use to dominate my opponents in.

Think about this; sport skills are achieved through learning experiences, and talents are given unto you from the day you were born. Only God gives the talents, but we are suppose to practice and practice to better the skills, which operate from the talent. Although, I am a two handed player, I still had to practice to better the skills that were connected to my talent. God is the man who supplied my brain with the talent and free-gift to be highly favored in sports. This particular talent (2-hand ability) or gift was given to me before and when I was born. When I was in the stomach or belly of my mother, my gifts and talents were there as well. As I grew older, the talent was unwrapped, and there I was realizing that I could play sports with either hand. I will never know why this gift was given unto me and not given unto you. As I think about it, it seems like the talents and gifts given unto me, is given to one out of every 100,000 athletes. But still in all, I haven't seen a man or woman possess the talent that I have, as of yet. I can only imagine how leveled my skills will improve once I make it to the big leagues.

It was somewhat phenomenal because I was born to be a lefty, but I grew up being a right-handed sports player. I knew I was left-handed because I wrote with my left hand, and I ate food with my left hand. My left hand and arm has always been my power limb, but in sports, my right hand became the limb that I trusted the most. One more thing, I can also, write in cursive with either hand. Can you do that? Oh wow, something just came to my mind; being able to write with either hand is a talent as well. Well, I must say it again; I am the best, I am the greatest, and there is none like me. Whatever sport my brain desires to play; it will always turn out to be the best.

Chapter 4
The Intelligent Human Brain

From the awesome handwork of God, a human was made. The first human made by God on earth name is Adam. When God used his hands to make Adam, skills were used during the entire process. Skills are always utilized through and by hands. I used my hand skills to play sports, but God used his hand skills to make a man. Since that is so, then my skills are nothing compared to the skills of God.

On earth, Adam is the first person to walk around on it with human brain. Although, more than 2000 years ago, Adam is the first person to walk on the earth with a human brain, however, in the 21st century **Brian Irons** walks on the earth with the same creative head system (brain). My brain and Adam's brain both operates the same. Yeah, Adam's brain, **Brian Irons** brain, and every human being on earth have a brain that functions and operates the same way. Not one human brain differs in the formatting of its system. From Adam to **Brain Irons**, an uncountable numbers of human brains have been in operation. My 2nd book, which is titled, "Thou Shalt Not Have Any Other Gods Before Me", (2008) speaks and teaches about God having a conversation with the first human brain (Adam's) on earth.

When God hand formed the outer body of Adam, he then gave it an inner body. Whether the body was formed first, or the outer body, I know not. However, the outer body was formed by the hands of God, but the inner body was activated by the breath of God. When God breathed into Adam, and life became a movement unto Adam, it was a creative act done by God. The body of Adam was dead dirt, until God breathed into his inner being. This inner being or inner body is called, "The Intelligent Human Brain".

When God willfully created "The intelligent human

brain", he miraculous placed inside of it, the amazing ability to search after life's necessities. Life necessities are things that are vital and important for a person's everyday living. As the brain seeks after life's necessities, while it's on that mental journey, it's been given the power and ability to discern right from wrong. Every human being on the earth knows what's right or what's wrong from the brain's intelligence. For example: when I was a child in the projects, although, I never knew there was a commandment that says, "thou shall not steal", the intelligent conscience worker in my brain caused me to realize that stealing was a wrongful event to participate in. People also know that it is horribly wrong to have sex with someone without the person's agreement and approval. That's called, "rape". Therefore, the creative work and breath of God, which supplied the brain with a righteous conscience (mental judgment), will awaken the mental body to know that it is deceitfully wrong to indulge in certain activities. Seeking life necessities and being alert to know right from wrong is part of the intelligent human brain's creative intelligence.

The word intelligence means: to obtain the ability to learn or understand how to deal with new situations when they arrive. When quarrels and other situations arise in our lives, we must allow intelligence to arise, rather than ignorance. The people in the projects did not allow intelligence to arise; they allowed their brains to operate under the influence of ignorance. God created within the brain, an automatic worker, which is the intelligent part, to learn how to adapt to life. When quarrels arise in a person's life, the brain is the intellectual power given to help people be over comers. Your high intelligence is created by God to provide you ways to defeat your own trials in life. Whether any situation is good or bad, the intelligence of the human brain will always intelligently search out any matter.

Before God breathed life into the intelligent human brain (Adam's), he made a hard helmet for its protection. A snail has a shell for protection, and so does a turtle. With a human, his head protection is called, "Skull". When God made and placed the skull over the entire brain, it became the brain's knight, and shiny armor. The skull loves the brain, because it is made to protect and stick close to it. The skull and brain are married, they have become one, and nothing can keep them apart but death. When the brain dies, the meat (head-flesh) will disintegrate, and only the bone skull will remain. Therefore, as I said, "nothing can keep them apart but death. A man thoughtfully made a helmet to protect the head of football players, and God thoughtfully made a skull to protect the brain. The human brain is filled with precious treasure, and God made the skull to secure it.

The skull is also called, "Cranium". The skull or cranium fits snugly around the entire surface of the brain. Just as shoes fits snugly on the feet, the skull fits tightly on the brain. The brain, which is located under the skull, it normally does not move, nor does it fluctuate. It sits under the skull, and effectively makes key decisions for physical performances to become active in every person's life. Although, a person may walk, jog, and or run, that individual still cannot feel the human brain in motion (floating in the skull). The intelligent human brain is perfectly fitted and compressed under the skull. If a person turns his or her head quickly to the left, or to the right, that individual will not feel the brain in motion at all. Although, the human brain is filled with massive amounts of liquid and fluid, it will not sail (move) while inside of the "skull". Therefore, as a person runs or jog, the human brain's job is to relax, think, and guide his or her next move. Even when a person is jogging across Natural Bridge and Kingshighway, the brain sits still, waiting for you to make a decision.

An unborn "chick", before birth has taken place, normally, it sits in an eggshell folded up. As the unborn chick lives in the eggshell with its body folded up, it has two covering for protection. The eggshell is the first protection, and the mom, which sits on the egg, is the other protection. Well, in the same sense, the intelligent human brain sits under the protective care of the hard bone skull folded up as well. The mother of the unborn chick shield's her egg so that predators will not have the opportunity to touch and destroy her unborn chicks. Well, in the same sense, the skull encircles the entire human brain and seals it from the outer predators. The eggshell is primarily a protective shield for the unborn chick, and the skull is the master "shield" for the meaty brain. Everything that has life on earth has a dreadful need for protection.

Why does the meaty brain need to be protected? The meaty brain needs to be protected because it has many vital coworkers within it. Every co-worker in the brain has a job, and a specific task to perform. Therefore, as long as a person has life on earth, the skull's lifetime job is to shield those workers. Forever the skull will protect the brain; forever, the brain will make decisions in your life.

The intelligent human brain is similar to the operation of the St. Louis Housing Authority. In the St. Louis Housing Authority, there are probably a hundred workers in it. Each person who works in the St. Louis Housing Authority has a certain task or job to perform. One or two workers may have the same job status; however, each person is appointed to perform at different task of work. For example, Chandra Moore, and Teresa Jackson works in section 8 department; Gloria Brown works in human recourses, and Delores Outlaw works in re-development. However, although, they all work in the same building, for the same company, they all have different tasks to perform. Although, the four of them work in different departments, somehow, they all have a connection that involves work to be done so that certain papers can be processed. In other words, the entire Housing Authority is a place full of workers, linked one to the other. What I am trying to say is this, the Housing Authority employees are seated under the roof of one big building for work, and the intelligent human brain of workers is seated under one hard bone skull for work too.

The brain has active network and channels within it. These active channels and networks have a permanent operation (job) and a particular movement to fulfill throughout the entire body. Every living intelligent brain has only one operation, which is to lead your body and life in the direction you have chosen it to go. Whether a person is Black, White, Chinese, Asia or of any other race, each brain is creatively designed by God to operate the exact same way. Yet and still, all brains have different activities of thoughts flowing through them on a regular basis.

God has given the brain a full lifetime supply of significant energy. The brain labors and toils consistently. The brain may come to a moment of rest or relax at times, but it never stops laboring. Automatically the brain continues to stay energetic, and automatically the brain continues to operate. Therefore, the brain never dies, it never stop functioning, only the body does. The brain is a thousand times more energetic than the energizer bunny, because it lives on, and on, and on throughout eternity. Even after death takes place, our brain's senses still lives, and I will explain unto you what I mean, later in the story.

It is said and recorded that if the blood ceases from traveling, or circulating through a person's brain, then physical death has come unto that individual. Whether the blood ceases its circulation from a stroke, or from a drowning in the water, once the intelligent human brain has experienced a halt movement of blood, physical death has come. If blood ceases from flowing through a person's brain approximately 4 to 8 minutes, physical death is experienced, or the individual's brain will be sent off into a vegetable state of unknown mental existence.

Centuries ago, when God rained on the earth until a flood was developed, all the living creatures died. When God caused it to rain centuries ago, small puddles of water were developed. During the period of the flood, as God kept on sending more and more rain, days turned into weeks, and the puddles of water all became connected, and inch-by-inch a flood was developed. The flood grew and grew, until it reached a height taller than any substance on the earth. Not a foot on mankind was able to stand on the ground, without the entire body being cover by water. Although, the brain is very energetic, however, it cannot perform continual living (breathing) while under water.

During the flood, mankind tried to use physical strength to outdo the flood's judgment. God rained upon the earth for 40 days, and 40 nights, and mankind cannot tread nor swim in water for an entire day, let alone for 40. A moment for rest is required when swimming is in session. Once a person's head is under the judgment of God, a sentence will always be pronounced upon it. The judgment of God can rain on your life, until it kills you. Oh my, you know what, when God sent a flood to destroy the earth, that was a time, that the death penalty had been used. God, through his flood's judgment, had sentenced all those brains to serve the death penalty. Physical strength will never be able to stand against the judgment of God. Physical strength, which is the body's character that activates wicked deeds, is what causes us to be judged. The flood came as a judgment unto the people, because of their physical and wicked deeds.

The intelligent human brain is very small. The entire brain can be held in hands of a person. Its average weight in the head of an adult is estimated at 3 pounds. Although, the human brain is small, it is still the strongest worker linked to the body. The intelligent human brain is the strongest worker because of the daily routine activities it performs. Every day, the brain's built in strength successfully demonstrates its authority. The intelligent human brain has been created to haul large amounts of weight randomly at will. For example, if a person weighs 700 pounds, the human brain has the power and strength to raise the person up on his feet for walking. Whether light or heavy, the human brain shows no signs of weakness to any size capacity. The physical strength of humankind cannot lift or raise a 700-pound man. However, the intelligent human brain can.

God is the discoverer of the intelligent human brain. God wonderfully made the brain to work effectively on your greatest behalf. Therefore, you need to personally guard and protect your brain with your all and all. Although, the skull is automatically the brain's protector, however, you as a person must do your part too.

Weakness within the brain may occur by a number of reasons. If a person is very sick or has a serious migraine headache, his or her walking ability is usually affected. One of the actual reasons why a person's walking is affected when ill, is because, illnesses affects the brain's maximum mobility to perform. If a migraine headache has touched your intelligent human brain, the brain will "think" about resting, not walking. Then the brain will compel and control your body to lie down and relax until recovery takes place. Sometimes the human brain will think of meds or medicine to take, in order to lighten the load of head pain that is active within it. The human brain is very intelligent; it is very smart to be only a piece of head meat. The brain will actually alert itself when any sickness has charged in.

The intelligent human brain is built and designed to control your every move that you will ever proceed to make in your life. Before any man or woman attempts to proceed to a destination, his or her brain has already visualized the place before the feet has landed there. Another fact about the intelligent human brain is; before you proceeded to go shopping, your brain gave itself all the thoughts of the products you desire to purchase. Not only does the brain guide the body to move, but also the brain is your "thinking center". Before any living human being makes a mental decision to do anything, the intelligent brain has thought it, before directing the body to operate toward completion. What I am truly saying is this; you will never physically step into any department store's entrance without your brain first thinking what is in the store or what could possibly be in that particular facility.

The intelligent human brain is the true master of the body because of its principal authorized power. The reason why "the intelligent human brain" is the grand master of the body is that, the body is the brain's slave. The body is under the complete control of the human brain. The slaves or servants of the grand master (intelligent human brain) are the limbs. Actually, the entire body is a faithful servant to the independent brain, because without it, the physical body is useless and inactive.

Slaves must do whatever the master has instructed them to do. Just as slaves are obedient unto their masters, the body is obedient unto "the intelligent human brain". The word "master" means, to be lord over. The word master also mean- to control by the commanding of words, or by physical force. Slaves are used for their master's purpose to carry out certain authorized task. A master has high rankings over all slaves. The master (the brain) gives orders, and tasks to its pupils (bodily limbs) so that they will know what to do next. However, whatever commands the master has commanded its slaves to do; they must and will perform the task, which has been instructed. Therefore, slaves are prime workers for their masters. Yes, the body is the brain's slave forever.

The intelligent human brain has many workers (sections) that perform different operations within the body. These sections or workers, which are in the intelligent human brain, guides the body and keep it active and ready for work. Here are some official names of these components or workers that are crammed inside the brain. In the brain, there are cells, neurons, cerebellum, cerebrum, hemispheres (left and right), four lobes, brainstem, memory, etc. Those components (workers) of the intelligent human brain operate mechanically, and they all ignite the body to perform different tasks on a daily basis. Meaning, each component has a particular task to instruct the body, when performing different physical reaction. Also, the spinal cord is the brain's greatest help for the body. The spinal cord is the body's backbone.

Many workers, which are in "the intelligent human brain", most people in the world, have no knowledge of their historical facts. Probably, 80% of the people who are in the world do not consider the knowledge and strength that the intelligent human brain truly has. Nor does anyone realize how important the intelligent human brain really is. Therefore, I am going to supply you with a brief hand written summary about the history of the many workers that are in the brain. I feel the need to inform you about the human brain, and its exalted performance it does with the body.

The first component or worker in the brain I desire to write about is called, "Memory". Memory plays an important key role when maintaining past and present commercial and non-commercial events. All of our past and present events we've experienced have turned into learning issues. When we learn from experiences, we remember them. When a physical or psychological activity has been done, our memory's center retains that information. When you remember what you did last night, or what you have done years ago, that experienced moment is gathered and held in the part of the brain called "Memory".

Even animals have a brain, which gives them the power to operate from memory. The memory in an animal will also retain important facts. A dog can remember where the food bowl sits, and never forget where it has been laid. A cat will not forget where the litter box has been stationed. Animals even remember pain, which is from the sense of touch. By vision, animals remember what their masters look like. Therefore, just like humans, animals have a brain that operates from the five senses, too.

Without memory being active in our brains, we would forget where our toothbrush has been placed. We will even forget where the bathroom in our home is. Therefore, memory is an important worker in every living species upon the earth.

Let me talk about a certain part of memory right quick. I am about to lay some information with facts in this chapter, which speaks about short-term memory. Short-term memory is mobile when helping a person to remember information that has just been received. Short-term memory operates very quickly. Information received, and used right away, comes from short-term memory. Short-term memory is active when a person's name needs to be remembered right away. Remembering what you ate for dinner minutes ago is a work from short-term memory. Short-term memory operates exactly as it is called, short term. Here is an example; when a person has given me his or her phone number, my short-term memory operates and holds that information. Depending upon how long my memory holds that phone number, however, later in life it is then transferred into long-term memory. Everything you remember is short term first, before it becomes long term.

The intelligent human brain has a number of mobile memory functions, which help us retain or hold information. One mobile memory is called, "Procedural Memory", and the other is called "Declarative Memory". Both of these memories, along with short term are always active in the brain.

This memory (procedural) holds and retains taught information from experiences you've already had. Once a task has been executed or performed in your life, that information is then gathered and held for long periods in your procedural memory. Once the procedural memory has gathered that performed action, you will never have to relearn that task or assignment again. For instance, when I first learned how to ride a standard bicycle, that taught data was sent into my brain's procedural memory for storage. When I first learned how to tie my shoes, that taught procedure went into my short-term memory. However, weeks and years later, that same shoe tying taught data now is located in my brain's procedural memory. Therefore, the next time I need to tie my shoes, or ride a bike again, my procedural memory awakens, and reminds me how I once did it. I do not need to be taught a second time on how to tie my shoes, nor ride a bike, because my procedural memory stored that learnt procedure within it.

Procedural memory applies to memorization of a person's physical movement and skills. From the procedural memory, you will never forget how to use a fork or a spoon. You will never forget that it takes both legs to pedal the bike to get it rolling. All performed activities and many more are stored in the procedural memory.

All actions done are performed by skills. When you really think about it, a skill is being utilized when feeding yourself. Taking the spoon directly to the mouth is a physical skill. Even while riding a bike, skills are being utilized. Eating, and riding a bike has become so common unto us, we fail to realize that it is a true physical skill, and that the brain's procedural memory held that learned data in its storage.

The other memory in the brain that I desire to teach unto you is called, "Declarative Memory". Declarative and Procedural memory are both long-term registered. This particular section of your brain's memory (declarative) preserves data concerning facts and details. Facts or details from your past, and current living are saved in the declarative memory. This memory holds information, after you have studied something, or has been taught a thing or two. After learning something in class, that information travels to short-term memory, then to declarative memory. In fact, information taught from your parent's years ago are stored in your declarative memory.

The God created memory in the intelligent human brain is similar to the memory of a personal computer. A human being must download memory into a computer, which will cause the system to operate. While on the other hand, God has placed a memory system in the intelligent human brain, so that information can be downloaded into its operating system (declarative and or procedure memory). From a compact disc, memory is down loaded into a computer. But the intelligent human brain's memory has been downloaded with amazing functions by the hand of God. Information and memory is added to a computer by a compact disc, and information and memory is added to the intelligent human brain through a person's living experiences.

There is a great difference between the memory of the intelligent human brain, and the memory of a personal computer. However, they both have been given the ability to obtained memory. A personal computer needs to be turned on in order for its memory data to operate. Even after a person has shutdown the computer, the memory is still preserved. However, the intelligent human brain's memory stays on always, and memory is active throughout a person's entire lifespan, 24/7. A person can go to sleep tonight, have a dream, and remember parts of it after he or she has awakened. The memory that God has built inside the brain will always be active.

The intelligent human brain is the handiwork of God; on the other hand, a personal computer is the handiwork of humankind. Humankind has processed within a personal computer the ability for it to perform several tactics of functioning. There is an extreme difference when God's hands make something (the brain), opposed to when human hands make something (electronics). When God makes something (the intelligent human brain), it lives and works forever. However, when humankind, with the hands, makes something, it is subject to breaking. Remember this; God's hands are awesome, and he has the creative power to perform works beyond what humanity can do, make, and or think.

Another worker in the intelligent human brain is called, "brainstem". The brainstem is said to be a person's survival kit. The brainstem's primary work is to control a person's breathing, heart rate, blood pressure, digestive system, and mental arousal. When God breathed into the nostrils of Adam, all of these activities became a head motion. Nevertheless, the brainstem is the worker that helps keeps you alive and breathing.

Let me provide you with more performances the brainstem does. When you swallow food into your belly, the brainstem is the active worker that has geared you into performing that act. Sneezing is also accessed by the brainstem. Activities we do not control by willful consent, such as breathing, the brainstem performs that activity on its own. No one motivates breathing to take place, it happens on it's on. God gave the brainstem the charge to breath, and it took over from there. Through the lungs, the brainstem does the inhaling and exhaling act for each living person. The only time and moment people consider inhaling and exhaling is at the doctor's office when asked too to do so, other than that, the brainstem automatically performs the breathing. Just as a person pumps air into a tire, the brainstem pumps air into the body. The brainstem mainly controls all the actions that you do not have power to control with your own ability. Just as a man cannot control his pulse rate, a person cannot control the breathing. If a person could control the breathing, then that individual has the power to keep himself alive on earth forever.

A newborn baby knows nothing about eating nor does the infant know anything about swallowing. When delicious treats (liquid food) have been placed into the infant's mouth, the brainstem encourages and compels the lovable toddler to swallow.

Since a toddler definitely knows nothing about breathing, the brainstem persuades the breathing to take place through the infant's lungs, through the nose. The brainstem takes care of all infants breathing, who are individuals that know nothing about life.

Injury done to the brainstem will cause a person to have trouble with breathing. Since the brainstem gives every person the power to breathe, then life itself is wrapped up into this international organ of power. If the brainstem controls heart rate, breathing, and blood pressure, then this vital component in the intelligent human brain should be guarded at all times. Actually, the entire brain should be guarded because it takes care of other bodily activities, than just your breathing.

Since heart rate and breathing (inhaling and exhaling) are controlled by this particular part of the brain, when this component has ceased from its natural use of performance, death and a burial place is next to be charted in one's life. Earlier in this chapter, when I spoke unto you saying, "whatever God makes (the brain)", it lives forever. Although, the body will die, the brain (brainstem) (spirit) of a man lives forever. The brainstem is your arousal or awareness observer; therefore, after death has taken place, you will still be breathing. Whether you go to heaven or hell, breathing will still be active.

Later in this interesting story, I will give you an example in full details where your mental status and spirit will live throughout eternity (forever). You need to know this, because I am sure that everyone desires to see the windows of heaven open up, and be received. No man with good mental sense desires to live in the intensity of heat, which is in the place called, "hell". Again, the body might die, but long lives the brain.

Another worker in the intelligent human brain is called, the "cerebellum". The cerebellum controls every person's physical movement. Unlike the brainstem, which controls our involuntary movements, the cerebellum controls our voluntary movements. Every limb you desire to move is done so by the cerebellum in the brain. This part of the brain is your physical movement enabler.

Here are some examples of my brain's cerebellum in action. When I rode my first bike in life, the cerebellum is the worker that controlled my legs to pedal the bicycle. As I was riding the bicycle, the cerebellum was graciously elevating my arms to be in control so I could guide it. When I was riding that skateboard down that hill on the day of my baseball championship game, my cerebellum was controlling my leg and ankle movement so that I could balance myself while riding. Also, when I performed a quick juke move, and dashed to the basketball goal, and dunked on "**Anthony Davenport**", my cerebellum help me put it down like that. **Anthony Davenport** did a few juke moves on me too. Therefore, **Anthony Davenport** cerebellum put it down on me before, too. In baseball, when I was on the pitcher's mound throwing the ball; as I went through the pitcher's wind up, my cerebellum was assisting and coordinating my body to balance itself. Even eating a bowl of cereal, the cerebellum controls the hand, and directs the arm to the bowl. Wow, the cerebellum helps me to do many things, and <u>I DID NOT KNOW it.</u>

When people use their fingers to type on the computer, the cerebellum is the brain's operator that guides the hands and fingers when performing this activity. A person with good common sense does not want to loose the mental strength that the cerebellum holds. Every physical activity you do, the cerebellum is the enabler to make it a work of success. Since that is so, there is not too many jobs on earth were the cerebellum is not needed to operate.

The cerebellum is my amazing skillful and talent performer. Therefore, this part of the brain is highly needed in order for me to stay active in all areas of sports, especially basketball. My cerebellum, when active in sports, turned out to be magnificently different from more than 90% of the athletic world. When it came down to physical ability (even handed sport player), my cerebellum had proven to be one of the greatest. Yeah, every person's cerebellum can't play sports even handed, but mine did.

Injury done to the cerebellum will cause a person's physical movement to become shaky and or unsteady. Injury done to the cerebellum will change a person's physical mobility. When injury is done to this organ in the brain, physical movement and coordination becomes a problem. Today, your body (limbs) moves at a normal pace, but when the cerebellum has been injured, your body's movement will be thrown off.

Another worker in the brain is called, the cerebrum, not cerebellum. Do not get these two, the cerebrum, and the cerebellum confused with one another. The cerebrum is the brain's performer that gives every person the ability to "think". This component (cerebrum) is our greatest head worker in life. Before a person decides to do anything, the thinking applicator reacts first. For the rest of your life, thinking will always be a necessity. Not too many things can be done without a person's thinking motivator being active. There are so many things that we do on a regular basis, and it causes us not to realize that a thought was done first. Before you open the refrigerator to grab that gallon of milk, a though was conceived first. Therefore, protect your intelligent human brain, so that you can effectively preserve the performer that arouses or awakens your ability to think. As you protect your cerebrum, which is your critical thinking tool, you are guarding your ability think accurately. Yeah, guard your thinking administrator.

Also, in the brain there are four other workers. These workers are located in the cerebral cortex of the brain. These four workers, individually, are called, "Lobes". Each lobe in the cerebral cortex consists of pairs, meaning, two of each is present. Every lobe has a specific name, and each lobe provides different functions within the head. They manage different operations, and perform key movement throughout the entire body.

The first sets of lobes are called, "frontal lobes". The frontal lobes play a role in the operating of your physical movements, along with the cerebellum. The frontal lobes and cerebellum both mechanically helps a person activate physical movements throughout his or her limbs. But let's not forget the spinal cord, because without, the body would not stand upright.

The frontal lobes are the workers in the brain that helps us utilize mental judgment. Mental judgments will be performed in our lives probably every single day. In everything you do, mental judgment will need to be assessed one way or another. Even when a person is driving a car down the road, acts of judgments must be assessed. As the cerebellum controls your hands to drive the car, mental judgment is needed to ride between the lines, which have been painted in the streets. When anyone is about to drive on the highway, in order to emerge into the fast moving traffic, you will have to use judgment before entering into the driving lane. Your frontal lobes will cause you to judge when it is time to emerge into highway traffic. Yeah, it even takes good judgment to before emerging into highway traffic.

Although, the cerebellum controls the hands and feet while driving the car, however, an act of mental judgment is in session to prevent car wrecks. In this world, many car wrecks occur because of the lack of good judgment, which operates from the frontal lobes. A person can make a sharp turn to quickly, and bam, a serious car wreck has just occurred. Most of the times, good judgment will prevent car wrecks.

The frontal lobes also activate your personal emotion. The emotions, that the frontal lobe displays, are the type of emotions that are connected to sensitivity, caring and loving. When you express your love and care at a funeral, you are doing that by the frontal lobes power. When you cry at a funeral or show your inner concern, the frontal lobes are the workers that gave you the ability to express your feelings.

When you fall in love with someone, and your heart has becomes broken, your frontal lobes gave you the emotional power to feel the event. I have fallen in love before, and I have been hurt before, too. Since I felt the emotional pain of being hurt, my frontal lobes were active at that particular time. Emotions aren't just active in pain; they operate in good times as well. When I finally received my high school diploma, my emotion rejoiced during that moment and time. Yeah, my brain's frontal lobes rejoiced.

The frontal lobes also play a big role in a person's speech and problem solving skills. When people have a conversation with one another, they do this by the frontal lobes' power. Since the frontal lobes deal with speech, problem solving skills, judgment, and it activates your inner pain, while you are protecting your brain from intruders, you are sealing up those works in the brain.

If injury is done to the frontal lobes, a number of mental abilities will become damaged. For most people, they will loose the ability to sort out simple problems. You will loose the ability to use accurate judgments. When your emotions once use to operate during sentimental moments, however, if your frontal lobes become damaged, you can loose that mental kindness. Anytime a person is always angry, his or her frontal lobes are going through some serious emotional pain.

The second sets of lobes in the brain are called, "parietal lobes". The parietal lobes deal with pressure and sensations. In my life, once I felt hot water with my hands, my brain's parietal lobes cause me to feel the heated pressure. It is also said, if injury takes place in the right parietal lobe, it may cause a person to have difficulty finding his or her way to already once known places and areas. For example; I know exactly where certain stores are located, but, if my right parietal lobe becomes injured, I may have difficulty finding where the store is located. The parietal lobes helps a person find his or her way back home. Although, you can remember what your home looks like, but finding your way to it, is a job done by the parietal lobes. When people park their cars on a parking lot at a mall, they might remember that it was parked over there somewhere, but to find it is a work performed by the parietal lobes. Since animals recognize their surroundings, I suppose they have parietal lobes too, because they know their way back home.

The third sets of lobes are called, "occipital lobes". These lobes are associated with vision, which gives a person the ability to see. Vision or sight is needed in mostly everything you do. A person needs to see exactly what he or she is doing while performing on any job. These lobes, which activate sight, are highly needed when driving a motorized vehicle. Although, good judgment is required while driving, nevertheless, sight is very important, too.

Sight is needed in all sports. When the ball was thrown unto me in football practice, the occipital lobes (vision center) played a key role. My occipital lobes enabled me to see the ball as it was coming towards my way. Also, in baseball, as I was pitching the ball to batters, I had to see the plate in order for me to throw strikes across it. Since these lobes (occipital) deals with sight, they also give you the visual ability to recognize shapes, sizes, and colors randomly.

The fourth set of lobes is called, "temporal lobe". The temporal lobes deal with the auditory system in the brain. When hearing is active in a person's life, the temporal lobes are yet working.

The four lobes mentioned above, of course, they all

do more than what I have explained. I just wanted to give you a small portion of information concerning them all.

Finally, yet importantly, the intelligent human brain has a worker in it called, "limbic system". It is also called, "the limbic lobe". The limbic system gives us the emotional strength to show a little fear in our lives. When a person shows fear in his or her life, the limbic system is yet active. I know my limbic system works because when a dog came towards me at a crazy speed, I jumped on top of a car. I think everyone's limbic system will operate when a pit-bull is approaching.

Emotions are a part of our feelings, and showing fear is a part of our being. Somewhere in your life, fear will need to be displayed. Somewhere in life, fear must be displayed in order to save your life. If you want to see another day in life, then fear will have to be active. Therefore, the limbic system in our brain gives us the adequate strength to express a certain level of emotions and fear.

The limbic system is one of the most powerful tools that operate in our brains. Since the limbic system is our emotion and feeling center, then the sensations to feel pleasure is connected here as well. At the same time, the limbic system enables our feeling, emotions, sensation, and pleasure to be active. When something causes you to feel good, the limbic system is the brain tool that has provided you with that reaction. However, the frontal lobes' emotion deal with our temper and compassion, and the limbic system emotion deals with feeling, pleasure, and sensation.

In the limbic system, there is a worker in it called, "Hypothalamus. The hypothalamus creates and regulates hunger, thirst, sexual drive, and other functions within the body. This part of the brain will create daily the need to have food. When you became hungry, your limbic system is at work. The limbic system will not delete the motion of hunger until food has been eaten. Once food has been eaten, the limbic system becomes satisfied. Once the limbic system sends a hunger mode to the brain, the cerebrum (the thinker) then becomes active. You will then begin to think of what food products you desire to eat. Once you have thought of what you desire to eat, the cerebellum (limb mover) will then guide the hands to pick up the food of your choice. After you have eaten your food, the limbic system becomes pleased, and the sensation of hunger departs.

Drug usage and sex brings about a mental pleasure. Sex and drugs both operates through mental pleasure, emotion, and sensations, which are activated by the limbic system.

The body's pleasure performer, which is the "limbic system", is where all addictions are held captive. For most of us, once our limbic system has been introduced to sex and or drugs, the gate of addiction soon opens up. When a person becomes addicted to sex or drugs, his or her limbic system becomes subject unto its authority. The more sex a person has, the greater the limbic system becomes dependent upon it. The more drugs a person intake; the limbic system will become dependent on it. Once the addiction of sex or drugs has kicked in the limbic system (brain), that person will become a slave unto either or. After the addiction of sex and or drugs charges in, a person's brain has just been conquered by its mental pleasure. Nevertheless, the limbic system is a part of a person's lust and desires.

Since the brain has more than hundredths and thousandths of subjects that can be taught on, if I decide to teach about the brain in its entirety, I will have to write the information in a different book. I can go on and on teaching you about the workings of the brain; however, I have provided you with enough information for you to consider the brain's creative power, which God made and created within it.

After reading this chapter, you have just been informed how the brain's system works. You have read the many of activities the brain does. Not one component in the brain works or operates alone. The entire system of the brain works with one accord. Although, it is said that the brain has thousandths of workers within it, however, the brain is so awesome that it never becomes confused when at work.

Every brain part knows its job.

From what you have just read in this chapter concerning the intelligent human brain, I think you and I both need to guard it always. There are many predators in the land, and they all want to destroy your brain. Those predators want to rip life up and out of your brain. Remember this; Life itself is in the blood, which circulates through the gifted power in the brain. Therefore, if any predator has your life caught in its cage, then surely your blood is there as well. When you keep your brain out of the reach of predators, you are keeping your life and blood away as well.

Chapter 5
Drugs Controlling the Intelligent Human Brain

In the earlier chapter (chapter 4), I have written unto you some basic facts about the operations and performances of the intelligent brain. In addition, chapter 4 spoke about which components of the brain controls every person's physical movement. Chapter 4 also spoke about the mental activity of the brain. However, in this chapter, which is chapter 5, I am going to write about what sections of the intelligent human brain that drugs will forcefully tamper with. In addition, in this chapter, I will write about how drugs will become the master of the entire brain's system. I will supply you with one or two examples of how drugs will cunningly control the human brain and body. I want you to understand what you are introducing your brain and body to, when putting drugs into the anatomy. Now I am about to reveal truths unto you concerning chemical intoxicants, and the mental effects when intoxicants touch your inner being (brain).

Ecstasy- Ecstasy usage began in the 19th century. In the 1980's, ecstasy became a popular chemical (drug) used by many people. Ecstasy is a drug that first comes in powder form. Normally, these days, the powder is compressed, and is then transformed into a pill. Since ecstasy is now used in pill form, in order to receive its negative and persuasive effects, it must be swallowed.

After the pill ecstasy has been swallowed, it then sits in the stomach whole. No matter what else has been put into the stomach, whether it is food or soda pop, ecstasy will relax in the stomach with other items too. Just like sugar dissolves in water, in the same sense, the pill ecstasy dissolves into the blood. It takes about 15 to 30 minutes for ecstasy to begin its mental activation.

As the intoxicant's from ecstasy connects to the blood, it becomes attached to the user's life, because life is in the blood. When people insert ecstasy into the body, very swiftly, the ingredients in it take a cruise to the brain. Just as ecstasy, when transformed from powder to pill, once it becomes fastened to the blood; a mental transformation will soon take place. Just as people go the hospital for a blood transfusion, however, when ecstasy's ingredient mixes in with the blood, a transfusion is in operation.

Have you ever seen a transformation take place? Have you ever dropped dye in water before? Have you ever dyed eggs on Easter before? If so, then you have seen a transformation take place right before your very eyes. When dye pill has been dropped into water, the pill dissolves, and is soon disintegrated. After the dye dissolves in the water, the water changes from clear, to the dye's color. If you drop blue dye in a bowl of water, the liquid will change into the color blue.

The same type of transformation that water does to Easter egg dye is the same type of transformation ecstasy does to the brain and body. When ecstasy has been put into the body, it disintegrates and changes the inner being of the person. After the transformation has taken place, the person's mental body has just been put under this chemical's authority for the next several hours.

It is said that ecstasy will compel a person to misinterpret the difference between reality and fantasy. Reality operates in truth, while fantasy operates in fiction. In the mind (brain), ecstasy will empower a person into believing beyond reason of facts, and then propel fantasy to prevail. Since this drug, when used, will cause an individual to misinterpret the actions of recognizing reality and fantasy, it sounds like a state of confusion is being adhered within the brain. When a person is confused about reality and fantasy, his or her thinking ability has been altered.

Many times, after a person has put ecstasy in the brain, that individual can experience not knowing where he or she is. The ecstasy user can be posted at his place of home, and still appear to be lost. That sounds like a state of confusion. When an ecstasy user does not know where he is, the parietal lobes in the brain have become confused. Remember, knowing your surrounding is a work done by the parietal lobes.

After ecstasy has set up shop in the brain, the organs in it become a marketplace. Ecstasy will begin to purchase several organs in the brain. Once ecstasy has purchased any of the brain's organs, for the next several hours it then becomes the owner of the head's components. Once a drug, such as ecstasy has been put into the brain, it will purchase your realistic thoughts, and sell back to you fantasy. Then, from out of nowhere, the thoughts of your brain will be taken on an evil tour. Strong mental and cognitive illusions will be imputed in the mind after ecstasy's powerful strength and intoxicants have met it. A state of becoming deceived will become a prime task, once ecstasy has taken over the thoughts of a person's mind. Nevertheless, our thinking performer (cerebrum) will be over powered by ecstasy's cunning motivation.

The critical thinking, which comes from our cerebrum's ability, is very important because we need it in order to make precise decisions in our lives. However, with the tremendous help of ecstasy, many repulsive or bad decisions will be made. Although, people, as well as myself, will make bad decisions at times in our lives even without the help of drugs, however, when ecstasy meets the brain's decision maker, it will force people to have unbalance thoughts, which will lead to making regrettable decisions. As this drug operates through your thinking ability, you had better believe awful decisions are going to be made. As your brain (cerebrum) is being influenced by ecstasy, many of your decisions made in life, will be choices that will cause you to break laws. Actually, if ecstasy is in your brain right now, the law has already been broken. Once this drug is put into the body, its illegal ingredients will possess the mind, body, and soul.

Ecstasy will never motivate the brain to think good

thoughts. Do you remember the drug stage of action that I clearly spoke about in the beginning chapter of this book (chapter 1- Growing up in a neighborhood plagued with wickedness)? First, the drug is used to get the brain chemically active, then comes violence, and then comes the attempted murder. Ecstasy users may seem cool and in control for the moment, but soon, wrath and rage will become a mental ongoing habit. If wrath and rage is continually being addressed within the mind, then soon, the physical body will be put to do a work of evil.

The brainstem is the ultimate motivator to get this drug active within the body. The brainstem is the worker in the brain that deals with swallowing. Once ecstasy is place into the mouth, the brainstem, which is the swallowing performer, gulps this drug. Once the pill is swallowed, it then becomes attached to a person's digestive system. The brainstem is our swallowing performer, and for years; people have been using it to swallow this illegal chemical control substance. The brain's organ that controls your breathing is the organ being used when taking ecstasy. Therefore, say no to ecstasy, and say yes to the living of your brain. The intelligent human brain is a terrible body part to waste!

One day, as you swallow this drug with the help of your brainstem, death can be your life's horrible experience. However, in a short period, this chemical will faithfully control every organ in the brain. Since this drug will lead a human being to doing many of the actions mentioned in the above paragraphs, then wickedness is associated with this pill of drug. Yes, ecstasy itself promotes wickedness to be assessed in one's life.

Ecstasy will become a close companion to the entire system of the brain. Once the limbic system, which is the appetite arouser, has become acquainted with ecstasy, then daily will the limbic system hunger for the taste of this drug. Nevertheless, in a short period, the brain cells, neurons, cerebellum, cerebrum, hemispheres (left and right), the four lobes, brainstem, and memory, will all be affected one way or another by this chemical controlled substance. The next drug that "I'm going to talk about is called, "heroin".

Heroin- comes from an agricultural seed that has been inserted into the ground (soil) by a human being. A living man actually, dug a hole into the soil, and put in it, a chemical controlled substance. Flowers, fruits, and trees grow from the ground to bring beauty upon the earth. However, this seed, heroin does not bring beauty to the earth; it brings deceit and wickedness.

After this grain or seed has been inserted into the ground, days later it finds root, then successfully make its growth. Out from the ungrounded, this drug grows into a bean shape like form.

After this seed finally grows from the soil, it becomes ready for usage. Once full growth has occurred, it then becomes a rigid substance of "Tar". The tar is pitch black, and is hard like a bean. The tar is then handled by a human, and then placed inside of an electric blender to be grinded up. As the tar is being grinded up, seconds later, it is transformed into a brown or white substance of powder. Then, suddenly, it becomes available for pathetic individual's to use for his or her own personal pleasure.

Since people have fastened their physical hands on heroin, it is now used for personal mental satisfaction or self-pleasure. Self-pleasure is what Heroin is being used for these days. Heroin or any other drug should not be used as a method to inherit self-pleasure. However, wickedness has caused many different people to do anything just to fulfill a mental rush. Why do people put drugs in their brains for mental pleasure? Well, the suitable answer is simple; wickedness is the psychological power that strongly persuades people to seek pleasure from drugs. Little do heroin users know that the drug, which gives birth to wickedness, has caused people to seek pleasure from it. Therefore, when people get pleasure from heroin, they are actually getting pleasure from wickedness.

This drug, heroin, was discovered in a country called, Asia. Although, heroin began its growth and discovery in Asia, somehow, someway, it stunningly found its abode in the United States. Since this drug has traveled to the USA all the way from Asia, then a demonic murder and deceiver has been brought to our country. Whether it was by plane, or whether it was by ship, nevertheless, the wicked predator and killer (heroin) is here, and seeking a brain to devour. This killer (heroine), just like ecstasy, is upon the earth being past around from city-to-city, and state-to-state. Yep, the killer traveled from across seas, and now the murderer is probably located in all 50th states of the USA.

Heroin's natural use and purpose was for killing extreme pain within the body. In other words, heroin was known as a medicine. If there was any affiliation of pain in the body, heroin was used as a medical treatment to take a dose of, and the ingredients from it would search and attack the area that is causing the aching. Actually, the plant, heroin (Pain Killer) was for general practitioners to utilize for medical handling.

A medicine as potent as heroin could probably only be handled when prescribed by physicians. License physicians wrote prescriptions to clients to be able to handle this drug. Nevertheless, heroin's seductive power has caused people to become personal practitioners because they go and purchase this drug at their own will.

Once the brain and body has been filled with the ingredients of heroin, usually, the user's brain is sent into a mode of nodding. Minutes later, the heroin user is cast into a mild and sometimes a deep sleep. After heroin has been sniffed, minutes later, the brain is then cast into a mode of wicked humbleness. A person does not have to be tired, exhausted, or anything of the like, heroin with its potential power will create a sleep mode within the brain. People actually; become mentally addicted to a drug (heroin) that puts them to sleep.

The limbic system in our brains deals with sleep. When heroin cast a sleep mode onto the user's brain, the limbic system and brainstem is being persuaded to operate from the abnormal. Heroin will cast a sleep mode in the brain, as if a person limbic system is ready for sleep.

Actually, the limbic system's performance is to alert the brain when it is ready for sleep. But heroin, with its manipulating powers will send sleep to the brain. Since heroin forces the brain to fall into a sleep mode, then the normal time for sleep to take place has been cast away. A person could have slept 15 hours last night, however, when he or she puts heroin in the brain, minutes later, the individual is sent back to sleep. It is so crazy to become addicted to a drug such as heroin.

Not only will this drug motivate its user to nod into a sleep mode, but also, heroin transports a bad temper (attitude) into the emotions of users. Once heroin has been put in the brain, the user's attitude is quick to jump from being friendly, to acting as if he or she is your enemy. Therefore, a change of emotion, which is controlled by the frontal lobes, has been ignited by this drug's evil and influential power.

Just the other day, I heard over the news that the predator, heroin had killed more than 40 people in one month. Not only did heroin kill more than 40 people, but also, those deaths occurred in one city. Wow, heroin is dropping, and killing people like houseflies. Wow, heroin has arrested people's hearts, and held their bodies in the chain of death. Many of those people were probably heroin users for years, I am sure. Then, suddenly, one day, heroin acted against their brain, and murdered them all. Drugs are never for you, because they are always against you.

People never know when their city is going to get a batch of dope so powerful that it kills. On the other hand, people never know what a drug seller has mixed with his heroine, as he tries to make it a more potent, and a longer lasting high.

Heroin and other street drugs go through a great number of hands before it gets to you. Those people (the 40 that heroin killed) put heroin into bodies expecting to feel its pleasure, however, the drug did a work beyond their expectation. Heroin went over the limit, and now 40 lives have had a funeral session. Right now today, 40 faces' are now buried under ground, covered in a casket.

Well, actually, wickedness is the power that has killed them all. Wickedness comes to life after heroin and other street drugs have been exposed to a person's anatomy (brain and body). As I said before, the murderer and predator is now in our country. Who will be the next victim to be killed by the evil and Satanic character called, Heroin?

However, in a short moment of time, heroin's intoxicants will become a close companion to the entire atmosphere of the brain. Soon, the brain cells, neurons, cerebellum, cerebrum, hemispheres (left and right), the four lobes, brainstem, and memory, will all be affected one way or another by this chemical controlled substance.

Codeine pills, morphine, crystal meth, and heroin; all present the same mental effects on the users of these products. Therefore, every drug just mentioned in the above sentence will influence the brain to operate in a negative way.

All drugs are like wicked dice; once a person put drugs into the brain and body, the ingredients from the drugs roll throughout the anatomy, and soon the lucky 7 will be seen. Once a person has been killed by heroin, the lucky 7 have just been rolled. Once drugs bring a tragedy into a person's life, the lucky number seven has just been rolled. Sooner or later, the gambler's dice will hit the number 7, and sooner or later, heroin's user will be hit with death.

Marijuana- is a plant that grows from the ground. Since this drug is a plant, which grows from the ground, it comes in seed form first. Although, this drug is a plant, it does not bring righteous character upon the earth. As soon as the seed of marijuana grows into a plant, a stem of wickedness has just stuck its face through the earth's ground. The earth's ground is like a stomach, because once marijuana grows from it, wickedness has just been birthed.

A great number of people once believed marijuana was harmful, but from the populations' daily usage, people now believe it's not so harmful after all. Since people do not believe marijuana is harmful, their minds have been converted to believing in an imaginary tale, rather than non-fiction. Marijuana has many people in the world mentally fooled. This drug creates within the mind of its users, thoughts on why this drug should be legal. People use the phrase, "God made the herbs", therefore; it can and should be used as a legal product.

So many food products take the name "herb", what makes people believe that marijuana was one of the herbs made by God in the beginning days of creation? People try their best to justify the use of marijuana, that it has become a pathetic shame. Within this book, we are going to find out, if God himself grew marijuana for humankind to enjoy. Just because people in other countries smoke marijuana at will, and has legalized it, that doesn't mean God made it right for them to do so. People are legalizing male on male sex too; do you think that is right? We can't even trust certain laws that are being passed. We all need God in our lives, so we will know the truth for ourselves.

This drug, marijuana has dumfounded many people in the world. People actually believe that there are no chemicals in marijuana. When it comes to marijuana, we've become so ignorant; it's a pitiful shame. Hey ignorant folks, anytime you put something in the brain, and it changes its normal ways, then that's a work performed by the chemical. The brain is made up of chemicals itself, and nothing can touch something that is chemical, but another chemical. We desperately put things in our bodies, before we learn anything from it. We so ignorant, that we rather learn from the experience first, rather than learning by reading. I do not care how well you try to minimize this drug's abusive power, it is still called, "a chemical controlled substance". In addition, it is also called, "a mind alternating drug". I do not care how dumbfound you are, God is still against such a drug called, marijuana.

There is only one earth, one God, and one law, for us all to obey. I do not care how many cities legalize marijuana, if God is against it in one city, then that goes for the other cities too. God doesn't show partiality toward places, or

elevate their cerebellum (limbs mover and controller). They think that they are in taking steroids for the body, but they have no idea that their brain's cerebellum is what's being affected.

A person who uses steroids might become stronger, but muscle strength is not the only enhancement given from this drug. As this drug enriches the user's physical strength, not only will it do just that, but also, at the same time, it works against the operation of the brain. As a person indulges in steroids, yes, he will become stronger, but the strength of wickedness will show that it is the strongest. When athletes put steroids into the body, often times they become sick. The wickedness from this drug will cause them to over look the ailing stage.

Steroids can be put into the anatomy in two ways. Either a person will use needles to insert this drug into the veins, or use the mouth to swallow this substance of wickedness.

Just like any other drug, when steroids have made a contact with the body, the intoxicants from it will then travel to the head by the blood. Just as a person in a boat floats on the water, the ingredient from steroids floats throughout the entire body. Just as water fills up the bathtub, however, when steroids are put into the body, the ingredients from it fill up the body. Now the user is walking around with a body filled with this drug's seducement.

Steroids affect memory, problem-solving skills, and it can cause aggressive behavior. I did not write too much about steroids, but I do want to let you know, this drug has killed many athletes throughout the years. Only a few deaths from steroid usage have been spoken of over the news. I am sure there are a great number of deaths that had not been spoken of. Whether you hear about it or not, steroids can and will kill you.

Alcohol- is a liquid substance that can be purchased from your local store. In every city and or state where a store has been built from the ground up, alcohol can be purchased. Not only can alcohol be purchased from all over the world, but also it is advertised daily over your television screen. Somehow, someway, you will see a bottle of alcohol.

I read an article the other day. The article talked about people being poisoned by alcohol. Well, the article did not use the word "poison", but what was said, was understood to me as a person being poisoned.

When a person has been drinking, then falls to sleep, and cannot be awaken, he or she has been poisoned by alcohol's ingredients. Doing things that you normally do not do, such as vomiting, is a sign of have been poisoned. Regurgitation takes place when too much alcohol has been consumed in the body. Also, when a person vomits while he or she is passed out sleeping, and still awakes not, the brain has been poisoned.

Now a day, a person only needs a dollar and a few cents to purchase a container or bottle filled with liquid dope. Yeah, that is all it cost to purchase liquid dope. A person actually goes into his or her pants pockets, pulls out hard-earned money, and then gives it to the store's clerk, to trade it for liquid dope. I call alcohol, "death over the counter".

When you purchase liquor dope from over the counter, and then begin to drink it while driving, you are asking for the creepy character called, "death" to come into your life. Although, everyone is appointed to die one day, however, when a person drinks and drive a motorized vehicle, death can come sooner than scheduled. A date and time is appointed to everyone when life on earth is to end. However, when you drink or put dope into the brain, it will create a time and day for your death to come. In other words, many people in the world die before their God given date, all because of alcohol usage. Drinking alcohol and driving at the same time, is like buying a farewell ticket to leave the earth today. Just as a traveler buys tickets to take a trip by plane, however, when a person drinks and drives that individual can be taken on a trip to "death". That is what chemicals and wickedness wants to do unto you; it wants to kill you before your God given date. By Brian Irons

When a person dies, or has been killed, two different

events has taken place. When a person has been killed, or when a person has died, those two deaths has approached a person's life from different aspects. A person that dies at 100 years old, most of the times, that individual has died at a moment when it was time to die. That's a normal way to die. On the other hand, when a person dies from a drinking and driving accident, that individual has been killed or murdered. That type of death has been experienced before his or her God given date. Therefore, dying, or being killed, takes the meaning of two different types of death.

Pouring alcohol into your brain and body, and then driving a motorized vehicle is practically like playing the college game called, "spin the bottle". Spinning the bottle is a game that college kids play, as they make up their personal set of rules. For instance, after a student spins the bottle, whomever the bottle stops and points to, that individual has to do something that he or she would not normally do. Whether, it is to kiss an unattractive person, or strip down naked in front of a group of people, when the bottle points at you, you must do what has been agreed upon.

Round and round the bottle goes, where it stops no one knows. Once the college student, with the hands spins the bottle, he or she never knows whom it is going to point too. At the same token, when people drink and drive, they never know when death is going to spin into their lives. Therefore, obey the laws of the land, and do not drink and drive.

Driving a vehicle while intoxicated from alcohol has become the number one killer in automobile car wrecks. Drinking and driving automobile accidents occur, because a person's thinking center has been deceived. People begin to believe that they are not too intoxicated to get behind the steering wheel of a vehicle. When intoxicating alcohol makes a contact with the brain, the limb's controller (the cerebellum) receives the intoxicant effects, and all physical movements will be hindered. Also, drinking and driving accidents are caused by drivers having a blurry vision, due to the occipital lobe (sight) impairment from alcohol's ingredients.

The "frontal lobe" in the brain is the quick judgment gate. Alcohol strikes within the frontal lobe and will bother your brain's ability to use accurate judgments. Many vehicle accidents occur because of the minimization of accurate judgment. Therefore, the cerebellum and the frontal lobes are being distracted when trying to make that driving task to become a complete success. When too much alcohol gets inside the brain, the cerebellum (limb controller) and the frontal lobes (judgment authorizer) are just a few of the affected areas of the brain's system. Not only are those two brain components under the influence of alcohol, but also, from the help of the brainstem this drug is swallowed into the body.

As people continue to drink alcohol, soon their brain will begin to feel its persuasive and potent power. From the intoxicants that are machine mixed into every bottle of liquor, the brain will feel its power physically. Depending upon the amount of alcohol swallowed, his or her physical movements, and coordination will be greatly bothered.

As we all have occasionally witness from our physical experiences, and have repeatedly observed with our own eyes, from watching folks who swallows too much alcohol in their brain and body, that their walking ability is altered from the norm. A normal walk would be for a human being to walk on a straight line, but when intoxicating alcohol makes a contact with the brain, a staggering walk will begin to develop. It becomes hard to walk on a straight line when alcohol has the brain under its influence. The cerebellum, which controls the balancing in a person's walk, is being persuasively afflicted at that particular time. Every time you see a person walking down the street staggering, many times it is because alcohol has his or her cerebellum under its control. The limbic system, which is a person's appetite arouser, once it becomes addicted to alcohol, it will began to hunger for liquor as if it is food. Not only does the limbic system awaken hunger, but also, it arouses your thirst as well. Once you become addicted to alcohol, your brain's limbic system will thirst after it, rather than healthy water.

After becoming addicted to alcohol, however, in a short time, the body and the brain will become depressed if alcohol or liquor has not been put into it.

Cigarettes & Coffee- I bet the users of cigarettes and coffee don't want me to expose facts about these two mental craved products, huh. Well, had I not provided you with information concerning these two mental craved products, it would not be a fine chapter. This chapter would not be a fulfilled chapter, if I had left these two chemical active products out of the chapter of brain chemical addictions. It would not be right for me to leave out the world's most highly craved addictive products.

Although, these two products (cigarettes & coffee) are the cheapest chemicals that can be purchased, yet, they still create a deadly addiction within the brain. Cigarettes and coffee both performs great works of negativity within the brain. Cigarettes are high in nicotine, and coffee is filled with caffeine.

Let me explain and define nicotine for you, so that you will have a better understanding about what you are putting inside your body and brain. From study; Nicotine is first an oily substance that is found in tobacco leaves that acts as a stimulant, which contributes to addictions. Also, nicotine is a poisonous alkaloid. Nicotine is a very powerful poisonous substance that is fatal to all the workers in the brain.

Nicotine, which is made from the tobacco leaves, is also used as an insecticide. Insecticide and alkaloid both are put into cans, that we call "bug spray". In other words, insecticide, and alkaloid is used to kill insects. Well, nicotine, which has insecticide ingredients in it, is a part of the formula when making cigarettes.

Insecticide, which is in all cigarettes, is being inhaled by humans, today. Humans, actually, inhale bug killer (insecticide) into their brain, and they do not know it. If insecticide is used to kill the lives of insects; then what do you think it will do unto the brain. Your brain and insects both have the same ending results in life when insecticide has touched them both. A human brain and insects cannot handle the fact that nicotine or insecticide has met it. When you spray insecticide on an insect, the bug usually never dies right away. It usually dies minutes later after the encounter of being hit by the insecticide. In the same sense, when you inhale insecticide (cigarettes), the brain does not die immediately, but years later; the brain will experience a growth of mental organ decaying, which will lead to a sickness unto death. We, as a people, really need to be careful about substances that are made by human hands.

When a person is addicted to cigarettes, he or she might be lead to try other mind alternating chemicals, too. One chemical addiction can open the door for another chemical addiction. Just as a person can "oops", slip and fall on a wet floor, a person can "oops" slip, and fall into another chemical addiction. Not only can smoking cigarettes lead people to other chemical active products, however, cigarettes have destroyed the mental minds of people over the past number of years.

Cigarettes have cleverly killed more than 100,000 people in one year. Wow, that is a great number of brains being sent to the graveyard for the usage of smoking cigarettes. Wow, that is a great number of brains becoming sick, and then suddenly appearing in a rectangular box at a funeral session.

When people smoke cigarettes for a length of time, they begin to cough heavily. The brainstem is the breathing operator, and it is being contaminated by the smoking of cigarettes. I sat and watched a person cough for exactly 5 minutes trying to gain normal breathing back. Once the normal breathing came back, he put the cigarette right back to the mouth to be inhaled. The brainstem, which gives life, is slowly being destroyed, but the cigarette user does not know it.

Many people have actually smoked cigarettes their entire lives. Although, many people have begun smoking cigarettes in their teen years, however, if you are over the age of 40 and still smoking, that's practically your entire life in which inhaling nicotine has been in action.

It is crazy because many people can be on their deathbed, and will continue to smoke cigarettes. Can you imagine a person on his or her deathbed, and crying out, "I need a cigarette". You would think that a sick person would have the mental empowerment to flee from the physical activity of smoking cigarette. However, the chemical addiction that the brain has been captivated too, will keep the erg and feelings to have the need to smoke, even while on your deathbed.

People do not believe that smoking cigarettes and drinking coffee will lead their bodies to experiencing future illnesses. As people, for years, we have over looked the negative power that cigarettes and coffee has. People often hear about sickness and diseases that smoking cigarettes can plague the body with, but people still smoke them on a daily basis. We believe that the illnesses given from either of these two addictive workers will not bring serious harm unto us. Everyone thinks he or she is hidden from illnesses that are created by smoking cigarettes. Nevertheless, if people continue to plague their brain with these two chemicals, the brain will unexpectedly receive a reward, which will be a mental illness.

The law does not enforce people to refrain themselves from drinking coffee nor smoking cigarettes, therefore, anyone can purchase and use as much as he or she desires. However, the brain has a law against them both. The brain's law is: "neither nicotine nor caffeine is needed. The only stimulant that the brain needs is its maker, which is God. Nevertheless, we disobey our conscious center and cause our bodies to experience the negative habits these intoxicants grants on the body.

Most cigarettes addictions begin after the age of at the age of 13. Most coffee addictions begin after the age of 19. That is just my own personal assumption. One addiction (cigarettes) comes from teen stress and ignorance, while the other addiction (coffee) comes from not having proper brain needed rest. Okay, I have a question for you. Is there an answer for your stress problems, and your non-resting habits? There has to be another solution besides shoving caffeine and nicotine in your head to bring about a mode of "calm".

Cigarettes are substances that have the ability to cause premature death to come into the user's life. In other words, a cigarette smoker can face death before it's truly his or her time to die. Just as a woman can have a baby earlier than 9 months, a person can die before his or her time by smoking cigarettes. Every person, who has died on the count of smoking cigarettes, has died from an illness that found its way into the organs of the head. Usually, cancer is the illness that comes from smoking cigarettes. When such an illness has found its way into the body, the individual is actually feeling the motions of death. Although, no one really knows that death can be felt, however, when a recorded sickness has attached it self to body, if death is with it, then death is being felt. Have you ever heard anyone say, "I can feel myself dying"? It is so true that chemical use and drug abuse will force a person's life to experiencing a death that can be physically felt, and emotionally aware of.

When people become addicted to cigarettes, as they purchase them, they have just bought their own personal killer. If you go to a store and buy a pack of cigarettes, you have willingly purchased for yourself, a substance brain killer. You have actually walked or drove to the store, and bought a box of cigarettes that is filled with 20 death sticks. Therefore, for you, it only cost less than 5 dollars to start the process of self-destroying your own brain and body. This killer (cigarettes) does not have to stalk you, nor follow you down the yellow brick road, because you, on your own went to the store and purchase it. With agreement from your mind, you have just purchased a two -inch (cigarette size) murderer. Remember, every time you smoke cigarettes, you are inhaling an illness creator.

Cocaine- is produced from leaves of the coca plant, which sprouts from the field just like marijuana and heroin does. Cocaine was once used as a numbing to certain areas of the body. If cocaine is shot into the body with a needle or put on the tongue, it will numb the touched area within seconds. The lobes in the brain that deal with touch are the parietal lobes. However, cocaine has the power to take the sense of touch from its users.

There are three entrances that cocaine users can do when putting it into the anatomy. The first way to utilize this drug is to snort it through the nostril, which is the brainstem's work because inhaling is being performed. The second way to use this drug is to inhale and exhale it through the mouth, which is the brainstem job again. The third way to activate this drug is too use a syringe to inject the dope into the bloody veins.

Jacking cocaine into your veins with needles is a job that your brain's body mover and coordinator (cerebellum) does. The cerebellum is the body's mover and coordinator; therefore, your own limb's controller guides the hands to stick the needle filled with dope into its own member (body). Whichever way you put cocaine into the body, the chemicals soon travels to the head by the blood. Once cocaine gets in the head, the strength of cocaine will prove its power throughout the entire system of the brain.

People that put cocaine in the brain and body are leading themselves to experience mental nervousness, and mental paranoia. One of the brainworker's that is affected by cocaine is the frontal lobe. The frontal lobes deal with emotional reactions, which is acquainted with paranoia. Since nervousness and paranoia are actions of emotions, the frontal lobes are being stimulated and animated by this drug.

Cocaine usage will cause its users to be on the streets night and day looking for the high, without eating food for days. The limbic system is the hunger awakener, but when it has become addicted to cocaine, it will ignore the desire to eat food. Cocaine will become the limbic system's new food for flavor. However, in a short period of time, the brain cells, neurons, cerebellum, cerebrum, hemispheres (left and right), the four lobes, brainstem, and memory, will all be controlled and demolished by this chemical control substance.

Inhalants- are substances that can only be inhaled. As a person inhales inhalants, vapors of air chemicals dashes into the brain. Inhalants come in a variety of products, such as; gasoline, cosmetic sprays, household cleaning products, paint thinner, nail polish remover, and many other products.

When this drug is inhaled into the brain, it starts to operate almost immediately. It is believed that inhalants clouds up the entire brain immediately after it have been utilized. Since the brainstem deals with the inhaling acts, then the brainstem is the primary actor to help this drug reach all users' inner being with success. Therefore, you are brutally murdering your own self by your own brainstem's activity. If you have willingly submitted to inhaling the product, then you have willing submitted to destroying your own brain's organs.

Years ago, it has been recorded that close to 10, 000 people have been led to visit the local hospital because of inhalant usage. More than 100 inhalant users have died in a one-year period. Yeah, I suppose the vapor and ingredients of this drug choked the brainstem (breathing regulator), and death became the user's reward.

It is said that inhalants will destroy your learning ability, your memory, and cleverly distract your problem solving skills. Well, short-term, procedural, and declarative memory will be destroyed after long periods of usage from this drug. Since the frontal lobes deals with our problem solving skills, this section of the brain is being affected during every usage of inhalant.

Every starting point of drug usage comes from a persuasion from a mental desire. As a person continue to use drugs, a higher tolerance level will be created. The chemicals within all drugs will create an amazing level of high tolerance. Meaning, when you once was satisfied from smoking one marijuana joint, you will be led to smoke 6 for the same psychological effect. You will never reach a level satisfaction.

From the information that I have written unto you concerning drugs and their power, once they become connected to the intelligent human brain, negative thoughts are always in effect. Now we understand why people are performing so many lawbreaking maneuvers. Now we know why wickedness is on the up rise in our land and community. It is all because of the way that drugs chemically alerts and controls the brain and body to do. Well, maybe I should say that wickedness is so exalted, because of how drug intoxicants exalt the thinking system of the brain. If a human being does not slide drugs in the brain, then the cerebrum will not think about committing a murder. If a human being does not slide drugs into the thinking processor, then the cerebellum will not control the hands to pull the trigger of a gun.

As you have just read in this chapter, that drugs have diverse task to perform. Drugs have a permanent job, they have a particular task to achieve, and they will not stop working in a person's life until payment is definitely received. When drug usage creates physical or mental harm in the user's life, that is the creative moment and time that drugs has received its paycheck (reward).

Do not think that drugs want your petty cash alone, however, also believe that all chemicals are after your life, and your physical condition (health).

Once drugs effectively leak its negative habits into your life, then it already has its unseen grip on your brain and body. Well, after you have finished reading this nonfiction story, it will expose unto you that any drug can and will take over a human being's life. Drugs utmost scheme for all users' are too unexpectedly kill, unexpectedly steal, and unexpectedly destroy them.

I have one more fact to present to you before I end this chapter. Since the brainstem is the potential controller of heart rate, which gives life into every human being, when drugs are put in the head, drugs are actually fighting against that which gives the tremendous support to live. The only thing that drugs want from you is your life. Although, drugs want your body, however, dope's utmost task is to make a connection to your brain, which controls the heart.

Therefore, as I have told you before, run for your life. If drugs have already captured your life, while you are reading this book, this story will introduce unto you to a man, which has the sufficient power to give you your life back. There is nothing wrong with starting life all over again. People start their lives over during different stages of life. Now it is time for you to start your life over, too.

SAY NO TO DRUGS AND YES TO THE LIVING OF YOUR BRAIN!

Chapter 6
Staying in School, and My Brain's First Drug Experience

Now you are about to see if chapter 4 (the intelligent human brain) and chapter 5 (drugs controlling the intelligent human brain) is actual information based on facts. I presume that I can say, "I am the mummy or the stuffed dummy" God used to show the world that such a hurting experience can happen. I believe, I am the person who has the testimony, which will reveal unto the world that drugs can manipulate, influence, control, and destroy hopes and dreams. Not only that, but I am the person who was used to show the world that wickedness is associated with drugs. It is time for me to get to the tangible (heart-touching) point of why I call this particular nonfiction story, I DID NOT KNOW.

On the bus, after basketball practice, the players and I were being driven home. This bus is called, "The Activity Bus". The Activity Bus is a bus that transports black athletes home every night after practice. Since all the black athlete's were from the City of St. Louis, a scheduled bus would transport us home everyday after basketball practice. Every evening, it was about 6 to 8 black athletes' traveling home. As we were all being driven home to our designated area, we would laugh, joke around, and sometimes sleep on the bus. A few of us lived in the south city of St. Louis, and a few of us lived on the Westside/north side.

Many times, the basketball players would inhale marijuana on the activity bus. Probably, 2 to 3 times out of the week, the players smoked marijuana on the bus. It was always a different person who brought some weed to smoke.

Many times, my teammates would ask me, saying, "Irons, take a puff of the joint". After I had been asked the question, my brain would immediately operate, and compel my mouth to say, "No, that's ok". It didn't take more than 2 seconds to decide if I wanted to participate in this drug event. I responded quickly by saying, "No, that's okay". The part of my brain (limbic system), which is my fear regulator, was doing its part. It was showing its fear, when it comes to drug usage. The players verbally asked me to take a hit of the marijuana on several occasions, and each time they asked, my brain would control my mouth to say, "No". My limbic system was afraid to participate in this drug-using event.

I did not have a thorough understanding why the players or people inhaled marijuana into their bodies anyway. Therefore, the desire to smoke it was not even a chance of thought. I had no desire to inhale this chemical substance. Smoke it for what, I want to be a star basketball player. To me, it was useless and meaningless to inhale and smoke anything. My health was far most important. More also, I've dreamed of showing my talents and skills to the world on television.

Smoking marijuana in high school was the grand performance to do. Many of my high school friends smoked marijuana. Their brains have been captivated by this chemical controlled substance (marijuana). I suppose none of them were thinking about the health of the body. They all smoked marijuana for their mental entertainment, I suppose.

As the basketball players and I were traveling home after basketball practice one day, it happened. The fellows (team players) spoke to me again saying, "Irons" take a small hit of the marijuana. This time I gave in unto their asking, and extended my arms and hands to grasp a hold onto that inflamed joint. I suppose, I finally empowered my mind to agree to take part in the act of inhaling marijuana. I took two willing puffs of the marijuana. After a few seconds passed, I said to my friends, "I don't feel anything".

Well, about 4 to 5 minutes later, unexpectedly, and out of nowhere, the operating chemicals from marijuana broke into my entire head. I then began to laugh, laugh, laugh, until my body exited from the bus.

I mentally caused my brain to make a decision to give drugs an accessed entrance into my life. As of now, while I am in high school, I've allowed the doorway of drugs to open up into my life. Also, immediately, this pathway of drugs, my feet have just touched, and I DID NOT KNOW it. Therefore, marijuana was the first entrance of a drug that ever entered into my anatomy (brain and body).

The uncontrollable laughter was the first effect that the marijuana brought into my physical and mental being. As I was laughing at any and every thing, the players were all laughing at me. They knew this was my first time getting "high" from a chemical control substance. As they observed how silly I became, while this drug became sovereign in my anatomy (brain and body), I became the hilarious comedy show of the hour. Every small reaction performed by me, was entertaining to them all. Nevertheless, my brain had been kidnapped from mental freedom, to a condition of being controlled by a chemical substance, and I DID NOT KNOW it.

Indeed, my brain has truly been kidnapped. Just as a kidnapper captures and abducts a child, and takes the infant away from home, my brain has been abducted in the very same like manner. Kidnap means to captivate someone, and hold him or her as a living hostage or prisoner. Seizing a person, and taking them away against his or her "will" is called, kidnapping. Kidnap and abducting someone is against the laws. Although, a human being did not kidnap me, however, marijuana imprisoned my thoughts, and is about to take my brain on the ride to hell, and I DID NOT KNOW it. Although, I am alive, and my body is yet with me, however, my brain is about to be toured on an ignorant mission; and I have no idea where I'm going, nor do I know what is about to happen next.

My brain became captivated to the mental pleasure of marijuana. After smoking marijuana, my brain had been taken on a tour in life where I did not want it to travel too. My brain became a prisoner unto the power of marijuana. Therefore, I am utilizing the term "kidnapped" because my brain had been taken out of freedom. Although, someone did not physically snatch me, however, my brain had been taken from the norm. My brain became captivated to this chemical controlled substance for a very long time. The chains of marijuana's ingredients shackled my life for many years.

Now that I think about my first drug usage experience, I actually controlled my cerebellum (the hand controller and coordinator) to guide my hands to handle that lawbreaking substance. Not only did I stretch out my hand to grab the marijuana joint, but also, I caused my brainstem to inhale the dope into my personal being. Therefore, I actually gave my mind and body the agreement to participate in the act of using this drug. Yeah, in high school, on the activity bus, is where my first drug usage encounter took place.

Since marijuana is on the school bus, then wickedness also is on the school bus as well. Wherever there are drugs, wickedness is always the reason why such is in the presence. Wherever there is wickedness, lawbreaking maneuvers are there too. Therefore, every person who was smoking marijuana on the activity bus, all were handling a substance that is against the law. So, not only am I lawbreaker, but also, I have performed an act of wickedness. Not only did I inhale a substance that is against the law, but also, I inhaled the seed of wickedness into my anatomy. Since a drug is now in my brain, then wickedness is in it as well. My brain as of now, has tasted the substance that exposes one's life to wickedness. Wickedness (marijuana) I saw on the ground in the projects, and the same substance has now been used by me.

In the bible, in the book of _1st John, chapter 2: 16 says, for ALL that is in the world; the lust of the flesh, and the lust of the eyes, and the pride of life._

Although, I turned down many opportunities to inhaling marijuana with the basketball players, however, something on the inside of me empowered me to try it. It is almost like having sex for the first time. When a person has sex for the first time, the person's mind became empowered to do it. That is exactly how I felt when first tried this chemical control substance. My mind became empowered to do it. My brain's high intellectual censor (the cerebrum- the brain's thinking member) was lifting up its self and persuading my mouth to say, "No" to inhaling marijuana. However, as I watched the team players smoke marijuana on the regular, my mind and body was obviously saying, try it, try it, try it! Moreover, I did.

My flesh lusted for that same feeling that the other players obviously had. My flesh (body) desired to have that drug encounter experience, too. My eyes viewed the amusement the team was having after they smoked marijuana, and my flesh eagerly wanted to become a partaker in this activity, too. No matter how long the basketball players have been inhaling marijuana into their brains, whatever it was that influence them to try it for the first time, is the same force that persuaded me. I am sure that, when they first tried drugs, they watched someone intake dope, too. Nevertheless, I immediately became one of them, by my first drug usage experience. I once use to look down on them, but now, I've actually become their equal.

Just that fast and just that quick, my brain and body had been cunningly exposed to the evil scheme of dope. In the twinkling of an eye, in the blinking of a moment, my brain and body was wrapped up in the magical ways of this chemical controlled substance. Although, I am sure that I have done many evil deeds in my life before, however, from my first substance usage, I have actually just met the author of wickedness (marijuana). Yes, the author of wickedness, which is marijuana, has found a way to operate in my life. From the first few puffs of the joint (weed), I have given my life to the power of dope and I DID NOT KNOW it. My hand has now touched a substance that leads a person into the ways of wickedness.

Once I had inhaled the weed into my brain, my body became impure from the first contact. This entire drug process became active, because of the lust of my flesh, and the lust of my eyes. Pride had not visibly kicked in yet, but soon, pride is going to break into my life, and set me up for the righteous judgment of God to visit me along with his anger. So here I am, with a chemical controlled substance inside of my brain and body. Not only have I just been exposed to drugs, but also, God's anger is on my back and I DID NOT KNOW it.

When I first smoked this chemical controlled substance called, "marijuana", I became disobedient unto three rules or three highly esteemed rules and instructions. First, I became disobedient unto the laws of God, because it is against the law to have drugs in my personal possession. Although, I did not physically bring the marijuana to school, as soon as I put it into my hand, that apparently caused me to be disobedient to the laws of God. Secondly, I became disobedient to my parents counseling because they verbally told me to stay far away from people who do drugs, and if offered, "walk away". Third, I became disobedient to my brain's conscience center, because my mind was telling me "not to smoke that weed" on several occasions. Therefore, when I first smoked marijuana, I disobeyed the cry of my brain's conscience center. Whether I realize it or not, my conscience center cried and cried out not to put dope in it, but I did it anyway. The brain is so intelligent, on its on, it knows what is good, and what's not so good.

For every teenager, once any drug has been accessed in his or her life it is because of disobedience. Teenagers as well as adults have overstepped or disobeyed their parents counseling, and their mental God created fear. No one in the world has ever used a chemical controlled substance, and his or her brain did not display a type of fear. Every human being that has ever tried drugs, before they tried it, a movement of mental fear became active. Since the limbic system is the brain's worker, which awakens the emotion to show fear, then that brain part of all drug users' becomes active first. However, I disobeyed my mental fear applicator and smoked marijuana anyway. Actually, when I first tried marijuana, I disobeyed every lobe and organ in my human brain.

I wonder how my parents are going to feel; if or when they find out that, their teenage son has been inhaling marijuana into his brain. My parents prepared the time to tell me about drugs being bad for the physical health of the body. My parents gave me talks and talks about staying away from drugs because of its detrimental agony. Yet, here I am inhaling a dope product into my own brain. Although, my parents have spoken unto me saying, "drugs will kill", which I did believe, but nevertheless, the lust of my eyes, and the lust of my flesh won in this battle. Nevertheless, I needed help to be freed from this chemical control substance even right now, and I DID NOT KNOW it.

When the basketball players would inhale marijuana into their bodies, they would return to school looking healthy and unharmed. If the basketball players smoked weed on Monday; then on Tuesday they returned to school in tiptop shape. From my personal mental point of view, I was looking for something harsh to happen unto them soon and very soon. I strongly believe that I was looking for a physical mishap to happen unto them that I could visibly see with my own two eyes. My young mind was mentally convinced that when someone does drugs, that something would happen to that dope user soon and very soon, and that my eyes would be able to preview the results from it.

Although, the basketball players offered me the dope, it was my own will to accept it. I am the individual to take the blame for participating in this puff-puff pass event. When the dope had been offered unto me, it became my own judgment to take part in this activity or not. Since I've inhaled marijuana into my brain, my mental status has truly become contaminated. My brain immediately went from not knowing what marijuana feels like, to effectively experiencing its amusement, and it's after effects.

Whether, I mentally realize it or not, I have actually entered my brain and body into a different world. I was 14 years old, still a young boy, so I DID NOT KNOW that I had just exposed my life to a completely new style of living. Actually, I am a changed man now because of what I had put inside of my brain. Although, I am still the same person, however, deep down inside, I became a different being. Since I have allowed marijuana's formula to touch my brain, the organs in my head are sharing space with a stranger. Yeah, one of the predators finally touched me. Not only did I allow marijuana to touch my brain, but also, from the usage of it, my brain's emotional center has become united with the tactics of wickedness. Although, it seems like I am still the same young innocent child, I DID NOT KNOW that a transformation has taken place in my life in a matter of minutes. From inhaling marijuana into my brain, it was almost as if, another inner being had entered into my brain's thinking center (the cerebrum).

I must verbally confess out of my mouth, "I did enjoy inhaling and smoking weed" because of the inner feelings that it "charged" within me. I became so addicted to this plant called, "marijuana" that I never sought the chance or the opportunity to rescue my brain from its subtle power. My brain spent more time trying to find ways to get high, than it did trying to find a technique to be freed from it. The intoxicants from Marijuana seemed as if they were glued to my intelligent human brain. My brain became stuck to the mental pleasure that it distributed throughout my entire head. Just as "crazy" glue sticks tightly to timber, my brain was welded to the potent active power of marijuana's formula.

Every since the first day that my brain experienced marijuana's rush, inhaling this mind alternating substance became an ongoing habit. Whenever I saw friends smoking marijuana, I always walked into the huddle, and took a whiff of the weed. In other words, my brain was craving for that immediate attention of the chemical fulfillment. My thoughts to smoke marijuana became a daily act for me. I believed my brain really enjoyed the overall sensation that marijuana stunningly inserted within it.

If I had not liked nor enjoyed the dynamic feeling that street marijuana produced within my brain, I would have been coaxing myself to cease or discontinue the actions of inhaling "pot". My days of seeking to implant my brain with marijuana would have been days of seeking to uproot the seed of marijuana addiction out of my anatomy. Finding a way to refrain myself from applying this substance into my brain, would have been my global authorized search. However, nevertheless, I enjoyed the feeling; therefore, I continued the use of directing marijuana into my brain. It seemed as if I was pulled by some unknown power, which kept me actively replenishing this chemical craved substance inside of my brain (flesh). So here I am, a freshman in high school living with a brain that has become addicted to the ingredients from marijuana.

Now that I have drugs (wickedness) in my brain, my physical limbs have been hired to do evil. Wickedness is now in my brain and body, therefore, it is about to put me to work according to its own evil pleasure and purpose. I have now been hired by wickedness to perform works of evil. Wickedness will cause me to work tasks of evil to fulfill its demonic desires. Just as any drug does not operate until it is put in the brain, well, wickedness does not work until a person has been hired to do evil. Wickedness is the boss, and all of its employees are commanded to do actions of evil. Nevertheless, just by smoking marijuana, I have been hired to perform at a position to do evil, and "<u>I DID NOT KNOW</u>" it.

The hideous secret of marijuana is to conceal its harmful addiction from its first time users. The most horrifying effect that springs along with any drug is the internal (inner body) addiction. Once the internal addiction has been registered in the brain, breaking the drug-craving habit will be hard to do. When I was a youngster, no one ever spoke about the addiction from drugs. Different people said, "That drugs could kill you". Well, here I am, utilizing a so-called killer, which is a drug, and yet, I am still alive. Death is not the first experience seen to drug users. The first reaction that I can see that happens to a drug user is the obsession and the craving for the drug. The mental addiction is what happened unto me, not death. Every basketball player on the bus who smoked marijuana had an addiction. However, no deaths, burials, nor funerals had been scheduled. Every basketball player on the school bus, at some point, their brain's limbic system was highly informed, and persuaded to accept drug's addiction.

Maybe parents should properly instruct, and counsel their children about the drug's addiction, and the controlling force that drugs have. Well, not too many of us know too much about the brain and body, therefore, we do not teach on the true riches that need to be taught. When you are done reading this miraculous story, you would have received much knowledge to teach your children concerning the works of drugs, and the operation of the brain. The written words in my book, which are filled with my life's experiences, are recorded in this story for your learning. Learn from it, and teach your children. Since most of us have already messed up our lives, lets seek to better the next generation, which many youths are about to enter into.

A generation comes into existence every 35 to 36 years, and I have proof of the matter. We believe that every time a person turns 16 or what not, that the next generation has just begun. However, I am not going to get into debates concerning generations and their presentations; but teach your kids about the brain, drugs, and wickedness. Since I have commanded you to teach your children about the above subjects, I cannot leave the creator of the world out; teach your children about God too.

Anyway, from my personal experiences, and observing the things that the basketball players did (inhaled marijuana on the regular), we all had marijuana's addiction floating around in our heads. I soon began to realize why marijuana's craving power is so hard to break. From its powerful character (the addiction) that it plants inside the head, it resembles the solidness of ancient iron, which cannot be broken. Ancient iron cannot be broken by human strength, nor can any drug's addiction. Although, I have seen a strong man curve an iron bar by human strength, but it was not broken nor split in half.

People and even myself have absolutely seen from watching digital television how chemical control substances can destroy a person's life. I did have a high level of fear in me before I first tried the marijuana, but I guess from repeatedly observing the basketball players inhaling dope (marijuana) into their bodies, I reckoned that it could not be that injurious. Once I physically caused my brainstem to participate in drug usage, every spoken word that was said badly about drugs had immediately departed from my mind. From my first usage of marijuana, all the counseling that my "declarative memory" had once retained had been blotted out. Marijuana deleted every negative word about drugs that my intelligent human brain had once retained within it. Now my memory has a new fact about marijuana, which is, how good it truly feels to my brain and body. The dangerous and horrifying information that had been spoken to me about drugs have been overridden, by the fascinating feelings that my brain and body had been exposed too. My brain no longer believes that drugs will kill; it believes that drugs feel great.

I smoked marijuana through my brainstem my entire high school career. Smoking marijuana became a driven escort of guidance in my high school days. Things became so hectic that I would skip classes. I skipped school and classes just to get "high" with a friend. Sometimes, after smoking marijuana at school, I would not even go and attend to any of my classes. I would rather walk down the hallways and interrupt other classes as it was in session. Skipping classes and physically bothering other classes was two of the ignorant performances I did while under the crafty influence of marijuana. Believe me, it is so true because I was physically led, and enticingly influenced by marijuana to do stupid things such as that.

As years passed by, dropping out of high school was heavily in my thoughts. I was having deep thoughts about not needing school academics in my personal life. My mind was thinking that I have a chance to become a pro-basketball player, so why do I need school. Since I am going to be a pro basketball star, I do not need the highest achievement award in education.

Since the thinking comes from my brain's cerebrum, and reasoning is from my brain's frontal lobe, marijuana was working on both of those two components or sections of my human brain. Remember, the brain already has its normal way of reasoning and thinking, but when drugs are inhaled into head, the thinking and the reasoning becomes chemically persuaded and influenced by the drug. Let the cerebrum (brain part that does the thinking) think on it's on, and not with the help of a chemical controlled substance. Once chemical control substances are in a person's thinking center, important decisions to be made can turn out to be the worst. Do not allow drugs to overlap your brain's normal thinking mode. Whenever you (my reader) and I meet, tell me how many times drugs have caused you to make horrible decisions. I want to hear your testimony. Really!

Take heed to this parable, which speaks about the painting of a house. A person owned a house, and the color of it was white all over. One day, the property owner decided to paint the entire house light blue. That he did. Since the house was once white and now light blue, a new color has now been applied. From that physical act of painting, the house is now a new color, which is blue. It's just the same as when I inhaled marijuana into my cerebrum and frontal lobes (brain); my normal ways of thinking and reasoning had been over lapped by the intoxicants of that particular drug. Therefore, I will never know, if I wanted to drop out of high school from a normal thought mode or not, because marijuana was in my thinking system (cerebrum) and my reasoning worker (frontal lobes). 90% of the people who did not earn their high school diploma, probably had drugs in their thinking system.

Marijuana was in my brain cleverly rambling from one brain component to the next. When any drug is inhaled into the brain, the dope becomes the brain's mentor and or tutor. Drugs will actually teach the brain how to become addicted. In other words, when you put drugs in your brain, it will soon become your brain's counselor, and or director. Do not allow drugs to over lap your brain from its normal ways of performance. God created the brain to do one thing, and that is to work on it's on without any lawbreaking help.

The brain is made and created by God to work solo.

As I was still putting this chemical (marijuana) in my head, being tardy from class became a major problem. Even as of now, I DID NOT KNOW or realized that this marijuana was powerfully enforcing me to have all these negative intentions and reactions. Most of the times when I was tardy for class, it would be because I willingly stayed outdoors to inhaled and smoke marijuana with a friend or two. Marijuana was a great hindrance to me in my high school years. During high school, I attended it more than four years. I was being a complete clown throughout the entire years of being in high school. I do consider myself an average student, but my grades said other wise. Well, I must not leave out the fact that, probably every report card period, I earned at least one F or two. The classes I've received bad grades in were classes I acted a complete "nut" in. Although, I did more than four years in high school, I was far from being what is called, "dumb". Nevertheless, from my first intake of marijuana, that was the dumbest move ever.

I had to go back to school to take up a summer course just to make up for unearned credits. Also, I had to go back to school for an extra semester. The reason why I pressed my way through high school and completed it is because my mother was not approving of me "dropping" out. My mother definitely wanted to see all of her children at least earn their high school diplomas, if nothing else.

I have another written manuscript, which is my 3rd book, and it will be published soon. This book is called, "Keep Your Vision". It speaks about people keeping their vision concerning goals they have been "set". It also encourages you to give God something to work with from your educational background. That is a good book for everyone, and definitely, the world of athletes should purchase copies of this up coming future book.

Now that I have my high school diploma (certificate), it does feel mentally good to have that achievement award in my home. Therefore, if I ever decided to go to college and further my education, I would not have to waste time with earning a G.E.D. A student cannot start college without a G. E. D. or a high school diploma. A high school diploma will quickly allow me to sign up for college immediately. No matter how many years I stray from school, a high school diploma will swiftly allow me to enroll, and begin college course classes.

However, if you do not receive your high school diploma, you will have to return to school to go through a required program to earn your G. E. D.. A G.E.D is not the same as a high school diploma; however, it will still allow you to sign up for college. Therefore, I advise all high school teens too at least earn that high school diploma while you have the opportune chance to do so. Trust me; there WILL come an unexpected moment in your personal life that you will consider registering for school again (college).

Many times, people are urged or mentally persuaded to go back to school to better their financial status. 85% of the people in the world go back to college to escape the mental pain of being in financial poverty. Some people go back to school to better their financial status so they can do greater things for their children. Therefore, little children, stay away from drugs, stay in school, and collect as much educational information as you possibly can. This is for the peace in the future of your earthly years to come.

In order for an earthly human being to have a decent living, that individual will need to be able to read and write, which are performances learned while in school. Learning how to read and write will help you to understand documents or contracts that you endorse your signature on. While you are learning how to read and write, you are preparing yourself for mental success, and less mental frustration. If a person does not learn how to read and write in English, then living in the USA is going to be full of frustrations that will easily lead the individual to mental aggravation. Everyone needs to be able to read letters on documents, and write complete words in sentences to fill in answers on job applications. So, stay in school, and as they say, "learn the golden rule". When striving to have a decent way of living;

you must know how to read and write.

I have witness or have seen many foreigners who came from across seas to the United States seeking to live their lives on this side of the world. Some of them traveled here, and cannot understand the English writing, which is the USA language. The USA's language is an interpretation many of us have learned shortly after birth.

Many foreigners who ventured to the USA came unprepared because they did not know how to read nor write in the English translation. If letters are not written in their foreign language, they are lost and without an adequate understanding. If the foreigner cannot read English, then it will be hard for him to understand the letters and words, which are written in English form. If foreigners, who have traveled to the US, cannot read the English translation, then it's most likely they cannot write in English.

People who are from the USA will attempt to get over on the foreigner when the opportune chance comes. I hope a foreigner does not come across the pathway of people who will try to get over on the over seas person. However, since the world is full of ongoing wickedness, there is a chance that someone will plot a scheme to get over on the foreigner. I bountifully dislike people who try to get over on innocent people just for a couple of dollars. People who try to get over on foreigners are sick-headed individuals. I guaranteed you, if anyone has pulled a trick on a foreigner; his or her mind was filled with drugs.

Also, little children, take the time to learn mathematics. Learn it! Adding, subtraction, multiplying, and dividing will always be a necessity throughout your entire life of earthly living. You can't dodge math, nor can you run from it; math will always be a mental work needed to be done in your life. When you earn your cash, you need to know how to count it properly. If you can't count numbers correctly, then your boss, or whoever finds out, will cheat you until you find out what's going on. Remember, there are many people in the world whose minds operate in deceit and wickedness, and humankind will cheat you whenever they get the opportune chance do so.

Let me put it all together; mathematics, reading, writing, and home economics are considered basic essentials for survival. Those four subjects (math, reading, writing, home economics) are daily necessities you need to learn in order to maintain an average living. Those subjects (math, reading, writing, and economics) are topics you'll constantly learn all through high school. Actually, those subjects you will learn in grade school, but high school will teach at advance levels. We all need to know the basics in life, so stay in school and learn how to read words, write with understanding, and add and subtract numbers. When you learn those things, that information will descend into your brain's center called, "Declarative Memory". There will be things that your declarative memory will probably let go, however, when you learn how to read, write, add, subtract, and basic home economics, I guaranteed you, you will never forget the basics of those four subjects.

Although, I smoke and inhale marijuana throughout my high school career, I did gain some learning techniques. I learned my basic reading, writing skills, math and home economic skills. Right now today, I am living off those four learned subjects that I learned in school. I have not been in school for years, but those 4 subjects that I learned in school stuck with me. Therefore, here I am, years later, living on the teachings I learned in school. Although, this book might have many errors in it, but as you can see, I learned, and kept enough English skills in my declarative memory to write a decent book. I am so glad that I learned the basic eight parts of speech.

You know what? Just by me writing the above paragraph, I have caused hundredths of teens to stay in school. That is my job, through writing, to encourage you all. This story is written to encourage people one way or another. This entire book might not teach you everything, but if one paragraph encourages you not to give up in life, then my book has served a great purpose. Since you are reading this book, that means, you have learned the writing is English translation. Keep up the good work, and never give up in school. We fell to realize that education and God are very important while living on the earth. Not to knock down education, but soon, within this book, you are about to find out that God's way is far more important than education. Education is important, but God is more important.

However, don't you dare quit school, thinking to do God's way. Education is a necessity every man needs, and God will never tell anyone to drop out of school. Only drugs and wickedness will tell you that education is not needed.

Chapter 7
Searching for Employment and Deeper into Drugs

Well, I did graduate from high school. Getting into my mother's car, I drove it to the high school to pick up my diploma. Putting my foot on the gas pedal, I was smiling inside. Before proceeding to pick up my high school diploma, I inhaled the flavor of marijuana into my brain. By now, my brain has become heavily addicted to this chemical mind-alternating substance. As of now, for four and a half years, I've been smoking marijuana. There I was, on the high way high as a kite in my mother's car. I was 19 years of age when my hand finally touched my high school graduation certificate. Well, time has now passed on.

My high school days are now over. I need to find a job so that I can earn a few dollars. I realize that money is exceedingly necessary and important in our society and world. Without cash, a person will not be able to buy nice materials and products from the local department store. If something is free, in most stores, you can believe it is a sample size product for the company's advertising benefit. Everything cost, and everything has been tagged with a price. Money has a special praise of necessity in this world. Any materials that you and I desire to own in life have a set price. Therefore, I must proceed in life and take care of myself by finding employment.

I went out into the world and walked into a couple of business places. In them, I filled out a couple of applications. Thank God, I already knew how to read and write. Since I already knew how to read and write, I was able to fill out applications with a decent understanding. Yeah, the reading and writing that I learned in school is now paying off.

While I was searching for employment, I found myself an occupation. Someone actually hired a drug head like me. Now I can put a few dollars in my possession. I am soon to receive an earned check or a financial payment. If I've worked for it, then I must be paid for my services done.

This job is a restaurant business. This restaurant is located a few blocks away from the old neighborhood I once lived in. I am not talking about my old neighborhood I grew up in as a child. This neighborhood is not in the projects. At this particular time, my family moved toward the South City of St. Louis. Therefore, I met new friends, and my job was located about five blocks away from the neighborhood.

At this job, my duties were to cleanse and stack dishes in racks for about 4 to 5 hours per night. Minimum wages is my hourly pay, which was $3.14. Of course, I did not want a minimum wage paying job, but I was led to do what I had to do. If I must wash and stack dishes to earn cash, then that's what I'll do. Although, I did not want an occupation that started payments at minimum wages, however, since I did not continue with my education, I was empowered to snatch whatever type of paying job that came first. Therefore, I hung in there, and took care of the dish room.

Since my high school diploma does not have specific qualification skills attached to it, walk on jobs, which do not require a certain skill level is what I found. A high school diploma does not have any additional personal academic skill award listed on it. Although, a high school diploma is great to have, but when seeking for high paying employment, your search is widely limited. However, if you earn a college degree, on it, will be the minimum hourly pay rate that a business must abide by, when salary is negotiated.

If your degree requires that you be worth a starting pay of $15 an hour, the company that has hired you, must abide in the area of payment. The business must pay you the salary that has been printed on your degree. However, there might be companies of your degree's field that may want to start you at $13.50 per hour. You might negotiate and accept that, or you might go and apply somewhere else, but the decision is all yours. Although, your college degree has $15 an hour printed on it, however, making $13.50 is a nice bargain.

There is nothing like being able to control your own financial living. You took your brain through college, and became a winner because you've earned that specialized degree. Your brain deserves the payment from all the mental trials and possible stress that it went through to accomplish that degree. You have been given the power to make your own financial decisions. But, me, my power is limited because I only have a diploma. Hey, do not get me wrong, because having a diploma can get you a nice job, too. But as I said before, with a high school diploma, your job search for great beginners pay is widely limited.

I cannot walk into a doctor's office with the intent to fill out an application for the RN position. The doctor or front desk clerk will ask, "Do you have a degree as a Registered Nurse". On the other hand, the front desk clerk might ask, "Do you have the minimum required hours of medical training? Well, for me, since I have no continuing educational skills, or the required experience needed for the RN position, 9 times out of 10, filling out an application would be a waste of time. They probably would not waste time with providing me with an application. By me having no degree, or hands on training, jobs that require a certain skill level, I became highly limited to receiving. Now a day, if you want the job of your choice, you must stay in school and earn that degree.

Anyway, the job that I had been hired at, the employee's payment plan is weekly. Earning cash once a week was cool, but the minimum wage payment was very weak. After I went shopping to purchase a pair of casual jeans or tennis shoes, and a bag of marijuana, my pockets became flat and empty. Oh yeah, I had to purchase my brain some marijuana because it craved for it. The hunger creator (limbic system) was addicted to the flavor of marijuana. Every pay period, I bought a great number of Fred Quickie joints.

Here I am working at this restaurant, and marijuana is

still working in my brain. If my brain did not get its food (marijuana), life would have become pathetically boring. Marijuana tricked my brain to believing in such a thing. It seems like my entire life is focusing on the mental actions and pleasures from marijuana.

Weed cunningly persuaded my friends and I into believing that inhaling marijuana brought all the "fun" into our presence. The power of marijuana had caused us all to believe, "if we didn't smoke weed, there will be no joy." Weed had our minds persuaded to believing that marijuana is the fun and excitement activator. My brain's functions had been mentally trained in high school to believing that; having pleasure and excitement was connected to the formula of marijuana.

Every friend of mine, which is from the neighborhood, we all inhaled marijuana throughout our entire years of being in high school. We all inhaled weed, for the purpose of fun. To believe in such a thing, my friends and I, we all were very ignorant individuals. I'm an idiot, my friends are idiots, and every drug user is an idiot too. If you are a weed smoker, then welcome to the idiot crew.

Even people on my job brain's were addicted to drug intoxicates. Sooner or later during the day, someone in the crowd would yell out, "I need to smoke a joint". Just about the entire shift of workers, brain's had a chemical addiction of some sort.

One day, an employee and I were inhaling marijuana while being in the basement of the restaurant. The owner of the restaurant became suspicious concerning the scent that was in the air of her personal owned business. Just as children smell weed in the home when their parents smoke it, and then become suspicious, my boss became suspicious in her place of business. The difference from children and my boss is the fact that, my boss knows exactly what the aroma is, but little children do not. Therefore, the boss confronted us, and asked, "Are you young men smoking pot in my restaurant"? Of course, Jamal and I nervously lied and said "no". We told the boss that some people were sitting on the back steps near the basement door of the restaurant smoking marijuana, and the scent blew inside the building by the traveling wind. The boss replied, "If I ever find out that you guys are smoking marijuana on my property, I am going to fire the both of you".

Already, as you can see, I have been led or forced to lie about my chemical abuse issue. Marijuana almost caused me to loose my first job. If the boss had fired me because of drug usage, I would have felt plain ole stupid. Nevertheless, there was probably not a day on the job, that my brain was not over flooded with marijuana's formula.

All the time, I would think about how I should be playing professional sports, and not washing dishes. My brain should be in college, damaging college basketball athletes, and possible on my way to the N.B.A. Day in and day out, I thought about the chance I had to be rich by playing sports. Sometimes, within myself, I still believed that I had the chance to play professional basketball; however, since I'm not in college, time is winding down. I am still young, and can still go and sign up for college.

Since I didn't graduate on time, and no basketball scholarship was offered, I thought I messed up, and could play ball for a college. Since I made my high school years so hectic, my brain was not thinking about going back to school, pick up books, papers, and attend classes again. If you make your high school years hard on you, your brain will not think about continuing education. Again, I advise you to go head and do the high school, and graduate on time. You have a whole lifetime ahead of you.

After a while, I became mentally exhausted with this minimum wage paying job, therefore, I quit. Not only did I suddenly cease from working at this job, but also, I sneakily crept out the back door when I was out of the boss's sight. The restaurant was still in operation, meaning, customers were eating, and the dishes needed to be cleansed. I walked out of this restaurant as the used dishes were being transported to the cleaning room. I did not care; I just wanted to be free from the sounds of dishes. My friend, who was my partner in the dish room, had to wash all of those piled up dishes by he lonesome-self. El. Jamal Goforth was in the dish room washing the dirty dishes. I ran out on the dishes, and I ran out on Jamal too. Hey Jamal, my good buddy, sorry I walked out and left you to wash all those dishes by yourself, (shaking my head) (over cracking too).

After I had ceased from employment of my first job, I soon began to search for another occupation to work at. I did have enough sense to remain active in searching of jobs. Besides, I needed to earn money, so I could feed my brain the substance that it craved and longed for, which was marijuana. Therefore, I was on another high pursuit searching for another job.

One day, I found another job. This job also was a restaurant food chain operation just as my first job was. As I said before, since I did not have any certified skills or advanced educational certificate achievement, walk in jobs were my primary leads. At this job, just like my last job, washing and rinsing the dishes after customers had eaten from them were my duties. I worked at this job for a total of 8 months. My first job only lasted for 4 months. My new job's payment period was every two weeks. Monday through Friday, I worked 6 to 8 hours a day. My hourly payment was minimum wages. So I guess you know I was not making a whole lot of money. However, I was still able to buy my brain medicine (marijuana), and a pair of Jordan tennis shoes from time to time.

Even while I was working at this job, many times, I thought about sports again. I began to realize that I really messed up my chance to have some financial stability in my life. Here I am washing dishes for minimum wages, when I could be getting paid 50 times higher.

Anyway, a time and day came when the owner of this restaurant had fired me. I was doing something in the restaurant that I had no business doing, and that was inhaling and exhaling drugs on the property of the boss's business. Of course, it is against all job rules to do drugs on the jobsite. Therefore, I was performing an act that was against the company's privacy and policy agreement.

Well, a few friends (employees) and I were smoking dope in the back area of this restaurant. We were getting high and having fun as we inhaled toxic substances into our anatomy (brain and body). Then, suddenly an employee yelled out, and said, "The boss is coming". We all physically scattered and went our own separate ways throughout the restaurant. Even though, we all scattered, the boss still smelled the strong scent of dope that filled the air in the building of the restaurant. We all thought that the owner of this restaurant was gone for the entire day, so we planned (frontal lobe scheming) to smoke a little dope in the back room of this privately owned restaurant. Nevertheless, I was the only individual who had been fired.

So there I was, feeling mentally stupid because I had been fired from my job because of drug usage. Being fired from my job because of drug usage was very embarrassing. It is shameful and embarrassing because, if anyone ever asks me, "why did I get fired from my job", I must tell that individual, "I was smoking dope on the job site, and had been fired because of it". As of now, only a few incidents have happened in my life concerning drugs, but to me, they were embarrassing moments.

I honestly believe that marijuana is the ultimate reason, why I did not graduate from high school at my scheduled and appointed time. Not graduating from high school at my appointed time was a terrible and an embarrassing event to experience. Graduating from high school later than I was suppose to, was the first embarrassing experience recorded in this book concerning "drugs and embarrassing moments". The second grieved or embarrassing moment is when I was fired from my place of work. For some reason, it never crossed my mind that dope was the "prime" reason for my embarrassing experiences. It also, never came to my thoughts that I needed some serious mental help from the usage of chemical controlled substance.

Every now and then, within this book, I will write unto you an update full of information concerning the incidents and experiences that dope has cunningly brought into my living.

Anyway, let me share with you more information in detail about the drug the employees and I were smoking which caused me to be fired from the second job. Other employees and I were inhaling into our brain a drug that is called, "pre-mo". Pre-mo is a chemical drug that gives the brain its effects from inhaling. Pre-mo is craftily put together in the form of a joint. It is smoked as a joint because cigarette papers (tiptop) are included to activate this drug product. Since two chemicals are put together to get the brain "high", it sounds like we conjured up a magic potion or something. Nevertheless, two drugs are mixed together to go inside one brain at the same exact time, and that is marijuana and grinded up crack cocaine.

Normally, marijuana is first spread onto the cigarette papers, and then grinded up crack cocaine is carefully sprinkled over it. Then, both drugs together are rolled up into a joint to be inhaled into the brain. Now that I think about it; that object I saw in the projects (marijuana) is now being used by me. I have actually picked up marijuana and brought its power alive.

Now that I think about it, I was fired from my job because of smoking a mixed drug product on the job site. Even though, there were a few of us smoking this drug, I was the only individual to be fired. One of the restaurant employees whispered the information to the boss, saying, **Brian Irons** is the employee who brought this illegal substance on the jobsite to be shared. Therefore, I was the employee to receive a verbal judgment, because I had been fired by the boss's voice.

As you can see, drugs have caused my life to receive a judgment from humankind. When I was fired from my place of work, this was the first commanded judgment that humankind has pronounced in my life concerning drugs. Yes, it was a judgment because I was found guilty, and had been charged for the act. In other words, in this situation, I suffered the consequences. Anytime you suffer consequences for your actions done, you have truly been judged.

The craziest information that I have gathered about this drug called, "pre-mo" is that, two drugs are drastically operating in the brain at the same time. Marijuana tampers with the memory worker in the brain (short-term or procedural or declarative), and cocaine tampers with your emotion worker (frontal lobe). Cocaine also causes paranoia to the brain. A person's emotions are in action when being paranoid. Since that is true, then the frontal lobes in my brain are being evilly worked on. Two drugs, which are inhaled into the brain at the same time is most definitely soon to cause brain addiction, and or a mental illness. Since I've been using drugs, from high school until now, my mental body has a serious illness and I DID NOT KNOW it.

Well, I must admit, my "limbic system" in the brain, which is my pleasure center, attained an addiction within it because I smoked pre-mo for a number of years. Therefore, it was an enjoyable feeling that pre-mo delivered into my brain.

I would like to say, "Drugs attacks a person's brain physically", because when dope has been inhaled into it, it immediately charges the organs in the head. When any thing charges at something, it goes after it physically. However, by charge and force, drugs will control your physical body when the body's mover (brain) is filled with dope. Just as a man will physically attack another person to harm that individual, drugs will also physically attack the intelligent human brain to harm it. Although, a drug has no self-made arms and legs, but once the dope is inhaled into the brain, it moves violently throughout the system in the head. You might not feel drugs physically beating on you now, but soon, you will feel the physical beat down and results in the near future. There are scars and marks that drugs are leaving on your brain right now, but you cannot see them, nor can you feel them. Trust me, when dope is sharing a space in your brain, the organs are truly being physically hit. Remember, your brain is the target, and drugs are throwing its power, and its might at it. You might not believe that drugs are physically hitting your brain; however, unexpectedly, one day soon, you are going to feel the harsh pressure. Just as charcoal will turn into ashes after fire has hit it, the cells in your brain will disintegrate after drug intoxicant's has hit it.

From the influencing power of drugs, dope causes all drug users to be blinded to many probable reasons. Sometimes it is hard for drug users to see why so much negativity and sickness is appearing in their lives and in their bodies. Let's say that an enemy of yours is out to kill you, or someone is plotting to do harm unto you. Your enemy will do whatever he or she has been plotting to do to you. Your enemy wants to get the opportune chance to get as close to you as possible. Once the enemy successfully finds away to get near you, that adversary (enemy) will do whatever it takes to physically harm or even kill you. Well, think about this, drugs are your enemy, because, they want to harm you. The unknown thing is this, your enemy, which is drugs, has you in its presence, and is so close to you, but you cannot see that the dope is working against you. However, myself, and the people in the world are mentally blinded from the fact that drugs whole purpose is too kill them, and give them an early release date from off the earth. Just as drinking and driving can give a person an early death date, putting drugs in the brain can do the same. Drugs have blinded all its users from the fact that they want to lead people's bodies straight to a dead man's coffin or a funeral's casket. Yeah drugs are powerful, because they put blindfolds on people's mental vision.

The clever power drugs beats in the minds of people is this; it will cause people to protect it, rather than speak against it. If someone approaches you, and say, "the reason why you are going through rough obstacles in life is because of your drug filled lifestyle. That individual will deny the fact that drugs are the prime reason. If someone would have came unto me and said, "The reason why you did not graduate from high school with your senior class is that marijuana hindered you". I probably would have replied and said, "That's not the true reason". Then I would have said, "The ultimate reason why I did not gradate with my senior class is because I played around in school, and did not do the schoolwork". From those words of quote, I would have been protecting the dope rather than speaking against it. That is what the power of dope does; it hides every reason from its user to believing that it is the true reason why problems are occurring or have occurred in their lives.

People will blame their problems on any and everything that they can think of. People will never admit that personal drug usage is the link to their broken down situation and problems. People will blame their friends, their jobs, their kids, their wives, their husbands, but will dare to blame chemical dependency. Drugs will cleverly disannul the fact that many current problems in life, exists because of being associated with drugs.

The working of a chemical drug in the brain is similar to the performance of a person wearing a black ninja suit. Usually, the person in a black ninja suit creeps, while plotting to do harm to the body of a living man. When the ninja plots to do harm to a person, a task of wickedness is soon to be performed. Actually, wickedness is already in operation, by empowering the mind of a person, which is seeking to do harm to another living being. Since the ninja is out to do harm, he now becomes a "wicked individual".

Let me clarify unto you about the evil plots, ways, and tactics that a wicked ninja does when preparing for an evil work. A ninja, most of the times will operate in dark or black attire, which is to make his identity unknown. The black attire is to hide the ninja's appearance from his enemy. When it becomes dark outside, that is when the wicked ninja does his creeping. The wicked ninja does not want anyone to recognize him. As the wicked ninja plots on his victim, he then seeks the moment, and time to creep up on his target or targets. In other words, the ninja kneels down, squat, and hides himself from the presence of his enemies. As the wicked ninja begin to creep up on his victim, he then leaps out, beats the victim, and leaves him for dead. That is exactly what drugs are going to do unto all dope associates. By its evil power, it is going to creep up on you one day, beat you in your brain, and leave you for dead. "The drug ninja" is good at its job. You cannot run, nor can you hide. When the wicked drug ninja jump out to grab you, there is nothing that you can do, but accept the pain and scars that he has plotted to do unto you. Nevertheless, the wicked drug ninja (drugs) operates through your body, to kill your brain. Actually, the wicked drug ninja already has my life, now he (the drug) is waiting for the right moment to jump out and damage me. Remember this; the wicked dope ninja is slick, sneaky, and surely, drug chemicals are after your life. Another translation for the wicked dope ninja is…"you reap what you sow" Even right now today, if you have drugs in your life, then the wicked drug ninja is creeping up on you from behind to finish its damaging work in your life.

Let me ask you a few questions; is the wicked dope ninja (any drug) operating in your local neighborhood or area? Did the wicked dope ninja creepily find a way to enter into your brain and body? Has the wicked dope ninja crept up on you, and has sneakily beaten on your wallet? If your answer is yes to any of those questions, then nevertheless, the ninja either is inside of you, or is lurking around you.

Every time a person intake a drug, that individual has given the wicked ninja (the creeper & killer) personal rights stop his or her heart at any given moment. On the other hand, the ninja can and will brutally destroy your brain functions at any given moment. The reason why I am using a "ninja", to be equivalent to a drug is that, awful personal experiences are going to creep into all drug handlers' lives, one way or another. That is what a ninja does; he creeps and creeps until he finds a way to injure his victim. Nevertheless, you just never know when the wicked drug ninja is going to jump out of nowhere and mess up your life, by adding more problems.

The wicked drug ninja did not kill me, however, when I willingly tried another drug product, that day and time crept up on me suddenly, and truly, it was unexpected. I mentally thought, and probably swore unto myself that I would never do any other drug, but marijuana. However, as you can see, I was easily moved into another drug addiction, which was cocaine (pre-mo). As I just told you in the earlier paragraph, the wicked drug ninja is good at his job.

Anyway, after I had been fired from my job, there was no income coming into my possession. I needed some money in my hands to keep my male dignity within me. As I said before, money is a true necessity in this world. Without money in my possession, my mind began to plot eagerly on how to make a nice amount of money that does not require school academics. Come to think about it, I should have consulted with a job counselor, or signed up for a trade school. There are many trading schools in my city that I could have signed up for, and earned myself an educational certificate to attach to my high school diploma. Nevertheless, a thought and vision had entered into my mind, and I began to visualize me making some quick and fast illegal cash.

In this vision, I had seen many great things happening pertaining to earning money. The vision that explored through my mind was about selling drugs. I felt within myself that if I operate it right, I could earn enough money to buy a few profitable businesses and then step away from selling drugs. If I earned a couple thousand dollars, that would be all that I needed to get my business going. The vision was completely about selling crack cocaine, which is against the law. Within this mental vision, not only did I see myself purchasing a business, but fine clothes, expensive cars, and having pretty women were in it as well. Nevertheless, I was led to selling an illegal product just so I can keep some money in my possession.

Since drugs already had infested my brain with illegal chemicals, they all became the controller and ruler of my thoughts and my physical actions. Since my cerebrum, which is my brain's thinking center is plagued with dope's formula; my thoughts about returning to the restaurant work place had been cast off. Drugs powerful scheme is in my thinking system, and they encouraged me to think from an illegal point of view. The organs in my brain have been given over to the power of drugs; my thinking system is what I really needed to make wise choices for my life. Since my cerebrum (the thinker in my brain) is soaked in the tactics of drugs, then making illegal decisions became very easy. Thinking from a drug point of view, my brain was persuaded to thinking of any and every kind of wickedness there is to do to earn some cash. However, as a human being, I must delete and X out those law-breaking thoughts. Nevertheless, when drugs are in the brain, it is hard to escape the plots, and scheming thoughts of wickedness.

Anything that was positive, my brain didn't seek to do. Therefore, my brain chose to break the law by selling drugs, rather than going back to school or finding another job.

I believe drugs had filled my mind with ongoing lawbreaking and wicked intensions. From the mind, I now understand why God spoke an angrily reply more than 2000 years ago to the people who were on the earth before me. *Genesis 6:5 and God saw that the wickedness of man is great upon the earth, and that every imagination of the thoughts of his heart was only evil continually.* I have actually become one of those wicked people God spoke about centuries ago. For the past 6 years, my heart has been fastened on the things of evil by indulging in drug activity all day everyday. Since drugs came into my life, brain, and body, I have been filled with the power to commit lawlessness and wickedness on a continual basis. Continually, I broke the laws, by handling wicked substances. I am no different from the people who God killed centuries ago by the continual dropping of rain, which grew into a flood. The people who God destroyed with death by the flood, they're thoughts, and imaginations were on evil continually, and so is mine. Those people from back in the days, and myself, are like-minded.

As drugs and wickedness operates within my brain, my heart has been continually devoted to relying on evil activities for emotional and financial support. When I think about that scripture (*Genesis 6; 5*), it makes me wonder what led the people to commit their selves to doing such daily wickedness. It also makes me wonder; did substances (drugs) find a brain to get in, back in those days? It makes me wonder; were the people in the Old Testament day's drunkards, like the people are today? It makes me wonder; was their brain being persuaded by chemicals to do wickedness, too? However, as we can see how the world is in action today, that a brain, which is filled with chemical control substances, will seal a person's mind to thinking on wicked tactics continually. Therefore, in today's society, every imagination of the thoughts of the people hearts is only on evil continually. Every single day, the people in the old days did evil, and every single day, the people of today do evil too. Therefore, I believe that the people who were here on earth before us, which *Genesis 6:5* spoke about, they also drank, and or inhaled chemicals into their brains too. However, in this book, you are going to read more truths about what led people to do wickedness more 2000 years ago, and what is leading people to do evil in today's society.

So here I am moving from one wicked action to the next evil act. I once was a drug user, and now, I'm a drug seller. My life had shifted from being a drug user, to being a drug seller. Wow, my thoughts have been devoted to evil continually.

When I bought this product (cocaine) to sale, I was very nervous. Nevertheless, I purchased a product that has an attachment to wickedness.

As I was selling cocaine in the neighborhood, I could not believe the amount of made. Customers were coming back to me to purchase more crack cocaine two to three times in less than 2 hours. Since my life has elevated from being a drug user, to a drug seller, it's almost as if, drugs and wickedness has given me a promotion. From wickedness to wickedness is what this promotion is called. Nevertheless, from high school and even until now, God has been watching me since the first day that lawbreaking and wickedness through drugs has been operating in my life. Wow, you mean to tell me that God is watching every move I make. Yes, indeed he is. Now God is about to watch me meet people and sell them drugs.

I bought this cocaine product with my last paycheck that was due unto me from the job I had been fired from. My paycheck for that pay period was about $200, and I anxiously invested the entire check on powdered cocaine. I bought 2 separate bags of cocaine, and each one cost $100. The separate bags of cocaine that I purchased, each bag is called, "teenager". From the power that cocaine possesses, the name, "Teenager" is an understatement.

Maybe cocaine should be called, "Strong Man", instead of Teenager, because of its strength and power it possesses. All dope chemicals have the physical power and strength of a big Strong Wrestler. Once a "Big strong Wrestler" gets a hold of you, and have you wrapped up in his arms, it is almost impossible to break away and become free. A person might try to fight, wrestle, or wiggle his way from the mental controlling power of drugs, but drugs magnificent power will "strong hold" you and pin its habits in your thoughts. The Big Strong Wrestler (the addiction) is stronger than you are. The "big strong wrestler, and the "incredible hulk" they both have control over my life. The Big Strong Wrestler is cocaine, the Incredible Hulk is marijuana, and they both have my life in the wresting rink of addictions.

I never thought that my life and body would be so caught up into drugs so deeply, that it would be so hard for me to say "no" to any of its law breaking motives. I DID NOT KNOW that my life would be led to hold on to drug habits or daily lawbreaking ways for so long. These things crept up on me, and I have been led to deal with drugs on a higher and more dangerous level. Meaning, I must meet hundreds of people who I do not know just to make drug sales to earn a few dollars.

My readers, beware of what drugs has to offer, and exclude yourself from them. Hey, you just never know when or what kind of evil experience dope is going to bring into your life. I had one small experience of smoking marijuana during high school, and my life is turning out to be like this. Never in a million years did I think that my life would be living like this.

I want you to remember this quote for your life; wicked actions lead to more wicked actions. Since I studied and learned my math during school, take heed to this addition problem; a brain on drugs + wicked thoughts = performances of evil. If the wicked character (drug) is dwelling inside of you, it will germinate its power throughout your entire body, and the strength or power of wickedness will develop continually within your brain. I have another mathematical equation for you; a man + a woman = a baby soon to be born. College + a degree = financial stability. Everything on earth is about addition. Also, remember this; what you do in today's society will always expose mathematics in your life. Whether you do good deeds in life, or do evil actions in life, there will always be addition in your life. As you can see, in my personal life, the mental usage of cocaine, and the physical activity of selling cocaine have been added unto my life. Believe me, when drugs are in your life, wickedness, and other actions of evil will be added into your existence. Math, math, math, somehow, someway, it will be a subject in your life.

I have another drug experience I'd like to share with you. In this experience, I was falsely accused. I was living with my parents at this particular time, and yes, I was a drug seller. One night I went into the house to get some sleep because I was tired and besides the day was late. This same night I was getting high with a good friend of mine named, Garren. We were in his car riding around together. Garren drove me to my parent's house to drop me off. He walked with me as I stepped upon the porch. After we had a short conversation on the porch, I opened up the door, went into the house, and dashed to my bed. My brain was high, sleepy, and tired.

Well, after Garren had dropped me off at my parent's house, he returned searching for something that he had lost. The item he was searching for was found on my parent's front porch. When he found the item, he reached down on the ground to pick it up. I suppose, as my friend reached down to grasp the item, my dad was sitting in his truck watching the whole scene take place. Well, my dad thought that my friend, Garren came to the porch to pick up a dope package. I guess my dad thought that I had laid a package of drugs outside on the front porch to be picked up; maybe my dad thought I had Garren to meet me at the house, to purchase from me drugs. Nevertheless, my dad thought that it was drug related, and he became upset about it.

When my dad came into the house, anger came along with him. Then he charged into the room where I sleeping, and immediately woke me up. My dad told me that he wanted me to be out of the house the very next day. He also said, "He does not want drug transactions being made at this house. So he wanted me to pack up my belonging, and be gone in the morning". When my dad had woke me up, and said that unto me, I was lost in mind, because I DID NOT KNOW what was going on. I was sleeping, and all of a sudden, I am hearing words of commotion. When my dad commanded me to depart from the house, another verbal judgment has just been cast upon my life.

Judgments do not only fall from Heaven, however, judgments will fall out of your own household. No one can stop judgment when it is to be pronounced. Wherever there is anger, there is always judgment.

When I had been kicked out of the house, prior too being fired from my job, I begin to sell drugs tough. I was already a daily drug user, and now that I am on the streets with no home to go too, I felt like I had nothing else loose. Being kicked out of the house did not make my dope habits too much of a difference, because my brain was heavily plagued with the venom of drugs anyway. Therefore, I kept on selling and using drugs, as if nothing happened. I did not allow my brain to analyze this situation; I shook it off, and kept on living a wicked life.

When judgments fall on us in life, after it is over, we will continue to do the same thing as if nothing happened. We need to stop for a while; analyzed things immediately, after any type of judgment has been pronounced upon us. Judgments are supposed to make a person stop and think carefully about what has just happened in life. Nevertheless, when wickedness is living in the brain, it will never allow you to rest.

As you have just read, drugs have brought another grieving pain to my heart. I was hurt when I had been kicked out of the house and had nowhere to go. I drank and inhaled marijuana as soon as I woke up and departed from my parent's house. Marijuana and alcohol were both heavily used by me all that morning and perhaps all that night. It was as if I was using drugs to heal my heart from the pain of being kicked out of my parent's house. Now that I think about it, if I was a hard workingman, such as my dad was, and I thought that my son was selling drugs out of my home, I would have kicked my son out too. However, the sad matter in this situation was that, drugs were not picked up from off of the porch, a gold chain was. Therefore, I was being kicked out of the house because of a gold chain, which my friend came back to the porch to retrieve. Nevertheless, this is the second judgment from "mankind" that has been pronounced upon my life because of drugs.

Well, I do must confess, I did keep ounces of drugs inside of my parents house. To my parents, this experience is more than a decade old, therefore, there is no since in getting upset now. The reason why I said that is because; people can hear a confession from someone about an act that happened 20 years ago, and they will become upset about it, as if it happened yesterday. Oh wait, my mother did find a package of drugs in the home, but that was a long while after I had been kicked out the house.

As I kept the ongoing affiliation of drugs, I still never thought that anything bad, nor an unpleasant thing would ever happen in my life. I inwardly felt that as long as I am taking good care of myself, then my life should be all right. However, as you have just read, I am not taking good care of myself because drugs are still bringing bad experiences into my existence. Yet, and still, I am putting drugs into my brain and body. Therefore, I am not doing a pleasant job at taking good care of myself. Taking good care of myself requires me to mentally beware and take cautious actions in my life, by not putting drugs in my brain and body. I must begin to do good things to my body, and not bad things, which are works of evil. The only works that I am performing in my life are activities that will damage it.

If anyone is putting any kind of substance/drug into his or her body, then that individual is not expressing proper care to it. Every time a person put drugs into his or her brain, that individual is feeding it poison. Just hearing the word "poison" sends a great level of fear into our minds. All drugs are lethal, and when put into the brain, immediately, the task of damaging one's health is in session. Once the word "poison" is heard in our ears, we immediately become skeptical, frightening, and fearing about the information that we have heard concerning its lethal power. Therefore, we keep our bodies far from its reach, because we think that anything that pertains to poison is dangerous to the touch. We also believe that poison is a substance that will bring sickness to our bodies, or peradventure kill us. We have become skeptical to handling or touching poison ivy, let alone, "true poison" itself. Since, I have been using drugs for a very long time, I DID NOT KNOW or realized that I had poisoned my own brain and body. As of now, neither am I providing my brain and body with proper treatment, nor am I expressing proper care. I am only poisoning it.

Drug users are actually putting poison into their brains. Poison produces diseases within the body. Poison will attack the surface of the body, or might force sickness to the internal organs in the head, and central nervous system. When a person has been poisoned, sometimes, vomiting will be an experience. Poison fights against the immune system and nerve cells in the body, and if too much of it gets inside of you, becoming sick unto death just might the your reward. Poison comes in many different types and forms. Poison is everywhere in our land. I believe that drugs are in every state on the globe; therefore, poison (any drug) is everywhere.

If you have ever seen a real snake on the outside or inside of your home, the first thought that travels through your mind is, "not to get to close too that reptile's reach". Then you begin think about the snake having deadly poison in its fangs, which the poison is sprayed from. You do not even think about becoming sick, you immediately think about dying from the lethal fluids that the snake might be carrying. Over the years of hearing about snake's poisonous venom, you were taught to fear snakes to the fullest. Therefore, you keep yourself far away from wild snakes at a nice distance. The reason why you stay far away from snakes is that you are afraid of being bitten by one, then becoming poisoned, which might lead to the experience of death.

A snake's venomous poison and a drug addiction both have the same physical and mental affiliation. A drug addiction and a snake's poison will sicken a person's brain and body. A snakebite and a drug addiction both share the same sickening power. They both lead to mental and physical illnesses that will soon force the body to see death. Since I have been putting this poison (dope) into my brain, no physical effects have occurred yet, but only in my brain, which is the addiction. Although, I do not feel any physical sickness or pain, however, my mental status has ailments in it because of my daily usage of drug. However, I do want to let you know that I have been bitten and poisoned by teeth marks of drugs that have been stabbed into brain. The day I became addicted to drugs is the day I became poisoned by its bite. It has not been manifested in the physical sense were it can be seen, but inwardly, the poison is slowly damaging my brain's organs to kill it.

Moving from one drug to the next (including alcohol) is a form of poisoning within the brain already. When a drug entraps you by its power, and you cannot seem to free yourself from substance usage, you too have been poisoned. Just like the snake venomous poison stays within the body until it kills the victim, drug addiction stays within your brain until it kills its victims too (you).

When a deadly snake, which has true poison in its fangs, bites down on a human being, and shoots its venom in the body, that bitten individual normally does not die immediately. It is the same performance with drugs, when you put drugs in the brain and body, you might not die immediately, but you will be forced to die soon. However, I have read and heard about people being bitten and poisoned by a snake, and dying hours later. Also, I have heard stories about people trying drugs for the first time, and died hours later. I know drugs are poisoning, because when I had slid drugs into my brain it change the entire course of my brain's mental focus about life. My life was once positive because I wanted to be a sport player. Now it is evil, because of being affiliated with drugs. That is how poison (drugs) work, it gets in the brain, and transforms the God given tasks in which it has been designed to do. God created the brain to serve him, but here I am, serving drugs with my brain. You need to order my second book. - (2008).

I remember an old statement that was once said by the older people, and it goes like this, "One thing leads to another". I now find that to be a true statement, because marijuana lead me too alcohol, and cocaine. Finally, yet importantly, I was lead to selling drugs. I am a true witness that one thing does leads to another. Lord please have mercy upon my soul!

Since so many unexpected harsh events have happened, I began to wonder, when will this dope madness end. I also, began to wonder, "How can I get out of this drug filled living? As I can now see, things aren't looking too good for me at this point in my life. For some reason, neither could I stop selling drugs nor could I stop putting dope into my brain. Yes, I do want to be free from drug money and drug usage, however, I've been poisoned, and my brain has been filled with the powerful venom of drugs. My entire life is now surrounded by dope, nothing more, and nothing less. When will my personal drug affiliation end?

Drugs will always keep the party going. From the poison that drugs sprays in the brain, the mind begins to believe, that, without drugs, the party will cease. Every time people go out to a party, the first ignorant question that come out their mouth's is this, "what are we going to drink" or "what are we going to smoke" for the party. Then when people get the drink, or get the smoke in their possession, they begin to feel calm. Soon, the people become highly ignorant and begin to say, "We only live once, so let's get messed up and party all night". That is one of the stupidest "quotes", to ever speak from the mouth. Since drug addicts say, "We only live once", that does not mean to go and make your life a living dope mess. How can you smoke or do any kind of chemical controlled substance, and then say, "We only live once". Well, I can't talk too bad about you because I have said that a dozen times as well. Therefore, I was ignorant, just like you are today.

The powerful drug addiction that is inside of people's brain will cause their mouths to speak words of stupidity. The dope in the brain is causing the lobe that deals with "speech", to speak ignorant quotes such as that out of their mouths. Actually, when people say the quote, "we only live once", what they are saying is this; if this drug kills me, then it is okay to die because "I only live once". Now think how ignorant that quote sounds. There are many ignorant phrases and words that drug users quote from their own mouth. Well, what do you expect to say or think when drugs are in your brain speaking and thinking for you? Stop putting drugs in your thinking and speech center. Stop being ignorant people, and become wise individuals.

People believe or think that weed or alcohol will be the only drug product that they will put inside of their bodies, however, that is not true. Smoking weed or drinking alcohol is a door opener for other drug products to come into one's life. From the entrance of weed, or the entrance of alcohol, other chemicals will soon become a temptation. While one door of drugs has opened up unto the user's life, eventually, another drug product of choice will become active too. When you use one drug, you have empowered your mind to try another chemical control substance. When you first try one drug, it then becomes easy to try another.

People try other chemicals (drugs) just to enhance that first chemical bodily "feeling" or "high". In doing so, people seek to make the drug "high" last longer. Whether you drink on occasions, or smoke dope every now and then, those chemicals are still going inside of your brain developing a hazardous addiction.

When people venture their lives off and get into drugs, their careers and goals are up for grabs. Unexpected situations will always appear in one's living when drugs are in the minds of people. Whether you are a drug user or a drug seller, unexpected situations will always arise into your life. Moments of evil will continually find ways to fulfill your commercial living. Oh my, how deeply and unexpectedly my life has shifted into a dangerous lifestyle of living. These experiences arose in my life because I had ventured off into marijuana. So people, stay in school, stay away from drugs, and keep a positive attitude in your life. Work hard for the things that you desire to have. Accomplishing your dream and goals will make life easier. Keep your mind on the adventure of your dreams, and stay free from mind alternating chemicals. Since drugs are classified as mind alternating chemicals, then surely they are dream changers.

Selling drugs does not require that the seller to have neither a certificate nor a high school diploma. That should have been a sign unto me, saying, "Drug selling is not a long lasting job, it is only temporal". A drug seller might earn large amounts of money, but when it starts to go down hill, the dungeon will be seen. Drug selling, which are actions of evil, will never keep you on top, it always take you down. Stay in school and work hard to have good employment.

A boss from an occupation might hire you because of obtaining a certificate from high school, which is a diploma. A college degree, or a certificate from a school of trade, can grant you to be hired on a lifetime job. Anytime you have a job, that does not require an application or a time card slip, you should never desire a job like that. If a job causes you to break the laws, you do not need a job such as that. A job, such as selling drugs will cease one way or another. Even with selling drugs to other people, you will "reap what you sow". For one, you are harming other people's lives when you sale them drug products from your personal possession. For two, your life becomes an open glove for either for the law to catch you, or for drugs to toss crazy experiences into your living. When the law catches you, or evil experiences come into your life, then you have been caught or captured by its glove.

Every living person that is living in the world will reap whatever he or she sows. If any man sows it, guess what, that man shall reap it. Every human being in the world is a true planter and farmer in life. Whether he or she realizes it or not, sowing and planting will always be a part of one's life. People will sow either good seeds in their lives or seeds of evil. When you sow seeds, you do so because you are a planter. Whatever you sow (plant) in your life, in the day of harvest (judgment) you will reap from that very same act.

Let's say, that you are a farmer, and you own acres of land. You, the farmer, have many planting areas in your field. In one area of your field, you planted tomato seeds. After the tomato seeds have been planted and buried, I am sure that you expect to gain positive results by growing tomatoes in the day of harvest. Oh farmer, indeed you will reap (grow) tomatoes in the day of harvest. Since you have planted tomato seeds in your field, then tomatoes is what will grow. Another example, lets say, that you have planted apple seeds in the field of your farm; of course, you patiently expect to grow fruit apples in the day of harvest. The word harvest means, to reap, receive, or gain from that which you have planted. Anything you plant or sow will grow in your future as a result.

Therefore, since I have sowed (inhaled) drugs into my brain and body, I am receiving the payments (harvest time) from the seeds of drugs. I sowed or planted drugs into my anatomy (brain and body) and negative results are what I am reaping in my days of harvest. To all farmers (living humans) who plants drugs into their bodies; your body is a field, and when you plant drugs in it, negative results will grow in your life. The reason why our bodies are an actual field is because; our bodies are made from the ground (field). My body is the acres of life, and I have planted drugs in it (my brain). Actually, our bodies are made of the dirt, and drugs take root in it as a seed does in the ground. When you plant anything, it will grow. Whether you plant seeds in your field, or drugs in your body, one thing that's for sure, the fruit of your experiences will be the results. The body will not grow apples or oranges, but judgments will be its fruit.

I have a scripture that I want to share with you, and it is from the New Testament. *Galatians 6:7 be not deceived; God is not mocked: for whatsoever a man soweth that shall he also reapeth.* As I was pointing out unto you, whatever you sow in life, especially in the body, you will reap true results in the day of harvest. In other words, a judgment from the law or biblical prophecy will be pronounced upon you. Without you even being summons to go before a judge in the court of law, a judgment from God can still fall down on you. When a person reaps from what he or she has sown, a court date is not require for this type of punishment. When a person reaps from what he or she has sown, a judgment can come down on you at any given moment. It does not matter where you presently are right now, your reaping shall come unto you at appointed times.

A person can even reap on the day of his or her marriage. Meaning, the day of the marriage, a spouse found out that his or her companion has been cheating. A person never knows when the day of harvest will be brought to the light. Therefore, I advise the people in the world to get their life in order, and stop sowing seeds of wickedness (evil), into their lives.

As I was still involved with drugs, from them, a tight grip had been clamped on my brain. Drug's tight grip had me bound for more than 6 years at this particular time. That's a very long time. I thought that I was only going to give marijuana a first time trial experience, and years later, here I am still messing around with this dope stuff. More than 6 years of my life has been under the command of chemical control substances. The seed of drugs sprouted great strength, and its power relaxed in my body, as a branch is attached to a vine. The net of drug's had every organ in my brain wrapped up in its power. Drugs are trying to kill me, and I DID NOT KNOW it.

Although, I planted the "seed" of death (drugs), inside of me, I decided to go back to school (college). Drugs were still in my thinking system, but I fought and fought, and a thought of doing something positive contacted my mind. Going back to school again was a positive thing to do. Instead of doing negative things, I decided to do something positive. When I went back to school (college), my high school diploma had already been earned. Therefore, I did not have to sign up for G.E.D classes. I did not have to take extra tests to begin my college courses. The only test that I had to take, was a test that will decided what course or classes I need to sign up for first. Even while I was taking this college placement test, my brain was high as a kite then. Yep, the seed of drugs were still planted in me because it had taken root many years ago. In my life, I might be a farmer, but I have not the power to hoe this seed of drugs and wickedness out of me.

The main reason why I enrolled in college is because; I wanted to give my basketball skills another chance to make it to the big leagues. I felt within myself that I still had the chance and opportunity to present my talents and skills to the N.B.A. world. I felt that if get the chance to present my basketball talents and skills on the court in college, then I'll have a chance to become free from selling drug. Basketball is the sport that I wanted to continue, since I was so dominate at it. Besides, I've vision myself showing off my talents and basketball skills to the world before the cameras. I did not want my talents and skills to go down the drain. Although, drug chemicals had poisoned my mind, my basketball skills were still top-notch, however, my decision-making in life were bad off. When I played basketball in all those street gyms, which I explained in chapter 3, I was on drugs then.

After being accepted to start college, the college

administrator told me that I signed up for college too late to play basketball. I was told that I had to wait until the following semester in order to participate in basketball. I signed up for college two weeks to late. I had to wait for about 2 months to play basketball. Therefore, I realize that I needed to take those college classes until it was time for me to sign up for the basketball team.

Patience is always a test in my life, and yours. In order for me to play basketball, I needed a rush of hard-core patience. With drugs working in my patience center (brain), it's going to be hard for me to abide with the rules of waiting.

While I was attending my basic college courses, it seemed as if the drug money had a mouth, because the cash would speak to me through my pager. In class, my wristwatch pager would beep and my mind became very distracted. When my watch pager beeped, I then peeped at the screen to see who it was, or what size package of drugs a customer wanted to purchase. As I was viewing the pager's screen, it showed how much money a customer wanted to spend; I would then boldly escort myself out the class, and go get that wicked money.

Sometimes I left class while it would be active in session. An instructor would be in front of the class explaining how to do certain assignments, and I would leave anyway. When the teacher was explaining how to do certain assignments, my mind was focused on that money. Therefore, I walked out of class on several occasions just to go and serve dope to a customer. Sometimes I left just to get high. My brain could not handle doing righteous things. When a brain is on drugs, and patience becomes a test, from the chemicals in the drugs, they will always win. The human mind it self, cannot defeat the awful choices that drugs will cause it to make. Your choices in life might not be the same as mine, but I know you made many regrettable decisions' while being on drugs.

One day I decided not to go back to college. College was hindering me from making money. Therefore, I quit attending college, and there I was on the streets with no more sport hopes. Actually, I was planning to play college basketball, and sell drugs at the same time. At least I thought! As you can see my reader, my entire brain's organization is highly plagued with getting high, and making that wicked money. Nevertheless, I went back to the streets, and left my mental education, or a definite chance to make it to the N.B.A, which could have helped me to earn money, which is not against laws.

I truly believe, if I would have stayed in college, and patiently waited for basketball to become available for me to play, most definitely, I would have been the star player on the college basketball team. I know, I would have been on the starting line up. Most definitely, without any doubt, either a bigger college, or N.B.A. scouts would have been observing me as the season toured to the end. I am so sure that I would have made it to the N.B.A. With the talents and skills that I possessed, someone, somewhere, would have caught a glimpse of my court performance. The only thing I needed was for one "big timer" (basketball scout) to watch me play one game, and that's it. Nevertheless, once again, drugs have unexpectedly performed another stunt in my life by causing me to quit school. Truly, drugs and the money are the direct blame for me quitting college. As you can see, drug's influences were in my thoughts, and there I was again, making bad decisions in my life. Since I quit going to college, the wicked drug ninja, surprisingly jumped out at me again, and caused me to quit school.

Now I understand why people say, "I wish I could start life all over again". That quote is in my mind right now. I am actually thinking, or wishing that I could start life all over again. I wish I had chosen another path in life, instead of choosing the road of drugs. Once I committed the act of engaging into drug, I became guilty of the actions that they led me to commit. When I first began to intake marijuana into my brain, the hands of time (clock) will not go into reverse mode and change already experienced events. Although, I am alive and healthy (so I thought), I still wish I could start life all over again.

Hey you, my reader, the hands on the clock has one charge to do, and that is to go forward, and never return and swing backwards. Once your actions have been committed, time shows neither sympathy nor pity. Time has one duty to perform, and that is to go clockwise forever. You do not have the power to go back in time, and correct any of your already made mistakes. Therefore, I advise you to be smart and make wise decisions in your life. Stay far away from drugs, as much as you possibly can. I have warned you!

My personal drug usage can be compared to a person who has lost his or her virginity. The very first time a person has sex, the virginity stage no longer exist. Willingly, 95% of the people in the world have given up their virginity. They've agreed to lie down with a human being, and then perform the pleasurable act of lustful sex. The other 5%, whose virginity has been taken, probably have been raped, or has been mentally seduced. For whatever reason it may be, the mental side of the individual will always have the remembrance of what sex felt like. Because of my drug usage, my brain and body knows what drugs feel like; and from the virgin's first sexual encounter, his or her body knows what sex feels like too.

Let say that a female, which was once a virgin, has been opened up for sexual pleasures. Once the barrier of virginity has been broken, there is no way that she can ever go back to being a virgin again. Her womb has been opened up by physical sexual admission. That is exactly how my life has been, because when my brain had been opened up by marijuana, I can never say, "I never did drugs before". My mind has become impure from drugs, just as the virgin has become impure through sexual submission. Therefore, my brain, and the virgin both have become impure from two different types of mental and physical pleasures. The virgin's mental and physical pleasure was sexual activity, and my brain's physical and mental pleasure was the act of slandering dope intoxicants into it. The reason why I said, "the virgin has become impure, is because, every person is suppose to give up his or her virginity on the night of marriage. I'll tell you more on that virgin subject later.

Sex and drugs both have similarities when it comes to personal and physical performances. The virgin, who was once sex free, has lost the testimony of being called, "chaste" or "pure". Eventually, the once known virgin will become sexual active with another partner. Loosing your virginity is the same physical and mental reaction as loosing your once known to be drug free brain. Once you loose your drug free mind to one drug, one day soon; you will become pressure and apt to try another. In the same sense, if that once known virgin is not careful, he or she will have many more sex partners over the years. Just like I went from one drug to the next to have mental pleasure, the once known virgin will go from one sex partner to the next to have mental pleasure as well. Therefore, sex and drugs both have similarities in mental performances.

In our world, sex and drugs are like twins in action. Sex and drugs both have similarities in performances one toward the other. They both are mental craving apprentices. By their pleasures, many hearts and minds have become captivated. All day, everyday, the people in the world have allowed sex and drugs to become high priority.

Here is another fact about them both; sex and drug are the two dominant killers in the land. Yeah, drugs can kill you by its powerful addiction, and sex can kill by its given disease.

Let me write an update of dope experiences that have approached my life since I have allowed drugs to be number one in my life. 1st my brain became addicted to weed. 2nd I did not graduate with my senior class in high school. 3rd I was kicked out of the house from living with my parents. 4th, I quit a job. 5th I had been fired from a job. 6th, I quit going to college. 7th I became a drug seller. 8th the usage of cocaine entered into my life. Those are the many experiences, which chartered in my life, after my brain had been plagued with an evil chemical. Whether you believe it or not, drugs were interceding with my brain's decision maker, causing unprofitable choices to be made.

Anyway, I am sure I am not the only person in this world that street drugs have hindered and have mentally influenced in a very negative way. I believe and know there are many people in the world who are wrapped up into the net of drugs. If people are not wrapped up into the mental pleasure of putting drugs into their brain, then they are entangled with the pleasure of making that wicked money. However, whether, it is the drug money, or the drug mental high, I am sure that drugs pulled a few awful tricks on you too. Nevertheless, with me, I was physically entangled with them both, the drug high, and the illegal money. My brain has been swimming in the aquarium of chemical additions for a very long time.

Chapter 8
More Drug Addictions along with
More Consequences to Suffer

Anytime a person sells drugs, he must first market it as if it is legal. As I was on the streets advertising and selling this illegal controlled substance (cocaine), financial gain became my work. I became more addicted to the dope money, than I did from getting my brain high from it. Anytime a person (**Brian Irons**) quits a job just to earn money through breaking the laws, that person has an addiction for money. If certain activities are programmed into your mind, then daily you will perform that which you have been programmed to do. Then, suddenly, you are captivated by its addiction. Anytime a person quits college, and messes up a chance to possible become rich, just to sell drugs to earn quick cash, that person has an addiction for money. When a person has an addiction to money, he must have it in his possession at all times. He becomes greedy in financial gain, and nothing else really matters.

Earning hundredths of dollars a day, my mind became spoiled. Everyday, I thought about more, more, more money to stash into my pockets. This sounds like the same "mind set" that I had when I first started getting high on marijuana. Just as I wanted more and more marijuana to get my brain high on, well, now I want more and more money to stash into my pockets.

All addictions have a link, and from the link, a chain will be made. One addiction leads to another and another leads to another. Before you ever come to your realistic sense, your brain will probably soar in the circle of addiction. Round and round and round she goes, wherever she stops, she'll never know. In the brain, round and round an addiction goes, and for the day it stops, no one knows.

Although, I was earning money from selling drugs, however, every dime earned serves one purpose; it is to be spent. Of course, the money earned from a job, or earned from selling drugs; they both grants payment from different resources. The money that's earned from a job is legal; therefore, no laws are broken, nor is the anger of God aroused. The money that's earned from selling drugs, about 4 to 5 laws are transgressed. When the laws have been transgressed, God's anger then awakens.

However, money, itself holds the same value when it comes to the spending. The 100 dollars a person earns from selling drugs can purchase clothes, and the 100 dollars you earn from your employer does the same thing. Nevertheless, the money earned from a job, and the money earned from selling drugs, will both spring forth-different outcomes in a person's living.

Whichever way you earn your money in this world, whether legal or illegal, an act of God's righteousness will always be rendered. Whether God is punishing you through his laws, or blessing you from doing what is right, righteousness from him will always be rendered. There is nothing righteous in selling drugs, however, when God judges you according to your lawbreaking deeds, that is God's righteousness right there. God will spill and expose truth through righteousness into your life one way or another. Therefore, the righteousness of God will always be proven though his judgments. If you do not allow God to make your life a righteous living, God will step his righteous self into your life with a judgments, and make his righteousness be seen anyhow. When God punishes you with judgments deserved, it is by his righteousness that such a penalty has taken place.

Let me share a biblical verse with you before I move on. *Psalms 19:9 The fear of the Lord is clean, enduring forever: The judgments of the Lord are true and righteous altogether.* I just wanted you to read a verse from the bible that speaks about God's judgments being observed as righteous. Your life might be filled with all manner of deceit and falsehood, but the spotlight from God's righteousness, through judgments will be seen. Every time you go in your kitchen at night and turn the lights on, you do it so you can see what you are doing. In the same sense, every time God judges you, he does it so that his righteousness can be seen too. You cannot get away from the righteousness of God. Even when the law convicts a person with the death penalty, that is a righteous judgment. When God drowned and destroyed all those people in the flood, that was a righteous judgment. If you read your bible, you will see that the death penalty is in there too. Over the years, I have heard newscasters speak about people who have been sentenced the death penalty. As I said before, humankind cannot judge or sentence anyone without the God's righteousness (the law's conviction).

Anyway, the more dope I sold in the neighborhood, of course, the more money earned. The neighborhood I sold drugs in, I call myself expressing love to every soul that dwelled in that town. Although, I did not have much, however, the name Lytskin (me) became known as one of the greatest throughout the entire neighborhood. This neighborhood was called, "Grape Street" or "Grape Hill". Andre P. or Rico P. gave the hood this name.

There was not one friend or person who dwelled in the neighborhood, that I did not help one-way or another. If someone in the hood needed a financial hand, Lytskin (me) would be more than happy to fulfill that individual's need. Of course, I could not help the whole neighborhood at once, but as time passed by, everyone received something from my hands. Not too many days passed by, in which I did not dish out money to someone for some apparent reason. Even if a person did not live in the hood, if he became cool with me, and the fellows, he received a gift from me as well.

In addition, I have given hundredths of dollars to help people with their housing bills. I have bought shoes for many people. I have given a little gas money to people who did not have the finances at the particular time to get to work.

Almost every female in the neighborhood, I have freely gave them money to get their hair done or just to put into their pockets. Fingernail and toenails I paid to be done. I bought clothes for people. I happily gave away money at will, as if I did not care.

Although, I was earning evil money through selling drugs, when it came down to it, I was never stingy or kept my money all to myself. Actually, money is charitable, good to have; and I will never watch an individual person or an entire family suffer hunger or need, if I could help it. Money was not a big issue to me, I mean, I did love to have money in my possession as you can see, but to be stingy with it, my heart was not filled with that hideous mess. My heart was pregnant with charity, and when charity gave birth so that I could give, I spread the money through out the entire neighborhood. I know that making money from selling drugs is horribly wrong, but as I said before, "all money does the same thing"; it spends. However, the money did not cause me look down on people who did not have any. It only lifted me up to help the person that had a need.

I had a girl friend at the time, whom I called "Chay". Chay knew, if she needed anything, Lytskin would get it for her. That young pretty doll was my heart. I was head over hills about her. However, being faithful to her was a very hard task to accomplish. Uh oh, oops, I had two girl friends at the time, and too many female sidekicks. Hello to my other girl friend named "Cat". Well, I am not going to get into all that relationship stuff, because I am not ready to reveal that lifestyle just yet. If and when I do reveal it, it is going to be a nasty mess.

As I was selling drugs and earning that unlawful money, there did come a time that I had been caught by the police. The cops caught me with cocaine in my possession. In my life, I had been charged for three drug cases in a 4 or 5-year span of selling narcotics. The three drug cases or charges that were cast upon my criminal crime record were two possessions of cocaine, and a cocaine sale to an undercover cop. These three drug charges were all crack cocaine cases, and none were powder. As you can see, drugs have brought more harsh events into my life. As of now, it seems like my life has a hex or curse upon it, because I could not free myself from committing the daily acts of breaking the laws.

After the police officers caught me the first time with cocaine in my possession, they handcuffed me, put me in the car, and drove me to the city jail to register my name in the criminal system. When the cops and I arrived at the police station, the name **Brian Irons** was then registered in the criminal system, along with other law breaking people (individuals that performed wickedness).

After my name had been registered in the criminal system, I was sent to a cell until further notice. This was my first offense; therefore, I was able to leave jail less than 24 hours. As I was being released from the city jail, I was then given a court date.

Since I had been summons to appear in court to stand before the judge (the law), my mind would be in great wonder. Thinking about what could possible happen unto me during my next court appearance, was mentally bothering. I would walk the streets, thinking, I could actually be sentence and convicted in court to serve jail time. I DID NOT KNOW too much, or anything about the law, nor attending court service. However, I was given a court date, therefore, I must return at the appointed time commanded.

After I had been released from jail, I was happy to see the outdoors again. I felt free like a bird loosed from its cage. My mental body (brain) felt relieved. Being in jail, which means being behind bars, made me feel like an animal at the zoo. Just as animals at the zoo are caged in, in jail I was caged in too. Being physically trapped behind cell bars, was a mental torturing experience. It seemed like those hours in jail were the roughest isolation that I have ever had to deal with.

After being released from jail, I was still attached to the law's system because my name had been assigned to return to court for a hearing and judgment. Yes, the name

Brian Irons must appear in court so that the judge (law) can provide me with my next move. My name had been freed from the jail cell, and my name will be called out in court whether I go or not. When the judge calls out my name, and if I am not present in court, I will be on the run. The name **Brian Irons** will be a fugitive on the earth if I do not go to court at my appointed time. Therefore, I must keep my court date, and present my body in the court of law.

For about 4 or 5 months, I was traveling back and forth to court presenting myself before the judge. At this particular time, I had a public defender representing me. On my last day of court, which was the day for me to hear a judgment, I pleaded guilty of possession of cocaine. I was caught red handed, and there was no way of escaping this. Therefore, there was no need for me to take this case to trial. After I pled guilty, I was then openly sentenced in the court of law. After the judge verbally gave the verdict, the judged beat the gavel on his desktop, and the sentence given to me was final.

Even though, I had been sentenced, I was still able to return to the streets. I left the court happy inside, because I was able to walk out of court, and not be convicted to serve time in jail. In a sense, I was free physically; however, my mental body was still locked up in the bars of drug's addiction.

When the Judge, through the law, gave me my sentence, it was required that I serve a period of 3-years on probation. The 3 years of probation is or was suppose to be ample amount of time to get my life on the right path. Being put on probation was a substitution for not going to prison. Instead of the judge, through the law, sending me to prison, he sentenced me probation time. My drug case was declared as a misdemeanor. As I now think about the sentencing to be on probation, actually, I allowed drugs to put me in a situation were my freedom was under the authority of another man's consideration (the judge). This judge consulted with God's laws, and from it, a verdict was given concerning my illegal activity. In other words, I was judge in court according to the laws of God.

So far, I've been judged by two voices from mankind: the first voice of judgment came from my Dad, and the other was heard from my boss. Well, this time, I have just been judged by the voice of God, through his laws. Since God spoke the laws into existence, when a person has been judged by the laws, that individual has been judged by the voice of God. My dad spoke a judgment upon me; my boss spoke a judgment upon me; and God has spoken a judgment on me too. I can now see that a person does not have to always be physically hit to feel a judgment. From the tongue, which sprays out words of judgment, your life will be hit. If you read my second book, you will learn more about spoken words of judgments.

While I was on the streets and under the law's judgment, which ordered me to be on probation, I went back to the streets to sell crack cocaine. My cerebrum (the thinker in my brain) was highly saturated with the poisonous asps of drugs. The only thing that my brain knew to do was lawbreaking activities. Drugs and wickedness have truly poisoned my mind. The venom from wickedness (drugs) kept my thoughts connected to the mental pleasures of law breaking activities, which became the desires of my heart. I sold drugs as if I had nothing to worry about. The law could not stop me; neither being sentenced to probation could stop me. I sold drugs for about a year or longer, and then I was caught with cocaine in my possession again.

When the cops (the law) caught me this second time, they handcuffed me, and escorted me to the police car. Here I am, on my way to jail again. Well, as of now, another cocaine charged is about to be typed upon my criminal history report.

This is my second time going to jail for cocaine. Well, again, here I am, in jail being finger printed. Well, here I am, watching my name (**Brian Irons**) being processed into the law's system again. After the processing was done, I was escorted to a cell. Well, again, here I am waiting to hear another verdict from the laws of God. Now, it is possible for me to face a little jail time because of this new drug charge. I knew for sure that God's law was going to declare me guilty, convict me, and then sentence me to serve jail time. I was so sure that the laws of God were going to send me to the penitentiary for an X number of years. I suppose I can use this as an excuse, "it is all because drugs have become triumph in my life". All because I made one bad choice in high school, my life has been on a wicked road. My heart and life has now been filled with the misery that drugs shot in into it.

About 6 months later, I caught another drug case. This time, I was charged for selling crack cocaine to an undercover cop. I sold dope to a cop who was dressed up like a dope feign. He was an under cover police, and I DID NOT KNOW it. The cop had dirty clothes on, and a full-untrimmed beard, which was a work of disguise. The beard actually caused him to look like a dirty crack head. As I said before, I will have to meet, and sell drugs to people I DID NOT KNOW. I did know many crack cocaine users because I have dealt with them on a personal level. However, more than half of my dope customers, at first, I DID NOT KNOW. Over the years, I am sure that I sold drugs to hundredths of people that I DID NOT KNOW. Nevertheless, I sold drugs to an under cover cop, and I now have 3 cocaine charges on my criminal history report.

Well, I was bonded out of jail again. Again, I was given a court date. Again, I was summons to appear in the presence of the judge to be sentenced. This is my third time having to appear in court for drug charging issues. Therefore, I was summons again to appear in court, to listen for name **Brian Irons** to be called.

By now, I realize that the judge, through God's laws, is about to pronounce righteousness (a sentence) upon me. Justification is about to be performed. God's law, through the judge, had mercy on me the first time of my appearing in court. Here I am again going before the law of God, for the very same wicked deed (selling drugs). I am about to face God's law in court for this same act, and now God's law is about to present a righteous judgment upon me again.

If any man is caught breaking the law, the laws of God can't wait to pronounce judgment upon the victim. The laws were sent to help us, however, on the other hand, the laws are sent to break your heart. Of course, the laws were sent to provide protection unto the world, however, if any man breaks the law, the law will act against him or her. Not only are the laws here to help us out, but also, if any man breaks them, God's laws becomes your enemy. Actually, if you break the laws, God himself becomes your enemy. Oh yes, God does become your enemy. If the law is against any performances that you commit, then God is against you as well. For example: if God says, "Thou Shalt Not" do a certain deed, and you do it, then who is against you? If I tell you not to walk in my house without knocking, and you do it anyway, then I am against you. I will explain more unto you later concerning God being your enemy, please read on.

The law is also sent to condemn your heart, meaning, when judgments are active in a person's life, it is never a pleasing feeling. Who in their right mind wants to go to court to be judged for committing wickedness? I do not care how much lawbreaking deeds (wickedness) a person does in life, that individual never wants to be summons to court, and then wait for a judgment to be pronounced. When a judgment has been pronounced in a person's life, it makes the heart sad. Then the countenance of the face will be transformed to look bitter. Therefore, after experiencing judgments, it will rule your life until time is served. Actually, one conviction in court can be on your record for the rest of your life on earth. No one wants to be under the court laws of rules for the rest of his or her entire life on earth. That will make a person's mind (thoughts) be plastered on facts of what can or cannot be done. People do not want to be under the law's judgment for one month, let alone the next decade or longer. Judgments never feels good to the mind, they only bring worries into the brain. When a person has worries for any amount of time, that individual's living is messed up. I will explain unto you later in the story concerning, "the law messing up your life". My advice unto the people in the world is this; cease yourselves from committing wickedness before the law through judgments messes your life up.

When I went to court for my first charge of cocaine possession, a public defender represented me in the court of law. The public defender help me escape a sentence that probably would have shipped me to the penitentiary. Well, I now have 2 new cocaine charges on my criminal history report. However, this time I felt within myself that I needed a paid lawyer, rather than a public defender. Therefore, I went and searched for a lawyer to pay, to fight, and stand up against the law for me. When I found a lawyer to pay, I told him my situation, and paid him the minimum fee. I signed the agreement papers, and this lawyer is now going to stand up for me in the court of law.

When I had been tried in the court of law concerning these two new drug cases, I pled guilty. I agreed with the sentence that the "law" tossed at me. Before I pled guilty to these 2 new drug cases, my lawyer told me that he can squeeze all my cases together, and that he could get me 5 years probation. I replied, "Yeah, that's cool, I can handle that". When I agreed to the 5 years of probation, with consultation from my lawyer, the judge immediately beat the gavel, and sentenced me, "5 years probation". Therefore, I knew that I could not get into any more drug trouble. Most definitely, I do not need another drug case added to my criminal history record. I DID NOT KNOW how much longer the laws of God are going to hold its conviction.

After the judge sentenced me to 5 years of probation, I then walked out of the court's building. I was so happy to leave the courtroom on my own, and not with the escorting of the police. As every individual in the world says, "I thank God for his mercy that has been upon life". So let me get my thanks on too; "I thank God for his mercy that has been upon my life".

Anyway, you know what is so weird, the world (people) has gotten so smart, that a person, who has broken the law can lessen his judgment by hiring a lawyer. In the

187

Old Testament days, when people did evil, wickedness, and broke the laws, God judge them accordingly. In the Old Testament, no matter what a person did, he or she was judged through the law. A paid lawyer was not granted to support the evildoer for his or her lawbreaking acts committed. In the olden days, God's laws required full restitution to be paid to every person who did evil (broke the laws). If I would not have had a paid lawyer, I believe the law would have demanded me to go to prison and serve jail time. However, it seemed like money minimized my judgment, nevertheless, I thank God, a paid lawyer can appear in court and represent a person in the New Testament days.

Even after my second judgment, which added more years to my life to be on probation, I went back on the streets to sell drugs. Every time I went to court, and had been sentenced, I always had thousands of dollars worth of crack cocaine somewhere hidden. Therefore, I was led to go back to the streets, and continue selling cocaine. Selling crack cocaine actually became my means for survival. It seems like I am cursed by this cocaine business. I could not perform my true desires (sports) that were once in my life. Yet, I was caught performing another task of wickedness, which added more years to my probation status.

For some apparent reason, I did not have the power to stop selling drugs. Neither was I able to persuade my mental to get rid of this wickedness. Trying to give up wickedness and drug activities is not an easy task to accomplish. My brain and body had been programmed through out the years to do drugs, drugs, and nothing but drugs. From all of the years of shoving drugs in my brain's system, my cerebrum (the thinker) only focused on ongoing schemes to access all my ways in life. My brain's cerebrum, the thinker for me, has become plagued and filled with works, which led to performing illegal activities.

After I had been sentence to deal with 5 years probation, the judge assigned my name into the system of probation officers. I must go to a place, and register my name in a place where probation officers are gathered. A probation officer is a person who supervises people who has been caught breaking the law.

I went to Cherokee street, which is the road that leads to the probation building. When I first walked into the probation building, I saw White folks, Black folks, Chinese folks, Mexicans, and other cultures too. As I said before, drugs does not discriminate color, race, creed, nor beliefs. When people (any nationality) give drugs the opportunity to prove its power, once it gets the brain, it cares nothing about ethnic background. Nevertheless, there were about 5 to 6 different nationalities in this building, waiting to see a probation officer. Therefore, not only has my name been given to a probation agency, but other cultures names had been assigned here too. As of now, the name, **Brian Irons** is registering in a probation agency firm.

After I had finally met my probation officer, she gave me all the rules and tasks that are required for me to complete the program. One of the requirements was to visit her at scheduled and appointed times. My probation officer told me that I must not be caught breaking the law for the next 5 years, or it will violate my probation. If I am caught doing any actions that are against the law, I will be sentence to prison to serve my jail time.

She told me that she was going to schedule a meeting for us to meet once every two months. As those 5 years of probation began to shrink, my probation officer began to get strict on me, and was having me to report to her twice or three times a month.

Throughout the years of visiting my probation officer, my brain stay filled with drugs. My brain and body was swamped with chemical controlled substances. Not only was my brain and body swamped with chemicals, but also, the limbic system in my brain has been hungering for chemical toxicants for years now. The brainstem is my survival kit, however, since I have introduced it to drugs, it has been made to believe that drugs are needed for survival.

The love for the feeling of drugs was in my heart and

body drastically. Chemical controlled substances tampered will all the insides of my brain for many years. From high school, even until now, drug chemicals have been operating inside of my head. That is a very long time. Nevertheless, after catching 3 drugs cases and being sentence to be on probation, my brain never deleted the acquaintance of wickedness from drugs.

Just as practicing sports everyday will promote better athletic performance, well, in the same sense, using drugs on a daily basis became my brain's practice as well. Daily I was practicing the motions of using drugs. The more I used drugs, the greater the addiction became.

After practicing drug usage for so long, I DID NOT KNOW that a skill was in affect. The first skill that drug's will perform in any brain is the active addiction. Here I am, on probation, because drugs have performed its skill (the addiction) in my brain.

All drugs/medicine have skills. Whether legal or illegal, all drugs have skills. When you have pain in the body, sometimes you will go and take a Tylenol pill to soothe the acing. Once the Tylenol pill has been put into the body, hopefully, the pill will perform its skills by deleting the pain. If the pill deletes the pain, then the skills from it have been performed.

The medicine in your bathroom's cabinet has skills. Nyquil has a skill to perform. Once this drug (Nyquil) puts you to sleep, and stops the fever from entering into the body, it has performed its skill. When I first tried drugs, the moment I became addicted, a skill had been performed. Therefore, yes, drugs have performed its skills in my brain because of this chemical addiction.

While I was on probation, it was required that I find a job. I needed to find a job to prove to my probation officer I am trying to better my living. Therefore, as I went out into the public to find myself a job, I still had drugs in my brain and in my possession to sell. I needed to be high, because I could not take the mental thoughts that my mind was dealing with. I did find a job, and you probably already know what kind of occupation it was. Well, it was another restaurant job. I figured that I should find any kind of job just to keep my probation officer off my back.

As I was working at this restaurant, I knew I could not leave the occupation. I must stay put and do my assigned assignments. Although, I was working here, I really didn't want to be here.

As I was working, beep-beep, there goes that evil pager. The pager beeped in college, and now it is beeping on my job. What shall I do? A decision must be made. Maybe I should not look at the pager. Since I am addicted to money, I had to look at the pager. It was powerfully rough to watch hundreds of dollars flash across my watch pager's screen, and not go and collect it.

Well, guess what, one-day as I was cooking, and making fish sandwiches, I walked out of the restaurant. Yep, there I go again, walking out on employment. In other words, I quit this job because I did not have the mental patience to work on a real job. At this point in my life, an employer's check could not mount up to the payment that drug selling provided. My patience was very bad within my brain.

As you can see my reader, drugs are really in control of my life because they are provoking my cerebrum to make awful decisions. This is the second job I quitted, and walked out on because of drugs. I worked at this job (McDonalds) for only two days. I know I am doing what is called stupid things. Actually, this is another payment that drugs provided me with. My brain could not take it; I had to get out of there. I didn't stay in school for the sake of financial freedom, and I didn't stay on the job for the sake of my personal freedom.

After quitting the job, an appointed time had come to visit with my probation officer. So I went to see her. I signed my name on the list to check in. Soon, my probation officer came to the sitting area, and called my name. I followed her to her office. As I was following here, I was very nervous. In my mind, I am hoping that she doesn't question me about this McDonald job.

Now I am sitting here in her office high as a kite. I

don't know why we as people do not think that other people cannot see that we are high. The eyes of a person will tell it all. When chemicals are in the brain, the pupils will look red. When the eyes of a person looks high from drugs, the occipital lobes are feeling the chemical's power.

Now she is questioning me. She asked me, "How things are going with the job"? My reply was a big lie. I told her everything is still going just fine.

Later on in life, my probation officer found out that I quit my job. As she was questioning me about it, I told her that I did not want to work there, and that I am looking for another employment.

As I sat in the probation officer's chair, she requested that I come back to see her the following week. Also, she said, "she is going to check my body's system for drug affiliation. Therefore, I was scheduled to take a drug test. Uh oh, another drug screening has just been scheduled.

I remember a time when I had been tested for drugs, and the results came back positive. Another time I was tested for drugs, I did an old trick, and mixed my urine with …??? And this test was under investigation. Although, verbally, I was declared clean in this test, it was still under investigation. Even though the test was under investigation, after my probation officer told me about test results, my system was declared clean. Therefore, the tricked worked, unless she lied to try to catch me doing it again. Actually, I had been tested for drugs a number of times, and many times, I was declared unclean. Many times, I've seen people leave the probation building by the escorting of the police. I guess it was because their body was tested positive for drug usage.

The probation officers never tell their client the day he or she is going to be handcuff, and sent to prison. Normally, they schedule a day and time for the police to come to the probation building. While the client is talking to is parole or probation officer, the police then walks in and handcuff the person.

Well, another day for drug testing was scheduled. I

was scheduled to go and visit my probation officer again, and I mentally feared going back to see her. I knew that my body's system was going to be tested positive for drugs usage. Well, this time I rejected going to see her. I must say, "That was one of the dumbest things that I could have ever done". Nevertheless, when a brain is on drugs, some of the stupidest decisions will be made. Wow, my life is actually being influenced by the skills of drugs. I quit two jobs, I quitted going to college, and now I quit going to see my probation officer, wow what great skills drugs has. Or shall I say, what great skills wickedness has when a person's life is filled with it.

You might think I cannot blame my ignorant decisions on drugs; however, as you can see for yourself how my life has become an illegal mess. I feel the need to blame something or somebody, because I know I am not this ignorant. Oh, well, maybe I am. After you are done reading this story, you will see the whole truth about drugs and its ways (skills). I realize that drugs will use every person's mind in many different ways. Meaning, each individual will make stupid decisions when drugs are tampering with brain's decision maker. Nevertheless, wickedness, and stupid decisions will be active in a person's life when drugs are in control of the brain.

Let me write unto you a quick up date about my drug-infested life. #1 an addiction from drugs developed within my brain. #2. I did not graduate from high school at my scheduled year to do so. #3. I was kicked out of the house. #4. I was fired from a job. #5 I quitted a job. #6 I quitted another job. #7, 8, and 9, are the 3 drugs cases that has been tagged on my history report. #10 I was placed on probation. #11 I quit going to college. #12 I quit going to see my probation officer. Those are the many situations, which arose into my life, while I was under the influence of drugs. These 12 events became my life's experience, because drugs performed its skills. You would think that enough is enough, but when drugs have heavily plagued its evil power in a persons thinking center, drugs will never stop working until completion. When drugs are in the brain, the human head becomes a device of ignorance. Now that I think about my drug usage and experiences, my brain is nowhere near of being intelligent.

As you have just read, I've had many personal explorations that happened to me while drugs were in my life. As I once said, when your mind is under the influence of chemicals, you are liable to think of the dumbest ways for escape. My brain was under the influence of chemical controlled substances, and I was led to live a life of all characteristics of negativity and stupidity. Here are two more mathematic equations for you: drugs + a brain = a life full of negativity. Drugs + a brain = bad choices to be made.

Since I quit going to see my probation officer, my living is now operating in secret. I am now on the streets (earth) ducking and dodging my probation officer. Not only am I dodging her, but also, I am hiding from the law. Actually, I am a fugitive, because I am on the run from the law. The law is the voice that gave me the judgment, which placed me on probation. Therefore, the law is after me to convict me and complete its job. I am not on the run from the judge, nor from the probation officer, I am truly running from the voice that sent the law. Since I am on the run from the law, actually, I am running from God himself.

When a person is on the run from God, what makes that individual think that a place of refuge will be found? Running from the law, which means running from God, you will never find a place of isolation. Well, actually, 95% of the people who are in the world do not have the mental revelation to know; when they run from the law, that they are running from God himself. Neither do people know that, when they disobey the law, they disobey God. Here I am on the streets running from the God Almighty, and I DID NOT KNOW it. Do you think God is going to catch me?

When people are on the run from the law, they become ignorant like Adam and Eve. Adam and Eve broke the law (God's command) and after doing so, they tried to hide from God. God planted the Garden of Eden, God created the earth, and Adam actually tried to hide on it. How can a person hide from someone who made the earth? Just like I can look at the ground and see thousands of ants working, in the same sense, God can look down from heaven, and see millions people trying to hide. Adam is ignorant, Eve is ignorant, and Brian Irons is ignorant too. If you are on the run from the law, then welcome yourself into the ignorant crew. You don't need to sign up; you don't need hold our hands, the only thing you have to do is run from the law, then automatically you have been grafted into the family of ignorance.

While I was on the streets ducking and dodging my female probation officer, she assigned a warrant in my name for an arrest. In other words, my probation officer signed papers, and sent out sheets for the law to come after me. The name, "**Brian Irons**" has become a fugitive to the world. No matter where I travel on earth, the law has the power to find me there too. Wow, it is so true, you cannot run, nor can you hide from the law's Day of Judgment.

As of now, the police are looking for me to place me in hand cuffs and arrest me. I dodged the cops (the law enforcers) as long as I possibly could. Even when I did not have drugs in my possession, I still had to duck and hide. My life is now in a horrible situation of mental conflict. I must seek to hide, each and everyday of my life because I do not want the police to approach me. Therefore, my brain became programmed to hiding from the police because of another ignorant decision, which I had made. I must seek to hide because drugs performed another skill in my life. It was from the skill of drugs that brought the idea into my head to stop going to visit my probation officer. Actually, because of drugs, I have been put on probation. So here I am, in the world, using mental dope tactics to keep my life in secret, and out of the view of the police. Drugs, drugs, drugs have made my life a living mess.

One day, as I was driving in my dopeman-dopeman car, the police drove up behind me. When the police (the law) had driven up on me, one of them shined the bright light on my car. The law finally caught me, and there I was looking and feeling stupid. The cops searched me for drugs, and they searched me to see if I was carrying a concealed weapon (gun). After the physical bodily searching was over, the cops wrapped cuffs around my wrist. Then they escorted me to their vehicle, and sat me down in it. There I was being escorted to prison because of the ignorant decision I had made. This is now my fourth time visiting the city jail.

When the cops rolled up on me, my brain was "high" as a kite from drugs then. As I was being driven to the city jail, I was sitting in the back seat, mentally hurt. When I arrived to the city jail, I was then taken to a room to sit in all by myself. As I was in the city jail, my mind began to replay all of the pass hurts and failures that drugs have caused in my life. Every drug experience flashed through my mind quickly. I was in a position where I could not do anything, but sit, relax, and grope. Every time something arose in my life, I was able to leave immediately and attend to that business. Now that I am in jail, I have no pager to answer too, I have no chemicals to put in my brain, and my brain needed its stress reliever. This day was really a brain-stressing day. I became a prisoner in the city jail, and I physically sat in a cellblock for two whole weeks. It was so depressing and so aggravating to be in a place where only walls can be seen.

In the city jail, I slept on a hard bunk, which was made out of metal. That was the most uncomfortable moment of sleeping that my life had ever experienced. A cot with a couple of blankets would have been more comfortable than this metal bunk. As I slept on this iron bunk, it did not give in; it was solid and stayed sturdy. Therefore, my body could not sink into it, as it would on a real bed. My neck, back, and shoulder begin to suffer intense pain. Crooks began to develop within my neck. My days in the city jail were rough on both, my mental status, and my physical being. I hope not to ever do the jail experience again.

The food was okay; I ate breakfast, lunch, and dinner. I even met my favorite snack in this prison, which is a honey bun. Faithfully, the inmates were fed honey buns every morning. As the honey buns were given to us, sometimes, the correctional officer tossed them in the cell, not caring where it landed. My meals were given to me on a tray, and the officers sat it on the edge of the cell bars. Now that I think about it, I am actually being fed like an animal. Honey buns were tossed into my cell, just as bananas are tossed into a cage of monkeys.

So here I am, sitting in the city jail patiently waiting for another court date to be scheduled. Then I must go before the judge, which holds the laws of God. The judge is about to present to me face to face, another hearing and judgment from the law's of God.

When the time had come for me to be released from being behind bars, the name **Brian Irons** was called. An officer came to the door of my cell, and said, "**Brian Irons** get up, its time to go". Then I arose upon my feet and began to put my clothes on. After I had put all my clothes on, I then walked to my cell's door. Then the officer turned me around, and put both my wrists in handcuffs. At first, I thought I was going to court to hear the judge. However, this officer escorted me to a van that already had about ten sad looking men piled up in it. It did not take long until I realized that I was on my way to the penitentiary. When I realized I was on my way to the penitentiary, I said unto myself, "I just know this is not happening unto me". Well, yes it is.

As I was walking towards the van, those prisoners looked like pitiful men. Every one of them (and me) had handcuffs clamped around the wrist. Just as Kunta Kinte was captured, handcuff, and shackled; well, every single last one of us had been captured, handcuff, and shackled too. We all performed a deed of wickedness, and now we all are handcuffed and shackled. Myself, along with these fellow prisoners, we all looked like slaves or animals wrapped up in the device of chains.

The van was filled with criminals from all over the city. We were so close to one another that sardines in a can had more space than we did. As I was in the van with these lawbreaking men, my eyes wanted to break out into tears. I knew I was on my way to the penitentiary, and my mental power was getting weak within. The only reason why I did not break down and cry is because, there were other prisoners in the van as well, and I felt that it was time for me to look tough or become tough. Although, one prisoner in the van did cry like a baby, I still held my true feelings in without dropping a tear.

Going to the penitentiary was truly unexpected for me. I never thought that I would ever be a victim to be placed inside of a penitentiary's cell. I knew there was a chance that I can go to prison because of the wickedness or wicked deeds (drugs selling) my body had been performing. However, I still never imagined myself being in a real penitentiary. Here I am going through another awful experience because of dealing with wickedness (drugs).

I am willing to bet my life on the fact that, every man who was being driven to the penitentiary; all were going because of something that pertained to drugs. Meaning, their hands were involved in a wicked act, which caused them to receive a convicted judgment that sent them to prison. Their hands, and mine, did a wicked deed, and the penitently will now be our home for sleep. Therefore, everyone who is in this van had drugs in the thinking system of their brain. Their cerebellum, which is the hand coordinator became mobile and performed a law breaking deed. No matter what judgment the law had convicted these people with, their hands were the tools used to commit an act of wickedness. Wicked acts are always unrighteous empowerment, which encourages our hands to do lawbreaking deeds. My fourth book, which is title; Lord Forgive My Hands, is a book of revelation about wicked hands. This book will be published in the near future.

As I finally made it to the penitentiary, I saw again, more than several different nationalities piled up in this camp. Wow, drugs must have the world of brains trapped in its evil net. Drugs have the world of brains filled with its poisonous venom. Wow, drugs have performed the ninja mode on people, by creeping up on them. Everyone in the penitentiary, somewhere in life, the drug ninja crept up on them all.

Drugs have the most cunning power that is in our world today. Throughout the world of cultures and races, they all have the same brain structured figure. The one and only difference of the brains inside of people's skull, is the fact that one IQ level differs from the other. Even with a brain that is diagnosed with a high IQ, however, from the power of drug, its intelligence will decline. Drugs are not afraid of brain smarts, or high intellectual intelligence. Actually, drugs are stronger than a person's IQ. Once any drug meets a person's brain's IQ or mental intelligence, that IQ level is destined for doom. As you already know, that I do have a little education (high school diploma), but drugs have cunningly made me look like a man that has no understanding at all. Although, I perceive my IQ level to be persuasively decent, however, from the usage of drugs, my IQ level has dropped tremendously. Here I am, now in the penitentiary because I allowed drugs to work its cunning power through my brain's organs. Drugs are very skillful.

In this world, a person's IQ level is based upon his or her smartness. However, that is not so. An IQ is based upon a person's mental intelligence, not upon the A's earned in class. Do not get me wrong, because being smart plays a high role in the IQ business, too. However, just by having a great level of intelligence to make wise decisions in life will rack up IQ points too.

Everyone in the penitentiary has earned a new name, including me. My name is not **Brian Irons** anymore; my new name is, "Big Dummy". My name is not **Brian Irons** any more; the law and God calls me, "The Wicked". Everyone in the penitentiary has earned rights to be called, "The Wicked".

When I was a child, I was afraid of the penitentiary. After viewing movie scripts and television scenes pertaining to prison, I never wanted to be trapped in a place like that. Movies and television showed prison to be a dangerous camp to dwell. Examples shown from television have displayed the penitentiary to look very abusive. Mentally, I was afraid of the penitentiary, but my mental fear didn't mount up to keep me from working ways to earn a cot in the penitentiary.

When you really think about it, every penitentiary is filled with brains (people) such as: murderers, serial killers, thieves, rapist, forceful acts of sodomy, armed criminal action, and drug users. All those wicked people, who have done evil with their hands, are gathered amongst one another. Since all those type of people (murderers, rapist, and drug users) are in one facility, then that place is a place full of wicked people and evildoers. The penitentiary should be a place we all should mentally fear. Although, I have not used drugs for more than 3 weeks, my mind still thinks from a negative point of view. These people in the penitentiary are wicked, I am wicked, and who can trust a wicked man. From the wicked deeds I have done with my hands, I must sleep in a prison every night, next to a bunch of wicked people.

This scripture, *Psalms -28:4*, which says, *Give them according to their deeds, and according to the wickedness of their endeavors: give them after the works of their own hands; render to them their desert*.

If anyone is in the penitentiary for murder, the hands performed that wicked act. If any man is in the penitentiary for theft, the hands performed the movement. If any man is in the penitentiary for rape, the hands performed that act as well. If any man is in the penitentiary for assault and battery, the hands were in session to fulfill that act too. All these people worked a worked of evil with their own hands; the scripture from Psalms 28:4 is talking about them.

Psalms 28:4 also said, "*Give them according to their deeds, according to their wickedness*". Since everyone is in the penitentiary because of a judgment from court, God is the individual who has given them what they deserve. Yeah, it was God, through his laws that pronounced a judgment upon these prisoners' lives. Therefore, everyone who is in the penitentiary performed an act of wickedness, and being sent to prison is what they deserved. In other words, every man in the penitentiary was hired to work wickedness, and the penitentiary was his paycheck. If a man's hands perform the evil act, and the penitentiary became his home, then he earned the ticket to get there. Wickedness and evil has made every prisoner a winner, and the penitentiary became their prize. There is no second place, nor are there third place winners, however, if any man is sent to the penitentiary, he has won the grand prize.

Since brain chemical infested people are all crammed up in the penitentiary, then violence and killings are committed in prisons on the regular. Drug users and lawbreakers are all locked up in one facility. Since I am here in the penitentiary because of my wicked deeds done with my hands, I have become one of them. We all have been sent to prison for one reason, and that is because we all did wickedness with our own two hands. Although, I did not commit a robbery, or performed a murder, I am still considered their equal, because we all have been labeled as "The wicked".

Going to the penitentiary is like going over seas to battle and fight for your country. Just like a person joins the army to serve his time, and fight for his country, well, going to the penitentiary, you have to serve your time, and may have to fight to save your life. A man can travel far away from home to fight in a war, and might be killed, and never make it back home to see his family members. In the same sense, a man can be sent to the penitentiary to go and serve time, and might not make it back home to see his family. Anytime, a world of lawbreaking people are dwelling together in one facility, anything pertaining to evil and wickedness can unexpectedly spring forth.

I advise you to stay away from lawbreaking activities (drugs) because the penitentiary has one more cot for you to sleep on. If you have never tried drugs in your life, do not start because you will end up like the rest of us who are here in the penitentiary. You will end up in a war because that is exactly what the penitentiary is, a place of war. From all of the hurts that drugs may have stamped into an inmate's mind, that individual is liable to snap and physically harm someone very badly. Just by being in the penitentiary is the far most hurt all by it self. Just to let you know, murdering is committed in the penitentiary very often. If a murder is not being committed in prison, then I guaranteed you that an inmate somewhere in the USA prisons, has been physically beaten badly. Therefore, even in the penitentiary, people are bringing judgments upon one another by their own personal means, and that's not God's ways of doing things.

As I was in the penitentiary, I was observing this inmate who was being released. He served his time, and now a portion of freedom is due unto him. This inmate was happy to be on his way home to be re-united with his family and friends. He had been here for a year and a half already. This very same day that the inmate was being released to go home, another inmate fought him. The inmate he fought against beat him badly. I saw the entire incident take place right before my very eyes. The wounded inmate had to go home to his family with a swollen black eye. His eye was sticking out so far; I could not tolerate looking at him. Nevertheless, both of these young men were in the penitentiary because of drug cases, which were charges against actions that were done with their own hands (fingers of evil).

The wounded inmate went home with a messed up face. I bet, when this wounded inmate lands his feet in his hometown, all of his friends and family will think that he's been getting beat up all the while during his jail time. Wow, that's a sad way to go home to be united with friends and family. When you live in a place full of wicked people, awful experiences will come into your physical existence unexpectedly.

Although, I was in the penitentiary, life kept on moving. There were times when we had dancing contests. So, I entered the break dancing contest. Yes, I would win them all. I was a great dancer. I was one of the best dancers around. I even won the break dancing contest while being in high school. If you could have seen my dancing skills, you'd think I was a great dancer too. In dancing, I've been called "Turbo," Well, let me get this off my chest; I am one of the best! As I said before, when my brain (body) participates in anything, and I like it, I become the best at whatever it is. Yeah, my brain is awesome.

I played basketball in the penitentiary too. The entire penitentiary of inmates viewed me as one of the greatest basketball players in the camp. There was this one-person name Ernie, he was awesome too. Ernie and I were considered the star basketball players in this camp (penitentiary). Ernie and I both grew up in the Vaughn Projects. We both lived in the projects were wickedness cleverly took over. I guess for the both of us, as we performed works of wickedness, from it, our names have been added to the criminal system of the world. When I got to the penitentiary, Ernie looked out for me. Actually, when we both lived in the projects, we were cool friends with one another. I have not seen Ernie in over ten years; however, from our performances of wickedness, it caused us to reunite in the penitentiary. If you have not seen many of your friends in years, if you ever go to the penitentiary, you just might run into one.

In the penitentiary, a few inmates were able to get their hands on some marijuana. The same drug, marijuana, which started this whole ordeal of wickedness in my life is actually in the midst of this camp (penitentiary). I have not smoked marijuana or used any other kind of drugs for about a month; therefore, my body's system was somewhat clean. Well, yep, there I go again, willingly causing my cerebellum to control my hand to grasp that dope. Yelp, there I go again, causing my brain stem to inhale marijuana. This is truly crazy because I am in the penitentiary-inhaling reefer into my brain's organs. Something has to be wrong with me mentally, but I DID NOT KNOW what it was. I should have been coaxing my brain to rehabilitate it self. Nevertheless, here I am in the penitentiary inhaling marijuana.

Of course, I was not the only idiot-smoking weed in the penitentiary. Ninety five percent of the inmates in this prison were inhaling dope into their brains too. The Penitentiary had become "a neighborhood" full of wicked idiots. We were smoking marijuana in the penitentiary as if we were gathered in "the neighborhood". If one of us would have been caught smoking marijuana, then more jail time could have been added to our sentence. I thought I was the only person who allowed drugs to cause ignorant things to happen too. As I can now see, these prisoners are ignorant as well.

Every drug related inmate in this place shares a mental status of the I DID NOT KNOW title of this book. As these people have allowed drugs to come into their lives, they have earned the true rights to say; "I DID NOT KNOW that drugs would lead my life to serve time in jail".

Before I went to serve time in the penitentiary, here are some names of all the drugs that I have put inside of my brain. I smoked marijuana, which was my first drug of choice. I have snorted cocaine, and I have smoked crack too (pre-mo). I tried "water" which is called "whack". I have crushed Tylenol 3's, and 4's, and mixed them in Benadryl cough syrup. I have swallowed volumes. I have snorted heroin. I have drunk beer and hard liquor too. From all drug chemicals I've put inside of my brain, do you think I have a normal brain operating mechanism (system)? Even though I felt and thought I was normal, however, it is impossible to be normal after all of those chemicals have operated throughout my anatomy. That is just too many chemicals that one brain has dealt with. Even right now, I am sure that many of my brain cells have been destroyed, but I DID NOT KNOW it.

Because of my drug addictions, I actually became a killer to my own life, brain, and body. When I had started putting drugs in my anatomy (brain and body), I was feeding myself death. When I was putting drugs into my body, I was literally giving death an invitation to come unto me and swallow me up. Every person that puts chemical control substances in his or her body is asking death to visit them. As soon as a person becomes addicted to any drug, death will be on his or her trail. Either death will come sooner or it will come later. Just as a person cannot run from the law's judgment, a person cannot run from death. You cannot dodge death. How can you dodge the killer, when you are inhaling the murderer into your brain? For many people, drugs are going to unexpectedly choke their brainstem and creepily kill them. Remember, the drug ninja is after your life.

People, listen to my counsel, and receive this message! No matter what great things your friends tell you how great drugs feel, do not be an idiot like me by submitting unto their words. Words are cunning, and they have the power to seduce you. You need to make up your mind, and be strong by saying "no" to drugs.

There may be a friend of yours speaking in your left ear saying, "give this dope a try, it will make you feel good". However, I am your friend speaking into your right ear saying, "drugs might feel good to the body, but it's not worth loosing your sobriety, peace, and happiness in life". Do not give your life to an addition. That is exactly what I did; I gave my entire life to an addiction. Say no to drugs because it is not worth loosing your mental freedom.

Your friend in your left ear is not telling you the entire story that comes along with the obsession of drugs. However, I am your friend speaking to you in your right ear telling you to stay away from drugs, because they will fasten a heavy and deadly addiction within your brain. I have told you the repercussions concerning drug use, and not just the good feelings. So, which friend should you listen too? Are you going to listen to the one that tells you only half of the story (friend in left ear), or the one that tells you the whole conclusion of the matter (right ear friend, me)? The only vision that the left ear friend is showing, is how good the drug will make you feel. However, I am telling you how your life is going to be a living mess. Even in my book, I am not hiding anything from you; therefore, I am telling you everything that you need to know about drugs. Take heed to this book, and say no to drugs, or you will be the next individual to experience a lifetime of "<u>I DID NOT KNOW</u>" tragedies.

If you hang out with people who do drugs, you have

two options before you. The first option is to disappear from your friend's presence every time they put drugs into their brains. The second option would be for you to find yourself new friends. There are many people in the world who do not use drugs. Therefore, you can always find yourself new friends. When you leave the presence of a friend who is utilizing drugs, it is a good decision that your brain has made. Do not feel bad, because you made a wise choice. If the police pull up on you and your druggie friends, the both of you will be searched. That is just one of the consequences that happens in folk's lives when they hang around people who are associated with drugs.

One day I had a bag of marijuana in my possession. This bag of marijuana was stashed away in my pants pocket. I was planning (brain's frontal lobe scheming) to smoke this bag of weed with some close friends of mine. Actually, with a few people who loved to inhale marijuana through their brainstem too. In the bag, there were ten fat joints already rolled up. I put the ten fat joints in a sandwich bag for safekeeping.

Suddenly, I saw a police car coming. The car was about a block away. When I saw the police driving towards my way, I became very nervous. A little fear began to work within me. Since a movement of fear had been accessed, then my brain's limbic system was at work. When I saw the police driving down the street towards my way, I quickly snatched the bag of weed out of my pocket and tossed it into the bushes. Then the cop pulled the squad car over, and got out. He started walking towards my friend and I. he searched us both. While one of the policemen was searching us, the other cop went straight towards the bushes, and looked in it. I suppose he saw something being sneakily tossed. Well, the cops found the bag of weed I had launched into the bushes. After the police found the bag of marijuana, they gave the drug charge to my friend. My friend is the innocent victim, but since he was with me, he now has a drug case, and a criminal record. For the rest of my dear friend's life, that marijuana charge will be on his earthly record until the day he dies.

Actually, that should have been a charge to my personal criminal record. I am the one who should have been charged for possession of marijuana. As I was saying unto you, when you are associating, or hanging around people who indulge in drugs, you might find yourself in the same situation as my dear friend was in. My dear friend was charged for possession of narcotics, when I should have been the one charged for the case. In other words, my friend was handcuffed, finger printed, and put behind jail bars for drugs, that belong to me. So stay away from chemical drug associates because you just never know when a false dope judgment might fall upon you. You just read how it went down with my friend and me. My friend had no idea, that this day would be an awful day for him. Well, all I can say is, Derrick Gray, I am sorry that the cops charged you for my bag of marijuana (shaking my head).

Another situation: a few of my friends and I were running from the police one day. It was nighttime. We all were running through this tight gangway, thinking it was an escape route from the police. I had a quarter ounce of cocaine in my hand to sale, which was wrapped in a plastic sandwich bag. Then all of a sudden, other police officers came from the opposite end that we were seeking to exit from this gangway. Therefore, I quickly tossed the bag of cocaine down on the ground. As the police hemmed us up against the wall, the dope that I had was on the ground near my friend. When the police officers saw the dope, they charged my friend with "possession of cocaine". Well, sorry Ron Kelly that the police gave you a narcotic charge case because of the drugs I had. As I was saying, you just never know, what will happen next in your life when you hang with drug users or drug associates.

I have two friends that have a drug charge that should not be on their account. I have two friends that have criminal records all because they wanted to hang out with the dope crowd. My two friends were hanging out with me because they wanted to get high. Because of the two friends of mine wanting to spill dope into their heads, narcotic charges are now posted on their law report. Now they have a criminal record, concerning drugs charges that should have been added to my criminal record. You know what, every friend of mine, has put at least 4 or 5 drug chemicals into their brains, and that's a shame.

Drugs have manipulated the lives of many women who are in this world. Women, have allowed drugs to be their tour guide on the earth. Being filled with dope, many women's feet have been led to walk to, and stand on the street corner.

Drugs have empowered many women to prostitute their own bodies. They actually take their clothes off; have sex with a person, just to get some dope or money. To all the women who give up their body (sex) to get high on drugs, that is an act of wickedness too. Just as I sold drugs to make money, you sold your body to make money as well. You have shamed your body just as I have shamed mine. Women, your brains have become wicked, because you will have sex, and then stick your hand out to receive a payment.

Most of you women are just like me. You thought you was going to get high one day for the fun of it, but not knowing, your drug usage and addiction would take your life this far. Just as I had no idea that I would turn into a drug seller; you had no idea that you would sell your body just to get high. Then before you know it, you will be prostituting your body for a great number of years. Right now today, I know a dozen women who have been prostituting their bodies for years.

In this life, we view women as being the weaker vessel in physical strength. Well, that may be true because she is physically weaker than a man. No matter how weak a woman may be, or how strong a man may be, when it comes to chemical addiction, drugs do not care about the physical strength of human sexuality. Drug's addiction will beat a woman's facial appearance into the dirt as if a man has brutally abused her.

In a woman's beautiful days, she could have been chosen to be the "Prom Queen" or even "Miss America".

However, when drugs perform its skill in her brain; her facial appearance will decline drastically. No matter how beautiful a woman appears to be, the power of drug's addiction will truly alter her countenance. After any woman becomes addicted to drugs, her beauty is soon to touch basis with decaying. Her beauty in the face will drop, why, because she is putting drug toxics into her face maker. Yeah, the brain is the worker that designs faces. Yep, God gave the brain such a power that it can make its own face.

The brain does it all: it even forms the entire body. It put dimples on people's faces. It makes the toenails, it makes a person's thighs, and all this work of creation is done in the belly of a mother. It takes less than nine months for all these bodily parts to be fashioned into one body--- a baby.

Therefore, when people put drugs into their face maker, the intoxicants from drugs, soon remakes the entire face. For example, do you remember how beautiful a young girl was when she was in high school? Right now today, I can think of a dozen high school girls who were so sexy, too sexy, nothing but sexy. Since these once known beautiful women have been on drugs for a great number of years, they all now look a "nasty hot mess". The sad thing is; these women still think they have that high school beauty look. Drugs are powerful deceivers, and I am being deceived right now.

When a woman becomes pregnant, what is the first body part seen? I believe it is the head, the brain. Everything starts at the head. When a woman gets her head or life together, everything else will follow accordingly. This same procedure goes for men too.

Women, get some heavenly help. Free yourself from the ugly force that drug living plagued on your life. Go get your mind cleansed. Earn your name back. Since many you women have been on drugs, you had been hired to do a wicked job. Not only that, but you have been given a new name. Your new name is, "wicked prostitute". You have allowed wickedness to give you a name. Therefore, stop, drop, and roll out of the drug game and earn your name back.

You and I both need to earn our names back. If you follow me, I will take you a place where people are given their names back. Not only will I show you how to get your name back, but also, you can get your life back too.

Some books say, "A person becomes addicted to something after repeating the same procedure for 21 days. Yeah, well, that may be true, but I have another quote for you to print into the encyclopedia of addictions." Whoever reads this; add this quote to the book of facts concerning "mental addictions". --- An Addiction can start as soon as your limbic system agrees with the pleasurable feeling that has aroused it. A person can have sex 3 nights in a row, and the addiction's plague can be engraved into the brain. Also, add this to the encyclopedia of addictions. ---When drugs are first tried, people can become addicted the same day, and some can become addicted next week, however, in each person's brain, different strokes for different folks. If you do something 2 two 3 times a day for a week, that is an addiction right there. Just because you cannot get your hands on something for a day or two does not mean you are not addicted. You just do not have the transportation to get it, or the money to buy it, but if you did, you would truly access it. Addiction aren't based upon your usage during time, it is based upon a craving desire. If you feel that drugs will settle your body down, then you are addicted.

Still as of yet, I DID NOT KNOW or realized that this drug addiction was setting me up. Once a person intakes dope, a certain path will be walked on. There are certain paths that the individual will walk on because of the mental enslavement of drugs. Your brain will control your legs to walk down certain roads that only a brain filled with drugs will go. If I had not drugs in my living, my legs would not have experienced running from the police. Since drugs were in my personal life, running from the police became my experience.

I have walked through many violent neighborhoods just so that I can buy some drugs to sell, and suddenly, out of nowhere, rapid gun shooting appeared on the scene. You just never know what you are walking into when you are on a pursuit for dope. Here I am ignorantly seeking to purchase drugs, and walked into violence, wrath, and random gun shooting. What I am trying to say is this, if drugs had not been in my brain, many of the places that I've visited, would not have been a walking ground for me. Many of the places I've visited would not have my footprints marked in the pavement.

A hunter uses bait and traps to capture his prey. The same way a hunter set bait on a trap to lure animals is the same way that drugs are luring to capture all dope handlers for the big catch. The trap is supposed to prevent the animal from escaping. After the animal has bitten down on the bait, and is captured in the trap, the hunter then tosses a net over the animal.

A meal for the hunter is now soon to be prepared. Now the poor animal is soon to be killed and slaughtered by the hunter.

When drugs had entrapped me, they were using me to destroy my own life. Just as the hunter set bait on the trap to lure animals, drugs have done me the same way. Yes, I fell into the net of drugs, now I am trapped, and soon to be destroyed, and I DID NOT KNOW it. The hunter catches animals, and eats them as a meal, and drugs have captured my brain, and are eating on my brain cells, but I DID NOT KNOW it.

A parable: A fisherman took a fishing rod with him to the sea. Along with the rod, he took a variety of hooks. Once the fisherman has arrived at the bank of the river, he patches bait on his fishing hooks. The bait (worm) is used as a scam. The worms are used to draw the fish toward the hook. The hook is for the catch. It's a plot. It's a setup. Nevertheless, in order to capture something, a plan for entrapment is needed.

Then the fisherman launches his rod into the deep sea. The rod has a hook on it with bait attached to it. The hook and the bait sits at the bottom of the sea idled, until it is aroused by a sea creature. When the fish takes a hunger bite on the hook and bait, he has just been captured. The fish had no idea that its life is soon to end. The fish did not know that the hook and bait was a set up. If this captured fish was able to speak for himself, I am sure the it will say, <u>I DID NOT KNOW</u>, the worm and hook was a set up to kill me.

Once the fish bites on the hook and bait, the fisherman then yanks and pulls on the rod. The fisherman pulls on the rod, so that the hook can pierce through the fish's mouth. Now the poor fish is the in the water being guided by the fisherman's rod. Now the poor fish is trying its best to swim away. The fish tries it's hardest to swim away, but the strength from the fisherman is too strong. While in the water, the fish realizes that it is being taken away from the journey that it was once on. This fish could have been living in this water for weeks or even months, and then suddenly, its life became trapped. The water is his city; it's his town, it's his place of dwelling. Once the fisherman reels in this captured fish, it is now being taken out of its city. Then the fisherman places the fish in a net on the bank of the river. Now the living fish has been taken away from freedom and among its peers.

The living fish is now in a net, and knows not what is about to happened next. That is exactly how I feel, because my life now resembles the life of that captured fish. The fish has been captured by the fisherman, and my brain has been captured by drug's addiction. Just as the fisherman tossed hooks into water to capture its prey, in the same sense, I have tossed the power of drugs into my brain, and the addiction has truly captured me.

I have biblical text that I would like to share with you concerning the fish, which, is compared to humankind. Maybe, one year, I will write a book, which might be titled, "The Life of an Animal, versus the Life of a Human". (I said maybe)

A Biblical text*; Ecclesiastes 9: 12 for man also knoweth not his time: as the fishes that are taken in an evil net, and as birds that are caught in the snare; so are the sons of men snared in an evil time when it falleth suddenly upon* *them.* As I have just said, I feel just like the fish, which has been captured and placed into a net to be killed later. Just like the fish did not know that the food (bait-worm) was used to lure him, capture him, net him, and then cause him to be killed, yet, I DID NOT KNOW that drugs were bait to lure me, capture me, net me, and then have the opportunity to kill me. Most definitely, I DID NOT KNOW that drugs was the setup bait for death. Just like the captured fish was enticed with fish bait, in the same sense, I was enticed with drug bait, and now the fish and I both are battling for our own lives.

However, the fish has more sense that I have, because the fish is squirming, and wiggling its body trying to get free. However, I am not doing anything but cramming more drugs into my brain. Even the fish realizes that he has been captured, but I did not realize anything. I guess the fish's brain is smarter than my brain, huh.

If a person's brain is on drugs, and that individual is not seeking to become freed from them, then a fish's brain appears to be smarter. The fish has detected or realized that something foul has taken place. Although, a fish does not have mental knowledge to know anything about life or death, however, it knows when something unorthodox has taken place when captured. Therefore, the fish panics and tries to become free. The fish does not want to be taken out of the water. The fish knows if it is taken out of the water, he has been taken away from life; because for him, life is in the water. However, my ignorant self, I DID NOT KNOW that life is in my brain, yet, and still, I am smothering it with chemicals.

Most drug addicts that have been captured by the dope's addiction will not fight for the living of his or her life, however, when a fish is captured, it will. The drug addict does not feel the pain of having a hook thrashed into the flesh, which means, "Have been captured". Well, I want to let you know, that if you are addicted to drugs, you have been "hooked" and "captured". Not only have all drug users been captured and hooked, but also, their life can end at any given moment. The fish ignorantly bit on the hook with the worm on it, not knowing that death was attached to it. However, I willingly put drugs into my brain, and death might be my life's results. Worms were the bait used to capture the fish to be slaughtered, and drugs are the bait I used to capture my brain for the killing. Somehow, or someway, as a person becomes addicted to drugs, his or her life is soon to end.

In every situation in life, a beginning stage, and an ending stage is always administered. When a woman becomes pregnant, a date and time is accounted, which marks the beginning stage of the pregnancy. Once the woman pushes out the infant from her belly, the pregnancy stage has just ended. Usually, a pregnancy is in motion for a total of 9 months. Although, an infant is a living species while in the belly of the mother, however, personal life on earth begins after the infant has been born. I was born on December 29th; therefore, life on earth had begun for me on that exact date. However, when I die, that will be the ending stage of life for me.

We understand that days, weeks, months, and years all have beginnings, and they all have endings, too. January is the beginning of every year. Every year expires (ends) on Dec. 31. Therefore, the earth has a beginning and ending stage. I have heard different people say, "God is coming back again", and when he does, the earth will be no more". In other words, even if God comes on January 1st, the earth will end then.

A person that runs in a track meet has a starting point (beginning), and an ending point (finish line). In a track meet, normally an air gun is triggered and fired into the air to get the race in motion. The runner already knows how many laps must be ran around the track in order to reach the finish line. Whether, it is the 50-yard dash or 3-mile jog, the runner knows how far he or she must run until the race is done.

However, the drug addiction that I have been captivated to, I DID NOT KNOW when or how it is going to end. When a person is in the drug life, he or she never knows when or how that way of living will end. For example, look at my situation; while I am in the drug living lifestyle, I knew how it all started but I DID NOT KNOW how it is going to end. Here I am walking in life, using drugs, and unaware of my true ending. When a person is into drugs, drugs will cunningly create an ending for that individual's life.

If your brain has been locked up on drug addictions, then from the addiction, the dope is creating unexpected experiences to come forth into your living. When something is being created in your life, the natural or physical eye will never see it in construction form. When God created the world, human eyes did not see it being done. Although, when God created the earth, there was not a human in the land to see it being created; however, creation is an act that causes things and situations to suddenly appear. In our personal lives', when anything is being created, it pops up in our view, and it has become a part of our living. When something is created, it just appears before your very eyes, and you never saw it being physically made. God said, "Let there be light" and all of a sudden, it appeared. That is how creation operates. A creative act appears, as if it crept up on you from behind.

Many people have filed bankruptcy because of the chemical drug addiction that dope has spanked on the user's brain. Drugs have created an act for people to file bankruptcy, and of course, they did not see it coming. When a dope head initially begins to spend his or her earns cash on dope to get high, a creative act to experience is in the makings.

I've dealt with many drug users who were wealthy, or should I say, financially stabled. They purchased dope from me often. Sometimes, 3 to 4 hundred dollars a day would be spent on crack cocaine. The spending of 3 to 4 hundred dollars on crack sometimes went on for an entire week. That is already $2100 dollars spent on crack cocaine in a 7-day period. The drug's addiction is the power that drove the "user" to go back and forth to the bank to withdraw money to purchase more crack cocaine. Before the drug user realizes that the chemical addiction has caused him or her to spend close to $15,000 on cocaine in 3 months, bankruptcy is about to be performed. The drug user does not even know that the chemicals, which he or she has been putting in the brain has created such a task, which led him or her, to file bankruptcy. As I said before, anything that's in creation form, the human eye cannot and will not see it being designed.

Filing bankruptcy is a devastating blow to the minds of the people who have been led to do so. When bankruptcy occurs, it darkens the heart of people because they have no materials to show for their hard-earned money. When the money should have been spent on bills and other important necessities in life, it was spent on drugs to feed the brain its on going addiction. Having nice and comfortable furniture in your home will make you feel somewhat good within yourself. Nevertheless, if you allow your brain to stay chained to the addiction of drugs, all your rightfully earned money will be spent on dope. Instead of buying things that will replenish your home, drug's addiction will cause you to spend the money to feed its habit. If you are not careful, drugs will keep you buying dope until it takes 90% of your biggest check.

Little do people realize that drugs love to prepare and create scenes with "big checks". "Big checks" are what I call, "your income tax check". Yeah, that fat yearly check that you call, "tax pay back", drugs love to get a hold of that. If you do not stop the uses of drugs, all of your "tax pay back" will spent on street crack rock.

When the paycheck was placed into the drug addict's hand, once it was cashed in, drugs prepared such a way for it to be spent. Most drug addicts will recite words in their minds saying; "I am not going to spend anymore money on drugs". However, when the money is placed into their hands, the chemical (drug) that is inside the brain ignites the addiction. The limbic system in the brain, which gives us the power to sense hunger, once it becomes addicted to drugs, it

216

then hungers after dope. Then the drug addict will search to feed the brain its addiction, and spend the money on dope. Once the limbic system becomes addicted to drugs, it will hunger for a substance that is not food. Go get yourself some mental help, because I do not care, I will sell you crack if your life was on the line. That is how all drug dealers are; they only care about themselves and that wicked money.

Drug's powerful addiction is equal to the performance of a big bully. A bully will always treat a person with indifference. Usually, bullies do their torturing work on either or younger and or smaller people. Most bullies are taller and wider in the body than their opponent. This bully (drugs) is more than 6 feet shorter than I am. The bully that my life is up against is only a couple of centimeters in height, but from its controlling power, it seems to be 90 feet tall. A bully will try to run your life to be Lord over it. That is truly, what drug's addiction has done unto me. Drugs bullied me; they ran my life here and there, and not only that, but also, they became ruler over my personal being. The bully (drugs) showed remarkably strength in my everyday living. Whenever there was an opportunity to get high or try another drug, I was boosted, compelled, and controlled to do so. From drug's addiction, the big bully controlled my brain. The big bully was touring my life on a path that leads to mass destruction and I DID NOT KNOW it. Drugs are actually my Goliath.

Destruction and misery are crammed in as a package when any drug addiction has touched one's living. Destruction to the brain and body is dope's greatest celebrations. When drugs have caused destruction or misery to be seen in a person's life, it has accomplished its utmost task. No matter how harsh of a scene drugs have awakened, they will never stop working a work of misery. Drugs are out to harm you; and drugs have the power, through the addiction to complete it utmost task. Dope has a continuous operation; never will drugs hesitate to make a person's life bitter, and never will it cease from directing your life into mass destruction.

Once a person causes his or her brain to accept dope's adequate power through smoking, jacking, sniffing, drinking or however, that individual has just submitted his brain and life into the trampling power of drugs. Once a person in-takes drugs, soon and very soon, that person become dope's tramp. Not only do you become dope's tramp, but also, you have submitted your life to a contract, even without the signing of your signature.

Most of the times, a contract is a sheet of agreement between two parties. Whether a certain contract requires one's signature, or a verbal agreement, every contract has rules and regulations. Usually, a contract is read over and viewed by the party, and then a signature is required. When the signature has been signed on the dotted line, it is to verify that, the policy plan on this particular contract has been agreed upon. When you submit to the agreement of a contract, you are saying that you are going to stick with that particular plan until the date of expiration.

Whatever the terms and policy plans in the contract is, you have agreed to it all. If the agreement or contract deal says, one year, 2 years, or 6 years, once your name has been has been signed on it, you are stuck with the plan. It is a sheet of agreement, and by you signing your name on the sheet, that means, you have accepted all the terms, which has been typed on the contract. A contract is a deal of binding. It is almost like being in jail. Just as I was not released from the penitentiary until my time was due, a contract will not release you until time is due as well.

Lets say that I have signed the name (**Brian Irons**) on a contract deal for some furniture. If this contract policy plan says that I must pay $125 dollars a month for the next 3 years, then that is what I must pay. No matter what happens in my financial living, the contract says I must pay up. Whether I am fired from employment, or anything of the like, I must still pay $125 a month for the next 3 years. A contract cannot be broken, until time has been served.

When a sports player has been drafted to a team to play professional league sports, usually, the player is asked to sign a contract of agreement. By demand, the athlete is told to sign a contract, in order for his name to be submitted to the team's roster. If the athlete, for some reason feels that he or she wants to be traded to a different team, once his or her name has been signed on the contract, the athlete cannot proceed to another team. The athlete must stay put until a specific date arrives, so he can be released. However, the contract that my life is on is very different.

As I was into the drug life, the power of addiction has been pressed down into my head horribly. I felt as if I was on a dope contract, because I could not free myself from this way of living. Even when I wanted to cease from putting drugs in my brain and body, I could not do it. It is hard freeing yourself from the practices of an addiction of any sort. Once I became addicted to drugs, the name, Brian Irons became the signature on a dope contract. Of course, I did not physically sign my name on this deal; however, when I bean to use drugs, the contract deal had begun on its own. As of now, my brain has been filled with drugs for at least 10 years. Even after all of the things that the power of drugs has taken my life through, I am still using them, because my brain's limbic system is addicted to its flavor. This has truly become a contract deal of wickedness, and I DID NOT KNOW it. I cannot be released from this lifestyle until time is served.

I have many friends right now today; whose minds have been locked up on a dope contract for so many years. Why? Because the addiction from drugs has not yet been broken. Indeed, the addiction its self, is a contract.

As I was in this dope game (selling drugs), I experienced being involved in physical battle with other men. These battles were fistfights. Of course, somewhere in life, disagreeing with people participated in this drug living lifestyle. I have been in so many fistfights that you would not believe. Frequently, I had to pay attention to my surroundings, and to those who were approaching on a daily basis. The craziest thing about my fighting battles is the fact that, every person I physically had an altercation with had drugs in their brains too. Whether, their brains were filled with alcohol's ingredients, cocaine, or marijuana, however, a chemical control substance represented us all. In other words, drugs were in their cerebrum (thinking center) and cerebellum (hands coordinator) controlling its God created movement. Yeah, we all are violent men. Drugs have brain washed us all. If your life is being controlled by drugs, then you are not being controlled by God; do you see the difference?

As my life was under the control of drugs, I remember being in 8 fights. Each fight, of course, I was the winner. In my first fight, sooner or later, I threw a one-two combination punch, and the fight was over. Yeah, I dropped him. The second opponent, I hit him with a one-two punch combination, and he ended up on the ground too. In my next 6 fights, I threw combination after combination, and dropped them as well. Therefore, I had 8 different fights, and all 8 of my opponents ended up on the pavement. I am the greatest, I am the best, and there's none like me.

A human being does not fight against my body; he fights against my amazing talent, skills, and techniques that my brain possessed. Although, my hands are the tools used while I'm fighting, however, my brain is the vessel in control of it all. My opponent does not know that my brain can control both of my arms like identical twins in physical power.

You may not believe it, but all of my fighting opponents that I put on the pavement, were done in less than 120 seconds. Once I viewed how an opponent holds his guards, and how coordinated his punch looked, I already envision the moment when I was going to speedily rush at him and throw my combination punch. Remember, in basketball, I can shoot 3 pointers with either arm. Remember, I can pitch a baseball with either arm. Remember, I can throw a football at a nice distance with either arm. Therefore, when it came to fighting, the same 2-hand talent and gift applies. By my arms being both perfectly coordinated one to the other, it was easy throwing a combination punches, and afterwards watching my enemy fall to the concrete pavement.

Since my combination punches knocked 8 people to the pavement, then I had to be extremely talented even in boxing. In the Wizard of Oz, Dorothy said, "there no place like home", however, **Brian Irons** is saying, there's no brain like mine. In the neighborhood, my name became, "LYTSKIN THE KNOCK OUT ARTIST".

After many of my fights were over, many friends would name me after pro boxers. I've been called, "Thomas (the hit man) Hearns. I've been called, "Mike Tyson". I've been called, "Sugar Ray Leonard". I've been called, "Marvin Hagler". I've been called, "Muhammad Ali". I've been called "Larry Holmes". I've been called "Leon Spinks". Lord have mercy, in my life, when it comes to sports, I've been called every pro name under the sun.

One day, I went to the mall and purchased 2 pair of boxing gloves. I presented the boxing gloves to the neighborhood. Of course, I had to be the first competitor to put on a pair of boxing gloves. In the boxing gloves, I was never hit were I fell to the pavement, but I remember knocking 3 of my opponents to the pavement, and several other people dropped the gloves and quit. If I had desired to be a boxer, I am sure; I would have been one of the greatest lightweight boxers in the world. Then I really would have been like Muhammad Ali…I shook up the world, I'm a bad man. You know what, I am going to go ahead and admit, "I SHOOK UP THE WORLD, too. Basketball, football, baseball, dancing, fighting……….I'm a bad man!

As chapter 3 (My Sports Position) stated, "I learned how to be defensive, because I was a baseball pitcher (defensive side), and I learned how to be offensive because I was a quarterback (offensive side). I owe it all to my brain. My brain is the vessel that performs all my talents.

If your brain is not as talented as mine, 9 times out of ten, I will sneak a few combination punches across your chin, and knock you out too.

Here I am in life, pronouncing judgment on people as if I am God. The people in the projects were handling situation though their own personal means, and so am I. The bible says, *Romans 12:17 recompense no man evil for evil.* That is exactly what I was doing; I was using evil tactics to solve my problems.

As I now think about the many events, which I witness years ago in the Vaughn Projects, those same events became my scenes in life. It's been more than 10 years since my family has moved out of the projects. In the projects, I saw much physical violence, gunplay, and random shooting, however, more than 10 years later, when drugs became apart of my personal life, those same events were performed by me. In the projects, I witnessed people running, and handling deadly weapons, such as guns. However, when drugs came into my life, I became a person that was running from the police and gun shooting as well. As I said before, wherever there are drugs, violence will become an active force. Just as the Vaughn projects was an area filled with violence, however, my brain and body became the area filled with violence too.

I remember, one day, a friend told me that a particular individual was walking through the neighborhood. This particular individual was in the "hood" searching for me. The human being who was looking for me was known for robbing and shooting the pistol. After I was told that this person was looking for me, the first thought that popped into my head was this individual seeking to rob me. This person has never robbed me before, but I felt that he was going to try too. Therefore, I darted to my house and grabbed my handgun from its resting place. Then I put the gun in my pants and charged outside. Once I got outside, I stood behind the corner of a wall in a gangway, waiting for him to come out of a certain house. I was standing in the gangway talking to myself and empowering myself to end this man's life.

This particular time, I was high as a kite. I was high from heroin, and only God knows what other form of drugs was active in my brain. My brain's cerebrum (thinker) was filled with heroin, and it created strong illusions of actually pulling the trigger of this gun. From the power of drug, I was uplifted to engage in this act of wickedness. Drugs were talking to me big time. Although, it was me talking to me, however, drug intoxicants were in control of the entire mental conversation. Drugs told me, "As soon as the guy opens the door, wait till he get off the porch, and empty the clip. I never felt this way before in my life, but I felt like, enough was enough. Drugs caused me to become so angry, that they almost caused my cerebellum (hand mover) to pulling the trigger of this pistol. If this person was seeking to rob me, I knew he would have had a gun, because nobody wants to get into a physical brawl with Lytskin. However, he never came outside, but if he would have, my brain was truly about to be tested.

I have already robbed 3 times already, and to watch and see another robbery occur, I was not about to have it. When a human being has been robbed 3 times at gunpoint, the only statement of words that individual has to hear is that a known robber is looking for him. When I heard that this known robber was on the hunt for me, my drug filled mind clicked, and suddenly I became defensive. However, just that fast, and just that ignorantly quick, a 1st degree murder could possible have happened.

If a murder had taken place, the case would have been called premeditated and non-self defense. Execution and being killed from a conviction of the law could have been my sentence and final judgment. Since only the law can execute the death penalty, and God is the law, then God through his laws would have probably killed me. As I said before, God has a law's judgment for every wicked deed done under the sun. There is no telling, what other broken laws I would have had to face in court for that particular murder charge. Another work of wickedness had almost prevailed in my life. Again, my drug filled thoughts made another ignorant decision.

Wickedness, wickedness, wickedness, how can I get help from the power of wickedness? Lord have mercy! Where can I find help? I need a doctor. I need someone to operate on my mental body. My brain has a real sickness in it, and I DID NOT KNOW it.

Chapter 9
Drugs Finally Damaged My Brain's Functions

After I had been released from the penitentiary, my heart was filled with joy. Being released from the penitentiary, and not having to get physically violent with an inmate, was joy all by itself. I did not have to use my brain's fighting talents and skills in that place. Although, at times, tempers were flaring on the basketball court, however, no fighting took place. Many of these inmates' bodies were solid and hard as rock, and I am glad that I did not have to wrestle with any of them. I came to the penitentiary in one piece, and I left it in one piece. However, I thank God for his mercy again, during the months of being lock up.

When I had been released from the penitentiary, immediately, I went to my old neighborhood. Yep, I was so happy to be home again. If felt so good to see the intersection of Rutcker and Ohio again. As I made my presence in the "hood", I saw all of my friends. Yep, here I am back in "Grape Hill". Yeah, I am home again.

Suddenly, one by one, my friends began to approach me. As they approached me, they began to put money into my hands. Maybe, they felt lead to supply me with some money, because of all the financial "love" Lytskin" showed unto them in the past. As I said before, there was not one person in the neighborhood that I did not give a helping hand too.

Before, I go any farther in my story; I want to thank Mike Nettles for sending me needed things while I was in the penitentiary. Thanks for your support Mike. Jackie Collins, Mona Collins, and Terrance Collins, thank you all for your support as well. To my girl; Chastity Brown, thank you for your support as well. Your letters that I was receiving twice a week really supported me. To my mother, you know I got to thank you for your support as well.

Anyway, after I finished fellowshipping with my neighborhood friends, I had to report to a place called, "The Halfway House". Although, I had to report to The Halfway House, it felt magnificently great to be in St. Louis again. Like Dorothy said in the "The Wizard of Oz", "there's no place like home", that is so true, because when I made it home, I felt just like that. Indeed, there is no place like home.

Also, there was no place like home so I can get into some sex. Sex is another addiction that I had, oh so badly. My limbic system was addicted to drugs, and it was also addicted to sex. I haven't had sex in 10 months, and when I got home, I had to get it. Anyway, let me get off that subject.

As I entered into the halfway house to make my presence known, I had to register my name (**Brian Irons**). After registering in the building, I was then giving a room in which I was to take my personal things. Once I sat in the room alone, I then counted the money my friends gave me. They supplied me with the exact amount of three hundred and fifty dollars ($350). That is a lot of money to come home and receive, after being locked up in prison for 10 months, and two weeks. That truly shows that I was one cool person to the neighborhood dwellers.

When I finally was stationed in the halfway house, I unpack all my belonging. It felt good to be unpacking clothes in my own city again. After a while, I learned a few tricks on how to escape the halfway house and return. Yep, I escaped numerous of times, but I made it back in the building without being caught. I snuck out the halfway house at times, just to get that sex. I was not the only ignorant man that snuck out the half way house.

When we would sneak out the Half Way House, we tied two to three sheets together, and were let down from it. We were let down on the blanket from the balcony. Two people would be on the one end of the sheet, and the escapee would be on the other. I was actually jeopardizing my freedom just to get that sex. My sex addiction was more horrible than my drug addiction. My limbic system was all messed up; it was addicted to a lot of stuff. Anyway, let me get off the sex subject, this book is about drugs.

Anyway, I slept in the halfway house for a total of 3 months. When I was released from the halfway house, I had to report to my parole officer. Therefore, I had to register my name to a counselor again. The name **Brian Irons** has been under the court's judgment for many years now. After I served my months in the halfway house, freedom I saw.

At this particular time, I was living with a friend. My parole officer came to my friend's house. She put a house arrest box on my friend's phone line, and tied a device box around my ankle. After a certain time of the day, I had to stay within so many yards of the house arrest box. If I walked farther than the maximum length provided, the house arrest box will record it. This house arrest assistance lasted for only 3 to 6 months. The whole time, while I was stationed in the halfway house, and while I was on house arrest, I was getting high as usual. I allowed drugs to skip into my life again. I allowed drugs to find its way back into my brain and body again. This drug stuff has to be some sort of witch; I must be under some sort of voodoo spell that I cannot break.

Before I advance any further in my story, let me submit unto you a scripture concerning "pride". _Proverbs 16:18- pride goeth out before destruction and a haughty spirit before a fall._ In other words, pride and having a haughty spirit will become active in a person's life, before destruction is tasted. A person becomes so lifted up in self-pleasure, that his or her living on earth is all about the rewards and personal achievements. Anytime, you have "pride" working inside of you, you are always on a mission to do things your very own "way". God hates the character called, "pride". Pride seeks to please it self, rather than to please God, who is the maker of us all. When a person has pride within in his heart, he speaks and credits himself on how good he has performed in a task, and how he has highly achieved his own accomplishments, rather than what God has done. Pride is a self-motivator, and will always lift up it self in you. When you have pride in you, you only think about you, you, and you. The evil condition that pride has is that it flosses about self-accomplished task, and having a haughty (prideful) spirit within you will cause you to put others down.

Pride kicked into my life, and elevated itself as I began to sell drugs again. As I made more and more money, I became the "man" filled with pride. I do not know how many years I had pride working inside of me, but it was there all the time, and I DID NOT KNOW it. Well, in all my sports, I allowed pride to be in them as I played.

Let me submit another scripture unto you as a package for you to open up unto your heart. *Psalms 7:11, says, God is angry at the wicked every day.* If a person is doing anything, on a routine or daily basis, and it is against the laws of God, consider yourself as being "the wicked". Consider yourself as an individual who God is angry at every day. Most of those people who were living in the Vaughn Projects were "The Wicked". The penitentiary of inmates is The Wicked, and since I have been living this illegal lifestyle, I am The Wicked too.

We as people always think that God is happy with us continually. The scripture hath saith, "*God is angry at the wicked everyday*". The scripture didn't say any names; it only called out "the wicked". What you do everyday, will determine if God is angry at you. Also, what you do everyday will determine if God categorizes you as the wicked. We think God doesn't get angry at us; we think he is only angry at other people, but never us. Later in this book, it is going to reveal unto you if God is angry at you, and if you are the wicked to him.

Did you ever experience your parents becoming upset or angry at you? Anytime a person breaks rules, the rule giver becomes angry with such a one. It is the same scenario with God; when people keep breaking his rules that he has set on earth, he becomes angry as well. No one pronounces judgment on anyone while being happy. Parents pronounce judgment on their kids, most of the times, from their anger.

When my dad had kicked me out of the house, he did it because of his anger towards me. Why you think God killed all those people on the earth centuries ago? It was because he became angry with them. We people have not the true understanding to believe that God actually gets angry.

This wickedness and evil, which I have been performing, started operating in my life ten years ago. When I began smoking dope in high school, that is the moment and day that God became angry with me and, I DID NOT KNOW it. The day I rushed drugs into my brain was the day that I can honestly say that God immediately became angry with me. When I began to put marijuana in my hands, immediately, I became a "law breaker", and God hates it when his laws are being broken. When God's laws are broken, it is all because wickedness led a man to perform an ungodly act. Yet and still, I lived in the drug life for ten years; therefore, God was angry with me for a decade, and even longer.

After coming home from the penitentiary, I reached a high standard of selling drugs. I went from profiting hundredths, and sometimes a thousand dollars a day, to earning $3500-$5000 daily and faithfully. I had finally reached the point in my drug selling life were I was selling enough cocaine to earn thousands of dollars a day. Collecting and gathering so much money, my mind became open to the thought, "You only live once".

As I collected so much money, I begin to celebrate. Although, drugs have already messed up my life, however, this day was more serious than any other day I've ever witnessed. I have celebrated hundreds of times while using drugs, but no day can compare to this one. During my 4 or 5 years of selling drugs, this day tops all. This particular day, I sold more than half a key of cocaine. More than 18 ounces of cocaine was sold from my possession. I sold whole ounces, half ounces, quarter ounces, and teenagers, which turned out to be more than $18,000. I didn't have $18,000 all at once, but I sold that much dope.

While I was in my pride, I was celebrating and

escorting chemical substances (heroin and codeine pills) into my brain and body. I was sitting on the passenger side of a friend's car. We were both getting high, and making drug transactions to customers from the car. I probably sold drugs to about 20 people this particular day, and no sells were 20-dollar crack rock. I moved up in drug rankings, and selling 20-dollar rocks to dope heads, became outdated.

The time had come for my friend and I to go our separate ways. I suppose, this guy drove me to my vehicle, so I could get in it, and drive myself home. However, in his car, I had fallen into a deep sleep. Heroin and pills caused my brain to be overly exhausted, and I dosed into a sleep mode. Right now, my brain has been cast into a spell of sleep. I suppose, the fellow who I was riding with in the car attempted to awake me, but I never woke up. Although, I was not aware of what was going on, my brainstem was still active because breathing was still in action. Nevertheless, the drug ninja finally snuck up on me again, and is about to violently mistreat my brain's organs.

I suppose, at this particular time in my life, I was slowly dying. Yes, this is truly, what the power of drugs has been trying to do to my life for a very long time. From the powerful stoke of drugs, I never made it to my car to drive myself home. Drug intoxicants were violently pounding on my brain. Usually, after getting high, I would awake from a push or shove, but today, nothing worked.

Since I never woke up, I was then driven to a friend's house. However, when I arrived at my friend's house, I was physically carried inside of the apartment. I was being carried because I was in a comatose state of mind, meaning, I was in a situation were I DID NOT KNOW what was going on. The brainstem, which is the worker that gives life, is the only mental active organ that is doing its job (helping me stay alive) (keeping the inner being operating).

When I was carried into the house, I was carefully laid on living room floor. It is possible that this household thought that maybe I was drunk and unconscious from the power of alcohol's intoxicants. However, I was not drunk, but I was "high" from drug usage. As I appeared to look drunk or high, this day was like a moment of disguise to the family of this household. From this household's visual experience, the people who lived here, all knew I was a heroin user, but as they watch me being toted into the house, I could have passed for being "drunk" as well. This family probably did not know what to think, as I was being carried and stationed on their living room floor.

The sleep patterns my friend and his family have witnessed after a night of me in taking heroin, sleeping hard was nothing new unto them. After a night of me snorting heroin, I would sleep heavily until the next day. Sometimes I slept until the next nightfall. To my friend's family, this type of sleep or un-consciousness is similar to the other nights they have seen, after a night of snorting heroin. The only difference remains to be seen is the fact that I was carried into the house. Other than that, sleeping overnight and halfway through the next day was a normal event.

As I laid on the living room floor unconscious, I strongly think my friend's family thought I would wake up the next day. However, I did not wake up the following day. I stayed on the living room floor.

Death is now trying to enter into my brain, and cause it to become its equal. Anything that's dead cant move, and death is trying to stop my brain from organizing itself. My cerebellum, which is my limb motivator had been forcefully inactive, therefore, my physical limbs was on lock down. The only actions my body could do, was to lie on the floor, and obey what drugs wanted it to do. After drugs sent my inner being in to this harsh mode of sleep, it was sent into a mode I did not want it to be in. My inner man was obeying the power of drugs, because it went into a mode (sickness), that I really did not want it to go. I never wanted drugs to put a mode on me that was so strict, that I could not wake up and do the norm.

My friend and I had a pet cat named, "Manic". I do not remember how the name "manic" came about, however, we called him that, and the cat answered. With this cat, if I caught my friend sleeping, or if he caught me resting, one of us would toss the cat on one another. My friend told me that he tossed the cat on me. I did not move, nor did I budge, nor did I show signs getting up. As my friend was tossing the cat on me, he did not know that death from drug usage was hovering over my body. I suppose the drugs were operating and reconfiguring my brain functions all through the night.

As the day traveled on, it was about 4-pm, and I was still lying unconscious on the living room floor. The family whose living room I had overlaid in had soon realized I was probably in the same position and spot all through the night. I do not know the time in which I was laid on the living room floor, but I heard that I had lain there overnight until 4-pm, which is the next day. I suppose the family whose living room floor I was in, walked by to check on me from time to time. I am sure I was not looking normal or healthy in my physical countenance. Terry, Mona, and Jackie, neither of them knew, I was slowly dying.

A member of my friend's family called my parent's house to inform someone about the scarce violent scene that is now taking place. My friend's family probably came to the living room, observed, and couldn't do anything but watch. As this violent scene was taking place, the family could not help me out. I call it a "violent drug scene" because my brain had been knocked into an unconscious state by the ferocious power of drugs. Anytime something knocks you out, the way it did me, that's a physical violent encounter. I may not have felt the physical encounter on the outside of the body, but my mental body felt the aggressive attack. My brain is now being manipulated by drug's power. Therefore, my friend's family called my parent's house.

When my friend's family phoned my parent's house to inform my family of this brutal event, my mother was not home, she was at church praising the Lord or listening to some gospel preaching. Therefore, this violent incident was in motion on a Sunday evening around 4-pm. When my friend's family called my parents house, they must have spoken to one of my sisters or my dad. After my sister or dad heard the torturing news, they called my mom's church to notify her of the horrible incident concerning her first-born child.

Can you imagine the thoughts that are floating through my mother's head after hearing about this drug event concerning her son? The only words or news that could have been recited over the phone is: "Gloria, I received a call from Terry's family saying", Brian has been laid out on Terrance's living room floor all night and half of the day". Since, my mother was at church hearing horrible news such as this, I am sure that the church service was interrupted, and special prayers to God went forth immediately. After prayers went forth, my mother leaves the church, and rushes to my friend's house, to see about her son.

Now my mother arrives on the scene where the brutal drug beating on her son is now taking place. A loving mother will always go and see about the malady of her offspring. No matter how light or heavy the issue weighs, a caring mother will make it her business to get there. I have always known my mother to love me no matter what. I knew that she loved me because of the passionate feelings and close relationship we held. I am confident that, when she arrived at my friend's house, as she beheld me, she put her hands upon my body to feel her sick son. Maybe she knelt down on her knees, as she was viewing my body. She, not really knowing, that she was watching drugs try to present death into her son's brain. After she realized my condition was far beyond of what her physical capabilities could do, she phoned the ambulance. She called the paramedics to come to the rescue.

Although, my mother's God (Jesus) did not answer prayers right away, as she may have desired, however, her God had a plan through his traveling mercy. Not only does God have a plan for righteous folks, but also, he has a plan for wicked ones too. God will use you anyway you allow him to use you. If you live in wickedness, God will use you through the reaping what you sow law.

In the projects (Vaughn Projects), gunshots, drugs, and violence would bring the police, and medical assistance to cater the area. However, in my situation, drugs performed a brutal physical attack on my body all by itself, and caused emergency help to cater to my unexpected illness.

When the medical emergency van arrived at the apartment, I supposed they quickly went into the living room to provide me with urgent care. Here I am lying on the floor in my friend's apartment, just as the person was lying on the ground after being shot and killed in the projects. The man in the projects, which had been shot and killed, his incident was probably drug related, and so is mine. Somehow, someway, drugs knocked us both down to the ground. We were both knocked to the ground by a performance of wickedness. Someone shot him, which was a performance of wickedness, and I put drugs in my body, which was a performance of wickedness too. We were both on the ground by something that is illegal to have in one's possession. A bullet from evil struck his body, and my brain was struck by the evil power of drugs. On the ground, we both experienced the power of evil. Yes, the reason why were both were on the ground is because of actions of wickedness, which are performed by people.

Wickedness is out to destroy lives and cities; and I found out that wickedness itself could be destroyed too. There is only one way wickedness can be killed or destroyed. It takes an explosive power to destroy wickedness; however, humankind alone has not that power. If you want to know how to kill wickedness, then follow me. I will show you the way, and the path you and I must walk so that evil activities will cease. Please follow me, and I will take you to someone who can murder wickedness.

Anyway, I suppose, the paramedics did CPR and hooked me up to a heart-monitoring machine. The machine is to motivate my brainstem, and keep it active for breathing. As the paramedics were performing all of their experienced skills to preserving my life, I was then placed on a mat. I was then picked up and carried into the ambulance. I am on my way to the hospital to check in. The name **Brian Irons** is about to be submitted into a hospital for mental and physical treatment.

As I was on my way to the hospital, my breathing was lethargic (in slow motion), meaning; my brainstem was having a problem with performing its normal breathing. In other words, my brainstem (brain part that elevates my breathing) is putting up a tough fight. Right now, my brain's organs are in a battle. I'm in the open field, and my breathing has been hit. Nowhere to run and nowhere to hide, my breathing is in a quarrel. Each intake of air is very important for me right now. Breathe in, breathe out, it must be done, or I'm a goner.

This is so sad, too sad, nothing but the art of sadness. Yep, the name **Brain Irons** has just registered in another place on earth, in the city of St. Louis. In a hospital is where my name had been registered. I signed my own name at the probation office; I signed my own name at the Halfway House, but someone else had to sign my name when I registered in this hospital.

When the ambulance arrived at the hospital, immediately, I was transported to a special area. I was transported to an area, were people who are diagnosed as "critical condition". "Critical condition" means, a person's life is in a fight to live. A harsh moment to live has become a living man's battle, when critical condition is his diagnose. Just like it is hard to drive any vehicle in the snow, however, in the same sense, when critical condition touches a living man's life it becomes hard to live. Lord have mercy, I am in a hospital surrounded by people whose life, brain, and body has met the wall of prevention. In every brain in this particular area of the hospital, all are fighting to operate for another minute of life.

When the paramedics placed me in the critical condition room or area, I was then pronounced "dead". My heart stop beating, therefore, the brainstem activity became inactive. My brainstem held on as long as it possible could, but the brutal strength of drugs was too powerful. My brainstem had shut down completely, and stopped its natural use of functioning. I actually sent my God created brainstem through all of that ignorance, stupidity, and insanity.

Nevertheless, the mercies of God were here at the hospital with me.

As I was in the critical condition department, it was said and recorded that my heart stopped for 11 minutes. The emotions of life, which are connected to my brain, had just tasted death. In life, my emotions loved the pleasure drugs released into them, but now, from the power of drugs, my emotions no longer works. Drugs finally hit the target that they have been shooting at for years. My brain was the target, and drugs finally hit it in a way that it has been trying to do for years.

I tossed marijuana's dreadful ingredients into my brain like a dart. After I tossed marijuana in my brain, I tossed other chemicals into it too. However, July 26, when I tossed heroin and pills into my brain, the bull's eye (the heart) was finally hit. The only sounds of celebrations being heard are heart-monitoring machines, which is to alert physicians of my heart rate, and my other inner being activity.

From all the talents and skills my brain possessed, I had the chance to shake up the sport's world; however, as you have now just read, drugs shook up and messed up my world. Wow, I DID NOT KNOW drugs would cause my heart to stop beating for 11 minutes. Wow, I DID NOT KNOW that drugs would cause me to be a patient in a hospital. Wow I DID NOT KNOW wickedness, through drugs had a plan for my life.

After 11 minutes of no brainstem activity (no breathing), suddenly there was a heartbeat. Suddenly there was a pulse rate in action. I suppose, the heart monitor showed breathing in action. If the lines on the heart monitor were straight, they immediately turned into zigzags. My brainstem received unknown strength and returned back to work. Yeah, my brainstem fought, and life came back in it. Just as a computer breaks down, and a human being is able to repair it again; yeah, my brain broke down, and through God's mercy, my breathing had been repaired. Both my heartbeat and my breathing were turned back on again.

Therefore, were my brain was once pronounced deceased, it now lives. I had no idea or I DID NOT KNOW that drugs would cause drastic danger unto my brain. I had no idea that the taste of death would be an experience for me. I have actually taste a portion of death for real. I must tell you this; death does not taste good.

Although, my heart rate became active again, my cerebellum, which is the mover of the body (limbs), was inactive. The reason why my cerebellum had been inactive is that, I went into a coma immediately following a first restored heartbeat. In a coma, the body does not move nor does it shifts. The body is at a sit still mode until a person comes up out of the coma. Although, my brainstem (alert center) had put up a good fight, it had not enough strength to awake me from this coma. Therefore, I suffered going into a cardiac arrest. When I say "arrest", I truly mean arrest, because going into a coma is like being cuffed in a deep sleep. Wow, drugs finally damaged my brain functions.

The deep sleep (coma) that the power of drugs put me in is similar to the activity of two people in a fistfight. In my fighting days, I hold a brilliant record of 8-0, with 8 knockdowns. Easily, I was able to handle each fight. I was able to see my opponent face to face, and duck from any thrown punches. Therefore, I was able to block most punches that were being physically thrown at me. As I studied my opponent fighting style, I used mental judgments before I threw my lethal combination punch. However, the opponents I am up against now are drugs. It's my brain against drugs one on one. I did not see the punch from drugs coming, and when it came, it hit me hard.

Drugs hit me with its one two-combination punch. The one two-combination punch that drugs hit me with, were heroin and pills. They hit me in the brainstem so hard that my heart stopped beating for 11 minutes. From the punch of drugs, I was also forced into a coma for 10 days. I have never heard or seen a man throw a combination punch, and from the punches, the opponent dies. However, when you allow dope intoxicants to operate in your brain, when they hit you, you will be hit you hard, and with all its might. Drugs have created another experience in my life. This incident was in the making for ten years, and I did not see this event coming. Another act from drug's creation has just prevailed. Another act from the wicked ninja had just been performed. Drugs are very powerful!

Drugs have a powerful punch; when they hit you, you will be hit at an unexpected moment. You might not be hit today; you might not be hit tomorrow, but it is a guarantee that the punches from drugs are going to be felt soon. Sadly, to say, but sometimes it takes a horrible punch from drugs and wickedness, for some us to understand that drugs are aiming to hit our life holder (the brain). When drugs punches on the body, there are no if's, and's or but's about it, because you will know that it was the strength and power from the upper cut of drugs. Take me as your prime example. When my heartbeat froze (stopped), an unexpected uppercut from drugs did that.

While my brain was in the coma, many dreams traveled through my mind. For some reason, I thought the dreams I was having in the coma, were events of reality. Even after awaking from the coma, my mind was in a confused state. Knowing reality from fantasy, I had no understanding of. Many dreams people have can be fantasy, and some can actually be reality.

In chapter 5 (Drugs Controlling The Intelligent Human Brain), it says, when people intake Ecstasy or LSD, their brain can be sent into a condition of not knowing the difference from reality and fantasy. In other words, when people intake ecstasy or LSD, something can happen unto them and cause their thoughts be to no different from mine when I awoke from the coma. After I awoke from the coma, I thought the dreams I had while in it were events of real life. Yeah, the ecstasy or LSD user's thoughts will be the same. A drug user do not have to awake from a coma to loose his mental awareness, the only thing he has to do, is keep using drugs, and his insights will someday be compared to a man awaking from a coma.

I have a miracle that I would like to share with you. The miracle is about my coma experience. I was told that my mother would ask me questions while I was in this deep sleep (coma). My mother would ask me to respond unto her by the movement of my hand. She would ask me, "to squeeze her hand if I can hear her voice". I suppose I heard her voice, because family members told me I squeezed her hand when asked. Since I did squeeze her hand, the cerebellum in my brain (limb controller) had just enough strength to perform that act. Of course, I did not squeeze her hand tightly, but she felt a slight squeeze on her hand. I am sure from that little squeezing of the hand brought a great reaction of joy into my mom's heart. Actually, since I did squeeze my mother's hand softly when asked, even in the coma, I still had a little mental sense to understand words. Maybe it was a sign from God showing my mother that her only son is going to be just fine. However, she still had to keep the faith, and keep praying, so that more miracles would be revealed and performed.

When a caring mother has a child facing death, there is no one on earth that will wail and moan to God the way she will. Of some sort, it was as if my life was under the power and decisions of my mother. My mother answered all questions from the doctors concerning my health. If the doctors had horrible news concerning my condition and life, the weight of it, and pressure from it was cast upon her shoulders. I cannot leave out the fact that God's mercy has been the greatest helping tool of power in this situation. God's mercy has been brilliant unto me; and much of my health success so far is because mother prayed to the God that she now has.

When the doctors thought, I would not live to see the next day, or make it through the night, mother prayed, my family prayed, and friends prayed as well. When the doctors thought I would be brain damaged for the rest of my life, mother prayed. Everything the doctors thought that would become a part of my life, if it was negative, my mama prayed against it all. Information that was given to my

238

mother from the doctors, if it didn't sound good unto her ears, then it did not sound good unto the ears of her God as well. Remember, mother was praying, therefore, she was communicating with God, and hearing his voice.

The doctors questioned my mother; what do you want to do? Do you want to take care of him for the rest of his life? Shall we pull the plug, or not? Not only did doctors have thoughts of pulling the plug on my life, but also, they consulted with my mother about amputating my leg. Wow, you mean to tell me that drugs put me in a position were thoughts of leg amputation was a suggestion. If amputation of my leg would have become an experience for my body and life, I have no idea, how I would have handled that situation. However, I thank God I never found out what life would be like having a missing limb. Nevertheless, if I had to live life with one leg, I am sure that I would have adapted to life, because "**I am one strong man**", even if I have to say so myself.

In a sense, my mother was like a female Moses. Just as Moses went to God to get a word concerning the people, my mother went to God to get a word concerning my life. If her God said, "**Brian Irons** is going to be "well", then it was a done deal. I think I need her God in my life too. Since God gave me a second chance in life, I need him in my life as well. I must grab a hold onto this God that my mother has, and find out what he wants me to do.

I remember a TV commercial that would come on the TV screen every now and then. This commercial talked about drugs, and spoke about things that dope will do to the intelligent human brain. The commercial was trying to shove fear in the minds of people concerning drug usage. In this commercial, there was a pan, which had two eggs in it frying. The message the commercial was sending out to the world is this; when someone put drugs in his or her brain, the chemicals from it, will begin to cook and fry the brain cells, as an egg does in a heated skillet. A person cannot physically feel his or her brain cells frying, but the example is somewhat true, because drugs do cook away the cells in the brain. People might not feel brain cells disintegrating at the point of usage, because it is a hidden mental performance. However, in due time, as a person continues to get the brain high on drugs, nerve cells will gradually began to be subtracted from his or her brain. A person cannot hide from what drugs are soon to do to the brain. The only way a person can dodge drugs future set up is to stop using them.

As long as you are inhaling the death helper (drug) into your lungs, dope is going to get the victory out of your life. Do not think consequences or repercussions aren't going to approach your living. Drugs are your wickedness, and your wickedness must suffer the consequences. Your consequences are the tragedies that drugs have taken you through. From every drug encounter, a wicked experience will be chartered into one's life. Obey the commercials on TV that speaks against drugs.

While I was in the coma unconsciousness, the doctors thought if I ever receive any kind of awareness in the brain, that I still would be a vegetable. From my mental understanding of what a vegetable actually is; a vegetable is grown from a seed that has been planted into the ground. Then the seed grows into a food product. The food product is filled with great nutrients, and vitamins & minerals. After the seed grows and becomes a food product, it is then washed or cleansed. After it has been cleansed or purified, it is then eaten in a meal by a human being. If a vegetable is a plant, and is to be eaten by people, then a vegetable knows nothing about life. If drugs had kept my brain in a vegetable state, I would have been just like that plant (vegetable), knowing nothing about life. Just like when people eat vegetables to gain inner strength to stay healthy, drugs had been eating on my brain's organs, trying to turn it into a vegetable, and I DID NOT KNOW it. If a vegetable state had become assessed into my brain, I would have been living life not knowing anything about my surroundings. Wow, drugs actually led me to experience a damaging tragedy such as this. Thank you again God for your mercy, which has brought my brain from a vegetable state of condition.

If my brain would have become the vegetable that drugs had been eating on, when my brainstem had stopped from its breathing, at that particular time, drugs had a lovely meal. Night and day drugs were having supper with my brain's organs until there was none left to eat. For 10 years, drugs had been eating on my brain's organs on a daily basis. Marijuana, cocaine, heroin, alcohol, Tylenols, and codeine pills, were all eating a meal, and my brain cells were the dish. From high school until now, I allowed my brain to become a 3-course meal a day to drugs. Therefore, drugs were eating cells in my brain for breakfast, lunch, and dinner. However, on July 26, drug chemicals ate on my brain cells, until all my cells became immobile. After my brainstem (the breathing center) ceased from its God given power, drug intoxicants had nothing more to eat. Drugs will eat on your brain until an illness is registered, or until death comes into your mental existence. If you keep putting drugs into your brain, someday soon, many of your brain cells will become a vegetable because they will not be in use anymore. That is the utmost plan that drugs desire to do unto all its users. People actually go purchase a chemical product that has the power to destroy their brain cells.

Let me clarify something right quick. All doctors, who have earned their physician's degree, many of them know what they are talking about. When doctors say, "a person is going to be a vegetable, they know what they are talking about". Then when the person comes out, and not in a vegetable state, that does not mean the doctor was wrong. In my situation, actually, from anatomy study, I was supposed to be a vegetable, but God's power through his mercy changed my mental situation around. So people of the earth, stop saying doctors don't know what they are talking about. Stop trying to make doctors look bad, because God's mercy can make any physician look like he does not know his study, when in fact he does. I wanted to stand up for the doctor's in the world, because people have been putting them down for years. I also will say this; hey DOC, know your medical studies.

While I was in the hospital, I really did not know why I was here in the first place. I did some drugs with the fellows one day, and woke up 10 days later. After I woke up from this coma, I DID NOT KNOW what was going on or why I was here? Imagine you waking up 10 days later after being put to sleep for any reason. That is what the power of drugs will do unto its users. Drug users will put its user in a situation that will cause them not to know anything about what's going on. I do realize that many people have been put in horrible situation because of the handling of drugs; however, the worst has yet to come.

I remember when I was in the coma; many friends and relatives came by to visit me. They explained unto me that I was looking like a human being that appears to weigh more than 200lb. I have never weighed more than 165 lbs in my life. Therefore, as I was positioned in the hospital, in this coma, I appeared to be a huge man. Maybe drugs were trying to expand my brain and body until my flesh stretched and leaked out blood. I was so huge that a couple of friends did not recognize me when they came to visit me.

I heard that, a group of friends came to the hospital, to view my body while it was in the coma. They thought the front desk clerk had given them the wrong room number. The front desk clerk did give them the right room number, however, my body expanded and swelled up to the point were I was physically unrecognizable. Drugs actually altered my countenance. Drugs finally did it to me; they wanted my brain to become deceased, or out of order. My reader, if you would have seen what my friends and family saw, you probably would have thought there was no hope for me. Truly, I looked like a man whose brain and life was going to be "out of order" forever.

Out of order! Did I say, "out of order"? The last time I saw or read the phrase, "out of order", it was on a vending machine filled with sodas. Well, I suppose the "out of order" phrase is the truth because drugs did knock my brain functions out of order. For the 11 minutes when my heart stopped, my brain had broken, and became out of order.

When people put drugs into their brains, they just never know when their brains will suffer damage, and be compared to a vending machine. Just as vending machines becomes out of order unexpectedly, your brain can become out of order unexpectedly too. Somehow, and someday soon, drugs are going to knock a functioning part of your brain out of order. Actually, if you are a drug user, I guaranteed you that many of the brain's cells have already been knocked out of order.

Actually, even right now as you are reading this book, many of you drug user's brain cells have already been destroyed. When certain brain cells have been destroyed, other cells in the brain accommodate for that which has been destroyed. The sad thing about it is the fact that you don't even know it. Doctors cannot detect, when brain cells have been destroyed, because there are millions of them.

When certain cells in the brain have been destroyed, other living cell will fill in the gap. A cell that deals with your memory, if destroyed, another cell that deals with another function in the brain tries to fill in the gap. Cells that are for thinking, needs to stay with the thinking. A cell that deals with memory does not need to go over to the thinking center to give support. The cells that leave its spot to help out in another area of the brain, is in a place where it was not born to be. Just as it is hard for a person to chew food when teeth are missing from the mouth, in the same sense, it is hard for a person to think properly when cells are missing from the cerebrum (the thinker). As certain cells suffice strength to help in another area of the brain; soon it becomes worn out, and then a person's mind is sent backwards. Say no to drugs, it is for the living of your brain's cells. Do not send your God created brain cells in phases of traumatic injury.

At this particular time, I was being fed through my stomach with a feeding tube. For 3 whole months, my body was eating liquid food. Being fed food through a machine was weird, but I needed to eat in order to survive. My cerebellum (limb mover and coordinator) was in action, but its strength was still very weak. Not only that, but also, my inner body was not even strong enough to handle heavy foods, such as meat. Therefore, liquid foods became my food while I was in the coma, and even when I awoke from it. Even after I awoke from the coma, breakfast, lunch, and dinner was served to me through a feeding tube.

I DID NOT KNOW drugs had such power to send me into a coma. Usually, when a person's brain is sent into a coma, it has been hit by something. Whether the brain has been hit by stroke, a serious car wreck, or a hard object has struck the head tremendously. Since my brain incident is not from the result of a car wreck, nor was I hit on the head viscously with an object, drugs have physically hit my brain all by itself. Because of me allowing drugs to drive my life, it's almost as if drugs have driven my brain into a brick wall. As of now, I feel like my life is completely messed up. I have to be a patient in a hospital because drugs thrashed my brain functions out of whack. Nevertheless, this harsh incident happened unto me, while I was under the mercies of God. I am starting to believe that the people who are in the world actually need more than just mercy alone.

In the hospital, there was a Foley Catheter connected to the private part of my body, which drained fluids from it. The Foley Catheter was connected to my private area because I DID NOT KNOW when it was time for me to use the restroom. My brain lost its mental mobility of letting me know when it is time to use the restroom. The "drug beating" evilly attacked my brain so greatly that the normal bodily procedures, such as, using the restroom had been stripped from my brain's knowledge. The doctors and nurses had my big over grown self in pamper, or diapers (yeah, that is funny to me too). Drugs deprived me of my adulthood. Because of my drug usage, I became an infant all over again. Drugs sent the mind of a 24-year-old man, into the mind and body of a 24-month-old baby. My physical strength (cerebellum) was going through the torture of what drugs had done unto it. Therefore, physicians, friends, nurses, relatives had to do everything for me, and when I say "everything", I absolutely mean "everything". From all the fun that I was having while associating with drugs, <u>I DID NOT KNOW</u> that so much fun would turn into so much disaster. Nevertheless, here I am in the hospital, sick, and going through mental harms from what drugs did unto my brain.

At this particular time, I wasn't able to do much for myself. The only thing I was able to do in the hospital was to lie down and allow nurses to come in: clean my feeding tube, check my vital signs, and plug more electrical operating devices to my body. If I can remember correctly, there were about 5 to 6 machines monitoring my body's health and condition. I was so sick and weak, that I could not even move my own neck and head. I couldn't sit up on the bed to relax. I am sure there pain was in my body, but I didn't know what it was.

I remember watching television, and the remote control was chained to the bars on the bed. I did not have the strength to handle the little remote controlled. The remote would slip out of my hands, and hang from the bed as it was on a chain. My cerebellum was not strong enough to close my hands to grip the remote control. I was very miserable in the days of being in this hospital. In life, I was use to doing any and everything for myself when needed, and now my life has turned into this type of living. Wow, drugs finally damaged my brain's functions!

While I was in this hospital for a about a month and a half, it was time for me to start doing a few things on my own. My physical strength was still very feeble. The coma zapped much strength from my brain's power. Well, actually drugs were the workers that initiated this physical attack, because I am going through physical ailments all because of them (drugs). It seems like my physical strength went another world, and never to be found.

It was very hard for me to perform physical tasks, such as eating One day; I was eating a bowl of cereal. As I was eating the cereal, my strength was being testing in a task such as this. Taking the spoon to the bowl to scoop up a little cereal was a true job of hard work and labor. When I would dip the spoon into the bowl of cereal, and then bring the food to my mouth to eat it, it would fall back into the bowl. Slowly I was able to lift up the spoon full of cereal, but guiding it to my mouth to eat it was the tough part. The cerebellum (limb controller) in my brain was still screwed up from the violent attack that drugs brutally spanked on it. At this particular, I knew nothing about the functions of the brain, therefore, I DID NOT KNOW, which part of my mental was suffering from this brutal drug attack.

The occipital lobe in my brain deals with vision; therefore, since I was able to see the bowl of cereal, this lobe had been activated. Even though I had sight, my bodily movements were very slow. As nurses would come into my room, I began look at them strange because I DID NOT KNOW who they were. I had no knowledge or understanding that those people were nurses. Drugs did my brain so bad to the point were, I did have sight, but I had no understanding about my present surroundings. The lobe in the brain that helps a person to recognize his surrounds are the parietal lobes, therefore, this lobe in my brain had been bruised. I am stuck in a position were I cannot do anything for myself at all.

For so many years, drugs became a companion or a special part of my being. Wherever I journeyed, drugs went along with me. Either dope was in my possession or in my brain; however, they were with me somehow, someway. Even when I went to the basketball court to hoop, with me being high from a chemical control substance, drug's power was present too. When I went to see my probation officer, drugs were there with me too. Even when I was attending court, drugs were there too. There were not too many places or areas that a drug high was not afflicting its influential power in my brain and body. When a person does any kind of drug, the ingredients from the dope stay in the anatomy (brain & body) for days, weeks, and sometimes months. Before this incident, I never went an entire 5 weeks, without having a chemical control substance operating in my brain. Well, during the 4 weeks I was locked up in jail just might be the longest time I ever went without surging drugs into my brain. Out of ten years of using drugs, 4 weeks was the longest time I can remember ever stayed clean from dope.

Anyway, while I was in the hospital, I realized this is the worst incident that ever happened to me in my life. No experience in my life can be compared to this dope tragedy. This tragedy was horribly disastrous. The process of having to learn everything all over again was mentally hurting me. Not being able to leave the hospital at my own power and will, brought great grief upon my heart and in my mind.

While I was in the hospital, people told me that I spitted on many visitors. I was told that I spitted on nurses as they were doing their job of taking care of me. In order for me to do something of that nature, I must have been possessed with a demon. Spitting on people is truly nasty, however, my brain was sick, and evil spirits were using me to be that way. I honestly believe I was demon possessed because of the attitude that proceeded from mental powers. Some people who came to visit me would stand afar off from my bed, fearing to come close to me. I guess they were thinking that I might spit on them too. At some point, it was as if the movie exorcist came alive in my life.

This accident happened unto me when I was at the young age of 24. I was very young as you can see. The age of 24 is a very young age for a person to suffer in any kind of harsh physical disaster. Actually, any age, is a horrible age to suffer from a tragedy such as this. If my brainstem and heart had not started to react again, or no pulse reaction became mobile, I would have died at very young age of 24. If I now live to see the age of 90, that would have been 66 years of living, I would have missed from being present upon the earth.

As I said once before, drug's job is to kill you, steal from you, and destroy you. At any given moment, those three activities (kill, steal, or destroy) can become your experience. If it concerns the drug money, or the drug's mental addiction, one way or another, a person's life will suffer. The age of a person means nothing when it comes to dope disasters. Even under the age of 13, drugs will hurt a child's life. Drugs do not care about your age, or a person's living background.

Who would have ever thought that drugs would be so powerful to have the strength to cause a person too suffer brain damage. Who would have ever thought that drugs could be so breath taking, that breath would actually be taking from someone for 11 minutes? Who would have ever thought that drugs would harm someone and cause that individual to be placed in hospitals for months? Who would have ever thought that heroin and pills would feel so good to the brain, then act against it, and send the brain into a coma? Who would have ever thought that drugs had the power to paralyze a person's limb? Who would have ever thought that smoking one drug product (weed) would open up a door and lead the same individual to experiencing about several other different types of drugs? Who would have ever thought that drugs could take athletic talents that were once attached to a person's brain? Well, I never thought that drugs could do any of the above actions that were just asked, or mention, but as of now, I have been made to be a true believer, because drugs it all to me. I am convinced that drugs can do almost anything that pertains to negativity. If you engage into drugs, then all these things can happen unto you. Say No to Chemical usage!

I would like to give a written example of the word "rape". First, I want to write unto you what the word "rape" means. The word rape means, to take or have physical intercourse with a person without his or her approval. It also means, to seize a person while applying sexual actions.

Most rape victims, who are captured and held down for sexual pleasure, are usually women. A woman does not want to have sex with this man, but he drives his private part into her vagina anyway. This evil act is done by physical abuse. Rapes are committed through physical brutal strength, which is called, "assault".

Well, look at the position that drug's put my body in. Although, I was not sexually assaulted, I was still physically abuse. Drugs snatched my bodily strength from me without my consent or approval. Drugs laid me in a position, and performed physical sickening pleasures with my body without my permission; although, in high school is the place were I gave drug intoxicants permission to work in my brain, but to go beyond that point, drugs took things farther. Drug intoxicants were operating inside of my brain, and performed intercourse with it. Of course, the intercourse was not sexual; however, it was an intercourse of mental abuse. Just as a rapist has sex with a woman, drugs had an intercourse with my brain. Well, maybe I cant call it rape, however, when I kept on putting drugs into my brain, I was giving drugs the right away to do unto me whatever it pleases. Not only was physical strength taken from me, but also, my talents have been raped as well. Everything has been taken away from me. My talent, my skills, and my bodily strength have been snatched up and out of my body. Yeah, drugs performed another skill in my life, by abusing and raping my brain.

Drugs powerfully took a big part of my manhood from me; drugs have taken every bit of physical strength I once attained. If drugs have ever taken anything from your physical stature, consider yourself a victim that has witness a "drug rape". Anytime drugs take something away from your mental or physical status, you have been successfully raped. Remember, rape means to take by force; therefore, if drugs have ever taken anything from you, it was taken by force, which means you have been raped.

Usually, when an act of "rape" has been committed, the rapist can be sued or prosecuted in the court of law. There are many laws in the script that cover charges for acts of rape. "Assault and battery" is one of the charges that a rapist can be charged with. Remember; there are about 4 to 5 laws that a person can be charged with when caught performing an act of wickedness, such as "rape". Well, I feel the need to charge drugs with, "assault and battery".

In a rape case, an "assault" took place when the woman was physically attacked. The "battery" happened when the man used physical strength, and held the woman down to perform sexual acts. Therefore, assault and battery is one of the preliminary charges the rapist can be sued or charged for in the court of law. Although, I was attacked physically (beaten in the brain) and held down (coma), I do not have a charge case for the committed act that was performed on me.

If I could take drugs to court, I would sue or charge drugs for "physical abuse", which is "assault and battery". The assault happened when the drugs had violently beaten up on my brain. Yes, it was a violent attack because drugs hit me and sent me into a coma. Not only was I assaulted, but also drug's power went beyond a physical attack and abuse. When my heart had stopped for 11 minutes, drugs actually performed a murder on me. During those 11 minutes of no heartbeat, I was considered dead, so murder is the case that drugs should be charged. Since I am the individual who put drugs inside of my body, which led my heart to stop for 11 minutes, there is none other to charge for the murder but me. There is none other to be charged for the "assault and battery", but me. Yeah, my fingerprints were molded on every drug that was ever put inside of my body; therefore, I am the guilty suspect to be charged with the "assault and battery" judgment. Death itself was truly my judgment, and most definitely, I was found guilty, and sentenced to die. Nevertheless, God had mercy on me one more time, and here I am still in a land among the living.

Using drugs have caused me to taste a portion of "self-destruction. Once I allowed drugs to operate in my brain, as well as in my body, the route that leads to self-destruction was in the process of happening. From the beginning, when I first began to use drugs (in high school) and up until now, the stages, which led to self-destruction, were linked to all of my experiences. Every drug chemical that I freely swished into my brain, were all links, which led to self-destruction experiences. As I was using drugs, I was self-destroying my own brain and body. It was me who willing used drugs, but the hazardous chemicals from it, caused me to check in at a local hospital. I allowed drugs to perform so drastically in my life until a vast portion of damage was done unto my brain. Now that I think about it, all of my dope experiences could have been prevented, if only I would have left drugs alone when I had the opportune chance. Then the hospital would not have been an appointed experience for me, and my brain would not have been a meal for self-destruction. Nevertheless, after my brain and body tasted drugs, physical death and destruction became my dessert. Yeah, God gave unto me that which I desert (deserved).

Once a person put drugs inside of the body, that individual has just made an agreement with drugs to become his or her physician. Once a person uses drugs, it goes into the brain and begins a task of surgical operation. Drugs will harm your body, rather than soothe it or heal it. When you put drugs in your brain and body, you have just given drugs the amplified power to take care of you through its magical and wicked powers.

When people go to the hospital for serious mental or physical issues, which may require surgery, usually a licensed doctor or physician is called upon. A license doctor is qualified to perform a number of surgeries. Surgery sometimes will help eliminate mental or physical distractions from a person's body. Let's say, surgery is required. Once the physician receives a verbal agreement or a written signature from the client, the doctor may then begin to perform the operation. After the statement of agreement has been agreed upon, the physician now has the right a way to carry out the procedures to perform the surgery.

Many surgeries will be required for the client to be put into a deep sleep. After the sleep has taken place, the physician then dives surgical devices into the body as he performs this surgery. Depending upon the type of surgery, which is about to be performed, anesthesia (numbness) to a certain part of the body might be one of the choices. Even a state of unconsciousness is required for certain surgeries. Nevertheless, when surgery is to be performed, the brain or body is about to be re-configured.

Look at my situation; I allowed drugs to be a

physician to me. Just as a physician puts his clients to sleep for surgery, drugs have put me to sleep (coma) in the same likeness. The doctor shoots dope (anesthesia) into the client's body, and I shot dope (inhaled or snorted) into my body as well. Just as a physician goes into the brain or body and reconstructs its functions, drugs went into my brain & body and reconstructed mine (brain damage) (paralyzed my left leg). This drug surgery was very brutal. I allowed drugs to become a physician unto me, and yes, surgery was performed. Therefore, from the doctor, which I call drugs; drugs damage my brain's functions by its surgical powers. Wow, drugs actually performed a surgery on my brain and body.

People put drugs in their brain and body as if the dope is their physician. When a person says, "I need a joint, cigarette or any other type of chemical" to calm his or her nerves, that individual is using a chemical substance as a doctor or healer. From the power of drugs, that person has been forced to believing that chemical controlled substances will heal bad nerves or pluck out intense stress. Therefore, a person puts chemicals into the brain to perform the duty as a physician. Drugs do not relieve you from stress. The only performance that drugs does; is to feed the brain its addiction that has been plagued inside of it. With every drug abuse, an addiction will spring forth. After the addiction has entered into the brain, the person now uses drugs in the place of a physician, but he does not know it. Marijuana and other drugs caused me to believe that I needed them in order to be entertained and feel good in life. Nevertheless, I allowed drugs to portray a role in my life, as if they were a physician.

Many people in the world have been tricked to believing that they need drugs in the life in order to function properly. That's how I felt when I became addicted to marijuana. Since people in the world think or believe that they need drugs to function properly, I think they all need to find another remedy to support them. Drugs have the power to force people to believe in falsehood. Before a person has ever put a drug inside of the body, he or she was doing just fine in life without it. You were able to think without drugs, you were physically active without drugs, and now all of a sudden you feel the need that drugs helps you function properly. I think people have forgotten how life felt before drugs were put inside of the brain. Well, I have been tricked just as the rest of the world has. However, I now know that drugs have a powerful character that will pull your mental mind away from reality to believing in fantasy. Every time you use drugs, to eliminate stress or whatever, you have been forced to believing in "fantasy". You can function properly without drugs and chemicals!

I realize a person does not have to be in the hospital to be declared sick. The only thing a person has to do is put drugs in his or her brain, and that is the sickness right there. Only sick people, such as myself, prances drugs into the brain. When I first put a drug (marijuana) in my brain and body, I was a sick individual to do something like that. I had to be a sick-minded man because I knew that drugs were unhealthy for my body, but I put them inside of me anyway. Therefore, even before I went into the coma, I was already sick in the head. I guess I was beyond sick; I was a psycho because I introduced about seven other different chemicals to my brain. If you are putting drugs in your brain and body, you are a psycho, just as I was.

When people in the world find out that a person either has murdered or have rape someone, they label that individual as a psycho. Well, in the same sense, if you are putting drugs in your brain and body, then you are a psycho, too. I think it is psychotic for anyone to put drugs in the brain, and then think to have fun while being intoxicated from them. People do not consider themselves as being psychos when they put drugs in their brain because they think it is a normal thing to do. Why do people (especially me) intake drug, and we know they will harm the body in the end. Therefore, every time you put drugs in your body, consider yourself a psycho or a person that is a pre-meditated killer. That is exactly what you are doing, killing your own self. We are nothing but psychos because we are killing our own personal being. That is what psychos do; they seek personal gain to satisfy their evil desire. There is no good profit in using drugs. However, as a person uses them, psychotic tendencies will be the person's life reward.

Chapter 10
Hospitals, Physical Rehab and other People's Injuries

St. Louis University is the first medical building I was transported to after this grieving drug tragedy occurred in my brain. In this hospital, things were very hectic and sad. I was bed ridden at Saint Louis University hospital for about 2 months. At this hospital, my therapy needs were done while being in bed. Although, I slept in St. Louis Hospital for only two months, it seemed like it was forever.

For a very long time, I thought the reason for me being in a hospital was because of a car wreck. While I was in the coma, I had dreams about being in a car wreck. All the times, doctors would ask me, "Do you remember or know what had happen to you"? After being asked, my reply was, "I was in a car wreck on Lafayette and Jefferson near the library. Yeah, my mind was really messed up in the days of being in St. Louis hospitals.

After two months had expired at St. Louis University Hospital, I was then transported to a second hospital. This second hospital is called, "Bethesda". The St. Louis University Hospital and Bethesda Hospital were both connected one to the other. My treatment in these two hospitals was the toughest times of coping. Many times, my eyes leaked gallons of tears in the presence of family and friends. I was so hurt from within. My heart could not understand why.

After the two hospitals in St. Louis did their fair share of providing my brain and body with treatment, it was time to go to another place for more attention. I was then transported to a third hospital. This 3rd hospital was located out of town. It was still located in the state of Missouri, but it was stationed in another city. Therefore, because of my drug usage, my brain and body was schedule to relocate to another city. Mount Vernon Rehab Center is my next destination for more physical and mental rehabbing.

This is the second time that I chose to do something, and was sent out of town. The first time my brain chose to do something, which was to sale drugs, I was caught doing it, and was shipped out of town to a state penitentiary. This time, which is the second time, I am about to be shipped to Mount Vernon Rehab Center.

All because of wickedness through drugs, the name **Brian Irons** has been registered throughout the state of Missouri. Wherever my brain goes, my name follows as well. The name **Brian Irons** had registered throughout the city of St. Louis, and the state of Missouri. The name **Brian Irons** had been summons to court a number of times. The name **Brian Irons** has even registered in drug rehab centers. The name **Brian Irons** has registered in the prison system. The name **Brian Irons** had a warrant for an arrest. The name **Brian Irons** had registered in the Halfway House. The name **Brian Irons** became wickedly great in St. Louis. Most importantly, the name **Brian Irons** had registered in an 11-minute death experience. The name **Brian Irons** has been everywhere in the state of Missouri. It seems like, names are very important in this life. However, follow me in this story, and I will explain unto you how important names really are. You need to know this. However, my name (**Brian Irons**) is about to check in at Mount Vernon Rehab Center.

From St. Louis, to Mount Vernon Rehab Treatment Center, it was a five-hour road drive. To me, it was far; it seemed like we'd never get there. My parents both drove me to this rehab center.

The third hospital (Mount Vernon Rehab Center) that I am being driven too; these people specializes in rehabbing people who have suffered head injuries, or serious bodily injuries. These people have dedicated their selves to learning and helping people whose bodies have suffered greatly. If this hospital cannot help an injured brain, then most likely, that individual's mental status is far beyond the help of physical therapy. Although, my brain injury was far beyond human help in the beginning stages, however, God has performed a merciful miracle upon me. God has done for me what a human being can't.

Finally, I made it to Mount Vernon Rehab Center. Before submitting in rehab an evaluation concerning my condition was done. This evaluation is an assessment, which will determine the type of therapy needs required to get my brain and body in better condition. Not only will this evaluation enlightened the doctors of my physical therapy needs, but also, the decision concerning the length of time for me to abide in this place was determined as well. After the doctors and therapists went over my medical report from St. Louis, they suggested I needed 5 months of physical and cognitive therapy in this facility. For the next 5 month, I will be living in Mount Vernon Rehab Center.

This drug encounter happened on July 26. I went home on March 25. Since I was a patient in the St. Louis hospitals for 3 months, and will now be in Mount Vernon for 5 month; a total of 8 months of is the length of time I've lived in hospitals. As you have just read, I have visited three hospitals for almost the total time of a complete year. ¾ s of the year I was stuck in buildings having mental and physical therapy. I was here in Mount Vernon on Christmas, and even on my birthday. However, I was not thinking about a birthday, I was thinking about going home, and getting better.

During my 5-months at Mount Vernon, the doctors and therapists were astonished after they read my medical report from the St. Louis. The 11-minute heart failure persuaded the doctors, and physical therapist to believing that I was truly a "special" case. I suppose that is the reason why I had two therapists walking along with me in the halls. I always wondered why the entire crew of therapists would watch me walk down the hall, while I was walking with therapy instructors. I guess from the conclusive report from my story, they were all so amazed to see me recover so fast. I felt like a celebrity in this place.

The reason why two therapists were appointed unto

me is because; when I would walk with the therapist, I would lean too far on my right side. One therapist was on my left side, and the other was on my right. My right leg was stronger. I trusted the right side more than my left (paralyzed side). I would be scared to walk on my left ankle because I could not feel the pressure when stepping down on the floor. My brain is not familiar with this kind of walking mode. I was very scared of stumbling or loosing my balance, and then hitting the floor. Nevertheless, I thank God that I never fell while walking in therapy.

Walking was a very hard task for me to perform. From my drug usage causing an injury to the sensation of my left leg, the left ankle has suffered paralysis. My walking balance was very poor. From this injury, the left side of my body is the side I had to work on. The paralysis mainly attacked my leg left (knee down). My thigh muscles do flex, which is a good sign that I can at least move a muscle. I was not able to walk long distance because of my lame ankle. Due to this paralysis, my walking has become slow, shaky, and uncoordinated. When my mental status came to the realization that my left leg will be a bit of lame, I knew I had to work hard in order to get better.

As I was being rehabbed at Mount Vernon Rehab Center, the therapists were doing a great job of rehabbing my body. Not only that, but also, they were doing a great job at teaching my mind how to cope with life from a brain injured point of view. If it had not been for Mount Vernon therapists, I would not have recovered the way I did.

My cerebrum (the thinker) had to plan and compromise with my cerebellum (leg mover). This way of walking was completely different. My brain was not used to this type of walking. It must be so true that, my cerebellum was familiar with a certain pattern of guiding my legs while walking. Then, suddenly, my cerebellum had to re-adjust its ways when it came to walking. What I am trying to say is this; my cerebellum has been operating in my brain guiding and coordinating my walking in a normal way for 24 years. Now, my cerebellum had to re-adjust itself because of this unfamiliar condition in my leg. Actually, my cerebrum, which is the thinker, had to think of new techniques and new patterns, as I was learning how to walk all over again.

Before this accident happened, I never had to think before walking. Now a day, I have to "think" first before taking steps. Before my brain suffered an injury, I walked willingly whenever desired. Usually, I stepped out there with my leg, began to walk, and never had to think about it. Although, I now have to think before I walk, my cerebellum is doing magnificently great.

Sometimes, on certain pavement outdoors, I have to think which leg to step out with first. Its not that I'm confused, however, certain pavement are unleveled and uneven. Therefore, I need to be careful about the leg I decide to step with first. I have lost my balance so many times on certain pavements, and almost fell. Actually, throughout the years, I have fallen probably a 100 times, but I thank God, I never been injured.

I have walked in many places, and came across floors, which had slight hills. If I had never had an ailment in my left leg, then, I am sure I would have never recognized uneven floors and pavements. I walked into a building one day, and the floor was uneven. It was like; a hill was in the floor. I was shifted off balance from the hill. Many people probably do not know that a slight hill is in that floor. The hill is a very slight one, and is non-noticeable to the human eye. However, only a person with a walking disability will feel that the pavement is uneven. My balancing while walking has become so sensitive; I can walk on any pavement, and discover that the floor or ground is slanted.

Listen, friends of mine, and people who are in the world today, stay away from drugs because you need your brain's power to keep you walking at a normal pace. People do not understand that the intelligent human brain is the performer that causes the legs to walk. The brain is so important; we fell to realize that it is our "overall" and "utmost" help in life, even when performing a simple task, such as walking.

I remember when I did not have the desire to come to this rehab center because of the weakened condition drugs had put my body in. I was scared to leave my hometown to go to another area to dwell. The reason why I was scared is because; I knew I could not protect myself from physical danger if anything happens to jump off. Besides, <u>I DID NOT KNOW</u> anyone at Mount Vernon Rehab Center. I suppose my mind was still thinking about how the streets treated me. However, I am truly glad I went and gave this rehab center a chance to rehabilitate my brain and body. If I had not attended Mount Vernon Rehab Center, I would have missed learning needful and helpful tips that are needed for everyday living, from a brain-injured point of view. Therefore, I needed to be here; so that the therapists and doctors could enlighten me on how to live after a harsh injury to the brain has occurred.

Before attending Mount Vernon Center, the surgeons in St. Louis took the feeding tube out of my stomach. My inner being had gotten stronger. Therefore, my body was receiving great physical strength as well. During rehabilitation, as I was getting stronger, I began to eat normal again; meaning the food was not dropping back into the bowl after I lifted it up to my mouth with a spoon or with a fork.

While I was living in Mount Vernon Rehab Center, I learned that patience is a vital asset to physical recovery, as well to everyday living. The physical status my body had been complied too, patience was the work that could only be displayed. Every since this injury has occurred, I had to wait on other people to do things for me, and it was hard tolerating such. I am use to doing any and everything for myself. When I had gained mental sense to allow patience to endure, I became relaxed in heart. I realized, I must sit, be patient, and let the patience of life take its course.

I was not able to walk on the treadmill machine to do leg exercises. The treadmill's speed was to fast for me. The physical therapists adjusted the treadmill to the slowest speed possible, and it was still too fast.

Neither could I ride the bike, which was a leg-exercising machine. My brain did recognize that I was on a bike, and that was a good thing. My procedural memory still held that taught bike-riding data within it. Therefore, my procedural memory is okay in that particular area. Although, the bike was hard for me to ride, I did remember that peddling is needed in order for it to operate. Since the bike was hard for me to ride, due to this paralysis, I never rode it while at Mount Vernon. No wait, I did ride it one time. The therapist tied my left ankle to the pedal with a brace, so I could peddle. Yet, it really did not work.

I want to thank a few therapists who help me get my brain back together: Joe, Mary Lou, Betty, Patty, Melody, and many others, thank you all for your support.

My brain, as well as a few other clients' in this rehab center, had suffered damage too. I sat and watched the therapist explains unto a man over the age of 40 how to ride a bike. This man's brain actually forgot the procedures on how to ride a bike. I am sure before this grown man suffered a head injury; that he rode dozens of bikes in his lifetime. However, in Mount Vernon Rehab Center, his head injury actually caused him to loose already learned bike riding information. He actually forgot how to ride a simple bike. Since past-learned physical activities are stored into the procedural memory, this person suffered an injury that affected that area of the brain. Wow, it is so true, that a personal experience can turn a person's life backwards. If I can remember correctly, I think his brain injury was from a car wreck; drinking and driving.

There is another patient in Mount Vernon I want to write about. This patient is a young man. He was a patient in the rehab center before I became one. When I met him, he was 16 years old. His story or tragedy is very different from my tragedy, but his incident was so serious, that Mount Vernon Rehab Center became a place for registration. No one goes to Mount Vernon, unless a person's brain, and or body have suffered a horrible tragedy.

This young fellow rolled around in a wheelchair.

Actually, 85% of the patients in Mount Vernon used wheelchairs. This 16-year-old fellow had shared his story one day with us all. He told us that he was walking with two of his friends one day. As him and his two friends were walking, they came to a bridge. When they reached the center of the bridged, his two friends physically grabbed him and tossed him off the bridge. As this teenage child fell to the ground, he landed on his head and suffered a injury to the brain. The injury he suffered had caused him to be paralyzed in one of his arms, and in one of his legs. This young man's body was in bad shape. I felt very sorry for what happened to him. Nevertheless, he and his friends were both drug users.

I supposed the two fellows who tossed this teenage boy off the bridge must have tried to kill him. This teenager was walking with some friends one day, and all of a sudden, he was attacked, handled, and tossed off a bridge. A case such as this, the law has about 5 convictions that can be charged upon those 2 men for their wicked deeds done with their hands. Just that fast, and just that quick, the power of wickedness led two men to perform an "assault and battery", or possibly, a 1st degree murder.

I want to throw this paragraph in as a bone for you to bite on. My reader, "drugs will get you one way or the other". If you have drugs in your life, how can you trust your "so call" fellow man (friend)? Your drug-filled friends are the one's who will set you up and turn their backs on you. Sometimes, your enemy is the same individual whom you are passing the joint (weed) too. My second book, which is title, "Thou Shalt Not Have Any Other Gods Besides me" is a great book to read. This book will teach you not to put your trust in humanity, especially people who snug chemicals into their brain.

I never did get the chance to hear the whole conclusion concerning the young man who had been tossed from a bridge. I do not know if it was a robbery, or a pay back from something he did in the past. However, I would like to throw my 2-cent in. Since he did confess that he was a drug user, I am willing to believe that the two people who tossed him off the bridged where drugs handlers of some sort. Yeah, their brains must have been operating from the cunning ingredients of drugs. Their minds had to be intoxicated from a chemical (drug and or alcohol). Who in their right mind would toss a live young boy off a bridge as if he was a piece of trash? Honestly, who in their right mind would toss a man off a bridge, and knowing that the there is a big chance that the young man could have been killed or suffered tremendously from a spinal cord injury. Well, let me tell you who would toss a man off a bridge. A person whose thinking center is filled with the murder weapon (drug or wickedness) will be lead to do such a thing. The person might not be "high" at that particular time, but drug chemical are still in the brain at one point. Once drugs have empowered the thinking mode in a person to do harm, it will soon cause the limb motivator (cerebellum) to become violently active, and then harm is soon to be done.

A person, whose thoughts are filled with dope, will think and act in a way that the chemical gears the brain to re act. When chemical are put into the brain, they became a person's director. People's thoughts should always be filled with mercy, but when drugs are in the brain, unmerciful ways are then promoted. When chemicals are in the brain, they become a director of its entire being. If you are directed by drugs to go to the left, then to the left you will go. If drugs direct you to kill, then you will commit a murder. It's almost as if a movie is being recorded when drugs are in the brain; yep-take-2. When drugs are in the head, wickedness will become a revealed act through physical performances. Nevertheless, this teenager's story is related to my book's title, because I am sure that he can profess and say, I DID NOT KNOW that dealing in drugs would prepare a scene, day and time to be tossed off a bridged.

A life filled with drugs will experience harm one way or another. Drugs and alcohol usage will either harm its user's, or they will provoke you to harm someone else. For example; the people who tossed that 16-year-old teenager off the bridge, he became injured; but the people that did the tossing, never felt harm. Therefore, drugs had empowered and encouraged those two people to harm that young man, which is someone else other than them selves.

Reaping from what you sow covers every evil deed that has been committed in your life. No matter what evil deed you have done, the prophecies, and the laws from God have a plan, which will be done. From the smallest act of evil, up until the greatest evil deed done with your body, a judgment is measured out for you. The two men who tossed the young boy off that bridge will suffer because God has required it to be so. The prophetic scripture that is written in the book of *Psalms 28:4,* which says, *give them after the works of their own hands; render to them their desert.* This prophecy will haunt them down, and provide punishment. The two fellows who tossed the teenage boy off the bridge, they might not be tossed from a bridge; however, they will reap from that evil act sown.

Every person in the world says this; "what goes around comes around". Well, since that is true, maybe something has crept into those two guys' lives and, which might have been damaging to their living. Actually, the said quote; "what goes around comes around", is not the phrase written in the bible, however, "you reap what you sow" is the true phrase to be said. Nevertheless, when we sow evil deeds in our lives, we just never know what type of judgment will be growth. Concerning the two guys who tossed the young man off the bridged, they could have been killed by now, or going through physical ailments right now today. Nevertheless, tossing a person off a bridge is an act of wickedness.

At Mount Vernon Rehab Center, I met another wounded patient that wickedness had touched. Someone injured this man through acts of wickedness. Yeah, someone was guided by wickedness to perform an assault on this man. Someone used illegal firearm and shot artillery (bullets) at him. His leg was the prime area of the body the bullets hit. When the bullet or bullets hit his leg, most of it became useless. His leg was damaged so badly, that most of it had been amputated from the upper thigh area. In other words, ¾'s of this man's leg has been chopped off. The knee is now gone. The ankle is now gone. Only the stomp of his leg remains. I wonder what the doctors did to the parts of the leg that had been chopped off. As I now think about it, ¾ of this man's leg was probably thrown in the trash. Wow, acts of wickedness striped a part of this man's leg from his body. Never will one of his feet feel the pressure of shoes and socks again.

The medical center he came from had amputated his leg. For 22 years of this man's life, both of his legs were active while walking. Since injury has been done, he now has to deal with one leg for the rest of his life. Each and everyday of his life, this tragedy scene will be reviewed in his mind. A tragedy such as his, and mine, and the kid who was tossed off a bridge, there is no way these events can be mentally forgotten. I am sure this one-legged man's heart had been crushed after this incident had occurred. However, just like me, he must stay positive and finish living his life on earth until death snatches his body.

This one leg fellow also uses a wheelchair just like the rest of us here at Mount Vernon Rehab Center. This one legman and I became great friends while we were in this place. We talked, laughed, and shared dark secretive experiences with one another. We shared stories concerning why we both were sent to this rehab center. He told me a 12-gauge shotgun was used, and that's how the leg became damaged. Hearing his story encouraged me mightily. After I told him my story he became encourage too. As the one legman was sharing his experiences with me, it was revealed unto me through confession that he was a dope head too. Therefore, wickedness is the reason why he had been shipped to Mount Vernon Rehab Center. He is another witness that can profess and say; I DID NOT KNOW drugs would prepare a scene, day and time for bodily harm would be my experience.

No one deserves to be tossed from a bridge; neither do I think that a man will ask to have his leg amputated from his body. However, when drugs are in peoples' thoughts, the fullness of evil will be performed. Once drugs empower the mind to seek after harm, there is no turning back.

People in the world are harming one another all because of drugs being in their brains. As of now, three people have been sent to this rehab center because of wickedness and evil. Someone performed an act of wickedness by tossing the teenager off a bridge; someone performed an act of wickedness by shooting the man's leg off; and I performed an act of wickedness by putting drugs into my brain and body. Nevertheless, wickedness is the blame for bringing bodily harm to our bodies.

I met two other people at Mount Vernon Rehab Center. At first, I did not remember who they were, until they both confessed that they both purchased crack cocaine from me before. After their confession, I began to remember their faces. Therefore, they were friends of mine through dope transaction. They both were from the city of St. Louis. They both lived on the south side of St. Louis too. Nevertheless, from the acts of wickedness, they both were shipped to Mount Vernon Rehab Center.

A horrible event happened in both of their lives. The event was so horrible that Mount Vernon Rehab become a place for them to be submitted in. They both used manual wheelchairs to travel through the hospital. To the one, he was shot ten times. Ten bullet wounds were found on his body. His flesh was pierced with marks the bullets left. Every bullet, which was shot into his body, left slashing scars. The slashes were once open holes; however, they are now closed. His body is marked for life. Wickedness did this unto him. He said that a few bullets are still in his body right now today. When I heard that, I was thinking about the organs in the body. Remember when I was a kid in the projects, and I wondered if bullets could remain in the body. After hearing his testimony, I now know that bullets can remain in the body. If bullets are still inside of his body right now today, then those bullets have become plastered to his inner being. He is another victim who can say, "I DID NOT

KNOW that drugs would create and prepare a scene for damage to be done to my body". Since weapons of war (guns) are the true reason for his injury, then acts of wickedness is what caused him to be shipped to Mount Vernon from St. Louis.

The other person I knew from St. Louis had been shot too. Someone shot bullets at him, and one had cruised into his neck. Probably, immediately, when the bullet entered into his neck, the spinal cord was interrupted. It became fractured. Once his neck bone became fractured, and the spinal cord suffered the drastic effects. The neck bone and the spinal cord are the most important bones that keep the body upright while standing. His wheelchair rims had rope twisted all around it. The rope was placed on his rims so he could grasp the wheels to get the wheelchair rolling. From the injury done to his neck and spinal card, he was unable to grip the wheels tightly. The injury that he suffered, took the strength from his hands to be able to squeeze. In other words, his cerebellum (hand coordinator) was still active, but it suffered great damage.

As you can now see, that not only will a brain injury cause legs (my leg) to suffer, but also a gunshot to the neck or spinal cord will savage limb strength as well. Even though the cerebellum in his brain is still operating, however, from injury done unto his neck, other parts of his body lost the power and strength it was once born with. When his neck became injured, the bones throughout his entire body became afflicted. As I said in the beginning chapter of this book, every bullet that is fired from a gun, counts the number of times that wickedness is set to be released. Therefore, not only did a bullet cruise into his neck, but also, wickedness proceeded into it too as well.

From personal experiences, I knew that the two men from St. Louis were both cocaine uses. They bought cocaine from me, and smoked it very often. I sold so much cocaine to these guys, I am sure an addiction had been created in their brain. I can only imagine why the trigger of a gun had been pressed, and why bullets were shot at them. I already knew their cocaine abuse history. However, since drugs were in their bodies and in their lives, they both have become witnesses of my book's title. Yeah, they had neither clue nor idea that a horrible drug scene would be created. Both of them have earned the rights and the ability to say; I DID NOT KNOW that drugs would prepare an evil mishap such as this.

In the rehab center, I've met a number of people who had issues in their lives. Every person in this rehab facility had been plagued with serious issues. Either the issues were physical or they were mental. If the issue was physical, the body had been beaten badly. If the issue was mental, the brain suffered an injury to the lobes. Every person in the rehab center needed to be provided with visual care. Since the brain is the duty of man's every reaction, from the injuries, most of these people had to be fed. Many of them had no control with restroom usage. I was looking at people who were going through trying times I once experienced. Grown men lost their mental ability to know when it was time to use the restroom. When a person has reached a certain age in life, and has lost the mental function to know when it is time to use the restroom, that hurts the heart badly.

As I said before, drug chemical will discriminate neither color, race, nor creed. In the penitentiary, there were many cultures. At the probation office, there were many cultures. Now, at the rehab center, there are many injured races (people) here. At Mount Vernon Rehab Treatment Center, I saw more than seven nationalities. All of them suffered from a tragedy that drugs had created. Every nationality in this rehab center is no different from the other. Wherever there is a brain, and if, drugs become mobile in it, it becomes powerless. No matter what nationality these people may be, drugs performed the same work on each of them all. Just as in the penitentiary, people were locked up because of what drugs empowered them to do, however, in this rehab center; drugs had empowered different races to check in for rehab. Drugs are not prejudice!

Many patients at Mount Vernon had experience

horrible car wrecks. From the car wrecks, many of these people were in bad physical shape. Some of them looked bashed up. It looked as if there was no hope for them. However, there was hope, because they were still alive. Some were pushed into the rehab center in nursing beds. They were in much pain, and loud noises of grunting could be heard. Their will power to live became weakened within them, I'm sure. As I looked into a patient's eye, I saw how hurt and miserable he now is. However, you just never know how far a person's rehabbing has come after a tragedy has occurred in life.

Electric wheelchairs were their means of traveling throughout the rehab center. Moving their risk to control the wheelchairs was a gift that was used by these patients. They could not move or control their arms the way I could. They could not stand on their own two feet, nor could they move their legs. Some of these people had been drinking and driving, and got behind the steering wheel of a car. Drinking while under the influence of alcohol is a breaking of the law. Since many patients were in Mount Vernon because of driving while intoxicated, they brought condemnation upon themselves. Now they might have to use electric wheelchairs for their rest of their lives because of driving while being intoxicated. Even when a person is drinking and driving, that individual never knows when damnation is due.

Why do people exit street bars or clubs thinking they are mentally okay to drive a vehicle? Many people believe it is okay to drink a few drinks, and then drive a motorized vehicle. They think they are beating the system by only gulping a small portion of alcohol. Even drinking small potions of alcohol effects and hinders the entire brain's operation.

Also, there are people who drink above the limit, and still climb in the front seat of a car. People never think about the brain's reactions when liquid toxicants have met it. People only think about how good it makes them feel. People are so hasty to get that intoxicating feeling into their brains that they do not think about the physical limbs, which are needed to drive and control the vehicle. The brain controls the foot to press down on the gas pedal to get the car rolling. The brain controls the hands for car steering. We never think about importance first, we only think about the great feeling alcohol slides into the brain. Whether you drink one shot of liquor or 6 shots, after doing so, you still should not drive a motorized vehicle.

When alcohol, drugs, or any chemical is released in the brain, never think that you are in a good mental condition to drive a car. When you do so, not only are you jeopardizing your life, but you are jeopardizing someone else's life as well. You are not in a great state of mental condition to drive a vehicle when alcohol is in the brain. It's not fair for you to damage or jeopardize someone else's life. You might not be the person to receive an injury, but as you are driving while under the influence of alcohol, there is a chance you might injure an innocent being. Time after time, you have been driving while under the influence of alcohol, and nothing has happened to you on serious note. However, your day of an evil experience is coming soon. If you keep driving motor vehicles while under the influence of alcohol, there is a chance that your name will be submitted and registered at Mount Vernon Rehab Center. Then you will become one of us. Either you will cause someone to check in for physical rehab or you will be in the need of rehab yourself. I am not wishing anything bad to happen unto you, but that's just "how the cookie crumbles" when drinking under the influence is in session.

People need stop thinking they can drink alcohol, and drive too. That is one of the biggest alcohol tricks in the world. It is a trick because alcohol will empower a person's cerebrum (brain's thinking applicator) to believing he or she isn't too intoxicated to drive. I call it a trick because a person can be drunk as a wino, and still believe within himself, that his driving reactions are normal. Alcohol is powerful, because it tricks the minds of its users. They believe they can drink, not be affected, and still drive a motorized vehicle.

I saw a clip a while ago. This clip was about a

beautiful young woman who had been in a horrible car wreck. A man was driving his car one day, and claimed to have only guzzled down a few drinks. As he was driving to his destination, his car smashed into the car of a young woman's vehicle. The intoxicated driver hit her car so hard, that her car doors became jammed. She was trapped inside. I suppose the woman's body was squashed inside of the car. She could not move her limbs. It was almost as if the car became a straight jacket to her body. This clip was horrible to see.

As this young beautiful woman was trapped inside of the car; the car was blazing with rapid fire. This woman is inside of her car with nothing but torturing flames breathing on her body. If her eyes opened up during this incident, I am sure her vision became impaired. I am sure she tried to fight the fire off, but who can win when fire is a person's contender. Even a person with great fighting skills as I have, can't fight fire off. The car had not the power to fight the fire, and neither did the woman. Nevertheless, the car and the woman both became the fire's contender. The longer the fire was able to punch her body, the greater the damage being done.

The woman did manage to escape from the burning car alive. Rescuers reached her before the fire burnt her flesh into complete ashes. Although, she was rescued alive from the burning car, her body suffered major burn wounds from head to toe. Her entire head of hair, the fire burnt to the scalp. The hair holes in her head, will never spring forth hair again. She was burnt to the point were all her clothes had burnt onto her skin. She suffered greatly from the flames attack. Her beautiful skin was stripped from her body. Even unto this day, she's suffering physiologically and physically from another person's lawbreaking motive. Yep, a man put his body inside of a vehicle, and drove it while being intoxicated from booze.

I saw pictures of this woman before the horrible incident had happened. I also saw pictures after this agony touched her living. As I looked at the photographs, she appeared to be at the age of 21-25. She is a very beautiful. She is a well-built looking young woman. She looked like the type of woman that never had difficulties with finding a man. In fact, I am sure men fell at her feet, just to have a local dinner date with her. If you ask me, she is so beautiful that Miss America would be fearful to loosing her title. Yeah, the girl is pretty; the girl is one of a kind.

Let's just say, this young woman had gotten off work, and was possibly driving home to be united with her family. The sad and heart breaking moment in her particular story, is that she never had the chance to walk down the pathway that led to her home. She never got the chance to unlock the door to enter into her home. Actually, she never got the chance to drive her car down the street she lives on. If her house is a 40-minute drive from her job, she could have been 5 minutes away from home, and a horrible car wreck prevented her from making it to her destination. Why? Because, suddenly she had to be submitted to a near by local hospital to be prevented from dying.

Her name became registered in a hospital. Treatment and physical therapy had to be administered unto her immediately. Hospitals became her home for the next several months. Medical attention became her worst nightmare. All she wanted to do was go home, possible take a shower, and relax. However, she never made it home because of an intoxicated driver hit her car. Another innocent victim's life changed for the worst. She had no idea that she would experience a horrible tragedy such as this.

Her appearance has been completely altered. I bet looking at a mirror was once a fascination unto her. Since the incident, she probably doesn't have the desire to look at one. Within, she probably cannot stand the fact that she has to look at a burnt face. For the rest of her life, she has to look at a face that blazing fire has harmed. All because someone broke the law by drinking and driving, her entire countenance has been changed. How do you think it feels to have beauty, and then loosing your glamour in tall "flames" of fire? That is sad, very hurting. Just thinking about this story of the burning car and woman, I feel like crying. Someone has messed her body just that fast. She has scars, burnt marks, and bruises all over her body that will never go away. The experience that unexpectedly arose in her life is a mishap that will be rehearsed in her brain for the rest of her life.

People, stop drinking, and driving! You know what, you can't stop drinking and driving, because the chemical addiction is plastered into your brain. You can't stop drinking and driving because you do not have the strength to do so. You have been poisoned. Your life seems to be cursed. The big bully has your mind, and the drug ninja crept up on you, and caught you. The hunter, the fisher, the strong wrestler, the wicked ghost chaser, and every form of evil worker have your brain in control. You have bitten on the bait of chemicals, and the snake's poisonous venom is in your brain. Now you need to go get some head treatment.

However, there is a doctor that I will to lead you to which will to help you. This doctor will save you from the schemes of ninja, the big bully, the fisher, the strong man, the hunter, the snake's venom, and from the strong wrestler. Finally, yet importantly, this doctor will cleanse you from your addiction. Do you want to know the physician's name who has the power to do such a work? Keep reading the story and I will lead you to his office. FOLLOW MEEEEEEEEEEE!

My situation is different from the woman in the burning car. I messed up my own life, but someone on the outside-brought damage unto her. I was the person that put the drugs into my own body. Therefore, I got what I deserved! Unlike the woman in the burning car, the only thing that she can say is this, "I was in my car driving one day, and all of a sudden, I became a victim trapped inside a burning car, due to a chemical intoxicated driver'.

The drinking driver physical situation is very distant from that of the young woman's. The drinking driver has neither scars, wounds, nor any harm done unto his body. He looks in the mirror every single morning, and sees the exact same image (face). His heart might feel a little pain and resentment; however, his heart of pain will never mount up to the pain that has been compressed into the heart of the burning woman. Nevertheless, the drinking driver lives up to my title, too. He can actually say, <u>I DID NOT KNOW</u> that I would cause damage to someone's life while drinking and then driving.

Now I am about to talk to all women of the earth. Ladies, you just never know what a man will cause to dissolve into your drink. Most women think drugs will bring a calm mood while out on a date. They believe drugs are the fun creator. Well, not only will drugs create fun on the date, but also, drugs can cause a heart hurting experience. For the rest of your life, an awful experience can haunt you. Just by using drugs on a date one time to many, you can suddenly be captured, and did in wrong.

Ladies, after you have just met a man, going out on a date with him is a normal event to engage in. Dating is cool; it is our way of saying; "I am interested in knowing a little more about the person". Dating is one of the practices people do before entering in a real relationship. Dating is supposed to be clean and yet sober. Now a day, people put drugs in the brain while the date is in progress. Not realizing it is a virtual mistake to do. I can only imagine the number of women who went out on dates, and had in mind not to have sex on the first date. Most of the times, when people have sex on the first date, it becomes a one-night stand. Also, they have wickedness or drugs in their lives.

Hey ladies, even become unconscious after chemical usage can be your experience. Once unconsciousness has come into the brain, that evil, wicked man will take your clothes off. He will perform sexual pleasures with a half-dead body. The only thing that is on that man's mind is to get inside your pants for mental pleasure. I know I lived a wicked life, but I thank God, I never did something like that to a woman. I am sure I've dated many women who didn't want to have sex on the first date, but since their brain was being controlled by a chemical substance, sex on the first date became an event.

Hey ladies, there are drugs out there in the world, that will put your brain to sleep, which will allow a man to take complete control of your body, without you even knowing it. If there are drugs in the world that will cause a man (me) to go into a coma, then you had better believe there are drugs out there that will put you to sleep. Drugs, which drags along wickedness, is so relied upon in the world, that men will drug a woman's brain just to have sex with her. Who will actually contemplate on a thought to do such a thing like that? Well, a person whose thinking center is filled with drugs and wickedness will be led to try to get away with such an act. Women, stop going on dates with the intent to use chemical controlled substances.

People of the earth, it is time for you all to say no to drugs, and yes to your intentional thinking. Know exactly what you are doing when going out on a date.

Think about all of the horrible scenes that drugs have already performed in your life. Although, you still have your health and strength (so you think), you mentally do not know what drugs are preparing for your next adventure in the future. The adventure (experience) might be light, or it might be heavy, but one fact that is for certain, drugs are preparing a particular episode in your tomorrow.

Chapter 11

Signs from God and My Heart is in Pain

In this book, you have just read how my usage with drug brought unexpected physical and mental hurts into my life. From those physical and mental hurts, my heart felt the motion of disappointments, and it travailed in pain. Instead of my mind operating in cheerfulness, it was stimulated through and by pain.

In life, I became a failure. I did not accomplish my utmost desires in life, which was to become a pro-athlete. My personal desires did not enter into prosperity.

As of now, the only thing I've earned out of life was a horrible drug resentment lesson. I became bitter; I was filled with anger, and much hatred arose from my mouth. My physical and mental body both learned what it feels like to not achieve its earthly desires.

From the pain that my life has felt, it made me feel as if my life has fallen into a deep ditch. As running water goes into a drain, my life went into a ditch. This ditch, which I've fallen into, was so deep, that human strength could not dig me up out of it. Human power had neither the mental nor the physical strength to pull me up out of this ditch. Neither did I have the knowledge to think of a way to get up out of this ditch.

From this wicked drug experience, the pain in my heart did prevail. When this dope disaster entered into life, a partial victory it got. I never wanted to be handicap, but the power of drugs made me to become one. It was human strength (my strength) against drugs, and dope intoxicants won the battle. Although, I'm alive unto this very day, drugs still earned a high percentage of my life's rewards. After drugs tossed my brain into a coma, becoming a pro-athlete was deleted from my living, and from my heart's desire.

Actually, when drugs caused me to quit college; and caused me to also quit going to see my probation officer, drugs prevailed even then. Yeah, drugs defeated my life in many areas, and the fight to live is not yet over.

Every since drugs performed this mental tragedy in my life, often times I became unhappy. This mental tragedy struck my life just as lightening dashes across the sky. Although, drugs struck me down like lightening, a miracle from God's out pouring mercy has truly uplifted me out of the chambers of death. When my heart stopped for 11 minutes, I was considered a dead man, but my brainstem had been activated by God's mercy. Now I am alive again. Nevertheless, I still have inner hurts and pains within my heart, which can lead a heart to sit on the table of solid misery.

I had so many plans for my life concerning sports. Every athletic plan my brain once held, is no longer a mental diagram, because my physical being has been beaten up. Never will I walk on the pathway, which leads to professional leagues sports again. Never will the ESPN sports casters mention comments about my dynamic moves displayed. Never will the NBA cameras catch a glimpse of my leaping ability. I actually, messed up my chance to win at least one or two awards in the NBA slam-dunk contest. There is no way I can play basketball with the physical condition I now have. Since my leg and ankle have suffered paralysis, to me, sports are now over. From the paralysis that my leg now possesses, playing sports is not even a desire my heart seeks to be involve in. I believe sports are now over for me; they have become corrupted to my living. The paralysis in my leg, and the weakness in my arms, remind me that sports are long gone. All my athletic plans, I once had, have been washed away by the power of drugs.

The great football quarterbacking skills I once possessed has been separated from my body forever. The active position as a football quarterback means nothing to me any more. I can barely throw a rock now, let alone throwing a football. The football is too heavy for my arms to handle.

Even balancing the football in my hand is hard to do. Every time I see a football, the quarterback position that I once played, becomes rehearsed within my mind. It hurts to see a football, and not be able to throw it more than 60 yards down the football field.

Even my great football catching skills has become inactive. The talent that I had to catch a football has been taken away from my physical ability. My heart pains, it pains, and Lord knows it pains.

One-day, two friends of mine, Mike and Darryl had a football. They both were in the middle of the streets tossing the football to one another. I was watching these two guys have fun as they were playing catch with one another. While they were playing catch with one another, I was sitting in the wheelchair watching. As I was in the wheelchair watching them play catch, I began to say unto myself, "only if they knew how far I once could throw a football, and how precise my throwing accuracy once was. As I was watching them play catch, I was on the sidelines building up my courage to participate in this activity. I wanted to catch a pass oh so badly.

When I finally motivated my mind to participate with them, "I yelled out saying, "aye fellows", throw me a pass. So, I began rolling in the wheelchair as if I was a wide receiver. One of my friends threw me a pass. When the ball had reached me, it hit me on the forearm, hard, and fell to the ground. Although, my arms did reach out for the ball; I did not close my hands to grasp it. It seemed like the ball traveled through the air too fast, and my brain could not react fast enough to close my hands. My cerebellum (hand mover and coordinator) did not close my hands together to catch the ball. My hands stayed opened the entire time. The ball was thrown to me on target and perfect. As I now think about it, I am glad the ball did not travel towards my face, or else I would have been in some serious pain. The football probably would have smashed right into one of my eyes. After this non-catching experience happened, my heart began to pain.

Even shooting a basketball is astonishing hard to do.

Not only was shooting the basketball hard to do, but also, handling one became a task as well. When I first put a basketball into my hands again, it felt good to have it in my possession. Every time I look at a basketball, my sport memories are brought back into my mind. My mental man (my brain) began to rehearse many of the splendid skills I once displayed on the basketball court. As of now, I cannot shoot a basketball, I cannot catch a football, and I am scared to play catch with a baseball because of its small size. I really messed up my life for real this time, and my heart travails in pain.

On occasions, people would ask me, "Do you want to participate in wheelchair basketball? Wheelchair basketball is probably a great activity. However, to me, I felt like my sports career was over, and I figured that I should move on to other things in life. I just could not put the love of basketball back into my heart again. Its not that I was afraid to play wheelchair sports, however, if I can't do a juke move and charge to the rim to dunk on <u>Anthony Davenport,</u> or <u>Ron Kelly,</u> I did not have the desire to play it. Drugs have forced me to retire from all sports at a very young age. I did not want to retire, but since I was dealing with wickedness and drugs, from their evil power, retirement was granted.

Well, one day I tried to shoot the basketball, and it did not even touch the rim. My arms were too weak to toss the ball that high. Not only that, but also, I could not even throw the basketball up there with one arm. Well, I guess I will never be compared to NBA stars again. I had already known that basketball was over for me, but when I shot the ball towards the rim, and it did not touch the rim, I was hurt within my heart all over again. I think I was so hurt that day that I cried in my bed the same night. Probably 95 percent of the athletic in the world does not know what if feels to be able to say, "I am one of the greatest athletes in the world", and then loose your talents and skills to drugs.

Even after this incident has happened, I am still being compared to many NBA athletes. Here I am now in a wheelchair, and still being compared to today's NBA stars.

These days, I'm being compared to A. Iverson, K. Bryant, D. Wade, L. James, T. Mcgrady, K. Garnett, Paul Pierce, Ray Allen, Anfernee (Penny) Hardaway and many others. For the rest of my life on earth, there will always be upcoming NBA athletes being compared to me. Sorry to say, but all the NBA athletes would have loved to have the talent I had. However, they all are awesome N.B.A. players with great talents and skills. When I meet any of them, they will all wonder within themselves; was **Brian Irons** really that great of a basketball player? Only if I could have shown them my talents and skills, then all would know that my basketball skills were true. Some people probably think I am exaggerating, but I know the truth, and so do God.

You know what I saw one day; do not get me wrong, because I might be wrong. I believe I saw Lebron James signing (writing) autographs with his left hand. He is a dominant right hand basketball shooter, but his left hand controls the pen. I also, write with my left hand, and shoots basketball with my right. However, I do not know if Lebron has the gift to shoot a basketball with any arm from anywhere on the court. Nevertheless, keep your eyes focused on him as his career journeys. He is young. He is awesome. Lebron is still developing his skills in the art of basketball. Hang in the Lebron, and stay away from drugs!

I actually missed the chance to be a franchise player. If any team would have drafted me, I guaranteed you I would have been a franchise player. There's not one coach in the NBA would have given me a chance to switch teams.

Just the other day, I was in the library typing this book. A basketball friend of mine walks in the building. From out of nowhere, he started talking about basketball. He said, "Hey, Lytskin, have you seen D. Wade play ball"? I said, I think I have. Then he said, well, D. Wade reminds me of how you played, but I think you have him beat, because you can play with either hand. The following week, I just happen to turn on a basketball game, and D. Wade's team was playing. I saw that young man do a move to the hole, and my mouth dropped. Then I said to myself, oh my goodness, I am being compared to a dude like that. Lord have mercy; I really messed up my life this time.

Although, my leg has a bit of paralysis in it, however, by the power of God it can be restored back to normal again. Whether God restore it back to normal again, or not, it is not a concern to me. I truly believe that God just might allow me to walk through life with a lame ankle. If he does, I should not complain about the condition of my leg. Neither should I curse God about it. If this paralysis lives within my leg for the next 60 years, I am content and totally prepared. Although, walking normal again would be great, but I realize, I am the one that messed up my own body, not God.

When I die, and be placed in a coffin, if my leg still has paralysis in it, I see nothing wrong with that. I see nothing wrong with it because I was not supposed to be here on the earth anyway. I am just so happy to be here in the land of the living, after facing 11 minutes of heart failure. Since I am still human, and not a robotic being, I still have an emotional side, and yet, I still have pains in my heart. A paralyzed limb does not mean that life is over for me.

This drug devastation concerning my heart's pain was in the makings for 10 years. For ten years, I had been tossed back and forth while this devastation was in the making. In High school, the evil preparation to negative disaster is where it all begun. As drugs were creating or forming links to my physical hurts, from them, I was almost destroyed. My brain and body had been banged up for 10 years by drugs. Day in and day out, I allowed drugs to be ruler over my life. Evil experiences approached me all because of drugs being head of my life. They (drugs) were torturing my physical body, which, in return lead to my physical hurts.

As you have just witness from reading my book, how the true power from drugs is hidden from the mental mind of humankind. During those ten years of being bound by drugs cunning addiction, its focus, and desire I DID NOT KNOW about. Most of dope's power and ways were not revealed unto me, until I began to fill my brain & body with the chemicals. Once I began to put drugs into my brain, afterwards, drugs prepared appointments of disaster to arise into my life. To all people who are pouring drugs into their brain & body, the true and evil power that the chemicals can do unto you, are hidden from the mental mind. One day soon, your entire brain center will be enlightened, and from your wicked encounters, it will be revealed unto you, that street drugs are evil, wicked, and powerful.

Although, the negative power of drugs was working in my life, I did learn many of its ways that follows the "drug use". I also learned that, drugs, wickedness, and evil are all associated. Also, the far and best implication that I have learned is, "one bad made decision, or one false move, can send a person through what is call, "hell and back". Hell is truly not on earth, but I would like to use "hell" as an earthen example. From what you have read in this story, concerning the evil situation I have witnessed, I have gone through "hell and back". Do you want your life to go through hell and back? Well, as long as you stay connected to drugs, "hell and back" will become a spoken phrase from your mouth. If the "hell and back" phrase doesn't come forth from your mouth, then I am sure, one of your friends will say it. Right now today, I have friends telling other people, "Lytskin" been through hell and back.

Many times, as I sat and thought about all of the horrible situations and drastic experiences that drugs have created in my life, I can honestly say, "God was doing his best in trying to help me. God was only trying, through his mercy, to steer me away from the evil lifestyle I was living". Every time a dangerous episode chartered into my life, it came unexpected. Time after time, as my brain and body was being snatched into dangerous and life-threatening situations, it is all because of the mercies God that I made it out alive. Whenever there is evil to be determined towards you, and somehow, someway, judgments have not been pronounced upon you, it is because of the unfailing "mercies of God". God's mercy is the parallel reason why many people have not been punished right now. God's mercy might be powerful, but it will only hold back the Day of Judgment only for so long.

God has allowed me to see many signs over the years. My own vision and mental knowledge has experienced the acquaintance of these signs. My own two eyes have seen every thing that pertains to substance abuse, and its controlling power. Whether the experience was from bodily drug usage, or a visual encounter, my life has seen and felt it all. The things that my eyes have beheld, "I would like to say", that only a great man of wisdom and understanding would have comprehended the insights of such events. Actually, only a freed man will foresee and understand such signs. To mentally understand and comprehend the "signs" of life in any situation, "good wisdom" is needed to discern certain events.

In my life, I did not use "good wisdom". Well, shall I say, I did not use "good judgment". I had wisdom of course, but it was my own personal wisdom. My personal wisdom needed to be filled or touched by God. My personal or "Self wisdom" did not mount up to understand that death is in the lifestyle that I chose to live. In high school, I thought about all the fun; never did I think about violence and death. However, good wisdom, which comes from God, is what we all need.

In the sentence below, is a scripture concerning wisdom. *Proverbs 9:10 the fear of the Lord (God) is the beginning of wisdom.* When a person fears the Lord (God), a certain type of "wisdom" is automatically engrafted into his or her inner being. A person's heart and mind becomes precious to the Lord when fearing him. Mentally, "Fearing the "Lord" is the kind of wisdom, that once it is active in the mind, it shall and will be pierced into your soul.

Having the fear of the Lord living inside you, is what I would like to call, "good wisdom". This wisdom, which shows a fear of the Lord, will bring great joy into the living of your life. Good wisdom, when you get a hold of it, it will sit at the seat of your thoughts and at the table of your heart. It will relax within you, and when it is time for it stand up and prove its power, it will boldly perform. This wisdom sits inside your inner being (brain and heart) waiting for the opportunity to prove its real power. Good Wisdom is a nutrient to your life. Get a taste of it! Let good wisdom become a meal to your life, brain, and body. Open up your heart and receive it. The organs in your body are all depending on being acquainted with good wisdom.

When you do not have the fear of the Lord, then good wisdom is not living inside of you. Good wisdom will give you educated power to help you make the right choices in life. Daily, will decisions and choices need to be made. When you grasp a hold onto "Good Wisdom", it will cause you to have a fear of the Lord in your brain (mind) and heart. Then you will learn and be empowered to make decisions that will lead you to safety.

Having not good wisdom living down inside of you will cause you to make many unwise choices. Those unwise choices will be made decisions that will lead your life down the road and path of ignorance and stupidity. Good wisdom is granted, not freely given. Let this wisdom come into your life, because it will teach you reasons on why you need to fear the Lord God. When you perform activities, that will cause the Lord to be angry with you, you have made a decision apart from good wisdom. Not allowing good wisdom to reign in your life is not showing the fear of the Lord. In life, I thought I feared the Lord, but my lifestyle proved me wrong.

There is a big difference between the "fear of the world", and "the fear of the Lord". Having "the fear of the world" is a fear that is obliviously a scarce about what an earthen vessel (physical being) can do unto you. For example, when I heard that a robber and gunslinger was searching for me in the neighborhood, immediately, I became fearful, and I fled to go and get my piece (pistol). I was scared of what this man might do unto me, if he came across my path. With my piece (gun) in my possession, I felt safe, I felt protected, and I felt physically guarded. That is an example of a person having a fear of the world. A person that fears the world is frightened about what can happen unto him or her, when someone is out to get him. Nevertheless, fearing the world comes in many different forms and fashions.

Many people often confess from their mouth that they fear God. Confession from the mouth that you fear God means nothing. As I said before, actions speak louder than words. You do not fear God, if you are not obeying his laws and commands. When a person fears God, that individual is skeptical to doing certain things. When fearing the Lord, you've realized that God is the judge, and you do not want him to pronounce judgments upon your life. Having fear of the Lord in you will cause you to live a lifestyle that he desires for you to live. You will fear the events that God can allow enter into your living. Not only what God can allow, but also, what he might send your way. Whether it be a judgment in court, or a judgment through biblical prophesy, you will fear of what can truly happen as you live on earth.

When God sends signs to humanity, he sends them all through the cerebrum (the thinker). Yeah, God watches things happen in our lives, which are suppose to make us all stand back and think. God created the brain; therefore, he tries to contact it one way or another.

In my 10 years of imprisonment with drugs, I have experienced many narrow escapes from the hands of death. Day in and day out, I escaped the gripping hands of death. Many times death reached out to grab me, but it did not pull me in. However, for 11 minutes, death did grab me, but God mercy caused death to unloose me. Whenever you make an unrighteous decision in your life, remember, from that made decision, invisible wicked hands are waiting for the perfect moment to grab you. Since I did not obey the signs from God, death had its paw on my fleshly body.

All my drug living life, I have seen many signs of cautions. While driving in my car, I have seen stickers on car bumpers saying, "Say no to drugs". Driving down the highway, I have seen many billboards displaying the same words (Say No to Drugs). I was walking on the sidewalk one day, and I reached down to pick up a piece of paper. On this piece of paper, were the same words, "say no to drugs". Those were visual signs telling me what I truly need to do with my life. Sometimes a piece of paper in the middle of the road has a message on it for you. There were so many signs flashing in and out of my life that should have been obvious unto me, nevertheless, drugs imprisoned my mind, therefore my life was locked its addictions. Remember, every time you see a sticker, or commercial that says anything pertaining to saying no to drugs, that is a warning unto you. You might not take it seriously, but if you are on drugs, it is a serious message, whether you realize it or not. God wants you to escape the death penalty that drugs are soon to present into your life.

Here are some of the signs that the mercies of God allowed me to see before drugs violently ran my brain into a solid brick wall. I have been in three cars that have been shot at. Each car had two or more windows blown out from gunshots. If only one car would have had blown out windows, I probably could get away with saying, "I was in the wrong place at the wrong time". However, three cars of mine experienced the same type of conflict. Therefore, those three gun-shooting experiences were signs saying, "Get out of the drug game".

People would drive through the neighborhood and shoot bullets throughout it. Cops have chased me all over town. I had been fired from a job and I quitted two jobs. I've been kicked out of the house because of being associated with dope. I ended up in the hospital over night one day, because of a night of heroin usage, which was an experience before this 11-minute heart stop tragedy. Actually, I have two hospital experiences because of the usage of heroin. I did not write about that tragedy because I am saving it for my second book. However, you still read enough information to see my full illustration, that I am trying to get across unto you. I went to the penitentiary for 10 months. Yes, those were all warning signs my life had seen.

Since, I did not obey the signs, which God did allow me to see, I actually forced God to allow my life to

286

experience one of the greatest acts of evil. From the tremendous power of drugs, God allowed me to suffer tremendously. I gave God no other choice but to let drugs have its own way with my brain, body, and life. So here I am, with pain in my heart and body because I did not obey the signs that God allowed me to see. Since I did not obey the signs, my heart has pain within it because I have to deal with a paralyzed limb probably for the rest of my life.

The way I walk now, opposed to the way I walked before, hurts me when I think about the many chances that I was given to take an exit out of the drug game. I did not go to the left, nor did I go to the right, I kept going straightforward in the life of drugs, without the fear of God even being in my thoughts.

I allowed drugs to use me, and play mental games with my life. That is exactly what drugs did unto me. They played me as if I was a "game". If I can use football as an example, drugs tackled me and I did not have any equipment on. Yeah, I was hit hard. Drugs hit my brain so hard; you would think I went head on with the great "Ray Lewis". There was not a helmet on my head, and the power of drugs charged straight for my brain, and injured its resources.

At times, I feel so ashamed within my heart because I have to ride around in a wheelchair. Actually, riding around in the wheelchair is not the shameful part. The shame comes when I have to tell people the reason why I am relying on a wheelchair. I have to announce to the public, "I am using a wheelchair" because I was getting high on drugs one day, and I suffer a brain injury. I have to tell people that my drug usage caused an injury to my brain, which caused my left leg to suffer the consequences. Also, I have to tell people that I was getting high one day, and I actually killed myself, but God sprayed the wetness of mercy upon me one more time. That is somewhat embarrassing to me.

I have to wake up every morning and wear a leg brace to keep my ankle and foot upright while I am walking. The brace keeps my ankle stable so that my foot does not hang while walking. I hate I did this to myself. Good lord, I should have obeyed the signs, and then my legs would not be going through this type of sorrow.

If there are no handrails on the wall when I go up or down the stairs, I have to either crawl or scoot to get to my destination. When a person has problems walking forward, then walking up or down the steps is definitely a problem. I think that I am doing a good job battling this physical weakness that has been fastened to my body. My legs were very important to me in my life; therefore, I do not like this type of living at all. Nevertheless, I am still content and thankful unto God because I was in much worse physical condition many years ago. Nevertheless, before this tragedy happened, signs were given, and I should have obeyed them. I should have stopped, dropped, and rolled out of the drug game, so that my body would not be going through this physical pain.

One day, I was sitting at a friend's house, and a glass of juice was offered unto me. I accepted the offer because I was a little thirsty. My friend went to the refrigerator and poured the juice in a cup. As he approached me, he then reached out to hand me the cup filled with juice. Once my fingers touch the cup, my friend would then let the glass go. When my hand touched the cup or glass, my cerebellum did not close my hands tight enough to have a full grip on it. Therefore, the filled cup slips through my hand and makes a complete mess. Sometimes, a friend thinks he's the reason for the spilling of the juice. Most of the times, it was my fault. Little situations like that hurt my feeling because I have been dealing with issues like that since the dope tragedy occurred in my life. It never fails; I always drop something, or knock over something on the table. Sometimes I fell like a little child all over, but oh well, life will still go on, and so must I.

People look at me crazy when I sometimes use both of my hands to grasp an offered glass of water. I now put one hand under the glass, and snuggle the other hand around it. I do it that way, so I will have a full grip on the glass at once. From all of the incidents that I have experienced pertaining to spilling water, using two hands to grasp a cup filled with liquid has become a safety tip. That is one of the new teachings (2 hands to grasp a glass) that my brain has taught me.

When people do unorthodox things in your presence, sometimes we need to consider having mercy on them because we just never know why people do things a certain way. We just never know what a person has been through over the years. Now that I think about it, although, my brain had suffered an injury; it is still learning and teaching my body how to cope with everyday living. Although, Mount Vernon Rehab Treatment Center taught me how to cope with life from a head injury point of view, however, the greatest teaching comes from my daily physical and mental activities. It seems like there is always something new that my brain teaches me. As long as my brain can function this way until the day I die, I am very thankful. No matter how the next day in life may look, I am so content with what strength that God's mercy has left my body to possess.

Although, I use a manual wheelchair in public on a daily basis, my legs are impressively beginning to receive satisfying physical strength. My brain cannot move the ankle up or down, but I can still stand up and walk on it. Although, my leg has suffered greatly from the ignorant decisions made in the past, I thank God; both legs are attached to my hips. My left thigh muscles have received great amounts of strength throughout the years. Everything in my life now evolves around my leg that has the numbness in it; therefore, regularly I must maintain it, and treat it differently from the other leg. I once use to cry, and shed gallons of tears because of the paralysis that has suddenly grabbed a hold onto my leg. When I came to the point to realize that the numbness has become a part of my leg's life, my heart and mind learned how to deal with the situation.

Right after this drug incident, not only was my physical strength weak, but my mental strength was weak as well. After I had put my tennis shoes on, tying up the laces was very confusing. I actually forgot how to tie shoes. The memory (procedural) had suffered greatly while my brain was under the attack of the coma. When I first learned how to tie my shoes, the procedural memory is where the taught data had been stored. Being a grown man at this particular time, and not being able to tie up my own shoes was another hurt that rested inside of my heart. Since I forgot how to tie up shoes, I would relax the strings inside of them. I did that for the entire 5 months while being stationed at Mount Vernon Rehab Treatment Center. My brain had to teach my hands how to tie shoes all over again.

One day a friend of mine came to pick me up at my parent's house. My body was already dressed with clothes. When my friend arrived, I begin to put my tennis shoes on. Then I begin to tie them up. As I was tying my shoes, I was having trouble doing so. My friend saw that I was having trouble tying up my tennis shoes. Then my friend stooped down on his knees, and tied my shoes up for me. Friends need to be caring friends in matters like these. The friend's name that tied my shoes is "Lamar Roger Pruitt".

Lamar Pruitt and I were cool with one another before this drug tragedy occurred. However, I never thought there would ever come a day in my life that tying up shoes would be a hard task to perform. Truly, I DID NOT KNOW that drugs would sift memory from my brain, by eating up already learned shoe-tying information.

Putting my clothes on was a task as well. I could not perform the normal routine of putting on own clothes. I once use to be able to stand up and put on pants, but now, I can't. I have to sit down or lay back on the bed just to put on pants. When I realize I was not able to stand and put on pants, my heart became tremendously shattered. I never complained about, nor did I question God; I did what I had to do to take care of me. If I have to sit on my bed to put pants and socks for the rest of my life, who cares, I will still thank God for what he has done.

Speaking of clothing! There always comes a moment that I need to wash my clothes. I can't afford a washer and dryer, so I take my clothes to a laundry mat, and wash them there. When I go to the laundry mat, I put my dirty clothes in trash bags. Then I put the same bag of dirty clothes in my lap, while I am in the wheelchair. My body's weight and the weight of the cloths, both I ride to the Laundromat in my wheelchair. The laundry mat is about a mile from my house. Therefore, in total, I u-haul my clothes in the wheelchair close to a mile. Since I take my clothes there and bring them back, then I am sure I do a mile in the wheelchair with clothes on my lap. I use to be ashamed to roll in my wheelchair, with a big trash bag full of clothes on my lap. Nevertheless, the shame has been washed away. I must to do what I have to do, by taking care of me. I have even had experiences were some of my clothes falls out of the bag, and into the streets or sidewalk.

In my wheelchair, I can get around quicker and faster. My wheelchair has become my physical means of transportation. I am grateful to be able to use a wheelchair. I definitely need my manual wheelchair, and no living man or woman on earth can tell me anything different. Sorry, to sound so blunt about the matter, but I love using my wheelchair, because I use it for more than one reason. Using my wheelchair gives me the power of not having to wait for people to take me anywhere.

It vexes me when people speak against me using my wheelchair. People do not understand why I really use the wheelchair. The only thing they know is that I can walk. From that fact of people knowing that I can at least walk, which has become known to many people in St. Louis, sometimes I get in debates with them about my personal condition. Sometimes I get defensive. When people debate with me about my wheelchair usage, I get so deep with them and say, "The day you stop smoking weed or drinking alcohol will be the day I will throw my wheelchair away. We all have holes in our lives that need to be patched up into perfection. So people in the world, do not worry about my wheelchair, if I am happy about the way my life has turned out to be, then let it be. If the truth were told, I am happier in life, than most of you perfectly physical in shape people are.

My wheelchair definitely comes in handy when I am going grocery shopping. I rather roll around in the store than walk through it. It is hard for me to carry groceries in my arms, then walk with a walker, and keep my balance at the same time. When I go shopping, it is easier to sit groceries in my lap, as I roll through the store in my wheelchair. Going grocery shopping is another reason why I use my wheelchair. Just the other day, I went grocery shopping, and put a loaf of bread, 12 pack of noodles, a bag of chicken, and a gallon of juice on my lap. I am good; I am courageous, and none of you have the power to put me down. Keep on reading; soon, I am going to tell every single last one a you a thing or two.

Many times, in the wheelchair, as I am rolling down the road, with grocery bags in my lap; I've experienced groceries falling out of it. In broad street traffic, groceries have fallen out of the bags. It is very embarrassing when the food falls out of the grocery bag, and onto the ground. However, most drivers on the road will kindly allow me to pick up my groceries before my food is driven over, and destroyed.

The wheelchair has become a motivator to me. I ride in my wheelchair everyday when I am outdoors going anywhere. When going somewhere outdoors, and I need to catch public transportation (city bus), taking the wheelchair along is necessary. When the bus arrives, the driver pushes a button from the dashboard, and a ramp slides out electronically. Then I roll the wheelchair onto the ramp. When I get on the bus, I then roll to the wheelchair parking spot. I love public transportation. My mind has become accustomed to it. Of course, I never wanted to be in a situation such as using a wheelchair, or in a position of being handicap, but as I said before, you never know where your life is heading when you indulge in drugs. However, there is always a moment in my life, that my heart ventures off into pain.

Sometimes, when I roll myself through the streets of St. Louis, I toss my hands high toward heaven, yelling out saying, "thank you God for sparing my life one more time".

Not only did God spare my life but also he gave my brain back enough inner sense to have a little understanding as well. Many people in the world have a brain, but are without realistic common sense. Well, if you have drugs in your brain, you are a person that has no realistic common sense. You have the sense of a chemical controlled substance. Although, at times, my heart still pains inside, however, in the wheelchair, my hands will continually be lifted up toward heaven.

As I said in the introduction of this book, that people are so fascinated with the physical being. I use to be so into to trying to get my physical strength back. I wasn't thinking about the intelligent human brain's power, I thought about the body's strength. I use to go to the gym to exercise and lift weights to gain pieces of my physical strength back. I wanted to keep my leg in the little shape that it is now in. Lifting weights is good for the physical body. The gym that I was going to, at that particular time, a price had to be paid. With my weakened financial status, I could not keep up with the payments. Therefore, I quit attending. I participated in this exercising program about 4 times. Not only did I have to pay the gym to lift weights, but also, transportation had to be paid too. Whether transportation was bi-state (public bus) or cab, a payment had to be made. I was feeling good about things, because I felt myself getting stronger just by attending a few sessions. Although, I could not afford to keep going to the gym room, God has provided strength in many areas where I was weak. Nevertheless, I was hurt that I had to quit going to the gym because of the lack of finances. I did have the mental persuasion to work towards getting my body stronger. However, the membership fee, along with the transportation fee was too much for me to handle.

There is an old saying that goes like this; "everything that taste or feels good is not good for you". Many things might cause the body to like the pleasure of it, but it might not be good for the body. I now find that to be a statement of truth, because drugs did feel good to my mind, however, they were not good for my body. Although, the formula of drugs felt good to the mind, my experiences proved that drugs are not good for the body. I was so naïve to put all of those different types of drugs inside of my body; and thinking it was a cool thing to do. What about my health? What about my brain? The physical health and mental status was never a thought that crossed my mind. I only thought about the feeling that drugs provided within the brain. I feel so disgusted right now. It is so true, that, everything that tastes good is not good for you.

Drugs have truly taken away my pride and joy (Figure of speech). My bodily limbs were my joy, and my talents were my pride. It was my pride (good feeling) to know that I was one of the best athletes in the world. It was my joy to know that I was skilful enough to play against three or four different athletes in a game of basketball and dominate them on the court. The great pride (good feeling) that I once physically attained has now been destroyed, because my joy (limbs) has become unavailable to participate in sports. I felt that there was none like me on the basketball court. Nerveless, I put drugs in my brain, and disaster was created. Yeah, drugs creatively destroyed my pride and my joy.

Many people in the world are like me: crazy, stupid, and ignorant. It takes near death experiences in order for some of us to accept the fact that drugs are harming our lives. However, many people who are reading this book have not experienced many of the events I've witness. So this word is for you; stop putting dope in your brain and body before your heart stop longer than mine did. My heartbeat paused for 11 minutes, but yours might pause, and stay in pause mode forever.

After my days of being in the hospital, I was living with my parents. About 3 years after this tragedy occurred, I moved out of my parent's house. I moved out to live on my own. It was time for me to go back out there into the world, and be on my own again. I felt within myself, it was time to step out, and not depend upon family. Meaning, a man needs to be on his own, and have his own space. So there I went, to live on my own.

When I had moved out of my parent's residence, and into my own apartment, a housing program was provided to help me out. This housing program is called, "section 8 housing". This housing program helped me pay a portion of rent on a monthly basis. Indeed, the housing program has truly helped me out a great deal. If it had not been for this housing program, life, financially, would have been so, so hard on me. I do not think I can pay full rent anywhere receiving disability payment, and survive in days like these.

I remember, I wanted to move into this newly built apartment building. This building had been renovated. No one has ever lived in it since its renovation. So I called the office, and spoke to the manager. We scheduled an appointment, so I could see what the inside of the apartments looks like. I wanted to see if this apartment building was compatible for wheelchairs.

This renovated building was located about two miles from where I was living at the time. I rolled my wheelchair the entire two miles to meet the office manager. It took me about an hour and 20 minutes to get there. Depending on how many hills I had to face, getting there faster could have been done.

The office manger was a nice person. She was very sweet. She gave me a tour throughout the entire building. She took me to a few apartments that were handicap ready, or shall I say wheelchair assessable. In each apartment, all of the appliances were brand new. New microwaves were provided. The carpet was new. The kitchen cabinets were new. Everything was completely new.

However, in order for the renters, including the owner of the apartment building to get inside of it, a key is needed. There were 21 apartments inside the building. There were only two entrances leading to the inside. After seeing this place, I really fell in love with it. I wanted to rent an apartment here oh so badly.

In order to have access to one of these apartments, an application must be filled out. I am so glad I learned how to read and write while in school. On the other hand, should I say, "I am so glad that my declarative memory held on to maintaining reading and writing skills. I am also glad that my cerebellum has the strength to handle a pen to write with. Not only did I have to fill out an application, but also I had to give the company 35 dollars. The $35 had to be given, so that the owner of the building could do a background check. Before I left the building, the manger gave me a time in which I could return to hear the verdict. Actually, this next appointment is like a judgment day, because, these people are going to tell me if I've been denied or accepted to live in the apartment building.

I returned to the apartment building to hear the outcome. Well, they told me that I was denied. It was a slap in my face. I had exceeding hopes on moving into this new building. The manager said, "my financial history did appear to be bad, however, the owner over looked it". However, my criminal record is what caused the company to deny me from moving into the building. My cocaine charges from years ago had haunted me. When I heard that my criminal history report was the reason for the denial, my heart began to pain. I was hurt because, although, those cases were put on my law's record many years ago, I am still reaping from it. Wow, those drug cases are on my record for the rest of my life. After I had been denied, I rode back home in my wheelchair with a heart beating while in pain.

As I was riding back home in my wheelchair; I repaired my mind, and put the sad news behind. My past is in the past. I cannot change that. Why let bad news bother me? That's minor mental hurt, compared to what I just came out of many years ago. I might not own a set of keys to one of the apartments, but I still have my "TESTIMONY". Therefore, as I was riding home in my wheelchair, I dust myself off, and still believe that things will change for me somehow, someway.

Yeah, life will go on, and so must I. Monday is going to turn into Tuesday, and Tuesday is going to turn into Wednesday. If you do not get with the program of life, then that is on you. Life will never stop for any reason. A paralyzed limb, a wheelchair, and a criminal record do not mean that life is over for me. Even in my weakened condition, time and life will keep on going. For me, it only means that I have to be mentally stronger and fight from the heart to gain what I need and want in life. The physical disaster has happened, so I must encourage myself every moment of my life.

The monthly or disability income that I am receiving is okay, meaning, it pays the bills, and not too much more. All bills have demands; and they demand payments. Bills want that money that is in your pockets. Bills do not even have a mouth, but they give out demands.

It is somewhat amazing how I once had strong athletic hands for protecting myself, and now they are weak and feeble because of drug usage. My hands are weak and feeble all because of the one bad choice, which was to smoke marijuana in high school. Listen to these facts: my hands, which were great in all areas of sports, were the same hands that caused sports to be deleted from my life. My own fingers, which are attached my hand, had guided marijuana to my mouth to be inhaled. My own hands and fingers were used to put heroin to my nose to be snorted. I caused my brain to control my hands to reached out and grasp a hold of every drug product that ever went inside of my anatomy (brain & body). My hands, which could have made me rich by playing pro league sports, were the same hands that cause me to live on a monthly payment plan (disability). All because of my own hands, I have no money unto this very day. All because of my own hands, disability checks have became a source of income for my life. Now I must patiently wait for a check to be mailed to me every 30 days (once a month). That has been hurting me for a very long time.

Although, I have many new physical limitations attached to my body, I know that there is a job out there for me in this world. Working at a fast-food restaurant will probably be too fast for me. Besides, my slow movements will probably cause me to be in the other employees' way. I hope to find an employment that will allow me to sit in my wheelchair. Standing up and lifting objects on a job, is a no-no for me. I desire to find employment because my monthly income was not enough to help me do things I desire to do. I didn't want to do a lot, but I do want to enjoy my last days of living on the earth.

Since I have been receiving disability income, the amount of money I receive is a little above $500 dollars per month. In today's world, 500 dollars is nothing, especially when it is received once a month. I have never had money in the middle of the month, unless given to me from a family member or a friend. Other than that, I was without money for more than 20 days out of the month. After, I had paid my bills; I was left with a small amount of cash.

After I had bought food, if I was able to buy food, you can say that the entire check was already spent before it was cashed. If I sought to buy a pair of pants, shoes or shirt, I most definitely would be without money. Not only did I need clothes, but hygiene products were a necessity too. Unexpectedly, out of nowhere, when I thought I had a few dollars to myself for the month, bam, I needed toothpaste, bam I needed new socks, bam, I needed soap, bam, I needed toilet paper, bam, I bought some white castles, bam, I needed bleach and detergent, bam I bought a play station game. Well, there goes my few dollars. The same things that you financially blessed people need, I need also. Nevertheless, I had to spend the little amount of money that I had, and think about being broke again for the next 20 something days. Wow, I was actually without money every month for more than 20 days, and this financial status has been with me for a very long time. Actually, right now today, I am still going through it.

If I wanted to purchase something more than a hundred dollars, I had to wait until the first of the month arrives. Probably two or 3 times out of the year, I sacrificed a hundred dollars to spend on something of value. I need a new TV for my apartment; therefore, a sacrifice was done. Moreover, that took more than 100 dollars. After I've made sacrifices like that, I was falling farther and farther behind on bills. Nevertheless, my brain did a good job with maintaining things, and paying bills. Hey, Brian K. Irons, you are doing very well in life, and don't let nobody tell you anything different.

I remember when I purchased a computer to do my writings on. The computer cost $399. You know that was way out my budget range. When I bought this computer, I did not pay a bill in my house. I did not pay my rent; I didn't pay my gas bill; I didn't pay my phone bill, nor did I pay the electric bill. Nothing for that month I paid. I took a chance and purchased this computer. However, the following month, I paid double on my rent. Oh my God, the next 6 months was horrible trying to catch up on bills. Well, (laughing) even unto this very day, I am still not caught up on bills. Bills run up so fast, who can catch them. Bills do not have legs, but they can beat your salary running.

Of course, I had to get my haircut; therefore, another bill was added to my check. Blessedly, I was able to come across a few awesome barbers, which cut my hair during the month, and allowed me to pay them on the first of each month. That hurt my pockets at times too, but I had to give those men their money. Even right now today, I am still paying barbers their money on the 1st of each month. I have been doing this for more than 7 years. I would like to congratulate myself because I do not owe any barber money. Only payments I still owe to this very day are bills.

I remember one day, my barber had a meal he was soon to eat. After he finished cutting a customer's head, he sat down and began too eat the food. After he ate all that he wanted from the plate, he began walking towards the trashcan, and was about to throw it away. I then yelled out, "don't throw it away, give it to me". He replied, "There's nothing on the plate, I ate it all". Then I said, let me see for myself. So, he passed me the bowl. As I ran the fork through it, there was nothing on it worth putting into my mouth. At first, I did not want to ask him for the bowl because I did not want to eat from of another man's leftover. Nevertheless, I was hungry, and survival was my tactic.

You would not believe how many times, I have asked for food from another person's leftover. Although, my heart pains in moments like this, I will never forsake the fact that God is still good! I do not care what goes on in my life; nothing can create within me to believing that God is not a good God.

Let me share another embarrassing experience with you. One day, a neighbor gave me some meat to satisfy my hunger for the moment. Yeah, well, I was hungry as usual. My stomach was growling, which was nothing new. I needed some bread to eat with the meat that my neighbor had blessed me with. The day before this meat was given to me, I tossed some bread in my kitchen's trashcan. I felt that it was getting old anyway, and probably was about to mold. The bread was sitting at the very top of the trashcan. Guess what, I actually went into my trashcan and pull the bread out of it. After I pulled the bread out of the trashcan, I said to myself, "oh my God, I actually went into a trashcan to get some food. If the bread had been in the trash for a couple of days, then no, I would not have pulled it out. Since it was at the top, and not in the trashcan for days, I did not feel too bad about it. I never told anyone about this incident before, but now that the world will read about it, the incident has now been told. I was too ashamed to tell anyone about this incident, but my shame has been wiped away, and I do not care who reads it. Besides, my entire written book is to encourage millions of people, one way, or another, for the next 3 centuries. I did not say 3 decades, I said 3 centuries. I know what I said. If the earth stays a live for the next 3 centuries, my books will still be here; and in a later chapter, I am going to tell you how I know so.

One day, I was sitting on my bed watching television with no shirt on. I decided to look down at my body (chest), for whatever apparent reason. As I was looking at my chest, my rib bones were sticking out of my body. When I saw the rib cage in my chest area sticking out, I became frustrated and my heart ventured off into pain. I knew it was all because I was not eating the proper amount of meals per-day.

Anyway, every year the government adds 10 dollars to the disability checks. Since, at one point, when I was receiving $500 a month, that means, I only collected $6,000 dollars throughout the entire year. After I calculated that total, my heart dropped to the floor. My heart was in pain once again. Although, my heart was filled with hidden pain, I never gave up on life. I knew there was something better that life had to offer me, than to live in financial pain.

I personally had gotten to the point in my life, were I was tired of paying bills, and then not having money throughout the month. I had a friend who came to my house often. He would go get a drink of water out of the refrigerator. After looking in the refrigerator for a drink, he sat down and drank his water. Then he said unto me, "Lytskin how you live, you never have food". Then I would say, "I find ways to eat". I'm a survivor, and I eat somehow someway. Even if the weather is bad outdoors, I get in my wheelchair, and go to a family member's house to eat.

One day, I joined a job-training program, which is for people with disabilities. I was hoping this program would help me find a job to put more dividends into my pockets. This program required that I participate 5 days out of the week, from 8: 30 a.m. to 2:30 p.m. I had fun in this program because I met more people who became my friends.

Many people who were here in this program had physical issues, and some had mental issues. Whether, the issue was physical or mental, they were encouraged to continue in life. I think it is so cool for mentally challenged people to seek employment. Although, many of them had mental issues, they still had a mind to know that money is needed to get what you want in life. So here I am in this place, about to participate in a program, which is supposed to enhance my skills for employment.

As I was in training, I was being taught both mental and physical skills. When the physical body is learning how to do something, the mental body is being taught as well. Doing training, I was able to stay seated in the wheelchair. The training and teaching only lasted for about 2 months. I felt within myself that I was doing an okay job.

Occasionally, a staff member monitored me. Proving a point to the staff members was my focus. Whether, I performed "good or bad", in the end, the staff will present unto me a verdict.

After two months of training ended, a staff member scheduled a time and day for us all to gather up. During this scheduled meeting, the staff is going to explain unto me the possibilities of being hired for a job. They (the staff) are going to present unto me a verdict concerning the physical and mental skills that I have displayed in this program. Whether they present unto me a good report, or a bad one, a verdict must be giving. Every thing I've done while in training, up until this point, the staff will explain unto me in full details. My future financial status is depending upon this meeting to be a good one. A judgment will be given, but I am hoping for a good one.

Well, after I heard the staff's verdict concerning my work performances, I was hurt about it. The mental part of me became vexed by the staff's words. The staff said unto me, "you move to slow to work for a real company". They also said", your ways of organizing an office was too slow and very poor. Actually, I went to this employment program twice. The second time I went, they said the same thing (I move to slow). Nevertheless, I left the program wounded and hurt within my heart again.

My body's reflexes and movements are still slow. This brain injury, which I suffered, was very brutal. For some reason, my brain orders my body to do things in a more difficult way. Even when a task is a simple one, to me it is a hard job. Since the staff said, "I was a slow worker", I then began to think about the injury that my brain suffered. From my brain injury, my cerebellum and frontal had been attacked violently by drugs. The cerebellum is my limb mover, and my frontal lobe is my organizer. The same function (frontal lobe, the organizer) that I use to organize drug gathering with friends, is the same brain function that I needed to organize things on a job. I was very good in organizing drug gatherings. Since drugs beat on my organizing worker, my job organizing skills was said to be poor. I cannot believe I put drugs in my brain, and now, I will be slow with physical bodily movements probably for the rest of my life. Also, when organizing things, I will probably do so the harder way.

After the staff had given me the sad report about my working performance, my emotions became hurt. My emotions, which are controlled by the frontal lobes in my brain, became bothered. I felt like my financial status would never change. I felt that life financially would be rough on me. However, when my feelings became hurt in situations, never did I allow sorrow to over take me for long periods. Emotions and feeling are created to experience change in life. Just as you will never see the exact same Monday, you do not have to live with the same hurting emotions. Each and everyday I awake, my emotions are being renewed.

However, I still decided not to give up. God did not give up on me; therefore, I should not give up on myself. I must keep on pressing my way through adversity that approaches. I will keep on pressing until a job has been found. Receiving under 7 thousand dollars a year, and less than 60 dollars worth of food stamps per month is quite a rough life to live. So here I am on a journey seeking for more. It is impossible to have a little fun with the finances that I now have. However, I did not sit and complain about it. I just kept on going and living life.

Through the years of being jobless, I still did not give up; I refuse to stop seeking another source of financial payment. Never will I let myself stay in the puddles of sorrow. If I gave up, personally, I would have lived life in complete bitterness. I would have allowed myself to drown in the pool of misery without water being present. Anytime a person gives up in life, that individual has drowned in complete bitterness. Do not let misery and the bitterness of life touch your living. Dry your weeping eyes, and get your thoughts right, do not stop now; you still have a race to run. By Brian K. Irons

One day, I went to a department store and asked the manager about a certain job position. I felt that I could perform at this position very good. This job did not require that physical ability to be a necessity. Hand speed and office organization skills are not an issue with this position. Being judged by a staff, this position does not need such. The only thing that can hinder me from working here at this company is they aren't hiring. This position is truly a very easy job. I was looking forward to working at this position. At this job, I wanted to work as a greeter or porter.

The porter or greeter's job is to welcome customers as they entered into the department store. Smiling and looking happy while greeting customers is a part of the deal too. Presenting customers with pleasant words is the porter's assignment. On the other hand, if I am hired, I can direct customers to a desired area in the store. This job can be done while sitting in my wheelchair. If I had to take a customer to his or her desired area in the store, riding in my wheelchair was perfect for that.

However, when I went to the manager of the store, I asked him, "Could I fill out an application so I can work as a "porter or greeter". Well, the manager of the store told me that the position is not an option any more. He said, "No one works as a greeter any more". I thought the company had recently stopped that position from being worked at, because just the other day, a greeter greeted me.

A couple of days later, in my wheelchair, I went to that same department store to buy some soap and shampoo. Of course, it was the beginning of the month because I had some money in my pocket. As I rolled into the department store, the "porter" of the store greeted me. After the porter greeted me, I became angry within myself. I felt like the manager of store lied. He told me the porter job is not an office anymore; yet, someone greeted me as I entered in. Within me, I felt as if the manager showed discrimination because of my wheelchair situation. Nevertheless, if he did lie, oh well, life is going to venture on, and so must I.

I do not care how crushed or hurt my heart becomes

with my financial status; my heart is strong, and I am relying on it to not give up and become defeated. I am not going back to the streets and sale cocaine again. I will find a job; I know I will. There has to be something I can do to bring myself out of this financial poverty. My financial situation is truly poverty level, and I desire not to live this way any longer.

My body might suffer from what I sent it through, but I refuse to suffer in financial struggle. If I can help it, which I am trying to do, this financial struggle has to end. I really want to get out of this financial poverty mode, because it bothered me heavily to ask people for $10 here or $20 dollars there. It has truly been hard on me. Although, I am hanging in there, and trying to do something with my life, it has been a rough 12 years as of now.

Now you know why I published this book without any professional editing. I had two choices to make: either publish this book now, or suffer financially another 2,3,4 or even 5 more years. I published this book hoping for a financial miracle. Trying to publish this book for $600 was hard. I did the best I could in writing and editing this book. If I was able to afford more electronic materials concerning my writing, I am sure, a better job of writing could have been done. I am proud of this writing accomplishment, but I know it needs lots of polishing done. For the pass twelve years, God has been good to me, but my finances have not.

I heard a married woman the other day share her testimony with the people in the audience. In her testimony, she said, "she makes over $60,000 a year". With $60,000 a year, I can do a lot with that. A person making over $60,000 a year, I was thinking to myself that she should have no complaints, not one. Then I began to wonder, "How much do her husband makes per year too? Actually, she probably makes more than $60,000; you know people are going to tell you what they make for real. This woman is very pretty, and from the way she dresses, and the car that she possesses, I can see that the $60,000 is taken very good care of her. After I heard her testimony, I became crushed within my heart because she receives more money in one year, than I receive in almost a total of ten years. Hearing testimonies like that only encouraged me to want more money in my life. Whether people acknowledge the fact that money is needed in one's personal possession or not, I realize that without it, living on earth will be full of pain. Since I was still happy while having no money, I realize that money never brings true happiness. I really didn't have money, but I was still happy. I still felt hurt and pain at times, but I was still happy in life. The main reason why I stayed happy, is because, I knew this book would be published and in stores one day.

My 3rd book will teach you to hold on to your vision. It is called, "Keep Your Vision".

Chapter 12

Opening Doors, and God's Word (Bible) Concerning Sin

At the approach of every door, a decision must be made concerning its entrance. Every door is connected to an entrance, and every door has an exit. All doors are available unto us to open. When you open a door, you have done so intentionally. It becomes our personal acceptance to open any door. Not only is it our personal acceptance, but also, each door is tag with numerous of tests. Remember this; your life is fully based upon the door you have opened. Whether good or bad, when you open any door, you can expect your life's experiences to be based on your entrance of that particular door.

If you need a cup of sugar, and salt is a door, then why should you open that particular door. Salt is not what you are looking for; therefore, the salt door should be kept closed. Go open the door of sugar, because that is what you desire. Stick with the plan, and do not change it. The directions said, add one cup of sugar, not a cup of salt. If sugar is what you need, then go after it. If you open the door where salt is; you have just opened up the wrong door, for the wrong flavor. By Brian K. Irons

In my life, when I opened up the door of drugs, I walked into a lifestyle full of stupidity, ignorance, and destruction. In addition, I also entered into the messy ways of wickedness. Stupidity, ignorance, and destruction became the activities in my living. As a mouse walks onto a trap filled with cheese bait, in the same sense, when I opened the door of drugs, I walked into a living filled with the bait of stupidity.

If you walk through a door were there is wickedness, you have just entered your body into a place possessed by demons. Wherever there are demons, you can bet they are there because of the performances of wickedness. Not only that, but also, you have walked through a door where the activity of breaking the laws are. The longer you stay inside a place where wickedness is, the stronger demons become. Demons will begin to become familiar with what you like to do in life. Demons will hold your mind, and never allow you to close that door back.

Demons do not gain their strength in time, only people do. People exercise continually, and lift weights to get stronger. However, demons gain their strength through daily personal acts of wickedness. I didn't see self-destruction the first time I smoked dope, however, from the gaining strength of demons, destruction I saw came ten years later. Through the power, and the strength from demons, the wickedness in my life had gotten stronger. When I had opened the door of wickedness, I was trapped inside for ten years. Nowhere to run, and nowhere to hide, my brain was captivated by the power and strength of demons. When I opened up the door of drugs, I DID NOT KNOW that I was entering into a living filled with demons.

Only demons lead people to experiencing disastrous and horrifying events. A demon is one that has the ongoing desire to do evil. When a demon is inside of a man, an evil task will be performed. Wherever evil is in operation, surely, demons are present as well. Demons do not travel in one's and ten's as we think they do. Demons operate in packs of hundreds and even thousands. Yeah, that many demons will enter into your life and mind after the door of evil has been open. Just as lent sticks to your clothes, after you have opened up the door of evil, demons will stick to your life. Why do you think that it was so hard for me to leave drugs alone? As my drug addiction level increased, more demons were added unto it. Drug addictions and demons go hand and hand. I advise you to know what you are getting yourself into, when you open any door in this life.

A drug's addiction is actually the demon itself. From the addiction, it became drastically hard for me to turn around and walk back out that door. The reason why the door of drugs became exceedingly hard to close is because; thousand of demons were attached to my brain's organs, and I DID NOT KNOW it.

Demons through drug's addiction actually use my brain as a home. Demons lived inside of my head. They became comfortable; they relaxed. Every time I kept putting drugs in my brain, it gave demons the power to live.

Every door (situation) that appears in life needs to be inspected. I am not talking about the doors at your local mall; I am talking about the doors of life. Before you walk through any door in life, observe it first. Once you walk through the entrance of certain doors, suddenly, and unexpectedly, demons will trapped you inside, and brutally beat you. You'll be in a place where there is nowhere to run and nowhere to hide. You'll become trapped inside with no outlet. Once you become trapped inside, a brutal physical bashing is about to happen.

Physical bashings are always performed by demons. Physical bashings are brutal, violent, and can kill when in action. Beating a man to the point of death is truly a work of evil. Read the example in the following paragraph about being trapped when walking through a door, and suddenly being brutally beaten by demonic led people.

I met a young man, who was 21 years old at the time. This 21-year-old fellow, I met him at Mount Vernon Rehab Treatment Center. I guess you know his mental and physical condition was so serious, that Mount Vernon Rehab Center was the place for admittance. Remember, no one goes to Mount Vernon Rehab Center with minor bruises or minor injuries. Although, my heart experienced 11 minutes of stoppage, and another person experienced bullet wounds to the body, however, this 21-year-old fellow's situation was one of a kind.

I believe his story went like this; this 21-year-old young man was in a street gang. The 21-year-old, and his other gang members had labeled themselves as bloods. This gang (the bloods) made a decision to go and check out this party. He and his gang associated friends decided to pull the vehicle over and park. After the car was parked, they proceeded to a door, and knocked on it. After knocking on the door, of course, they entered therein. They had just entered through a door were a party was going on.

I suppose loud music was heard. Or maybe people were going in and out of the door, which probably drew the blood's attention. As my friend and his other gang partners entered through the door of this party, they did not know it was a party full of crips. Actually, this house party was a gathering of a gang of members who are enemies to the "blood" association. In other words, the 21-year-old man, and his friends (the bloods) opened a door and walked into a house full of enemies (crips &demons).

All "gangs" are demonic promoted. Nevertheless, my 21-year-old friend walked through a door, not knowing what was on the other side. Soon and very soon, the bloods are about to find out what type of door they had just walked through. When my 21-year-old friend and his group entered though the door of this party, the "crips" recognized that a couple of "bloods" entered therein. The crips is a gang that wears dark colors, preferably blue. However, the bloods wear red colors. I suppose my friend and his partners with him, all had on red colors. When the bloods entered through the door, immediately the gang called, "crips" rushed them. The crips physically mishandled the bloods badly. The bloods were out numbered, so they were physically bashed and violently manipulated by the crips association.

The bloods walked into a party, which apparently was the wrong party. Nevertheless, the gang of bloods came dreadfully close to meeting the character called, "death". Just by entering into this door, I am sure they did not know that the faces of death and demons would be seen.

I am sure the bloods and crips does some sort of drugs. All gang members put some sort of chemicals into their brains. No gang has parties without drug usage in action. Therefore, the party was filled with wickedness, evil, and demons, because of the presence of drugs. Since the "crips" are filled with demons, and the "bloods" are filled with demons, when the two gangs fought against one another, it was a battle against demons on demons. Therefore, a situation is never won because demons will never solve a demonic problem.

When you open up the door of drugs, and walk through it, a brutal day of beating is soon to happen in your life. Some door openers of drugs will be beaten on the first day of entry, just as the bloods were. On the other hand, some will be beaten in a ten-year span, just as I was. A gang of humans has never beaten on me, however, a few men did surround me a couple of times, but I manage to flee and escape from their presence. However, another gang did beat up on me, which was marijuana, cocaine, codeine pills, and heroin. I opened the door of drugs one day, and they beat me on July 26.

People of the world, never think that one drug by itself cannot kill you. Anything that awakens demons can also awaken death. Demons are inside of all street drugs, and I have never in my life, known a demon to be a good servant. That is why drugs are not good for the brain. Once drugs intoxicants are put in the brain, the only activities done, are events demons persuades the body to do. I advise you to close the door of drugs and wickedness, which will prevent demons from coming into your life.

Just as a new movie being advertised on your TV screen saying, "coming soon at a local theatre near you", it is the same order that drugs will do unto you. Once you put dope in the brain, the beating from drugs is coming soon within your local brain that sits inside of you. The only difference between the bloods being beaten, and your brain being beating is the fact that; you are beating your own life when you put drug intoxicants inside of the brain. From the intoxicants of drugs, a demonic force then becomes active, which will use your life for its own purpose and pleasure to do evil.

People already know that entering through the door of drugs is the wrong entrance to take. Our conscience worker bears witness that it is wrong. A drug door is a door that we should never open up. It is best that every door that pertains to drugs and or wickedness be kept closed. Let that door stay shut forever. If you let the door of drugs stay closed, you have just stopped demons and wickedness from entering into your living. Stay free, and do not even knock on the door of drugs. If you knock on the door, it will be open unto you. Through wisdom, know that it is wrong, rather than finding out by harsh physical experiences, which is a taste of sufferings.

Once a person has entered into the door of drugs, that individual has just walked into an apartment full of trouble and frustration. Being disappointed is an ongoing task when a brain has been exposed to the pleasure of drugs. After I had opened up the door of drugs, my life became mentally frustrated and very much disappointed. Events started happening in my life that I never thought would be a part of my being. Once I opened the door of drugs, it did not take long for the windows of crime, court appearance, and violent activities to open up in life. When I first entered through the door of drugs, I actually walked into the "house of horrors" and I DID NOT KNOW it. Not only is it called, "The House of Horrors", but also, it's the "House of Planned Destruction".

After I had experienced all of these dope tragedies, which caused my mind and body to suffer physical and mental disaster, the thought of attending church smoothly popped up into my mind. Now, my cerebrum in the brain, which is my thinking center, is thinking about a different door to open up. When the thought of church popped up in my cerebrum, I went to this one church called, "**Old Landmark Temple C.O.G.I.C**". Pastor Albert G. Hollins and assistant Pastor Ronald Moore are the heads in this place.

This same church prayed for me, when I first became ill at my friend's house. When I approached this church, the doors became open, and I was about to enter. As I came to the front door of this church, the assistant pastor (Ronald Moore) and two of the associate ministers, Stanley Smith, and Clifton Brown picked me up while I was sitting in the wheelchair.

As I was sitting in the wheelchair, they rolled me to the front area of the church. The church people were now able to see what God had done. Well, also, the entire church was now able to see what drugs had done unto me as well. There I was, sitting in the front row of the church, bruised up in heart, and beaten in the physical from the bashing of drugs.

As I sat in the front of the church, the power of God was so strong in the place that I broke down "crying". Oh, although, I am a grown man, and was very tough on the streets, I am not ashamed to cry in front of people. Besides, when the power of sorrow hits anyone in church, he or she will shed cups of tears.

At this particular time, my tears were of great sorrow. This was my first experience of feeling the presence of God in a church. Although, I was a man, and very tough on the streets, when I attended church service, I became a big baby under the power of God. I cried because every drug scene that my life had witnessed swiftly flashed through my mind. Incident after incident, robbery after robbery, drug use after drug use, and finally, my sports career is now over. I cried, I cried, I cried!

Not only was I opening up the doors of the church, but also I was opening up a bible on a continual basis, or as much as I could. In my life, my thoughts never did conceive the mental pleasure of reading a book at all, especially during school. I do not remember ever reading an entire book in my life. Reading was not one of my desired motives. I could not seem to prepare my mind for the mental session of reading. Reading a book filled with a bunch of words, I just could not do. There was no power in the world that could excite or motivate me to read a book. However, since I began to attend church, reading the bible became one of my daily chores. Now a day, I really enjoy reading other author's stories, and most definitely, I enjoy reading the bible. I wish I had the mind to read years and years ago.

As I have been attending church and reading the bible, I learned that, being the physical man that I am, I had not the potential strength to stop the persuasive force of drug usage. Neither my physical status, nor my mental power mounted up to defeat the warring temptation of drugs. Although, I did have great physical strength to protect myself from physical danger, however, when it came to protecting my inner body, I was dumb and weak in that area of life. I did not have Godly power to protect my inner man (brain) from the enticement of drugs.

You need to read your bible too, to learn the power that it has. If you go and grab a hold onto your bible, if it has dust on it, that means, many months has passed by, and you have not been reading about the power God.

True seekers of God, and people who have a relationship with him, will read the bible regularly. The bible is a spiritual strength builder. It's your peace creator. When you read it, it will become living words unto you. My next book, which shall be released in 2008, is called, "Thou Shalt Not Have Any Other Gods Besides Me". This book will teach you that the words in the bible, which have been truly blown from the mouth of God, are in the earth's facility. Just like in the movie Poltergeist when the little girl stretched forth her arms, placed her hands on the TV screen, and said, "They're herrrrrre", well, the words in the bible are herrrrre on earth as well.

People in the world will never have the full strength to cease their bodies from performing actions that feels so remarkably good. A person's body is fascinated by good feelings, which the brain's limbic system plays a high role. The limbic system interacts with the body to give it the treatment of pleasure. Your brain will strive to get that good feeling and sensation as much as it possible can. When the brain becomes fascinated by the explosive sensation of pleasure, the body becomes trained, and begins to feign for that same feeling. Once you put the drugs in your brain, the body then becomes a prisoner to the pleasures of that operating chemical. Now that your brain and body has become addicted, the mental power to sustain from drug affiliations has been cast away. The hidden operation of drugs is to imprison the brain with its pleasures, and at the same time, it will weaken the user's strength to flee from the wicked usage of drugs.

I read a scripture in the bible that I DID NOT KNOW nothing about until I started reading it. The biblical book's name is called, "Romans". In the book of Romans, chapter 5, and verse 6 is a scripture that I feel the need to share with you. This scripture enlightened my mind (brain) concerning the strength that every man and woman possesses on earth. The scripture reads as this, *Romans 5:6 "for when we were yet without strength, in due time, Christ (Jesus) die for the ungodly*.

Allow me to enlighten your mind about that scripture. It says *"for when we were yet without strength, in due time, Christ (Jesus) died for the ungodly.* The ungodly are people that do not obey the rules of God. People who do not allow God to give them a new way of living, or that do not accept the "blessing" plan of God is called, "the ungodly".

People are called ungodly because their minds are constantly concentrating on wickedness, inventing evil things (drugs), and searching for ways to commit demonic activities. We all were once led to do many acts of evil. None of us had the strength of God dwelling in us at certain points in our lives. We all have knowingly lied before. We all did something sneaky before. We all were without strength. You may not have done the ungodly deeds I've done; however, I am sure you've done something evil before.

When I first begin to inhale drugs into my brain and body, afterwards I continued to use them on a regular basis. On my very first experience of inhaling dope, which was marijuana, I DID NOT KNOW that something was on the inside of me that helped, urged, and led me to become aquatinted with this chemical controlled substance. You mean to tell me that there is something on the inside of me, and I DID NOT KNOW it. That is quite naturally weird or mentally scary to have something on the inside of you, and not even knowing what it is. It makes me seriously think, and mentally wonder, how it actually got inside of me. How long has it been inside of me? Who or what is it that's in me? From what I read in the bible, it was something inside of me that led and empowered me to try drugs, and definitely caused me to break the laws of God. After breaking the laws of God, that, which was on the inside of me, led me to harm my own brain and body. Nevertheless, when I was living the street life, I continued to do drugs on a daily basis, because of an inner being. It was a hidden character living inside of my brain and body, and I DID NOT KNOW it.

Here is the scripture concerning this hidden character; *Romans 7:19- for the good that I would, I do not: but the evil, which I would not, now that I do. 7:20, now if I do that, I would not, it is no more I that do it but sin that dwelleth in me.*

Many people right now have no idea what that scripture means. Again, you need to get God in your life and read more about the words he actually spoke from his mouth to be recorded on biblical paper. That scripture is a mere fact about life that I DID NOT KNOW about. Throughout my years of living on the earth, I DID NOT KNOW what sin fully meant, neither did I know that sin was dwelling in my body. Of course, I DID NOT KNOW that sin was the main reason and purpose why my life ventured through "hell and back". Finally, yet importantly, I DID NOT KNOW that "sin" was the ultimate reason why my body almost ended up a dead man's casket at a graveyard ground site. Although, drugs were the substances that messed my life up, however, sin, which was in me, was the head leader of all my lawbreaking decisions made.

Allow me to plainly explain, and provide you with a simple example of that scripture (*Romans 7:19-20)*. Consciously, you know wrong from right. Remember, God has provided the brain to know right from wrong automatically by the conscience center. However, *Romans 7: 19-20* is saying; we know it is wrong to indulge into certain activities, but sin is the character that leads us to indulge in the act anyway. We know it is wrong to indulge in drugs, but through the power of sin, we did drugs anyway. We know it is against the law to have drugs in our possession, but we still secretly hid dope inside of our homes, automobiles, pants pockets, or anywhere thought of. We know it is wrong to have sex with a woman without her approval, but sin caused a rape to be committed anyway. Sin is the controlling power that has led us to do all activities of evil. If sin is not living inside of you, then going to court to be judged will never be an experience. Sin is the controlling power that has caused a world of people to break all of the "Ten Commandments".

When human beings first put God's blessed plan into their lives, and make church their place of fellowship, instead of the nightclubs, many hidden facts about sin and drugs will be revealed. He (God) desires to teach and reveal unto us all every "good" and "bad" outcome that happens in your life. God is the truth revealer to all humankind. God is able to teach and reveal unto you great facts. Since God is a teacher, then willingly you should become one of his full time students. Whether you cause your body to do good deeds in life or bad deeds, God's word (bible) will to teach you concerning both perspectives.

Results from committing sins are actually occurring in people's lives right now today. Everyone is ignoring the signs and warning that are being displayed unto them. I know that I am not the only person in the world God has tossed warnings at. If I was the only person in the world who God has sent warnings too, I would be the only person in the world whom God loves. However, I am not the only person who God loves. God loves us all, whether clean or dirty, he still loves us. Even as we all are committing acts of sin right now, God still loves us. Nevertheless, God desires to get the most out of our lives, than what sin is getting. Sorry to say, sin is doing more influencing in the world, than what we are allowing God to do. Its not that sin is more powerful than God is; it's just that, the people are filled with the strength of evil, rather than the muscles of righteousness. It's easy to do wrong things, but it is hard as ancient iron to do what's right.

When people were seeking to end my life by the shooting of bullets, truly, sin and Satan had the biggest impact. Whenever Satan leads a person to do anything, that individual is doing something against the commands of God. Anytime someone seeks to kill a person, that individual is being controlled by the strength, force, and power from Satan. Satan is the entity that leads humankind to participate in evil. Yeah, Satan is the demon in this world. Therefore, when I was in that gangway, plotting to commit a murder, sin and Satan were operating through my mind, encouraging me to commit a murder. Satan and his demons cause us all to sin, and when sin is committed, he gets the glory.

Therefore, every time I did something that summons me to face the law in court, sin, and Satan helped me to get there. In other words, sin and Satan are the provokers that lead people to face the laws of God' in court, to be convicted, judged, and sentence. Now I know why God destroyed the earth many years ago. It was all because, sin had lead people to break his laws on a daily basis.

Although, more than half of the world is not spiritually inclined to claim being in a true relationship with God, more than half of the world knows why Jesus was killed. More than half of the world has acknowledged a biblical fact that Jesus died on a cross for our sin. Many of us have never read about the story of Jesus, however, most of us heard about it. We heard that Jesus was beaten, nailed to the cross, and killed on the account of our sins. Since Jesus was beaten to death, it had to be human hands that did it. Since Jesus was nailed to the cross, we know that it had to be people, which primed iron points though his hands. However, these things were done, because Jesus agreed to die for our sins.

Even though it was the plan of God for his son Jesus to come to earth and die for the sins of world; an additional work was done through the people, which killed him. People who look and act just like you and me, actually laid hands on Jesus and brutally killed him. A "gang" of humans gathered up in numbers, surrounded, charged, beat, and killed Jesus. Just as a gang of members charged and beat up my friend, who was in a gang called, "The Bloods", the same scenario applies with Jesus. Yeah, Jesus was surrounded, charged, beat, and killed too.

Jesus did not die from an old age ordeal. He was crucified and murdered by the hands of people in the sight of men and God. The people who forcefully laid their evil hands on Jesus were led to do so by the operation of sin. As I said before, anytime an individual or a group of people commits a murder (or assault); it is sin, and Satan, through demons in complete control of the entire scheme, plan and plot. Even before the people murdered Jesus, God saw how it was all going to transpire. However, Jesus was led by God to face death for the sins of the world. Nevertheless, God led Jesus to face death, and sin led **Brian Irons** to face death. Do you see the difference yet? If not, let me break some more stuff down unto you.

There is more to realize and understand, than just to know that Jesus died for the sins of the world. Actually, from my spiritual understanding, God has given me another revelation why Jesus came to earth to die on the account of our sins committed. The other reason why Jesus came on earth to die is that, while the raging and violent acts of the killing of Jesus body took place, his bruised and damaged body is an example unto us what sin will do unto our bodies as well. When we look at the cross of Jesus, we see a man bruised, beat up, and whose physical appearance looks like a worth of nothing. That is what sin did unto me, it bruised me, and it beat me, and made me look like a piece of nothing. Although, the death of Jesus means everything to the world, however, when **Brian Irons** face death, it meant nothing but a body's of waste. Jesus faced death by the will of God, and I faced death by the force of sin and Satan.

When we allow sin to operate through our bodies, it will empower us to become murderers to our own lives. Just as sin led the people to harm the body of Jesus, sin led me to harm my own body. With my own personal hands, and with the help of sin, a murder was almost performed. Drugs, when they are operating in a person's life through sin, they become a team. Yes, sin, Satan, and drugs are a team. They will always win; you are not clever enough or strong enough to conquer sin and drug tactics alone. It is time for you to accept the blessed plan of God for you life, rather than, being led by sin, which in return will bring death in your life. Yeah, sin's job is to kill those who allow it to work through their bodies.

Roman 6:23 says; for the wages of "sin" is death. In other words, when sin is operating in a person's body, his or her payment, or wages will be death. If you continue to operate and work in sin, you will receive a salary. Committing sin is a job; every time you break the law, God looks at that as a job of evil performed. Therefore, a payment of sin's results is to be expected. Sin will persuade a person's body to work, until death becomes the payment. Every time sin causes a person to perform acts of evil, his or her body is being toured to the graveyard (death). If sin is controlling your body, as drugs physically controlled mine, you are heading for unexpected danger, in which death will be your wages.

Even when we were infants, we all have sinned. *Psalms 58; 3 the wicked are estranged from the womb: they go astray as soon as they be born, speaking lies.* This scripture speaks about people actually born speaking lies. Infants, toddlers, babies, all speak lies as soon as they are released from the womb.

However, I am not going to talk about being born on day one; I am going to take it 2 years later. I am about to talk about you committing a wicked act even at the age of 2 years old. When a two -year-old baby has shattered a glass lamp, or has broken an object of great value, that little infant will look the parent square in the eye, and then lie about it. When the 2-year-old child lies about the event, a sin has just been committed. The sin that the baby is born in will ignite the infant's brain to cause the mouth lie. The two-year-old child does not even know what the word lie truly means, and yet, an act of dishonesty has been performed. Now I know why the bible says, the wicked are estranged from the womb, because infants have the cunning power to lie, even at 2 years after birth.

The parent is not dealing with the fact that the baby has cleverly lied from the mouth; the parent is dealing with sin that the baby is born in. That same child can do the exact same thing (break something) the next day, and then lie about it again. That is what sin makes us grown folks do; we do the same ungodly acts repeatedly for years. If sin causes us to go astray from God, and we perform lies 2 years after childbirth, then the ruler or master of evil is born with us. Nevertheless, for most of us, God's mercy has been operating in our lives long enough until a decision, which is to seek freedom can be made.

Lets say that a 2 year old baby, which the bible says is born in sin, has died or been killed. Although, the baby died, in sin, that child still has a place in heaven. The child still goes to heaven because he or she never reached a mature age to determine right from wrong. That child never reached an age to have the understanding to make a free will choice to go to Jesus. However, my over grown self lived to see the age of 24, therefore, I had ample enough understanding, but I did not seek freedom. Therefore, the "gates of hell" opened up to receive me, along with my sins.

If God had not showed mercy on me when my heart stopped, a picture of my face would have been scanned on an obituary sheet being passed around at a funeral session. My obituary would have said; young black man by the name of **Brian Irons** dies during the night from drug usage. Actually, the obituary should say this; sin, wickedness, and drugs killed **Brian Irons** on July 26. It is the truth isn't it. All because of sin and drugs led my own hands to work wickedness; a funeral was about to be arranged. If God's mercy had not done one more work for me, then on July 27, my family would have been seeking a building to have my funeral.

Not only would have death been my life's reward,

but also the place called, "hell" would have been my home throughout eternity (forever and ever). From the wicked life I was living, hell almost became my inherited place. The bible states, in *Psalms 9:17-the wicked should be turned into hell, and all the nations that forget God.*

As you have just read, my life has been filled with the works of wickedness, which characterizes me to be called, "the wicked". A long time ago, my name had been changed from **Brian Irons** to "The Wicked". Although, sin is the true worker of wickedness, but if I allow it to live in me, wicked actions will be my daily motives. The bible speaks the truth, and it will not bite its tongue. If it says, **"the wicked shall be turned into hell"**, then guess what, the wicked will be turned into hell. If I let wickedness live inside of me, and I die in it, then wickedness and me both go to the lower parts of the earth, which is hell. If you are living a lawbreaking life, then you are called "the wicked". It's not hard to earn rights to be called the wicked; and it's not hard to be sent to hell. Only thing you have to do is keep living a wicked life, and hell is all yours, because you've earned it.

I thought the penitentiary was rough, my Lord, I do not want to go to "hell". Hell is a place that is worse than any number of penitentiaries put together. At least in the penitentiary, you can run, and protect yourself, however, in hell, you cannot do anything but sit, and be tortured forever. Wickedness almost brought my life down to the grave of hell. Anything that takes you down, or bring you down, there is no place for you to go but down. The wicked one, which is the devil, once you've became an employee for him, he then has prime rights to take your life downward, instead of upward. Hell is the place where the wicked one lives. If you are working with him, then death and hell just might be your eternal reward (payment).

Just the other day, I overheard a young woman make a statement concerning a person going to hell. We as people can see how wrong someone else is, but we never see our own flaws. Every time we see someone doing wrong, we say, "He's going to hell". Well, do you break the laws (do

322

drugs)? Is your life an evil mess? Is wickedness living inside of you? Do you lie to get money? If so, what makes you think it's not possible for you to be sent to hell with that person. You folks need to stop it! We love to examine others, but we won't examine our own selves. If you look at your own self, then I am sure you have no room to talk. Michael Jackson spoke a message years ago, but it got passed all of us. "Man in the Mirror"!

People in the world always say, "God knows my heart", well, of course, that is true, but if you not seeking righteousness as the bible speaks, then God knowing your heart means nothing. When you begin to walk upright with God, that's what moves him. People have been walking on the earth for decades confessing, "God knows my heart". If your life has never came to a point were God has forgiven your sins, then hell will be your home, after you die. How can you say a person is going to hell, and your living is fully filled with all unrighteousness. This world is truly off course, and we do not know it. Everyone thinks he or she is so right, and then proclaims the bible to be a book of false advertisements. Anything that pronounces statements against our personal righteous, we become so ignorant, and begin to proclaim our ways or reasoning. Anyway, back to the story.

The bible has a scripture in the Old Testament that I would like to willingly share with you. *Ecclesiastics 11:9 Rejoice, O young man, in thy youth; and allow thy heart to cheer thee in the days of thy youth, and walk in the ways of thine heart, and in the sight of thine eyes: but know thou, that for all these things God will bring thee into judgment.*

This is what God is saying through the scripture written above. God is saying this; young man, young woman, go ahead and do whatever your heart desires. Whatever your heart desires, and whatever your eyes behold, go after it, and get it. Go ahead and celebrate concerning your earthly accomplishment. Do whatever you want to do. Me, God, I give you the right away to do drugs if you want to. I give you the right to choose your own road to walk on in life. I, the Lord God will not step into your life and stop you.

If you want to drink alcohol, and intake drugs, then go right ahead, and while you are doing it, salute yourself. You do not have to follow my blessed plan if you do not want to. You are a man, you are a woman, and you have been given full rights to make your own decisions in life. However, _know thou_ this, I (God) do want you to know that I am going to judge you for all actions done. If you want to live a dangerous life, that is your business, but my prophetic words are going to do whatever they say. Do what your heart desires, but know thou this; my judgments have desires too.

As you have just read in my story, I was rejoicing, celebrating, partying, and having ongoing pleasure from the methods of drugs. Sin, along with drugs persuaded my heart to do all acts of evil. My heart was glad in the days were I was able to purchase cars and spends loads of money. My heart became cheerful, when I was able to buy clothing at will. Whatever my heart desired to have, I sold drugs, collected enough money, and then purchase whatever I wanted. In my youthful years, I did every thing without the mental persuasion of "good wisdom". In my heart, it was all about the cash, sex (with women only), and materials. Whatever my eyes perceived, and whatever they lusted after, I did not withhold anything from them. If my mind had creatively thought it, if my heart willfully desired it, once my eyes beheld it, I had to have it in my possession. I was not thinking about judgments; I was only thinking about being cheerful (or satisfied) in the days of my youth.

As a bottle is filled with soda, my heart and mind was filled with the pleasures of wickedness and evil. Just as soda is drank by a person, my inner man drunk up the fluids of sin. As the blackness of tar covers the roof of any house, sin and evil covered the inner parts of my soul. As the queen bee searches for honey to satisfy its appetite, my brain searched for more sinful activities to satisfy my lustful desires. As an eagle can see miles ahead of him, God saw this wicked drug disaster coming 10 years before it happened. By Brian K. Irons

Let me share with you a few categories that sin will

persuade you to perform when it remains in your brain and body. These sins are categorized as "the works of the flesh". There are 17 works of the flesh, which sin empowers people to perform. The 17 works of the flesh, which I am about to mention, are physical performances by people who live their lives in sin. These performances are done because people have decided to do the desires of their own heart.

The book of Galatians 5: 19 says, now the works of the flesh are manifest, which are these; adultery, fornication, uncleanness, lasciviousness, 5:20 idolatry, witchcraft, hatred, variance, emulations, wrath, strife, seditions, heresies, 5: 21 envying, murders, drunkenness, reveling.

1. - **Adultery**-is an unfaithful sexual performance done by two or more people. When two people get married, a scene called, wedding has taken place. In a wedding, a bride and a groom are both present. A man and a woman stands chin up at the altar. Face to face, both parties exchange words, which are vows of commitment. Not only are the words vowels of commitments, but also, those same words are words of promise. When the couple exchanges vows, usually, an authorized minister is present to read the holy script. Yeah, that's how a wedding is usually done.

As the couple is looking into one another eyes, a licensed minister asks both of them questions. One by one, the minister ask them this question; do you take this man/woman to be your lawfully wedded spouse? After the minister asks the question, he is expecting the answer from them both to be "yes, I do". After both parties have said, "I do", the two have just become married. These two have agreed upon the covenant of holy matrimony. Not only did this couple commit and make vows to one another, but also, a vow has been committed unto the Law as well.

When two people finally become married, I hope they do not think they have the fullness of God in their lives. Just because being married is a righteous act before God, that does not mean you have been freed from sin. People can be married and still live wicked lives. People can be married, and still be live in the same lifestyle I was living.

We all know that, after a marriage has taken place, it becomes automatic that neither party is to perform sex with none other, but with the spouse. If one does have sex with a person other than the spouse, adultery has just been committed. The person who commits adultery, has just shared his or her inner being with someone else.

God has a commandment that says, "Thou Shalt Not Commit adultery". If adultery is committed by anyone, that person is being disobedient to God. Not only to God, but also, to the spouse as well. It's by vows that the married spouse is not to have sex with someone else other the spouse. And it's by the command of God not to do so as well.

Adultery is committed through deceit and crafty scheming by a man and or the woman. When adultery has been performed, it is from the strength of sin, that such an act has been committed. Sin is the forceful power that strengthens two people to activate this deed of adultery. Never can one person commit adultery alone.

When adultery has been committed, an act of deception has been performed. Constantly, during the committing of adultery, deception is always an active force. Although, at the altar of marriage, most ministers do not mention the word "adultery", however, whether the word adultery is mentioned or not, the two who have been given in marriage, they already know that having sex outside the marriage is a horrible act to commit. When I say it is horrible, know that it is horrible.

The adulterer (the cheater) will tell ongoing lies to get this act of adultery in session. Lies will always be rehearsed into the ears of his or her spouse when adultery is being planned to be committed. Married people who are caught up in the sinful ways of adultery, they will lie about where they are going. They lie about going to work. They will lie about going to the gym. They lie about going to the grocery store. They even lie when they say; they are going outside for a little walk. Lies, lies, nothing but lies will be told when a spouse is caught up in the evil practice of adultery.

When a person's body is caught up in fulfilling the act of adultery, that individual is never at the place where he or she is said to be. The spouse thinks his or her mate is at one place, and all the time the companion is somewhere else having unlawful sex. Then, when the spouse finds out about the sin (adultery) that his or her mate has been committing, it is possible that thoughts of murdering the cheating companion will enter into the mind. If thoughts of murder do not travel through the head of the innocent spouse, then thinking of ways to get "pay back" might enter in. Adultery is one of the powers that sin has led many people in this world to commit.

Another evil act that happens when people are caught up in adultery, is not answering the cell phone. Now a day, these cell phones are used as evil gadgets. Every time a married person is with someone else other than the spouse, and the mate calls the cell phone, that person will not answer the phone. Then, when the cheating spouse goes home, and the spouse asks, "Why didn't you answer your phone", he tells his mate, that the phone did not ring. Although, at times, the cell phone might not ring for real, however, these days, you don't know whether to believe your spouse or not.

Because of sin being an active living force in the world, from it, many people have become true idiots. I've heard people say, in the Old Testament of the bible, King David had two wives, therefore we should be able to do the same. The Old Testament is actually a book written about people who God allowed to do the cheerful things of their own heart. Just as God is watching you do ignorance, he watched them do it too. God never intended a man to have two wives; however, since the people were filled with so much self-motivation, he allowed it to carry on. Just as you are disobedient by sleeping with a married person, King David was disobedient too.

Before a person commits an act of adultery, a mental movement is activated first. The cerebrum (the head thinker) becomes mobile before this act of adultery is committed. Then the cerebellum becomes active for the physical aspect of it to come into play. The cerebellum guides the hands to put the man's private parts inside the woman. It does not matter; whose cerebellum guides the male private body part into the woman; the only thing that matter is the fact that adultery is being committed. People cheerfully commit the sin of adultery. They disregard or care nothing about the judgment.

As this act of adultery is being committed, the limbic system in the brain causes the person to feel the sensation and pleasure. Now the person's limbic system has become sexually addicted to a person that is not your be wed spouse. After the addiction has kicked in, this person has just lost the control to stop having sex with this married person. Once you hit it the first time, you will be mentally pressured to hit another 99 times. Now you know why adultery is categorized as "the works of the flesh". People stop believing that you can control sin! Yes, my sinful and drug filled body, has slept with married women too. God please help me!

2. - Fornication - is having a sexual encounter with someone, that's not your husband or wife. Biblically, if you are having sex, and not married, then fornication is the active sin in your life. Single people are the ones who commit fornication. They are not in a marriage commitment with another person, but they are having sex all the time. People commit fornication so long, until their conscious does not even operate anymore. They commit fornication so long, and they care not about the judgment. In the days of our youth, we cheerfully commit fornication, and care not about the judgment.

When people live their lives in fornication, they do activities with others as if they are truly married. Neither marriage took place, nor wedding vowels were spoken into the ears of one another nor the presence of a licensed minister, and yet, sexual activity is in motion. The Holy sacred altar has not been seen in this relationship, but you are performing sexual pleasures anyway. Having sex while not married is considered a sin in the sight of God. Since more than 85% of the world is committing fornication, judgment has come upon all those who indulge in such a practice. Eventually, it will be revealed that you are having sex (fornicating), while not being married. We've become so ignorant, we think, certain things are happening in our lives by mistakes, when in fact, its judgment.

When I see teenagers who are pregnant, I already know, they were caught up in the sin of fornication. In this world, you might find one or two teenagers who became pregnant while being married, but not many of them were virgins before marriage took place. Since fornication is a sin, every time a woman performs this lustful act, and becomes pregnant from it, that's judgment. Just as I was using drugs, and suddenly became physically exposed to the world concerning my sinful drug habits; teenagers when pregnant, and not married, you've become sinfully exposed too. As I said before, do not think all judgments are only executed in court. Even having sex without being married, you reap what you sow.

Let's say that a teenager is pregnant, and not married. As this teenager walks around the earth pregnant, her known friend's approaches and ask, "Are you having a boy or girl"? On the other hand, they might ask, "How many months are you pregnant? Nevertheless, the pregnant teenager thinks its pretty, she thinks it is cute, but she does not realize, she is bringing a baby into the world because of the performance of fornication. Now I see why a baby is born estranged (in sin) from the womb, because most infants were born through fornication.

Everybody is running around on the earth having sex with any and everybody, and not even thinking about the judgment. Every time a woman commits fornication, and become pregnant, or contracts a disease, she has brought judgment upon herself. This is even so with the men. When a man has sex with a woman, and she becomes pregnant, or a disease is brought forth, he has brought damnation upon himself. All these kids we are bringing into the world were never supposed to be. We have been lead by the works of the flesh (sin) to have sex with people, and God never intended to be. I have had sex with more than 50 women, and you think that was the blessed plan of God. I shot the seed of sex in more than 50 women. What if ten of those women would have become pregnant? I probably would have kids by ten different women, who I was not supposed to be having sex with. These women, when I saw their faces, and viewed how sexy their bodies looked, I went after it. Therefore, I was driven to these women based upon my own lustful desires. And that is not the blessed plan of God. If people keep sowing fornication into their bodies, then sicknesses, diseases, and kids will be their judgment and or promotion. We have become so comfortable with fornication that we forget it is sin, and it is to be punished too.

We people are so ignorant. We have taken the quote from the bible, which says, "be fruitful and multiply", out of content. Single women walking around on the earth pregnant saying, "God said be fruitful and multiply, so that's what I am doing". We take biblical quotes for our own personal satisfaction, because we have no realistic understanding. When God spoke the quote, "be fruitful and multiply", he was talking to two people he gave to one another through marriage. God was talking to two people, that he gave one to another, Adam and Eve. These days, fornicators are walking on earth thinking that the "be fruitful and multiply quote", it is speaking to them. Sin has our minds so far gone in fornication that we've become messed up from it. The sin of fornication is powerful. Why, because people are still searching for physical relationships first, before seeking a spiritual one with God.

Every sin committed has an ending act of misery. If we would do it the way God intended, many children would not be fatherless. In the beginning, God intended the sex drive to be performed only in marriage. But the sin fornication is so strong in the land, that having sex before marriage has become almost automatic. The sin fornication has our minds programmed, and it has gotten out of hand. I mean, honestly, if fornication (having sex before marriage) is a sin, do you really think God want us performing it? Do you really think God it is okay with it?

Then we wonder how the disease aids came into our land. We go from one relationship to the next, to the next, to the next. Are you still wondering how aids came into the land? Look at how many people we have had unprotected sex with. Me, myself, when I was in the drug life, I am sure I had sex with 15 women different in 6 months, and didn't wear a condom. Even if I had to pay for it, I got it. If I didn't have to pay for it, I still got it.

I have had sex with so many women, that I can't remember them all. I am sure, in my wheelchair, I have rolled across the path of more than 25 women whom I had sex with, and didn't even know whom they were.

One day, I saw two women. They both approached me. One girl said, hey Lytskin, do you remember her"? I said "nope". Then she said, Lytskin, that's a shame you don't remember that girl. I said, "Well, I am sorry that I don't remember her, who is she?" As I was riding in the wheelchair going to my destination, my mind began to wonder. I said to myself, "is that a girl I had sex with back in the days, and just don't remember who she is. I took so many women to the hotel from the nightclub, had sex with, and that was it. I don't remember a whole lot of women I had sex with; and that's a nasty shame. I know I suffered a brain injury, but good Lord. It makes me wonder, how many women have seen me, and remembered that I sex them, and I said nothing to them because I DID NOT KNOW whom they were.

Just because condoms are in the world, does not mean God gave such an idea. We are some ignorant folks. The other day, I over heard a woman say, "If God didn't want condoms on the earth, then they would not be here". God's protective way from diseases is for you to not fornicate. Man's protective way from diseases is to wear a condom. Which plan do you think is perfect? If you wear a condom, it can break, and you can still contact a disease, or the woman can become pregnant. If you do not fornicate, there is no way you can catch a disease. Whether using a condom or not, it is still looked upon as fornication, and God is against it.

Actually, deadly diseases such as aids were here before us all. In the past, sexual deadly diseases had another name. Now in the 1900's, the disease has been named Aids. Just as our ancestors passed these sins unto us, they passed unto us aids, which had another name. I don't know what the sexual deadly diseases were called in the 16 hundreds. However, since it was deadly, it might as well have been called AIDS.

Aids didn't just pop up from out of nowhere. People through sexual encounters created Aids. Let me tell you how I believe aids made it onto the earth. I am going to give you one example of how I believe Aids came into our nations. As they say, "it takes two to tangle". Well, let me make up a saying, too; "it takes two or more disease to form another disease". One day a man and a woman were having sex. The woman had gonorrhea, and syphilis, and the man had a horrible case of hepatitis. As these two diseased filled people were having sex, all three diseases mingled together, and Aids was formed from it. Diseases come from germs. Dozens of germs get together to form one name of sickness, such as, "Aids". I am not saying that my statement is a scientific fact; however, my statement just might be true. With all the sin and free sex being performed these days, Aids is not the only sexual disease earned.

Anyway, even in fornication, a man and a woman will actually live together in the same house, as if they are truly married. The man and woman actually believe that the relationship is God given. The bold character sin has really forced people to live in a relationship that God hates. Many people are so caught up in fornication that they are going through rough times in their so-called relationship. If fornicators would go to God for truth, there is a high chance that you are living with someone that will probably never be your marital spouse. God will show you that he or she is not suppose to be your future mate; neither now nor in the years to come. The reason why people think that a certain individual is his or her future spouse is because; they are caught up in the sin of fornication. Living in fornication will cause you to believe that every boyfriend or girlfriend just might be your wedded spouse.

What is a girlfriend? What is a boyfriend? Who made those words up? Those two words were never supposed to have a definition. They were never supposed to be in the nation's translation. It was always suppose to be, "Husband and Wife". The sin of fornication has our minds so messed up, that we claim boyfriends and girlfriends, before we claim righteousness.

Let me say this also; there are many relationships in the world that God did put together. Although, God lined you two up for marriage in the future, you both still need to refrain yourself from fornication. If you two do fall into fornication, you have still committed sin, and God is not happy about that. There is a great reason why God desires people to be married before sex is practiced.

Another reason why God does not want sex to be active before marriage is because: when you are trying to get to know someone, and fornication becomes active, your feelings for the individual will grow sooner than suppose. You should be trying to get to know the person, not having sex with.

Now a day, most people's minds are operating from lust. They think a spouse has been found, but lust was in it from the start. There is a difference from finding a soul mate, and finding a lust mate. These days, we have sex before we actually get the chance to know someone. Actually, we need to spend time with someone for about a year or two, before thinking of marriage and having sex. We so quick to become attached to someone, that we think we are going to die next week. As I said before, sin is causing us to do things our very own way, rather than God's way.

Well, I've slept with many women, and never been married; therefore, I committed fornication too. While I was out there in the world of sin, I have practice fornication for years. Day in and day out, I was with different women. Never did I stand before a holy altar. Never did a minister ask me pre-marital questions, nor were there vow exchanges. Nevertheless, I have had sex with many women through the sin of fornication. During my moments of committing fornication, I have earned two kids. Now you know why fornication is categorized as one of the works of the flesh. God, please help me?

3. - Uncleanness- is an illness from sin that leads people to having a spirit of perversion. Lesbian, gay, (homosexuality), and bestiality (sex with animals); these are activities that operates from an unclean spirit. Not only does having sex with the same agenda, or with animals, operates from an unclean spirit, but just by having sin in your life marks the uncleanness.

An unclean sprit was operating in my body while I was on probation. When my probation officer tested me for drugs, and the results came back positive, I was declared unclean. Many other works of evil operates from an unclean spirit. Now you know why uncleanness is categorized as one of the works of the flesh. I need some help! Will someone please help me?

4. - Lasciviousness- is a sin that plays many roles in its practices. The prevailing role lasciviousness plays, is the sneaky and crafty ways, in which a plan to do evil is accomplished. You become so deceitful, just to get that plan of evil to happen. You want it to happen so bad, that you will do anything just to experience the event. Even if your life is on the line, lasciviousness will lead you to go after it anyway. If it takes days, weeks, or even months to get that event to happen, lasciviousness will cause you to stick with the plan, until it's experienced. If it is a thought of evil, and you are trying to bring the event to pass, then lasciviousness is in action.

The work of Lasciviousness will cause a person to work through mental envisioning. When attempting to experience a task of evil, it actually becomes your far most and utmost obsession. Your mental body becomes fascinated, just by the thought of it. After the mental movement has worked in you, soon you'll become spellbound to make it happened.

Here is a written example of how lasciviousness operates: a person who commits adultery is sneaky, and uses crafty (schemes) ways to carry out the arrangement. When people plot, plan, and arrange to have adulterous sex, from the plotting of it, lasciviousness is very much active. Since lasciviousness is a sin that gears people to arrange and organize events, then the frontal lobes in the brain is working to get this evil event scheduled. Lasciviousness operates when you are arranging to commit sin.

When my friends and I thought of places to smoke dope, the sin of lusciousness caused us to do that. Together we plotted, planned, and arranged moments to get high. Therefore, the sin of lasciviousness was dwelling in my body, because I planned and plotted to do many acts of evil. Now you know why lasciviousness is categorized as one of the works of the flesh. God, please help me! Free me from the net and chain of sin.

5. - **Idolatry**-is active in a person's life when the individual perceives an object to be his or her on going source of power or help. Idolatry is also practiced when people are giving their full attention to what is before their very own eyes. They become fascinated by what the object does for them. Whatever it maybe, it becomes plastered to their hearts and minds. When a person's living is caught up in idolatry, it is all about the object more than anything else. The object becomes a person's daily devotion in life because the heart has deep reverence and relies on it for support.

Well, drugs were my objects of idolatry practice. I trusted and relied on drugs to help and do great things for me in my life, rather than God. When you trust in something, your thoughts are captivated by it. Hey people, it's not hard to be caught up in idolatry. Even the cars I owned became objects of idolatry. Therefore, my cerebrum (my head thinker), and my brainstem (heart regulator) were plagued with idolatrous ways and its formulas. Idolatry is another sin that was being operated from my body as well. Now you know why idolatry is categorized as one of the works of the flesh. Will somebody help me, because as of now, five sins have been in operating within my body? I have been committing idolatry for ten long years, and I DID NOT KNOW it. Lord Help me!

6. - **Witchcraft**- when people believe that certain things can change their living situations, other than God, that is witchcraft. Only God has the power and authority to change a person's living. Many people believe that zodiac readings and chemical substances will change their present situations. Zodiac readings or chemical control substances will only sell you pretense visions. Just because you read a zodiac reading, and the words in it really did relate to your current living, does not mean it is your prophet. Let's say a zodiac reading gave you a true-life experience quote on Monday; do you think it is going to relate to your living next Monday? Well, probably not! People actually believe readings can match them up with a relationship. Go read a bible; only it will give precise future living endeavoring events.

Witchcraft takes up numeral accounts in its meanings. However, people who put chemical controlled substances in their bodies are filled with witchcraft. They have been made to believe that dope relieves them from stress or whatever. From the power of drugs, people have been made to believe that drugs are party enhancers. Although, filling your brain with drugs does increase the intensity level, however, a witch, which is your drug of choice, has forced you into believing in such a thing. Their minds have been cursed, and their heart has been cast into a "spell". Who or what gave you the mental power to believe that intoxicants kill's stress, and enhances the movement of a party. I believe a witch apparently did. What led you to believe such a healing will take place from chemical controlled substance? Sin did, well; a witch did. Just as a witch or a psychic will advertise false words unto you, and show you lustful visions of future actions, putting chemicals in the brain has done the same thing unto you and me.

No need to wait for Halloween to see a wicked witch. I also thought that the wicked witch was only on "The Wizard of Oz". However, since the world is the way it is, then the wicked witch is located in every state on the globe. Every time you put any type of drug, or chemical controlled substance in your hand, you are handling a product that causes "witch tendencies".

When we think of witches, we also think of evil and curses. Well, when I begin putting drugs into my brain, evil was contracted, and a curse within my brain developed. Therefore, the witch operates through drugs. When I was filling my brain with drugs, I was actually putting in it a witch. My brain was filled with witches and I DID NOT KNOW it. I was led to try drug after drug, because of this chemical controlled witch had cursed me. That lousy witch! Lord have mercy, please save me from this witch!

2nd Samuel 15:23 says, for rebellion is as the sin of witchcraft. As you have just read in this book, how rebellious I was toward the laws of God. I became rebellious after putting drugs into my brain. Since I was being rebellious, my mind was filled with the works of witchcraft. In other words, when a person is rebellious unto God, the unseen power of a witch is operating through his or her mind. My, my, my, I need some serious help in my life. Oh my God, you mean to tell me, that as of now, I have six sins working in my body. Lord have mercy! Please help me? This stuff is ridiculous. All this time, I DID NOT KNOW that witchcraft was operating in my life.

7. - **Hatred**- is an activity of two or more people who are involved in drama. When I think of the word "drama", I think of screenplays, TV shows and movies. Yeah, dealing with drugs and wickedness, that's exactly how my life has been looking; just like a movie. Actually, all the drama my life was having, it became a movie to God, because he kept the cameras rolling. Just as I watched drama on the TV screen, God was watching drama take place in my life.

Each and everyday of my drug filled living, the film

and cameras were rolling. As the cameras of God's eyes were rolling, nothing but actions of hatred was being recorded. My life became a screenplay. In my life, the eyes of God were screening every manner of hatred performed. Much hatred lived in me because of my enemies. They did not like me, and I could not stand them, therefore, the sin of hatred was working through me as well. Lord Help me!

8. Variance - is the sin that brings conflict and disagreements between two or more people. Arguments stay active when people are trying to get their point across. When people use their mental energy to prove a point, soon, the situation grows into negativity. Allowing the sin, variance, to live in your body will soon persuade your mind to think from a hatred point of view. After hatred has become active in the brain, soon, physical violence is then being brought into play. Having debates and battles all the time is called, variance. As I was living the drug life, many conflicts and disagreements approached me through other folks. My life was filled with much conflict; therefore, the sin of variance was plugged into me too. Is there anyone who can help me from the sins that are reigning in my life and body?

9. - Emulations- means to strive to be in control or ahead of someone. A person does his or her very best to be seen as the better person. Well, I was a drug seller; the only thing that I knew was to seek and strive to look better than the next man. I fixed my cars up just to be seen. Therefore, the sin of emulation was connected to my brain and heart too. Lord have mercy, already, nine sins are living inside of my body, and I DID NOT KNOW it. God please help me!

10. - Wrath- means to have anger in you, which tends to lead to violence, which is an activity that causes people to pronounce personal judgment. When a person has wrath in his or her heart towards another human being, usually, physical violence is next to be brought forth. When physical violence is brought forth, people actually recompense one another *evil for evil*. Yeah, the sin of wrath was definitely in high pursuit within me, which soon led me to plot a murder. We know that all homicides are performed by physical violence, through personal wrath and anger. Yes, I was filled with much anger, violence, and wrath while living the drug life. Now I know why sin became my master; Look at all the evil acts that were committed by me. God please help me!

11. - **Strife**- means, not agreeing with one another, which turns into violent tendencies. Two people can be in the same neighborhood, doing the same thing (selling drugs). Then a person might try to run another person off the premises. The person feels like he want to sell drugs and make all the money, therefore, he seeks to run the other drug seller away.

A certain person came into my neighborhood, which tried to run me away so he can sell his drugs. He was against me, and I was against him. Strife was going on. Not only was strife in action, but also, quarrelling was in progress too. Therefore, one day, I gathered up my friends to watch my back, just in case his boys would try to jump me. So, I called the person out to a one on one fistfight. Yeah, I dropped him, hit him with my combination punch, and the fight was over.

Always being against one another is a sign of strife. Well, of course, this sin was in my life as well because I was performing much strife in the streets of St. Louis. I need some true help, for real. Lord God please save me!

12. - **Seditions** - is being rebellious against righteous rules or disobeying righteous statues. When the police caught me with drugs in my possession, afterwards, I continued to handle dope. My life was filled with the sin of seditions. I was rebellion against many laws. The power of sin (sedition) strengthened me to do so. Therefore, the sedition sin was wrapped up inside of me as well. Lord have mercy! Please help me!

13. - **Heresies**- is a denying of a truth that has been revealed. A cousin called me over the phone one day. She was telling me about a vision she had seen of me. In the vision, she saw me being killed. When my cousin told me the vision that she had seen, I guess I did not believe her. I did not accept the fact that a truth has been told; I kept on

hanging with the fellows, and kept on selling and using drugs. No matter what truthful heresies I've heard, sin empowered me to push it all to the side. However, the greatest sin of heresies is not to believe what the word of God (the bible) says. Yep, I had this sin in me too. I need some help.

14. - Envying- is a work that exposes jealousy and or resentment toward another. When a person has something that you do not have, and you become jealous, envy is working in you. People even envy other people because of how another person looks. Men have this envying problem bad, but women have it grossly. I can raise my hand up, and admit to God, that this envying sin is reigning in my body, too. This is ridiculous, as of now, I have 14 works of the flesh (sin) operating within me, and I DID NOT KNOW it. Lord help me!

15. - Murder- to take a life of person by physical force. Although, I never committed an act of murder, however, I ruined many lives by introducing people to the to drug game. Although, I did not commit a murder, however, when my heart had stopped because of my drug usage, God would have judged me just as if it was a murder. Actually, in the sight of God, I would have looked like a person who has committed suicide. The person who puts a gun to his head, or slit the wrist, both are no different from me. They used a tool to kill themselves, and I used a tool (drugs) to kill myself. Nevertheless, hell, would have been my home. Therefore, I believe I am capable of saying; I almost murdered myself. Lord help me!

Another murder I want to talk about concerns women and abortion. Yeah, when women go to a hospital to have abortions, they actually become murderers. A living soul (infant) is actually living inside of you, and you will make an appointment to visit a doctor to kill that baby. Not only are you murdering a baby, but also, it was premeditated as well. You made plans, and scheduled an appointment to kill this baby, and this was done by lasciviousness. Wow, you know what, in the sight of God, if any woman have an abortion, she has just committed a first-degree murder. See, that's what women agree to do, when they conceive a child in the works of fornication.

16. - Drunkenness - drinking booze or alcohol over the limit. Yes, I had the drunkenness sin in me as well. Hennessey was my flavored drink. Gin and juice was second to Hennessy. Every party given has drinks in it. Anytime a person drinks at a party, 9 times out of ten, when going home, he or she is driving while intoxicated. I use to drink and drive all the time. However, I thank God I never experienced being in a car wreck. Well, I must confess, I did hit a dog one day on Grand Ave. near Tower Grove Park. If I would have hit a person, even if I was not drunk, if the police would have given me a breath examination test, and if it came back positive for alcohol usage, I still could've been handcuff. The law does not care how much you drink. The law only wants to find you guilty, so it can provide you with a penalty. However, the dog did live, but I'm sure I broke his jaw. I had many horrible experiences while being highly intoxicated from alcohol. Lord please help me!

17. - Reveling-when people take intense pleasure in performing actions of evil is called, "reveling". Taking any situations to a higher level is called, reveling. When someone has a fistfight, and then go get a gun, that is taking the situation to another level. Many people start arguments because they love to take things to a higher level.

When sin cleverly lured me into using drugs, I inwardly attained within me, every sin that was just written, and mentioned above. By the power of sin, those 17 works of the flesh captivated my life. Daily, weekly, monthly, yearly, my life had been mesmerized by sin. All 17 works of the flesh became moving events in my life. I smoked one joint (marijuana) and, afterwards all 17 works of the flesh were performed by me. I DID NOT KNOW that one person can have so many sins in the body. My mental status became attracted to the phases of evil by the explosive power of sin.

Now I see why I had so many demons in my life. From all of the sins I've been committing, demons were being added to my personal being. One sin led me to another sin, and another sin led to another. Yeah, sin literally persuaded my brain to think, and then mobilized my body to perform wicked actions.

We all are naturally approached, and lead to do bad things at different stages, and moments in life. My first experience with drugs was in high school as a freshman. While on the other hand, someone else may have been sinfully led to experienced drugs in middle school. Whether your first experience with drugs was in middle school or in high school, sin was the motivating power. Mentally, you were persuaded to try drugs, and physically you were led to activate the chemical.

Every time I hear about a murder, it alerts me to know, that someone has allowed sin to control his mind and hand. Every time I smell the scent of dope, I already know, someone has allowed sin to toy with his or her life. Every time I hear about a rape case, I already know, someone was empowered by sin to perform an unwanted sex act. Every time I hear a person cussing and speaking foul language, I already know, sin is in action in his or her life.

Who would have ever thought that one bad choice to try drugs would lead a person life to be in a position were his or her "brain's power" would be up for grabs? Your brain is up for grabs each time you rush drugs into it. Tell me something, who gave you the power to know that the next time you smoke that blunt that your brain will not trigger off into the wrong direction. I guess you do not realize that chemicals hinder the brain's normal ways of functioning that God designed for it to perform. I do not care how weak you think that little bitty marijuana's power is, once it is in the brain; any of the head's organs are up for grabs. The only mental reaction that it takes for marijuana or any other drug to dysfunction one of the brain's members is if God raises his mercy from you for a split second. Then, there is a wide chance that your brain can be sinfully transformed into a vegetable for life.

God presently has a will and a plan designed for

every human soul who is upon the earth today. When people do not live in the "blessed" plan that God has designed for peaceful living, they are living a lifestyle, which is very dangerous. When people live their lives against the shielded and blessed will of God, they will always awaken moments for judgments, sentencing, imprisonment, and physical punishments. However, always hiding from the law (police) will be his or her daily activity. Denying God's blessed plan is sort of like running your head into the head of a ram's horn, which is not a fair match for any human being. People need to stop bumping heads with God's blessed plan for their lives, because they will loose every time.

Actually, in this life, God has set forth two plans on earth. One plan of choice provides health and protection. The health and protection plan, if chosen, it will lead an individual to experiencing, happiness, joy, and peace. While the other plan of choice will lead a person to experiencing sadness, sorrow, and death. God has set a path before all humankind, to choose to walk through.

Deuteronomy 30:19 I call heaven and earth to record this day against you, that I have set before you life and death, blessing and cursing: therefore choose life, that both thou (you) and thy seed may live.

This scripture represents the two opportunities before your mental mind to choose. One of the two choices will be made as you live on the earth. It says, *"God has set before you, "life" and "death", "cursing and blessings"* which means, two plans are presented pertaining too life. However, only one can be chosen. No if's, and's or but's about it, one of the two choices will be your made decision. Even right now, as I'm speaking unto you, a choice has already been made. Actually, whatever you are doing right now today, verifies the choice you have made in the pass.

If you choose to live in sin as I did, then you have made a wicked choice from your heart's desire. Freely you have chosen the plan that consists of curses, in which your brain will be lead to face death. When you choose to live in sin, you will be walking on a dark and evil road. Meaning, you just never know what evil experience will face next. If you are performing any of the 17 works of the flesh, then you have chosen the cursing and death way. To make a long story short, if you are being rebellious to God today, then your living has become acquainted with a witch. Then the judgment from God will continually fall upon you, and death will be your final sentence.

On the other hand, if any living person chooses the plan that consists of life and blessing, he has chosen the path that will lead him on a road to all the goodness that God has to offer. Choosing the plan of *"life" and "blessings"*, your life will be protected from sin's power.

I have read in the bible, and realized that God is the person who gave humankind life. Since God is the one who gave life unto man, and has put breath into his body, then we as individuals should work with him and not against him. However, sin has led us all to magnify it, rather than magnifying the maker of breath and life (God).

When we work against the power of God, it is the same scenario as your 2-year-old child becoming angry, and then trying to wrestle you down to the ground. How would it look for you and your two-year-old child in a brawl? A two-year-old child does not have physical strength to match up against the parent; in the same sense, you are no match against God. Neither in mental powers nor through physical strength, you are no match with God. No man in the history of all the earth will ever mount up to be a fair contender with God Almighty. If you show me a man that thinks he is stronger, mightier, or smarter than God, you have just shown me a true demonic idiot. I advise you to work with God and not against him. Since God is the one who made you, let it be known that you need him to pick your life up from out of sin's ditch. Our inner being, which sin has marred and made filthy, it needs to be washed by God. Our lives have been horribly blemished up, because of our sinful actions.

In the book of *Isaiah, 1:16 it says, Wash you, make you clean; put away the evil of your doings from before mine eyes; cease to do evil.*

Isaiah is a prophet who God spoke too in the long past. Isaiah had a relationship with God. After God spoke to Isaiah, Isaiah's interpretation of what was said he wrote in the book called, "Isaiah". Whatever words God had spoken to the prophet Isaiah, this is what he wrote as he interpreted it; *wash you, make you clean; put away the evil of your doings from before mine eyes.* We already know when sin is in a person body, that he or she will be led to do evil. However, the prophet Isaiah said, *"wash yourself, make yourself clean".* In other words, sin is needed to be rid out of our bodies, because it makes our bodies unclean before the eyes of God.

Actually, Isaiah is not telling you to wash and clean your own self. That's a hard job for you to do. Remember, we have sin in our bodies, and we love fulfilling the works of the flesh. Therefore, sin's filth will never be cleansed by mortals (human beings). Why, because we do not have the strength to do so. We love committing fornication; we love having sex with someone's spouse, we love using drugs, we love fighting, we love causing havoc, yeah, we love doing the 17 works of the flesh. Therefore, we will never come to a point and position in our lives, were we can cleanse our own ourselves. Written by Brian K. Irons.

When we accept the life and blessing plan of God into our lives, a wise choice has been made. The cleansing process begins. If you had the power to clean your self from evil, then you have the power to clean yourself from sin. Only God has the power to *wash you, and make you clean.* Therefore, Isaiah is saying, "go get God", let him cleanse you, and follow his blessing plan for your life.

For many years, I have said to people and myself, "I need to clean myself up before attending church". I also remember saying, "I need to get my life together, then start attending church. Sin is a powerful character; it will actually make you believe that you can or need get your own life together before attending church service. However, you cannot clean yourself; you cannot wash yourself. Millions of people actually believe they can and need to clean themselves before going to church. People; stop fooling yourselves; stop allowing sin to make you believe you can clean yourself. That's a myth! How long, or how many years have you been saying, "I need to get myself together". You have been saying that for years, and the cleansing hasn't happened yet. Stop being fooled, stop being tricked; I want to let you know, if you are trying to get your own life together, it will never happen. Sin will cause you to believe you can clean your own self, until it kills you. People have been saying they are going to get themselves together for more than 30 years, and if you are not careful, you'll be one of them. Can you just imagine how many people in the world have said, "I need get myself together, and it has never happened". Can you imagine how many people have said that, and were killed or died in all their committed sins? Do not allow sin to trick you from going to church. If you allow sin to trick you any longer, sin just might kill you before you make to the church. The church is a place to be forgiven and cleansed from your sins.

Isaiah 1:17 learn to do well; seek judgment. Whether we realize it or not, we have been taught by sin to do much evil in our lives. We have been taught by sin; in return, it has made our bodies feel sick, rather than well. Anytime a force (sin) has led you to do evil, you have been taught. Just like when parents lead, and teach their children to do healthy things, well, sin leads, and teaches people to do un-well things. Why do you think the scripture says, "*Lean to do well*"! It says learn to do well because God has to teach you to do well. As God teaches you, then, good deeds from your body will be done. When you learn to do "well" from the written word of God, your life will turn out sweet, prosperous, and healthy. If you allow God to teach you to do well in life, then your name will turn out to be successfully great.

Isaiah 1:17 also says, *seek judgment.* When people seek this type of judgment, they are seeking to find out how God feels about what they are doing in life. Before we do anything or go anywhere, we need to find out what God has to say about it. The prophet, Isaiah is saying, go to the judge (God), and seek his help. Let God judge you, before the law's judgment have its way in your life, as it did mine. When you ask God to forgive you, you are asking him to clear you from sin's judgment, punishment, and guilt. Go ahead, go boldly to God, get him in your life, and get your judgment over with, and final. This judgment is different from the judgment done in the court of law. It's different because you're going to God to be judged, rather than forcing God to send the law's judgment, or biblical harsh prophecies into your life. I will tell you more about this form of judgment in a second. Don't worry; I will remind you because this is too serious for me to forget. Your life is counting on me to deliver unto you this revelation.

Anyway, the problem with us (the world) is that we think we know it all, when in fact, we know nothing. You can be the smartest man in the world, but without God's teaching in your life, you are truly one of the dumbest individual's on earth. Without God in our brains, we will continue to make ignorant choices day in and day out. Everyone needs help in his or her life. No matter how old a person may be, that individual needs a touch of help, and a lead of God's guidance. God is the teacher; and guider, let him lead you to a place where sins are forgiven. All sins must be forgiven before entering into a relationship with God. When Isaiah said, _seek judgment_, he is saying, seek God, because he has provided a way for your sins to be forgiven.

Guess what else I found out from reading the bible; I found out, when a person has been summons to appear in court to be judged, the very same act shall be done when a person dies. When you go to court, you face God's laws, because judgment is to be pronounced. When you die, you face God at the point of death because judgment is to be pronounced even during that stage of life also. Read the scripture that I found in the bible.

Hebrews 9:27-it is appointed unto man once to die, but after this the judgment. Well, you have just read it for yourself. Since that scripture, which speaks about dying and then being judged, I advise you to receive what God is miraculously presenting unto you. Although, God's mercy brought me back from the dead, however, when my heart stopped, that was judgment. God could have allowed me to come back from the coma physically strong as before. However, I was judged, and a price was paid. My mental and physical body suffered greatly after this slight death experience became apart of my life. Judgment fell upon me hard, but since I am still alive, the judgment was not final (eternal).

God does not want you to die in your committed sins. God is presenting unto you the opportunity to get yourself clean from sin. No man in the world can dodge or run away from being judged by God. You can run and live on earth for 125 years, but know this; your brainstem and heart will give out one day. Death will be experienced. Therefore, when you do die, you will face the judge (God). Whether you live or die, judgment will be administered.

Hey people of the earth, follow me; I am your spiritual Harriet Tubman. Just as Harriet Tubman led slaves to become physically freed from their masters, I desire to lead you to a man who can free you from the master of sin and evil. If you are living a life in sin, then sin is your master. However, I will lead you to a place called, "spiritual and mental freedom". God sent me back to the earth, to lead people away from sin. To all my friends, male and females, many of you have followed me into drug living, and have been in slavery for years. Now I desire that you follow me again, so that you can become free from sin and drug's penalty.

Although, I realize that God's mercy is great, powerful, and is located throughout the entire earth on every living being, I was still missing something very valuable in life. There has to be something more of a potent protection than just mercy alone. I am not down setting or underestimating the power of God's mercy, because you've just read throughout this entire book about what it did for me. Mercy is the active reason why I am here writing this book unto you; therefore, I will never exalt myself to speak badly against it. However, mercy alone in one's life is not a full-satisfied life to live.

Chapter 13
Come to Jesus

From the drastic sicknesses, that my body experienced, I finally concluded, that I needed to get more of God into my life. From this personal dope disaster, I realized that I was missing something. I realized there is something on earth or in life I did not have. I was in a world, doing all the things my heart desired. Nothing could persuade me, other than to realize I needed help with my life. What more does God has that I need to get a hold of?

God has been pulling and pulling on me for a very long time. For 10 years, and even longer, God has been pulling on me. God, through his mercy was doing his best to steer **Brian Irons** into another direction, which was the way of peace. There was something or someone that I emotionally realized that I did not have as my helping hand in life. I believed the worker who I was missing is none other than "Jesus Christ" himself. Therefore, the heavenly God tugged (drew) on me one more time. I inwardly (from the heart), and physically (with the body) went to see the man who God named Jesus.

If God is mercifully "drawing" you in any direction, trust me, God is drawing you to grab a hold of his son Jesus. If you do not submit to God and accept his drawing, you are wrestling against the blessing of God for your life. I have wrestled and fought against the "drawing" of God for many, many years. When you are fighting against the pulling of God, you actually become God's contender. Although, I submitted my life to the plan of death and curses, God was still drawing me toward his son, so that peace can be applied into my life.

When you feel low and down, and begin to say within yourself, "I need to go to church"; that is God pulling and drawing you towards freedom. Let's say, "Your life is a living mess". "You are on your way to work, and everyday is the same, horrible. While you are driving to work, your conscience character begins to operate. You are actually thinking about going to church to get rid of the way you've been living. You inwardly feel that you need some serious help. You are tired of living a certain way. Everyday appears to be a day full of foolishness.

Written below are some examples of God drawing me to receive a better way of living. However, I wrestled, and kept allowing myself to content against Almighty God. Example #1: When I had been robbed three different times at gunpoint, and after each gunplay, a thought appeared into my mind saying, "get out of dope game before I get shot and or murdered". Nevertheless, since my mind was full of wickedness and witchcraft, I sinfully kept on selling drugs. Example #2: When three of my cars had been plagued with bullet holes from gunshots, the thought to leave the dope game alone approached my mind but I never took the action to do so. I sinfully kept on selling drugs to get that evil money. Example #3 When three drugs cases were placed upon my earth's record, the thought to leave the drug game floated through my mind, but I still hung in there, and kept on selling drugs. I often saw with my own two eyes many dangerous drive-by gun shootings, and I never moved a limb to follow my conscience that God was dealing with. I can go on and on in listing the drawings from God, but enough has been shared for you to understand. Those were actual moments were I wrestled with the thought (drawing) that God was dropping in spirit (brain). However, after those 10-12, and a dozen other conscience drawings were performed by God's mercy, if I would have had enough sense to stop, drop, and roll out of the drug game, then my body would have been preserved and protected, rather than suffering from a serious evil final drug effect. Nevertheless, after all of that bitterness had poured into my life, I realized that it was time for me to try something new. As God pulled on me one more time, I accepted the "drawing" from God, and I finally went to his son Jesus.

Although, after my incident, I attended church, however, a time came, where I began to smoke marijuana again. I was going to church, I was hearing about God, but I did not give my life (brain/spirit) to him. Yep, I was smoking marijuana again. In my mind, I knew I was not going to try any other drugs after what I just went through. But you just never know how far sin and drugs will take your life again. Actually, I should not have even done marijuana again. Although, I was going to church, I didn't go to be cleansed (washed). I was going to church because I felt like it was a good thing to do. Although, attending church is a good thing to do, however, only going to show your face means nothing. All the sins I've committed before the coma experience, were still in my body, because they have not been forgiven. Even as I started to smoke weed again, God drew (pulled) on me again. God must truly "so love the world".

When people attend church service, if they are not going to be doctor on, and be freed from their sins, then what's the point? We should be going to church for either two reasons: 1st-church is a place to be cleansed from your sins through the preaching of God's word (bible). The other reason for going to church is too learn how to have a true relationship with God.

Harsh experiences, many times do not deliver us from things that may have caused harm in our lives. If the sin remains in a person's body and life, then deliverance from it has not been performed. I know three people right now today who had been shot from being in the drug game. They now use wheelchairs, and are still selling and using drugs. Their sins have not been forgiven. Their sins are still active in their lives, because they are still doing the same performances. People can attend church, and have not been forgiven of their sins. Many people think Jesus has fully come into their lives because they attend church. In this chapter, you will know if you have Jesus the way you think you do.

I remember at one point, after I had been cleansed and washed from sin and drugs, I began to attend church seeking for the outpouring of God's spirit. I attended church 8 months strong and faithfully. I wanted to be baptized with the Holy Ghost (spirit of God). I wanted this experience to be shared in my life. I use to watch Evangelist Jesse Harris praising God, speak in tongues, prophesying to the church, and I wanted that same bold spirit she had.

This particular day, the church praise service was filled with the power and presence of God. The church has always been filled with the presence and power of God, but this day was a very special day for me. This day was amazing. The music in the church was playing. I was up doing my little praise dance for the Lord. I've always thanked God in the testimony, and I've thanked him in my praise dance too.

As I was giving God praise in the dance, I was holding on to my walker for balancing. Suddenly, Clifton Brown, and Stanley Smith both grab me. They both put my arms around their shoulders, and we three kept on dancing for the Lord. As I was crying, drooling, and dancing for the Lord, I begin to speak in tongues, which is a language from God. I didn't speak in tongues for a long time, but it was still a language given from God. Now that I've received the Holy Ghost (spirit of God), God's son Jesus has come into my life, brain, and body.

When people attend church desiring God to give them the Holy Ghost (His spirit), timing varies. It took me 8 months to finally receive it, while it might take you 5 days. God knows your heart; he knows when you are truthfully ready to seek a better way of living.

Jesus is the individual, whose job is to help and receive openly every person that the man above (God) sends unto him. The moment I received Jesus in my life, is the moment all my sins were forgiven. Also, when I received Jesus in my life, I became a partner with God. Everything that you and I need in this life has been miraculously placed inside of one man's life and body, and that is Jesus Christ himself. Whether, we need healing in our bodies, or whether we need relief from mental stress, and most importantly, a need of forgiveness of sin, Jesus is the true source of help. Healing is plugged up into Jesus body, and every human being must be willing to go after it and get it.

Every person that goes to Jesus, God has evidently touched his or her mental conscience and persuaded that individual to march towards that way. When you finally accept the drawing from God, by going to Jesus, Jesus is standing with open arms ready to receive you.

In the New Testament, *John 6:37 Jesus says, all that the father giveth me, shall come unto me; and him that cometh to me I will in no wise cast him out.* From all of the years of me performing works of wickedness, no matter what sins I have presumptuously done in my life, or what laws I have broken, Jesus cannot cast me away. No matter how filthy my life and body is, Jesus cannot deny me. God sent me to his son Jesus, so that he could help me with my life, and give me the power to make wise choices in my life. Although, I've been baptized with the spirit of God, sin is still in the world, and I must be prayerful and careful.

When I went to Jesus, he did accept me, and pulled me in unto him. As I ran unto Jesus, I went unto him in all my filth, shame, and sin, and he did not reject me, nor did he cast me away. When I went to face Jesus, I was filled with all 17 sins that *Galatians 5:19-21* spoke about. Jesus performed the task that his father gave him the power to do, and that is to clean me up from my sinful past. When Isaiah said*, wash you make you clean*, he was saying, accept the drawing from God by going to Jesus. I thank God that he made and created Jesus mental (inner body, the spirit) to act differently from all the people, which are upon the earth. Now you know, the only way to be cleansed from sin is through the power God gave to his son Jesus. As I said before, you do not have the power to clean or wash yourself. If you want to be cleansed, go get Jesus right now, because he is the only one who has the power to do it.

When people, especially women, hear my testimony about all my wicked deeds that I have done in my life, and why I am using a wheelchair, many of them reject me immediately. However, Jesus already heard and seen every wicked deed that I have willingly committed, and he still pulled me in as his own kin. Therefore, Jesus pulled me in to have a relationship with a filthy, and pitiful, sinful man like me. God knows how wicked and how filthy my life once was. Since God gave a command to his son to fulfill, Jesus had no other choice but to look pass all my faults and evil ways, and cater to my needs, by accepting me as I am.

That's what the scripture means, for Jesus to accept us as we are, yes, he accepted me as I am. People in the world take the saying, "accept me as I am" the wrong way. Women and men of the earth both take scripture's meaning the wrong way. Women will go to church wearing skirts high above the thighs, and shirts showing every centimeter of breast, and then say, "God said come as you are". Men go to church, wearing all kinds of stuff, and then say, "God said come as you are". The world of people have messed up minds. We actually do what we want to do, and then try to give God the glory somehow.

I saw a pretty woman the other day. She is one of the prettiest women that you ever did see. She was wearing some short shorts that were ridiculous. I asked her, "What you think God thinks about wearing shorts like that? She said, God doesn't care what I wear, he loves me". She also said, that's why God put clothes on the earth, to be worn. You people think every piece of clothing is okay by God to wear. When sin is in your life, you will think any and everything is okay to worn, even to church. Certain clothes we wear, we wear them for self-satisfaction, and not for God's satisfaction. Remember this, every item made by a person on earth, is not heavenly thought of. This book that you are reading, is heavenly agreeable, because it is clothed with the righteousness of God. But some of the clothing many women are wearing is no different from the nudeness of Adam and Eve.

The bible is not saying come to the church just as you go to the nightclubs. The bible is spiritual, and we take many of its quotes physical tense. When the bible says, *come unto me*, or *come as you are*, it is saying, no matter what sins you have committed in your life, "Come to Jesus even while in them. In other words, if you are filled with all 17 works of the flesh (sins), that's okay, come to Jesus as you are. Don't worry about what you did in the past. Every sin you have committed under the sun and under the moon, "*come to me as you are*". The scripture is not talking about your clothing. This scripture is speaking about going to Jesus, and realizing that you need a forgiveness of sins. Ladies, present yourself before the altar fully clothe. Show some respect at the altar of new life. If any woman needs to know how to present herself in the church, then go view my sister in the Lord, LaTonya Bishop.

When God sent me to his son Jesus, he miraculously took away all the creepy characters out of my life. When Jesus cleansed me from my sins: the drug ninja, the big strong wrestler, the hunter, the fisher, the death bait, the big bully, the wicked ghost chaser, drugs addiction, and the plan of wickedness were all taken out of my life. Thank you Jesus!

If you want to follow me, then you are following a good man. This entire book was written for one fact, and one fact alone. That is to bring unclean people to Jesus. I brought you to the physician, but you must be willing to let him do surgery on you. Jesus has the power to give your brain a new makeover. You might have to lie out, and wet your face with tears, at the foot of the altar, so Jesus can perform a miracle on you. Whatever works, then let it work. However, you must have a great act of sorrow in your heart. You must be so regretful of the things you've done in the pass. Go to a church, because the physician dwells there.

Matthew 11:28-Jesus said, come unto me, all ye that labor and are heavy laden, and I will give you rest. Well, now that I went to Jesus, and truly have him in my personal living, I am not working in hard labor, which sin and drugs led me to perform. I am not under the power or labor of drugs any more. Every time I broke one the laws of God, it was because I was empowered by sin and drugs to do such labor. The longer my life was under the power and labor of sin and drugs, the heavier the load became. Although, I was working in heavy labor with sin and drugs for ten years, when I came to Jesus, it was still lightweight for him to remove. When your brain and body is weighed down with the pounds of sin, take it to Jesus because nothing is too heavy for him to lift out of your life. Sin might have caused your life to be low (heavy), but Jesus has the power to lift you out of sin's tomb. *COME UNTO ME*!

My life is no more under the command to rush out the door to answer a "pager". I now presently have rest in my life and body because I finally accepted the *"life and blessing"* plan of God. In fact, I do not own a single pager at this particular time. In my past, it did not matter, what time of the day or night it was, after the pager sounded off, I physically scurried to the destination to go and collect that sinful money. Every time I tried to get some rest from selling drugs, my pager would beep. Then, immediately, I drove my car to meet a customer to sell cocaine. All during the day, and all through the night, I had many drug selling appointments. Now that God has led me to his son Jesus, those actions are no longer an activity in my life. If anyone wants true rest in his or her life, Jesus is the one that will supply you with it. The wonderful love about Jesus inviting people to come to him is the fact that he knows everything that you have done. As you have just read in my story, I almost did not make it to receive the invitation of Christ, because an 11-minute death experience came before the righteous invitation.

When I came to Jesus, he became my new master. My old master, which was sin and drugs, had bruised me very badly. This new master, which is Jesus Christ, he bandaged me up, and sealed all my inner wounds.

It is time to take heed to the voice of God, rather than obeying the voice of Satan. Satan's voice is usually not heard from him himself; however, he uses living people to activate his voice. The master of sin intentionally uses others to speak to your mind. Satan and sin never speaks about good or holy things. Satan's job is to master and rule your life, so that evil can be done all the days of your earthly living. Once the mind or brain agrees with the works of sin, then the body will perform that which it has agreed to do. Even while a person is operating in fullness of sin, Jesus is still saying unto that individual, *"come unto me"!* However, you are not familiar with hearing Jesus voice. You are use to hearing the voice of evil. Now that God has spoken unto you though my writings, you have heard his voice, now go to Jesus.

I have another scripture that I want to write unto you, and I am sure that you have heard this biblical passage before. *John 3:16 for God so loved the world, that he gave his only begotten Son, that whosoever believeth in him should not perish but have everlasting life.* Although, eternal life is a living that never ends, eternal life in heaven is granted to those who believe in God's son Jesus. Since eternal life comes through believing in Jesus, you have to go to get Jesus in order to inherit that heavenly dwelling. However, in my sinful drug dealing years, when my heart had stopped, do you honestly think that I would have lived in eternal life with Jesus? If you actually think or believe, I would have been in eternal heaven when I died in the 17 works of the flesh, which was a dead body that broke many laws, you do not want to find out by dying in your unforgiving sins. You can believe in Jesus, but in order to inherit eternal life with him, a certain work in life must also be applied. Not only that, but also, a certain path must be walked on, which will lead you to heaven.

Now that I have Jesus in my life, the existence of God's grace has been given to me as well. The bible says, *John 1: 17, for the law was given by Moses, but grace and truth came by Jesus.*

The law was given to Moses to give to the people of the earth; however, grace was given to Jesus to give to people who get a hold of him. Since I have gotten a hold of Jesus, I now attain "grace and mercy" both at the same time. Once I opened up my heart, and allowed Jesus to come in it, grace came in too. The reason why I know this is because; it is not written any were in the bible that Grace is upon those who walk not in the "blessing" plan of God.

Every person in the Old Testament who grace became acquainted with, God saw that the person wanted to be used by him. Most of the Old Testament prophets' said, "I have found grace in the eyes of the Lord", meaning, they hearkened to the voice of the Lord, and became God's friend. God saw that they wanted to be on his side, and he used them as witness for righteousness. The Old Testament prophets were granted grace, because the Spirit of God used them. They search for a better or godly living, and unto them grace was added.

In the Old Testament, many times it is said that God found favor in someone. When God found favor in the people in the Old Testament, his grace is what he saw in that individual. When I went to Jesus, and was forgiven of my sins, God found favor in me too. When a person wants to be used by God, that is when God shows him or her favor. When God shows favor to someone, that individual's heart is seeing for a change of living. God can't show you favor, when your life is filled with drugs, fornication, witchcraft, idolatry, and all the other 14 works of the flesh. There is such a scripture that says, *"Now if any man have not the Spirit of Christ, he is none of his"*.

John 14:6-Jesus said, I am the way, the truth, and the life: no man cometh unto the father (God) but by me. When humankind does not read the bible, to build a relationship with it, it becomes a book of mysteries. People believe they can, or is going to heaven by their own righteousness. People believe they are going to heaven just because they haven't committed a murder or have even cheated on someone. They have no heavenly understanding of what certain scriptures mean. They do not understand, nor believe, that God has preserved a system that leads people directly to heaven. God is in paradise (heaven), and Jesus has plainly said, *"No man can come unto the father but by me"*.

The only way to get to the father, who is in paradise, is to be escorted there by Jesus Christ himself. When a person first walks into a church, usually, that individual is escorted to a seat by the Usher. In the same sense, Jesus is the one who will usher you into heaven. In other words, if anyone desires to see God, Jesus claims to have the directions and plans to make this event possible. If you do not have God's beloveth son in your life, then it is impossible for you to meet God. That is why God directs us all to Jesus so that his beloved son can clean us from sin's filth, and then he can show us the "way" (directions) and the procedure to get in contact with heaven.

Remember, everyone one earth has instructions and rules in this world, and God has instructions and rules that will direct you to heaven. In order to get to heaven, Jesus has the instructions, and he knows the directions that will lead you there. Jesus has the keys that will open up the doors of heaven for you. Well, I suppose that Jesus, himself is the actual "rule" of God. Yep, it is by rule that Jesus is the Son of God, and it's by divine instructions that Jesus knows the way to heaven. *Jesus said, I am the way, the truth, and the life: no man cometh unto the Father but by me.* Well, now you know, if *no man can come unto God but by Jesus*, then Jesus is the only, I mean the only way to get any man to where God is.

I DID NOT KNOW that I actively needed Jesus to prepare a way for me to get to heaven to see God. Since I was living a certain lifestyle, and doing everything my own "way", then I was not doing things God's way. I was doing everything the "wicked way". The "way" that I was living in life, broke God's laws, therefore, God was against me because he judged me. However, if I walk the way that God has provided for me, which is to follow his son Jesus, then there will not come a moment that I should have to reappear in court again. Jesus said, *I am the "way"*, which means, he wants me to follow him because he is the only "way" for you and I to have an appointment to see God. Jesus is God's escort and "way" to heaven. People in the world, GO GET JESUS! Go get God's escort!

Heaven is an eternal home. Heaven is a place where

the almighty God lives. Jesus is not going to take any and everybody into his father's house. If you die in wickedness, which are actions of law breaking maneuvers, do you think Jesus is going to escort you to heaven? An order and sequence must be first met, so that living in heaven can be your place to reside, after death calls you in. First, you have to meet Jesus to have a chance or the audacity to live above the clouds. Jesus is the only one who is accepted by God, whom gives prime rights for heaven to receive you. Jesus will show you the way, in which you must go in order to walk around in heaven.

I have another scripture for you to read. *John 14:2-in my Father's house are many mansions: if it were not so, I would have told you. I go to prepare a place for you.* Do you mentally think that Jesus went boldly to his Father's house, which is in heaven, to prepare a mansion for me to live in? Again, when I died in all of my sins, do you think Jesus took the time to prepare a mansion in heaven for me? If you do not have Jesus in your life, brain, and body, then Jesus has no righteous reason to go to his father's house (heaven) to prepare a mansion for you or me. Whatever lifestyle you are living today, it is preparing you for your eternal place to abide in forever. Whether it is heaven or hell, a place is being prepared for your eternal abode.

Read these examples of my life's preparation: I went to sleep one day, woke up the next morning, took a shower, put my clothes on, went to work, and bam, being associated drugs caused me to be fired. I went to bed another day, woke up the next morning; took a shower, put my clothes on, dash to school, and bam, being associated drugs caused me to quit going to college. I went to bed one night, woke up the next morning, took a shower, put my clothes on, and bam, I quit two jobs. I went to bed one night, woke up in the morning, took a shower, put my clothes on, went to get high, and bam, drugs sent me into a coma. I went to bed one night, woke up in the morning, put my clothes on, and bam, I am on the run from the law (probation officer). I went to bed one night, woke up the morning, took a shower, put my clothes on, went outside to sell some dope, and bam, I got robbed. I went to bed one night, woke up the next morning, took a shower, put my clothes on, and bam I am on my way to the penitentiary. I went to bed one night, woke up in the morning, took a shower, put my clothes on, and bam, I came so close to committing a murder. Those were times, dates, and appointments that drug experiences had appeared into my life. Since my life was drug filled, drugs created or prepared all those unexpected scenes to occur in my life. Drugs will prepare situations to happen in your life, and you will never know what is going to happen next. Bad things might not be happening unto you this very minute (you think), but in the near future, horrible events will become experiences. Drugs want to prepare an opportunity to kill you! I know you do not want death to be your manifestation of a drug penalty, do you? Do not give drugs the opportunity to prepare scenes for your life in the tomorrow! Now that I have Jesus in my life, he is preparing a mansion for me to live in, which is being built in heaven. Either a person will be escorted to heaven, or commanded by Jesus to be sent to hell.

Now I am about to explain unto you about the brain still being active and alive in hell. Also, I am about to explain to you, that being rich does not mean much too God. Having money or the finest earthly materials, will never stop hell from becoming a person's home. As I said before, the brain (inner man) never dies, only the body does. Therefore, let me share with you a story written in the bible (New Testament) about a rich man who is now living in hell.

Luke 16:19 there was a certain rich man, which was clothed in purple and fine linen, and fared sumptuously everyday. This rich man clothed himself in purple. In the biblical times, wearing purple is a sign that shows royalty. The color purple symbolizes a high praise upon a person's living. It shows that a person has a high ranking a certain area of life. Meaning, the person who wears purple can do what many people in the world cannot do. Also, in the New Testament days, royalty means; to have power and authority. Every single day, the rich man was blessed to be able to keep himself looking good. Daily, for himself, the rich man is able to purchase all the wants and necessities at will. If any financial situation pops up surprisingly, the rich man is able to handle that business immediately. When a person is rich, or should I say wealthy, he or she feels superior. Being able to do for yourself at any given moment is a lifestyle of living sumptuously. When people are rich, they live their lives in luxury. Not one day went by that the rich man was not able to do for himself whenever desired.

The rich man has all the goods in the world. Money kept him happy. This rich man is living a lifestyle I could have lived, if I would have signed a sport contract deal. When people would have found out how such a great basketball player I am, there would have been many endowments granted unto me. From TV commercials, to my name being printed on my own shoes, I would have become rich. However, my drug usage stopped riches from being attached to my living.

Luke 16:20 and there was a certain beggar named Lazarus, which laid at his gate, full of sores. Lazarus laid at the rich man's gate, and his body was plagued with sores. The bible says the beggar was "full" of sores; therefore, his body was probably covered with them from head to toe. I can only imagine how the beggar's skin looked, as he laid at this rich man's gate. So many sores were on his body; his skin probably looked like it was embedded with something contagious. Looking at a body full of sores is a nasty thing to see. Just the other day, I saw a woman whose skin was full of black bumps, and it was not a good sight to see. Therefore, I can only imagine how the beggar's skin looked, since it was full of sores.

Why the beggar, whose skin is filled with sores at the rich man's gate anyway? The beggar feels that the rich man has something in his possession that he needs. Even if the beggar didn't see what he needs with the eye, he knew the rich man had it to give. Whatever Lazarus, the beggar, saw in the rich man's possession, his inner being was empowered to beg for it.

Let's find out why Lazarus laid at the rich man's gate, and what it was that he begged for. *Luke 16:21 And Lazarus was desiring to be fed with the crumbs, which fell from the rich man's table: moreover, the dogs came and licked his sores.* Now we know what this beggar, whose name was begging for. Lazarus wasn't begging for the rich man's money, nor was he begging for his man made materials. Lazarus beg for food, which is a substance that will keep him alive. Lazarus was probably a poor man, and was hungry for the most part. The beggar's limbic system (brain) was yearning to be fed food, to stop its hunger.

This is truly a work of homage, or shall I say respect. Anytime a man stretches out his body on the ground, and hoping to receive anything, he is asking for mercy to be shown unto him. Any person who does such a thing, has come to his last resort of being helped. Lazarus probably did all that he could to get some food, so he decided to do what was most embarrassing, and that was to lay stretched out at the rich man's gate begging for food.

When people are going through rough times in life, and are at the point of hunger, they will be led to beg for food. Lazarus was hoping that the rich man (the man with the goods) would have compassion and sympathy on him. Lazarus didn't desire much. Lazarus didn't even want a whole meal; he would have been satisfied with just the crumbs (or a small portion), which fell from the rich man's table. The crumbs are probably the portions of food that the rich man throws away. Better yet, Lazarus probably would have eaten from the rich man's plate. There is no telling, how much food, after becoming full, the rich man throws away.

You know what, a thought had just entered into my mind. I actually asked for some crumbs before, too. This hungry beggar probably lowered his self- esteem many times, just to have a meal. **Brain Irons** did the same thing many times before too. When I had asked my barber to give me the plate of food, that he was about to be tossed in the trash, I lowered my self-esteem just for a meal. Therefore, actually, I asked for crumbs, but no food was on the plate worth eating. My situation is different from the beggars, but we both were lead to ask, and do what we could for survival. My story is different from the beggar, but we both share the same heart hearting experience. I do not know the length of time Lazarus begged the rich man for crumbs, but later in life, both Lazarus and the rich man had died.

I must tell you folks something before I proceed with this story. Some of you folks are mentally slower than the man who has suffered a brain injury. Anytime a woman or man, ask for your left over; it is possible that he has no food. It is possible that the person has no food at home. You folks are so quick to quote scriptures, but none is quick to let the scriptures live through their giving. Let me leave that alone, but I am going to pick it back up in one of my upcoming books.

When a person has sympathy or pity on someone, usually a work of compassion is in action. However, the rich man did not show any compassion toward the beggar. I am sure that the beggar laid at the rich man's gate on several occasions. It was obvious that Lazarus, the beggar, wanted food for the belly. It was not a hidden agenda, nor was it a secret. It was openly revealed unto the rich man that Lazarus desired a meal to serve his body. I am sure Lazarus even opened his mouth and asked for a meal a number of times.

However, you know what, personally speaking; I know exactly how Lazarus, the beggar feels. People can plainly see you going through a stage of suffering, but will not lift a finger to help. For years, people saw as well as heard that I had a need. Yeah, many of you St. Louis folks knew I needed a helping hand. I was like the beggar, he didn't desire much, and neither did I. Although, I needed a financial helping hand, and Lazarus wanted a meal, my situation is not too much of a difference. Actually, the beggar's situation and mine are very similar. Just as the rich man saw the beggar suffering, many of you saw me suffering too.

In this beggar's story, it is said; *moreover, the dogs*

came and licked his sores. In other words, the dogs came and catered to one of the beggar's need. The dogs licked the beggar's sores, which was a work of compassion shown from a beast (animal). Not only did the beggar need food, but he needed love to be shown unto him as well. The dogs supplied the beggar with medical attention, but the rich man did not provide the beggar with any. When a person is hungry, food is the substance that will satisfy that need. Once that hungry individual eats a meal, the inner being becomes healed, because food is a potent medicine to the hungry body. After a person has eaten a meal, the hunger mood soon departs from the brain. The dogs were moved with compassion but the rich man didn't move with any. The dogs freely approached the beggar, but the rich man kept his distance.

Luke 16:22 and it came to pass, that the beggar died, and was carried by the angels into Abraham's bosom: the rich man also died, and was buried; when the rich man had died, I guaranteed you that his family put these letters, R.I.P over his dead body. Engraving R.I.P. over dead people, has become so common unto us, that we fell to realize that many people really aren't in peace. People may die quietly, but some will lift up their eyes on the other side of terror. We are about to see if this rich man is actually resting in peace.

Luke 16:23 and in hell he (the rich man) lift up his eyes, being in torments, and seeth Abraham afar off, and Lazarus in his bosom.

Luke 16:22 says, *the beggar died, and was carried by the angels into Abraham's bosom*. The beggar died, and being transported by the angels, he was taken to a place where Abraham is now living. The rich man died, and God sent him to his well-earned place, hell.

Luke 16; 23 says, "in hell", the rich man lift up his eyes. As I explained unto you before, that; *"The Wicked and all those that forget God shall be turned into hell"*. Since this rich man is lifting up his eyes in hell, he is not resting in peace. Since the rich man is in hell, which is a place of eternal torture, then how can he have peace within.

The rich man is in hell, because God turned him towards that way. Maybe the rich man was once living righteous, and his heart became attached to selfishness. Think about it; the rich man had to be going in a certain direction in order for God to turn him another way. Hell became the rich man's home. Therefore, God categorized him as "The Wicked. I believe the rich man treated the beggar horribly wrong. This rich man was probably so proud and arrogant, he probably laughed in the beggar's face as he ate his food.

Since the rich man lifted up his eyes in hell, as the scripture has said, he even has sight in this place. Since the rich man lifted up his eyes in hell, his pupils are still in operation. While the rich man is having active sight from hell, he actually sees the beggar in Abraham's bosom. There once was a time, when the beggar respected, and looked up at the rich man, but now, the rich man is in hell looking up at the beggar who is in Abraham's bosom. From hell, the rich man is now looking at the person he showed no compassion, too. If people aren't careful about how they treat others, God will recompense you your reward. It is so sad, because God rewarded the rich man with an eternal brain torturing home...hell. As of now, since the rich man is in hell watching activity take place, then his occipital lobes in his brain is yet active. Yep, in hell, the brain still performs sight.

Luke 16:24 And he (the rich man) cried and said, Father Abraham, have mercy on me, and send Lazarus (the beggar), that he may dip the tip of his finger in water, and cool my tongue; for I am tormented in this flame. Oh wow, the rich man is in hell crying out for mercy to be shown unto him. The rich man is actually in hell, crying out to Abraham that he might send Lazarus (the beggar) to bless him. The rich man is now begging that Lazarus be sent to him, so he can supply him with a little water, when in fact; he did not give the beggar any food. The rich man now realizes that he did not show compassion and love toward this beggar. Although, the rich man's story speaks about him and the beggar, I guaranteed you; the rich man looked down on many other people in the world who had needs.

Anytime a person is sent to hell, it is evidence that Jesus and the love of God is not being active in one's heart. But you know what, I believed the rich man was once a child of God's righteousness. The rich man called Abraham, father, which signifies that he was of the seed (son) of Abraham. Anyone who is of the seed of Abraham's faith is a child of God. Therefore, if the church folks, who are the seed of Abraham aren't careful, hell can become their home too. The entire bible is written with true series of stories that can become our personal report if we show not the love of God abroad. Since this rich man is in hell, as the bible quotes, then you people who have the world's goods need to be careful when turning down someone who has realistic needs.

Not only will a person have the mental authority to know that he or she is in hell, but also, speech is active while in there. Yeah, the rich man had conversation with Abraham, which means, a person can speak while in the place of torment. The lobes that deal with speech are the frontal lobes. Therefore, these lobes are still active in hell. When a person goes to hell, he will be fully alive in there.

Even a person's emotional side is performed in hell, because the rich man desires mercy to be shown unto him. In hell, the rich man was feeling regretful. He now realizes that he showed not the love of God to the beggar (the needy).

Hey, people who are in the world today, we all need to show mercy to those who have needs. Showing mercy unto the needy, or to those who have real needs, is imitating the love of God. God performed mercy on you, therefore, perform mercy on someone else. Show some care; stop being stubborn with substances that has dead president's faces on it (money). Show compassion because you just never know, how your life is going to make a turn about.

Luke 16:25 But Abraham said, Son, remember that thou in thy lifetime receivedst thy good things, and likewise Lazarus evil things: but now he is comforted, and thou art tormented. Here is when Abraham tells this rich man why he has been sent to the place of eternal torture (hell). God is not going send a person to hell wondering why he or she is there. God is going to tell you exactly why hell became your eternal home. If being sent to hell would have become my judgment, "I believe God would have said unto me, "you allowed drugs to be your God, and you broke all my commandments"; everything you call a work of compassion, was from the work of evil.

Abraham said to the rich man, _son, remember that thou in thy lifetime receivedst thy good things, and likewise Lazarus evil things: but now he is comforted, and thou are tormented._ In other words, Abraham is telling the rich man; you had enough substances to help and feed the beggar, but you didn't. The rich man probably had enough to get the beggar on his feet to purchase a business.

Anyway, since Abraham spoke to the rich man who is in hell, then from hell the rich man heard his voice. Every word Abraham spoke to the man in hell, he heard them all. This is a prime example that a person's hearing is active even in hell. Not only can voices be heard in hell, but weeping and gnashing of teeth noises will be heard too. The bible says that, hell is a place where weeping and gnashing of teeth operates. Weeping and gnashing of teeth is probably a noise that will be heard as people mourn and cry out for an escape to be freed from hell. Weeping and gnashing of teeth takes up many definitions in its meaning. Nevertheless, once a person goes to hell, its over, there is no coming back to earth for another chance.

While this rich man is in hell having conversation with Abraham, he wanted Lazarus to be given the power to do another act for him. The rich man stated_; he has five brothers_, and he asked Abraham if Lazarus could be sent to his father's house to testify to them, lest they be sent to hell too.

Maybe his five brothers have the same attitude he had. The rich man knows how his brother's attitudes are. He grew up with them. The rich man knew, if his brothers keep living the way that they are living (not having the desire to help the needy and the poor) that hell would become their eternal home too. Who knows, a financial inheritance could have been left behind for the family to share, which caused them all to be rich. The brothers probably were treating those who had needs like trash, and showed no compassion, just as he didn't show any. When the rich man was alive on earth, he didn't show any mercy, and probably, neither are his brothers. Really, think about it! Why does the rich man want to come back to tell his brothers about hell? If his brothers were living compassionate lives, then there is no reason for him to come back to earth to warn his brothers.

Since this rich man wanted Lazarus to come back and speak warnings to his brothers, he was still able to remember earthly events. Yeah, his declarative memory is still in operation, even while in hell. The declarative memory memorizes facts, and information. As I said before, the memory of a computer can loose its data, but the human brain lives forever, and will remember the smallest thing when you least expect it. Do not let your brain visit the place of torment (hell), go get Jesus today!

The rich man's story is a true living example of this scripture written below in the book of Matthew; *Mathew 16:26-for what is a man profited, if he shall gain the whole world, and lose his own soul? Or what shall a man give in exchange for his soul?* Yep, this rich man gained the whole world, but he still lost his own soul. He profited with money, but when it came to spiritual or godly profit, he either didn't inherit it, he lost it. The rich man lost his soul to hell. The rich man was filled with the motivation of pride. That is what rich people do; they gain the whole world, and lose their own soul, all because of not showing compassion to a person who has a need.

Many rich folks rely on money to make ways for them, rather than God. They believe, because they can pay their way out of every situation, that it is the gift from God, when in fact, its not. Don't get me wrong, because being rich is a gift from God, but using money to pay your way out of situations, is not what the gift should be used for. Rich folks might be able to pay their way out of court, but when they all die, the tomb of court will be seen, because its judgment day. Financial riches mean nothing to God; the way you live on earth is all that matters. The rich man, and the poor man, is both alike to God. They both must obey the commands of God.

This next scripture speaks about a purpose and plan of God. _1ˢᵗ John 3:8 He that committeth sin is of the devil; for the devil sinneth from the beginning. For this purpose, the Son of God (Jesus) was manifested that he might destroy the works of the devil._ Jesus has the actual power to destroy the works of the devil. Jesus is God's new way for destroying wickedness and sin (the works of the devil). If you allow Jesus to destroy the works of the devil, you have accepted God's plan. Instead of wickedness destroying you, let Jesus first destroy it. Through forgiveness, the works of the devil are destroyed. Jesus must first destroy your wickedness, before a relationship with him is built. I have just told you the plan that God came up with to destroy wickedness, and it alone. Year ago, God destroyed humankind, along with their wickedness. Now the plan to destroy wickedness has been changed. What a merciful God he is!

Chapter 14
God Making Your Name Great Through a Relationship

The only thing people know about God and Jesus are their names. Also, people only know that God is the creator of the heavens and the earth. The only thing many people can say about Jesus is that he died on a cross for the sins (men) of the world. Other than that, people know nothing more about Jesus. Actually, you do not know anything about God or Jesus until you have read up on them. The bible is filled with facts about who God and Jesus really is. If you do not read the bible, you will never learn whom they are.

Another thing we believe; when we present the name God or Jesus in our conversations, we feel that we know them both. Bringing up the name God or Jesus in our everyday conversation does not empower us to know either of them. We grew up from childbirth (youth) hearing those names. Therefore, our minds have been programmed on the fact that those names do exist. Yet, we really do not know the "deep" understanding of why those names do exist in this violent world. Actually, many people believe, or think that Jesus is still dead.

You have to learn about the things God loves, and the things that he hates. To know God or Jesus the way you need to know them, you need to read the bible and learn historical facts about them both. Just as you read about me in my book, and have gotten a chance to know me, well, in the same likeness, you need to read the bible, and learn about Jesus and God. Many of you have never met **Brain Irons** before in your life, but since you have read about me, you have learned hidden facts about me. Well, now it is time for you to crack open a bible, and learn the hidden facts about God and Jesus.

Many of you picked up my book, read it in its

entirety, but has not ever read a bible's chapter. From reading my book, a relationship between us has been built. Now you need to pick up a bible, and begin to read it, and it will interact with your being. Throughout the years, many of you have purchased dozens of books, but have not even considered buying yourself a bible. Most people have more than 15 books lying round the house, but not one of them is a bible.

Throughout the years, we all have heard of the things that the bible speaks against. The true reason why many people will not pick up, or read the bible, is that it speaks against un-married relationships (having sex before marriage). That is one of the main reason why people do not read the bible, and build a relationship with God--- it speaks against having sexual pleasure while not being married. Once a person hears, that the bible speaks against having sex before marriage, immediately, he or she professes, "Man wrote that book". People are always against anything that speaks against the works of the flesh. When the bible speaks against having sex before married, it is only saying so for your own good. However, people take it so negative that they think something is being taken away from them. If none of this un-marital sex (fornication) would be in the land, then diseases would not be a high rated killer in our world. Since the world of people wants to get into personal relationships anyway, then sexual transmitted diseases will continue to multiply. The bible (God) is only giving commands to make our earthly living--- a great living, but we are so caught up in "self mode" that we neglect its heavenly support.

We learn everything from books. A book is all we have in this world to learn about God. When you learned how to do math, you was taught how to do so from a book. When you learned about science, you've learned it from a book. When you learned about world history, you've learned it from a book. The same thing applies when seeking to learn about God and Jesus. You will learn of those two names from a book called, "The Holy Bible". Read it; build a relationship with God, because you really need too.

When you have a relationship with God, you become a follower of him too. Abraham became a follower of God. Although, Abraham was a follower of God, it is recorded in the bible that he performed a few ungodly acts as well. Abraham did a few bad deeds in his life, and so did I. One of the great historical facts about Abraham, is the fact that he came to a point in his life were he could hear the voice of God. However, with me, there is no way I was hearing the voice of God, because drugs filled my hearing center (brain) completely. If I thought to do what was right, drugs led me to do what was wrong, which was to break the laws. Even though, Abraham did some evil deeds as he was growing up in life, all of his evil committed deeds were forgiven. The reason why I know Abraham evil performed deeds were forgiven is that he now lives in the high place called, "Heaven". Oh yes, he does lives in heaven now. Remember, from heaven, Abraham had a conversation with the rich man who *lifted his eyes in hell.*

When you are in a relationship with someone, not only do you learn about the individual, but also you will learn the person's voice as well. God's biblical word is his spiritual voice, as well as his physical voice. Therefore, if you are not reading the bible, you are not hearing the "Voice of God". If you are not learning to hear God's voice, then you will never come to the realization of knowing who God really is. God talks, he speaks, but if you do not give an ear to hear what he has to say, you will always be lost. If you do not read the bible, then you will never learn what God has to say about the living of your soul.

When two people are in a relationship, they learn one another voice so well, that they can distinguish one another's voice in a public area. If I was married, which means I am in a relationship, and my wife walked up behind me and called my name, immediately, I would know it's her voice. I have learned the sounds of her voice through this commitment. Depending upon the length of time two people have been married, they will learn one another's voice and language in a short period. As it is mentioned in the bible, that Abraham did learn and did hear the voice of God.

There's a recorded scene in the bible concerning the voice of God, which went out unto to Abraham that I want expand on. God, spoke to Abraham from heaven, and Abraham heard God's voice. *Genesis 12:1 now the Lord said unto Abram (Abraham), get thee out of thy country, and from thy kindred, and from thy father's house, unto a land I will show thee.* After Abraham heard the voice and command from God, he left his country, left his kindred, and left his father's house. God commanded Abraham to go somewhere, and he did just that. Abraham had a relationship with God; therefore, he was able to hear God's voice. If you never hear the voice of God, how can you obey it? Although, you have ears attached to your head that does not mean you are hearing God's voice. There are many voices in the world, but there is only one voice of God. The things you are doing today, signifies the voice you've heard and is obeying. Which voice are you hearing? Listen people, God's voice in the bible, I advise you to read it, and give heed to what it has to say about your life.

There is not one living man on the earth that God does not have a task for. God created the world and us, therefore, not only does Abraham have a command to obey, but also, we have a command to obey as well. I do not know the task God has for you, and you do not know what job God desires to give me. Everyone must go to God through Jesus to find out what it is that God wants you to do. Read this next scripture, which is a continuation of what God said to Abraham, after he was commanded to leave his country, his kindred, and his father's house.

Genesis 12:2 and I will make thee (Abraham) a great nation and I will bless thee, and make thy name great, and thou shall be a blessing. This scripture speaks about God making the name of "Abraham" great. I am going to explain unto you how Abraham name became great. This scripture (*Genesis 12:2*), also speaks about God blessing Abraham. Abraham must obey God, in order for his name to be made great, and for him to be blessed. In the bible, there is a biblical story about Abraham's seed (name and descendant) becoming great. Abraham name became great through his seed (children). However, I am not going to explain all of that. However, I will supply you with an earthen example that is easy to understand how Abraham name became great.

When I was attending middle school, my music class would sing a song, which was about the name of "Abraham". This song has a written verse within it, which said, "Father Abraham had many sons". When my class was singing about the name of Abraham, that marks the "greatness" right there. The entire class probably did now know who this Abraham is, but we were singing a song concerning his name. Although, I was singing the song with the class, I DID NOT KNOW him at all.

Abraham was giving the power to know God. Many people in the world actually think they have a relationship with God, when in fact they do not. It takes being in a relationship with someone, in order to know that person. Also, it takes power to believe every written word and fact in the bible. People believe, when they receive new homes to live in, and being able to afford new cars, or earning a big promotion from the employer is because of being in a relationship with God. Please, I can probably name about 100 people who know not the Lord, and they get great promotions on the job yearly. We actually believe that, knowing God is based upon financial promotions, and the gathering of material. Purchasing the biggest house, or earning the biggest annual check, does not mean a person is in a relationship with God. If you are not walking with Jesus then you have not a relationship with God. As the scripture has said in an earlier chapter of this book, "what profit a man to gain the whole world and lose his soul? You can have everything you could possible want in this life, and still not have God. As the scripture has just said, "you can lose your own soul". The rich man did not have God at the time death pulled him in. He was driven to hell, and lost his soul to the underground world. When walking with Jesus, which means being in a relationship with God, your soul will never be lost.

Not only does God desire to make the name Abraham great, but also, God's thoughts are overflowing with the pleasure of making our names great too. God desires to make every earthly being name great for the purpose of his own glory. Once we become connected to God, and begin to hear his voice, the "great name" process is in the making. However, you have to get a relationship with God, in order for this "great name" process to begin. There is a plan and order that you and I must personally receive from God to be led in the right direction as God purposely makes your name and mine great. First, as I said in the earlier chapter, you have to get Jesus first.

God will never venture into the world, and make your name great, without participation. You have to be a participant, and receive the plans from God. If you do not become a participant, you will never learn the plans, which will make your name great. When God has made your name great, you have prospered from his righteousness. Nevertheless, you must obey God's rules in order to inherit the "great name blessing".

When you allow God to make your name great, God is the one doing the making, and not you. As God prepares to make your name great, the makings of will unfold, piece by piece. Just as a movie is developed scene-by-scene, well, when allowing God to make your name great, it will be done seen scene by scene, too. God can only begin to make your name "great" when you submit your life according to his divine plan. The suggestion I have for you; give your life and body to God so he can make your life and name shine like the brightness of the sun during the day, and the twinkling of a star, which shines every night. Just as God made the moon to give great light on the earth nightly, however, if you allow God to make your name great, your name will shine greatly, day and night. In God, your name will touch basis with his solar power.

However, people always go out into the world, and make their own names great just for worldly publicity. When people decide to make their own names great, it is the individual doing the making, rather than God. As I now think about the lifestyle I was living, I was making my own name great. In fact, I did make my name "great". My name was known in many areas of St. Louis, Missouri for playing sports. Although, sports are okay to be known or great in, however, if I had become that great professional athlete, I probably would not have God in my life. If I would have signed a multi-million dollar contract to play basketball, that doesn't mean God is in my life. If the truth were told, God wants to be in everyone's life (brain), before any become millionaires.

People desire to make their names great first, and then try to let God become a partaker of their lives. People work hard to get college degrees, but never work to get God in their lives first. People work hard for years to get that financial promotion, before they seek to have a relationship with God. People work overtime hours for more money, just to buy houses, but do not work overtime getting to know God. Many athletes train daily to get better in sports, but they never exercise the mind to build a better relationship with God. People shop for the best car to ride around in, but never seek to put God in the vehicle with them.

The bible says, in _Mathew chapter 6:33 but seek ye first the kingdom of God and his righteousness, and all these things shall be added unto you._ Everyone is working for personal gain before seeking the righteousness from God. Even I, was seeking to be a basketball star, and never sought the righteousness of God. My personal desires came first, and God righteousness I never sought. However, God righteousness through divine judgments found me first. Before I decided to seek God's righteousness, the laws judgments, and prophecies had beaten on my life.

Being a good athlete in sports means nothing to God. My basketball skills mean nothing. There was not one basketball shot taken that I was able to give God the glory. After the basketball games were over, immediately, I went to perform lawbreaking maneuvers. That's not God, that's not having a relationship with God. My baseball pitching skills means nothing. There was not one strikeout were I gave God the glory. My quarterback skills mean nothing. There was not one thrown touchdown were I gave God the glory. Therefore, a million dollar contract means nothing. If my name would have been signed on a basketball contract, my name would have become great, but drug activities and other evils would have continued to be performed. Probably, without a doubt, I would have stopped selling drug because I would have been rich by playing basketball, but I am so sure that I would have still been putting drugs into my brain. What I am trying to say is this; if I would have become a sport's millionaire, how can I truly, I mean truly, thank God when lawbreaking maneuvers were grossly apart of my life. I mean, I never asked for forgiveness of sin. I was in the world lost, without any heavenly guidance, just as some of you rich folks are today.

In one particular neighborhood (grape-street) that I dwelled in, everyone that hung in it sold drugs for me at one point. At one point, I supplied a person with a package of cocaine to sell. Whether a person profited $20, or a $1000, I gave a specific amount to be returned. I probably gave drugs to more than 30 people in this particular neighborhood. As of now, every single last one of them probably still owe me money, but that life is over, therefore, I do not care what has happened to that evil money. It would look so ignorant for me to approach someone, and request money to be paid.

However, right now today, the name "Light skin" (**Brian Irons**) went down in history as one of the most successful drug dealers who sold dope, took care of wicked business, and made large amounts of money. I was so greatly known in this neighborhood, people jokingly still ask me this question right now today, "where all that money that you hid and stashed away"? Not to be putting down others that associated in the hood, but everyone knew that **Brian Irons** (Light Skin) was the man. Whether, it was playing basketball, fighting, or selling drugs, the name "Light Skin" (**Brian Irons**) became greatly known. In my 4 or 5 years of selling drugs, my name became great in the neighborhood (south side). My name became great through the helping of drugs, and not by the guidance and makings of God. Do you yet see the difference?

As you have just read, throughout the years of selling drugs, I made my own name great. However, God told Abraham that he would make his name great, meaning, he (God) was going to create a way for it to be done. When God says he is going to do something for a certain individual, he does not need any help or human assistance to carry out the plan. When God gives you a task to perform, he already sees the beginning of it and its ending. Let's not forget the middle, because that is the central point when God is making your name great. God's title and power is God; therefore, he is sovereign at whatever he desires to do for you. The only work that you or I have to do is to be available to hear him when he speaks. Just as drugs spoke to my mind through the basketball team, and my name became wickedly great throughout the years, however, God wants to speak to my brain and make my name righteously great in due time.

As I now live in the blessed plan of God, he has given me a job. The job that God has inspired (hired) me to perform is to write books probably until the day I die. My next two books will be written about dope. These next two books will save many lives from personal self-destruction. This job ((writer) that I now have, is far distant from the job of selling drugs. This job will not bring any harm to my mental body or my physical body. Nor will it empower me to break laws.

Within myself, I felt that I needed to find myself a job to make a few dividends, so that selling crack cocaine would not revive itself into my life again. Writing is a job that God is going to work with me on. If I stay with God and keep the faith, financial avenues will be open unto me. Although, I could have been rich by playing five different sports on a professional level, God has given me a charge to express my brain's talents through writing. God is going to provide a way for all of my necessities to be met. As long as I keep the vision that God has given me, and keep a relationship with Him, great things will happen for me, and the name, **BRIAN K. IRONS** will be made great throughout the earth.

Its time for me to trust what God can do for me, instead of trusting what drugs can. I have already experienced the power and control of drugs, now it is time for me to experience the power and control of God. God Almighty, I want to see how far you are going to take my writings. Yeah, all my writings are for your glory. Since God has hired and given me a task to be a writer for him, I do not have to search for jobs any more and fear of being rejected or turned down. God, show me what you can do, your servant Abraham is no different from me. You made Abraham name great, so make **Brian Irons** name great too. Yes, God, make **Brian Irons** name great!

When people go to the store, mall, or library searching for my book, it is because God is working on making my name great. Now that God has raised me from the dead (11 minutes heart failure), the name "**Brian Irons**" will probably be heard in your city, town, and or state. This book, which has my name printed on it, will be purchased, and become greatly known throughout the history of the earth. Yeah, I am soon to put on the same shoes that Abraham wears. Abraham name is known, and my name is soon to be known too. Abraham feet traveled from place to place, and my feet are about to go state to state.

God has made many names "great" upon the earth. We know that Dr. Martin L. King is known and famous for the message that he spoke called, "I have a dream". In fact, God made Dr. Martin Luther King name so great, that his birthday is acknowledged on the earth every year. Phyllis Wheatley was once a slave, and a person known to be a Christian. You may not have ever seen Ms. Wheatley, but you've heard of her. Phillis Wheatley's story is in many history books. Yes, God made her name great too. Phyllis Wheatley name has been known as a poem writer for holy admiration. Also, Ms Wheatley was the first black female poet. Pastor Illona W. Dickson name is great too. Pastor

Dixon's name has become great as a warrior and preacher/teacher for God. In her godly greatness, she is one of a kind. Pastor Author R. Johnson name has been made great by God too. This pastor will tell you the truth, even if it hurts. Paula White, another great preacher. Her name God made great too. Judge Greg Mathis, your name is great too. Rev. Larry Rice, God has made his name great too. His ministry helps all St. Louis citizens with housing needs, and he is a great preacher also. Pastor TD Jakes and Creflo Dollar names have been made great too. The prophetess Juanita Bynum, her name God made great too. The great Evangelist Caroline Gilbert, by God, her name is great, too. Joyce Meyers, Bishop Green Lee, Jesse Duplantis, Rod Parsley, Myles Munroe, through the will of God these names have been made "great". My young sister in the Lord, LaTonya Bishop, her name is great too. I call this young female preacher, "LaTonya Bishop the Great". To LaTonya Bishop, God has you so deep in my heart that he is going to give me the power to open many doors for you. (I GOT YOUR BACK). Evangelist Sheila Mack, and Minister Aretha Patterson, names are great too. Many singers, such as, Nicole Mullins, Bebe and Cece Winans, Shirley Caesar, Dottie Peoples, Marvin Sap, Hezekiah Walker, Kirk Franklin, their names have become great on the earth too. Pastor David Battle, your name is great too. Pastor Ronald Moore, and Pastor Hollins, both your names have become great, too. Hey, Jesse Battle, I remember you visited Radiant Life in Christ Church one day. You taught the congregation on how to prepare a sermon scripture by scripture. Well, I Did Not Know, that I would be using your teachings to write all my books. All of my books will be written based upon that one day of teaching you provided at Radiant Life. This book, I Did Not Know, was re-planned entirely from your teachings. Well, Pastor Jesse Battle, your name is on the great name list too. God has made talk show hosts and actors names great, too. Gloria Irons Brown, (my mother) her name is great too. Gloria is the person who was used by God to make careful decisions for my life while I was in the coma.

All of the people I have just mentioned in this paragraph; have a relationship with God. God spoke to them, gave them a command, and they obeyed that which was commanded. Not only have these names been made great upon the earth, but also, their names are written in the Lambs Book of Life (in heaven) (in the bible) Actually, if your name is written in the Lambs Book of Life, that's the greatest way to have your name in the "Great Name Spot". Well, you can add me to the "great name" list too, because God spoke to me, and gave me a charge to write books. Since I wrote this book, I obeyed, and now my name is in the making of becoming great. Yeah, the name **Brian Irons** will be known for the book, which is titled, I DID NOT KNOW.

When God makes your name great, whatever the business is, often times you will mention his name. You've understood that, you could not have accomplished certain goals without him. I truly realize that without God, my book would not be displayed on the earth. Not only that, but my name would not have the opportunity of becoming great. When God makes your name great, your business name becomes great too. God is the "great" name maker, and by him, the work of "Great" is performed.

I now have revelation to know why Dr. Martin Luther King stated in one of his poems, which is titled, "I Have a Dream". In this poem, Dr. Martin Luther King Jr. proclaimed, "that all men are created equal". The reason and conclusion that I have found concerning all men being created equal is this; God created many brains in the heads of many people, and every one of them have a brain that looks alike and does the same thing. God created all brains in the same fashion and in the same form. Not one living brain differs from the other. Although, every person looks different and even act different, however, every brain is designed by God to operate in the same like manner. Therefore, when Dr. Martin Luther King said, "All men are created equal", he is so right, because all brains functions the same. By Brian K. Irons

This book will free millions of brains that are

experiencing the enslavement of drugs. Wherever there is a bookstore in AMERICA, the book, which has my name on it, can be ordered there. When the cashier person looks up my book's title on the computer, the name **Brian Irons** will pop up as the author. Yeah, my name is in the makings of becoming great. Hallelujah, to the Lamb of God!

From the mental (spiritual) guidance and preparation from God, I will pass this story to my children, so they can pass it to their children as well. I will teach my children how to run a book business, as God provides me with the understanding to do so. This book will go from my possession to my kid's possession. This book will stay in the family. God is not going to allow this true story to fade away as grass does. I believe God is going to make sure that this book stay available to America forever or at least until Jesus comes and take away earth. Just like every generation, another family member revises the movie "roots", and keeps its historical facts and scenes on the TV screen; my books will stay here and travel from generation to generation as well. I truly believe that wicked affiliations will be in the land always, because people will not delete the activity of chemical usage from their personal lives. Just as Martin Luther King died, and his name is still with us, well, when I die, my name and book will be here as well.

Hey people, do not perceive the wrong understanding from this chapter. Even if your name has become great before God being fully in your life, it is never too late to go and get him. You only have to get Jesus, ask for forgiveness, and Jesus will intercede with you and your business. However, if you've built an empire from selling drugs, God is not going to promote that. You will have to start all over again. For some of you, that will be hard to do. However, it will be worth it all. Also, remember this, God is not going to sign his name on every personal own business in the world. For example, if you are running a porno business, you actually think God is going to promote that. You know what, let me stop, I have to go. But I will tell you more in my second book.

Chapter 15
Just a Few Personal Words to Share

This book (I DID NOT KNOW), I like the thrashing episodes and scenes that are written within it. However, I do not like the order of the paragraphs in which it is written. Although, it is a great story, however, my brain is not satisfied with the writing thereof. When I first began writing this book, I was lost on how to write it. I first wrote this book without chapters. Then I had to dive through the entire book, create chapter names, and re-organize all the paragraphs. I wrote the rough draft of this book a very long time ago. In less than a week, the rough draft was written. I thought it would be a good idea to keep adding more words to the writing until publication arrive. Well, personally speaking, it was not a good idea to keep adding more and more words to the story. However, only if you knew the things I went through, just to get this book in this kind of shape, then truly you would disregard the content order. While writing this book, I had to write it over more than 20 times. Never did I give up on my vision to be a published author. My computer kept loosing my book's information. My floppy disks were breaking on me. Oh my God, you have not a wishing clue of all the things that tried to cause me to give up. I am so glad the book is finally published. Just a few personal words to share!

Every time you share this book with some one, it is possible that a life will be saved from the glued power of drugs. Also, every time you share this story with your friend or relative, it is possible that they will purchase this book. When a book has been purchased, that is a dollar earned; I can give to my children. Of course, I am going to do great things for myself, and you had better believe that. That little brown pretty lady on the book cover is my precious daughter. She needs me, and I need her. Just a few person words to share!

Dierra Brown (my daughter), I am so glad I will be able to do great things for you. I cannot wait to take you out to eat, shop, and do many fatherly things with you. I am daddy, I am the man in your life, remember that. I get the first REAL date with you girl. I need to take you out as often as I can, so you can get a feel of how a man is supposed to treat you. To my son, Deantae Richardson, I need to do great things for you too. I need to teach you how to respect a woman when she comes into your life. Parents need to take their children out on dates at times, and teach their kids how to present themselves when out on a date. Parents should take their child out on dates at a very young age, because once the child becomes a teenager, it's too late. While the child is young, he or she will listen. Once the child becomes a teenager, the child already thinks he or she knows it all. Also, parents need to take their children on dates to teach them what to expect from the opposite sex. Of course, you shouldn't talk about sex to your 10 year old. But be open-minded and honest about expectations. The younger you start teaching your child, the better chance for success. And of course, mention the rules of God while on this date. I did not get the chance to do these things two my kids, and I am hurt about it. But God put it in my spirit to tell the world, about an activity that needs to be done. I am sure most of us (parents) have experienced awful dates before. Nevertheless, we parents went through what we went through so we can warn our children about those things. Just a few personal words to share!

Hey, you men in the industry of rap music; there's not one rapper or musician who differs in the mental. You people are no different from me. We all have the same brain mechanism, and drugs will do us all the same way. Stop putting the violence enhancer (drugs) into your brains, so that the percentage rate of violence in the rapping community will decline. If the violence enhancer had not been in many rap listeners and rappers brains, there is a great chance that Tupac, Biggie Smalls, and Jam Master Jay would still be alive unto this very day. I am not saying that another rapper killed them; however, those 3 were killed, and probably by a brain filled with drugs. Please, do yourself a favor, and get God's son Jesus in your life. Remember this, if drugs are in your rapping business, then violence will soon show its face. There is so much hostility in the rap business it's pathetic. Once violence shows up, then shortly, guns will be brought into action. Then a body will be filled with the metal formula of bullets. Then, just that fast, and just that quick, another dead rapper will be viewed at a funeral. One more thing I have to say; to all you musicians; how can you call women B's and hookers in your music, and then thank God for the CD's success. People actually believe God is in everything they do and say. Also, you black men who dwell upon the earth, go back to school, get a higher education, and earn for yourself a positive life. I know I was once a wicked man, however, God has changed my living. Besides, you do not know how long God's mercy is going to keep you from the danger of physical harm. Life is truly too short! Just a few personal words to share!

Pro athletes and Celebrities from all over the world, I am sure this is a great story for your teen child. I suggest that, if you have kids who are in the 6th grade or higher, a copy of this book should be purchased for them. Also, pro-athletes, buy a copy of this miraculous book for your teammate. Cause a link of my book to be extended throughout the world of professional athletes and celebrities. Yes, you all (celebrities) need to read this book too; because every week, there is an awful drug or alcohol scene being displayed on television. Every week, I read a celebrity story in the newspaper concerning drugs and alcohol. I have seen many celebrities be charged for driving while under the influence of a chemical. I have seen many celebrities catch drug cases. Although, most celebrities are financially secured, however, sin and drugs will not hesitate to mess up celebs life. Money has no power against sin. Sin and drugs has the power to mess your celebrity's name up, too. I am not going to say any names, but the enticement and power from drugs has net many celebrities. Therefore, pass this story to the next. Just a few personal words to share!

The other day I was rolling down Cherokee Street in my wheelchair, and came across a man. This man had heard that I was writing a book. Him and I were having a conversation on the sidewalk. In our conversation, he made a confession to me. He confessed that, "he thought I was talking trash about writing a book". He thought that, since I use a wheelchair, that I didn't have the mind to write a book. Well, guess what old man, here is my first written book, and I just might give you a copy. Throughout the years of having a disability, many people in St. Louis have looked down upon me. I know they have. I have proof and facts to show it. Either they all have looked down on me, or they all were jealous, which is a thing I have been dealing with all my life. In fact, you all are jealous, and I must destroy that envying spirit that now worketh in you all. Everything that my God created brain has dominated in, has always brought forth jealous folks into my view. Jealousy operates from one of the works of the flesh, and it has lived in many people who have known me. Check this out; people were jealousy of me in basketball, baseball, football, dancing, fighting, and even in the street life. Now that my brain wrote a book such as this, that jealousy spirit is still against me. To all those who have looked down on me, guess what, my brain is an entrepreneur. What is yours? If you have not given your brain to Jesus yet, your life is worse off than a sorrowful man in a wheelchair. However, from my writing, which has been inserted in this book, this wheelchair man, just shook up the world! Hey, Mr. Ali, I finally did it; I shook up the world, too. Just a few personal words to share!

Let me present unto you statistics and fact-recorded crimes that happened in St. Louis, Mo. I am going to tell you about the year, "2006". In "2006", 129 murders have been committed; 337 forcible rapes; 3,147 robberies; 4,992 aggravated assaults; 8, 510 burglaries; 23,596 larceny thefts; 8,645 vehicle thefts. If you add all the crimes that were committed in 2006, it equals 49,356 crimes committed in one state. In a full year, all this wicked madness had been in action. In a total of 365 days, 49,356 crimes have been committed and recorded. If these online facts are very much true, which I truly believe, then that is more than 35 crimes committed every single day in one state. Oh my goodness, do I have my mathematics right, because that's too much wickedness done in one state. However, I can only imagine the number of crimes committed that were not seen nor recorded in the article of law breaking facts. If all those crimes were committed in one year (2006), then I'm scared to even imagine the number of crimes committed since "1993". Oh my God, we need to find a solution, so that crime committing will cease, and the high rating of wickedness will decline. Well, guess what, my testimony is the answer to solving this crime committing madness. My testimony is not the ultimate answer to solving crime, but it is a link to it. Jesus is the ultimate answer, and my testimony will lead many people to his name. God brought me back from a brain injury, and supplied me with a powerful testimony. None of you folks allowed my testimony to be heard. Of course, I testify all day everyday on the streets, but you folks know exactly what I am saying. Only in three churches, I was called upon to present my testimony. Other than those three times, no one else has allowed me to even speak a 15-minute message in their organization. St. Louis actually ignored my testimony, and I can't believe such a thing went forth. My testimony is just that powerful, that I should have been schedule to give words of exhortation throughout the city of St. Louis. No need for you to get upset at what I am saying here, because 15 years gave you all ample amount of time. I can't believe none of you were high-minded on my testimony. Everybody keeps saying, "Our teenagers need to hear your testimony". If our teenagers needed to hear my testimony, then why didn't you set me up a time and date to present it? I can't believe, I was in this city for 15 years, and only spoke in three places. Just about every pastor, every principal, every athletic coach, every minister, every Christian in St. Louis, have heard of my story. Then you folks wonder why I backslid from the church, and wonder why our city has this wicked crime committed curse upon it. You folks actually looked passed a man, (me) who God has given the power and mental sense, through a testimony to help all the churches in St. Louis. Then you people wonder why the black community is being shot down because of drugs. You folks aren't allowing God's people with these amazing testimonies come to the forefront to be told. Just a few personal words to share!

Jermeine Irons (my cousin), you know I got your back girl. I thank you for your ears of listening to me, and your food support as well. We have spent so much time with one another. Although, you are my cousin, you're also my precious friend. Hang in there; things are going to get better for the both of us. For years, people have put us down. For years, people have talked about us. For years, our lives have been looked at as the tail, and never to be the head. Guess what Jermeine Irons, lift your head up, you are a warrior; you are one strong black woman. When God bless my life to touch a little financial stability, you might as well get your praise on, because you will be blessed as well. Just a few personal words to share!

I want to thank the so call friend of mine who ignorantly laughed at me over the years. Many times, this so-called friend played on my phone about being a book publishing deal. You and your cousin both played on my phone. You even had your ignorant female friends to use their voices too. It was so hilarious to you and them. You did not upset me, however, you knew I was going through a suffering period, and yet, games were played on me for laughter. Through your laughter and ignorance, it only empowered me not to give up. I kept myself focused on my writing. I give you great thanks, because from your ignorance and stupidity, you actually motivated me to work a little harder. In this book, I already explained how sin and Satan operates, and guess what, sin and Satan actually used you and your friends to play on my phone. If people would realize how messed up their lives are, and how much they need Jesus, there will not be time for them to play around. I know this is small talk to the world, but you do not play games with someone that is going through a period of suffering. You know exactly who you are, and so do I. You are the same person, who said unto me over the phone, "Lytskin", you have been trying to get that book published for more than 5 years now, and you need to give it up". When you should have been the one trying to help me, or buying a little food at times, you did nothing. Only thing you did was talk about me, to all your friends, and all you family members, or to whomever you came across. Although, I shake your hands at times, and I show no expressions of grudges while being in your presence, I look you square in the eyes, and shake my head on the inside. Friendship within the world never stays the same, remember that people of the earth. Hey people in the world; sometimes it is time for you to move on with your life, and find new friends. In fact, since I am a Christian, I should not have been hanging with them anyway. There is more to this so call friendship story, but I will not get into all that. However, to you, the person who played games over my phone, I still love you bro, because I know through your ignorance you did it. Never will a Christian do something like this, and I do not care how much you folks talk about church folks. Trust me; church folks might fall into sin at times, but they do not play games with folk's lives. I wrote this paragraph to show the world that even so call friends will think of the ignorant things to do, no matter how a person's situation or condition is. Humanity will turn his back on you every time, just to have a moment of laughter for 30 seconds. Nevertheless, my friend, you need Jesus in your life too. Actually, most of my so call friends were empowered to see me down and out, because I have always seemed to be on top. Hey church folks; you would not believe the number of folks who are jealous of you, all because you have Jesus in your life, and they are trapped in the curse. To all you jealous foes, my book has just showed you how the wicked ghost chaser can be taken out of your life. Just a few personal words to share!

I have to get this off my chest; when you people in the world find out that a churchgoer has committed an ungodly act (me), how can you talk about that individual. See, you people do not read the bible: the bible speaks against people talking about others and their faults. In Mathew 7:3 it says, *why beholdest thou the mote that is in thy brothers eye, but considerest not the beam that is in they own eye.* In other words, you are talking about someone's failures; when you yourself is caught up in: fornication, lying, witchcraft, idolatry, drugs, lawbreaking activities, adultery, drunkenness, stealing, lying to get money, and many other acts evils. People do not have time to talk about church folks; you need to be focus on getting your life together before death creeps up on you. People's minds are really messed up because of the devil. The people in the world say, "Why should I go to church when the church people are committing sin too. Oh, please stop it. I guess you people going to stay away from the church altar, which is the place of forgiveness. God does not care about your complaining. If you die in your unforgiving sins, while complaining, then you and the rich man both will be complaining in hell at the same time. Everyone out there talking bad about what certain people are doing, however, I wonder what God is watching you do behind closed doors. Anyway, let me leave that alone. Just a few personal words to share!

I have to get this off my chest; I cannot stand people who think they know more about a person's life, than that individual does. To make a long story short, can you write a book? Just a few personal words to share!

I need the church people to keep me lifted up in prayer. So many times, I came close to telling someone like you how I really feel. It's been rough; it's been hard, I am still a man who has on a jacket of flesh. If I had allowed my flesh to activate itself, I probably would have cussed many of you folks out. However, I thank God I allowed his spirit to hold my tongue. In fact, put my name on the church wall "prayer's" list. Keep the name **Brian Irons** lifted up before the presence of heaven. Pray for me that God keeps my brain in his "blessed will" for my life. Just a few personal words to share!

When I am outdoors in my wheelchair, I ride about 3 to 5 miles a day. On very good days, especially during the summer, I ride even farther. To all the people in the world, who uses wheelchairs, go back out there in the world and do your own thing. Do not wait on people. I know many of you cannot get around the way I can, but ask God to give you a job. God can use you too. Go back out there in the world, do not let the wheelchair situation defeat you; you defeat it. Get God in your life. My friend **Rick Wynn** has been in a wheelchair for more than two decades, and the lifestyle he lives, has really encouraged me. He even drives. He's been working for years, and he does a lot on his own. Hey, **Rick Wynn**, you are one strong man. Just a few personal words to share!

Although, I am the one to blame for the struggling, I have really learned something from observing people. From watching you all, I can see that money is very powerful. No one wants to struggle the way I did, however, since I went through it, I learned a lot. Never do I want financial stability, if I am not going to help people. Never will I do what the rich man did to the beggar. Just as quick as I get some money, very quickly I am going to give it away. Of course, I am going to take care of my kids, and myself, but I have to give most of it away. When I die, the money will not go with me, and I am a true believer of that. I thank you people for allowing me to see, that money is not what we cake it out me. Never will I have extra money, and not think to help the next man. From what I have seen over the past decade, when it comes to money, you people are pathetic. I am not to a certain individual; I am talking to a city of people. Just a few personal words to share!

Before Jesus gave up his life or spirit on the cross, he gave a verbal reply. Jesus said, "It is finished", meaning, he did what God commanded him to do, and then submitted himself unto death. When my book became published, I realized that my financial struggle is "finished". Just as Jesus gave up his spirit and life to God, I gave my life and spirit to the God, too. Now that my life is in the hands of God, my financial status is soon to change. Since I have both God and Jesus in my life, I've been given the power to be called a son of God, and the brethren of Jesus. I've become a son of God, and the brethren of Jesus. By the adopting power from God, I have been engrafted with the tribe of Israel. By faith, Abraham is now my father. Just a few personal words to share!

Check this out; I was awesome with a baseball in my hands; I was great with a football in my hands; I was one of a kind with a basketball in my hands; I was superb with boxing gloves in my hands; now that I have a pen and paper in my hands; you tell me what I should say? Did you just see my brain's talents unfold right before your very eyes? Just a few personal words to share!

I could have met many people who millionaires on earth. I could have met and played against Michael Jordan (basketball). I could have met and played against Bret Farve (football). I could have met and played against Mark McGuire (baseball). I could have met and fought against Sugar Ray Leonard (boxer). However, my drug usage caused me to miss the opportunity to meet these rich celebrities. God is so good; he has put me back on the road to meet big league people. Yeah, Creflo Dollar, TD. Jakes, Joyce Meyers, Benny Hinn, Juanita Bynum, those are big league names I have the chance to meet. Also, Dionne Sanders, Michael Irvin, and AC Green, I have the chance to meet them all. Even if I never meet millionaires, somehow, someway, they all will hear about my story. Wow, hey people, God will line your life back up if you go get a hold of his son Jesus, and you must believe. Not only believing, but obeying him needs to be accessed too. Just a few personal words to share!

This will be revealed unto you all in the near future; Jesus is not dead because he lives in me. Guess what, also, the Apostle Paul is not dead, because his teaching lives in me too. **I AM THE APOSTLE PAUL IN THE 20TH CENTURY**. Of course, I am not Apostle Paul in the flesh, but his ministry is my ministry, which came from God. Paul and I, we both love to write stories and letters unto the churches. If your church receives a letter in the mail from Paul and me, it is a good thing. Well, I really don't want to leave you, but I must go and finish writing my next book. Just a few personal words to share!

To my family, David Brown, Gloria Irons Brown, Neco Irons, Tiffany Brown, I thank you all for your support. You four individuals have shown me great love. Kim Gilbert and family, thank you all for your food support. Darren (from Cali), Robert (Bobbo), and LARKIE-LARK, and wife, what's up people! Larkie Lark, ever since I've known you, you have been a real friend. Ebony from back in the day, greetings to you. Brian and Judy Jones, in my time of need, your family has been there for me, and my blessings from the Lord be upon your household forever. Tracy Douglas (me-me), you know I got ya back. The Jackie Collins family, blessing be with you all. Chastity Brown, and Cathy Richardson, my blessing from the Lord be upon your household forever. Lamar, Rico, and Andre Pruitt, what's up? Lashelle Berry, and Mike what's up. Chico and brothers, whats up? Joseph and Jamal Goforth whats up? Keith Gilbert, I can't wait to see your face big cousin. Bernard Scott whats up? The house of Radiant Life in Christ, may the Grace of God be with you always. Blessings be to the house of Old Land Mark Temple C.O.G.I.C. Blessings to the house of, The Bread of Life. New Evangelistic Center, may the grace of our Lord be upon your ministry continually. To those whose name is not mentioned in this closing paragraph of the book, don't take it personal. If you do take it personal, think on this, what have you done for Brian K. Irons in the past 15 years?

Below is the sequential order of the publishing of my upcoming books:

1st- I DID NOT KNOW, which is the book you have just read.

2nd-Thou Shall Not Serve No other Gods Before Me

3rd- Keep Your Vision

4th - Lord Forgive My Hands

5th- When God Says Move, You Need To Pack Up And Go,

Or the fifth book might be titled- A Blind and Rebellious City

Again, I am one strong African American!